First Edition copyright © 2013

All rights reserved. permission in writing must be obtained from the writer before any part of this publication may be reproduced or transmitted in any form or by any means, electronic or mechanical. including photocopy, recording or any information storage or retrievel system.

CONTENTS

CHAPTER 1 – ALGEBRA
1.1 Order of operations...5
1.2 Decimals and fractions..6
1.3 Percentages...17
1.4 Prime numbers LCM and GCD..28
1.5 Types of numbers..31
1.6 Roots and rationalization...36
1.7 Interval notation and inequalities..38
1.8 Exponents...46
1.9 Equations..52
1.10 Expanding and factoring..73
1.11 Evaluating expressions..78
1.12 Equations with absolute value...79
1.13 Logarithms and logarithmic equations..................................86
1.14 Sequences and series...96
1.15 Significant figures..120
1.16 Scientific notation..123

CHAPTER 2 – GEOMETRY
2.1 Geometry...126
2.2 Geometric transformations..157

CHAPTER 3 – FUNCTIONS
3.1 Introduction to functions...168
3.2 Linear functions...176
3.3 Quadratic functions...204

CHAPTER 4 – TRIGONOMETRY
4.1 Degrees and Radians..242
4.2 Definition of the Trigonometric functions...........................247
4.3 Trigonometric functions..263
4.4 Sine and Cosine Rule..278
4.5 Trigonometric Ratios...283
4.6 Inverse Trigonometric functions..289

CHAPTER 5 – SETS
5.1 Sets..294

CHAPTER 6 – STATISTICS
6.1 Statistics..305
6.2 Mean, Median, Mode and Frequency diagrams...................309
6.3 Probability...316

CHAPTER 7
7.1 International system of units...319
7.2 Common errors..321
7.3 Fractions review..324

CHAPTER 1 - ALGEBRA

1.1. – ORDER OF OPERATIONS

1. $5 + 3 \cdot 2 =$
2. $2 \cdot 3 - (-3) =$
3. $-5 \cdot 5 - (-8) \cdot 2 =$
4. $-2 - 5 - (-2) + 2 =$
5. $(-2)(-5) - (-2) \cdot 2 =$
6. $25 \cdot 2 - 7 =$
7. $15 + 4 / 2 =$
8. $14 / 7 + 3 \cdot 6 =$
9. $5 / 5 - 30 / 2 \cdot 5 =$
10. $1 + 4 / 2 - 8 / 4 \cdot 5 =$
11. $20 / 4 / 2 + 4 =$
12. $12 \cdot (2 + 3) =$
13. $5(3 \cdot 2 / 3 \cdot 2) + 2 =$
14. $1/2 + 3/2 =$
15. $6/3 - 20/10 =$
16. $5(1 + 3 \cdot 2) + 2/2 - 8/4 =$
17. $(15 + 3) \cdot 2 - 2 =$
18. $0 / 5 + 3 \cdot 2 =$
19. $5 / 0 + 3 \cdot 2 =$
20. $(1 + 1) \cdot (2 - 2) \cdot (4 \cdot 5 \cdot 5) =$
21. $(5 + 3) \cdot 2 =$
22. $(5 \cdot 3) \cdot 2 =$
23. $5 \cdot (3 \cdot 2) =$
24. $5 \cdot 3 \cdot 2 =$
25. $100 / 2^2 + 21/3 =$
26. $(2+1)^2 / 3 + 13 =$
27. $2(3^2 - 4/2)^2 - 1 \cdot 3 =$
28. $3(1 - 4/2^2)^2 - 4^2 / 3 =$
29. $10(2^4 / 2 - 1^2 + 1) / 2 =$
30. $2 + 3(2 - 20/2^2)^2 - (5^2 + 3)/2 =$
31. $5 / 0 =$
32. $0 / 4 =$
33. $0 / 0 =$
34. $(2+4) \cdot 5^2 - 2/2 =$
35. $-1 \cdot 5^2 - 2^2 + (-2)^{3-1 \cdot 2} =$
36. $(-2^2 - 2)^2 \cdot (-2)^{1-1} =$
37. $(4 - 5 \cdot 2)/2 - 1 =$

1.2. – DECIMALS AND FRACTIONS

Write the fractions as decimals:

1. $\dfrac{1}{10} =$
2. $\dfrac{1}{100} =$
3. $\dfrac{1}{1000} =$
4. $\dfrac{1}{10000} =$
5. $\dfrac{2}{10} =$
6. $\dfrac{5}{100} =$
7. $\dfrac{-31}{1000} =$
8. $\dfrac{766}{10000} =$
9. $\dfrac{55}{10} =$
10. $\dfrac{101}{100} =$
11. $\dfrac{-335}{1000} =$
12. $\dfrac{20000}{10000} =$
13. $\dfrac{1}{2} =$
14. $\dfrac{1}{5} =$
15. $\dfrac{1}{4} =$
16. $\dfrac{1}{3} =$
17. $\dfrac{1}{8} =$
18. $\dfrac{1}{9} =$
19. $\dfrac{2}{5} =$
20. $\dfrac{2}{4} =$
21. $\dfrac{3}{5} =$
22. $\dfrac{4}{5} =$
23. $\dfrac{3}{4} =$
24. $\dfrac{7}{5} =$
25. $\dfrac{5}{4} =$
26. $\dfrac{9}{5} =$
27. $\dfrac{2}{9} =$
28. $\dfrac{1}{20} =$
29. $\dfrac{3}{20} =$
30. $\dfrac{8}{5} =$

Write the decimals as fractions

31. $0.3 =$
32. $0.2 =$
33. $0.1 =$
34. $0.01 =$
35. $0.02 =$
36. $0.11 =$
37. $0.26 =$
38. $1.3 =$
39. $1.42 =$
40. $0.011 =$
41. $0.312 =$
42. $0.16 =$
43. $1.4 =$
44. $2.043 =$
45. $43.3 =$
46. $4.12 =$
47. $1.302 =$
48. $1.111 =$
49. $102.32 =$
50. $2.346 =$

Perform the operations <u>using fractions only</u>; give the answer as a decimal and fraction:

51. $50 \cdot 0.1 =$
52. $85 \cdot 0.01 =$
53. $45 \cdot 0.001 =$
54. $6 \cdot 0.0001 =$
55. $5123 \cdot 0.001 =$
56. $435 \cdot 0.01 =$
57. $15 \cdot 0.001 =$
58. $-236 \cdot 0.0001 =$
59. $1228 \cdot 0.1 =$
60. $1085 \cdot 0.01 =$
61. $4500 \cdot 0.001 =$
62. $0.16 \cdot 0.0001 =$
63. $12 \cdot 1.2 =$
64. $25 \cdot 0.22 =$

65. $2.5 \cdot 1.8 =$

66. $7.2 \cdot 8.8 =$

67. $0.15 \cdot 2.01 =$

68. $87.5 \cdot 0.2 =$

69. $31.5 \cdot 0.3 =$

70. $0.215 \cdot 1.38 =$

71. $0.5 \cdot 1.23 =$

72. $1.02 \cdot 2.5 =$

73. $31.7 \cdot 0.18 =$

74. $21.2 \cdot 1.13 =$

75. $0.42 \cdot 5.56 =$

76. $3.1 \cdot 0.642 =$

77. $13.7 \cdot 8.9 =$

78. $1.07 \cdot 0.03 =$

Perform the operations using fractions only; give the answer as a decimal and fraction:

79. $\dfrac{1}{0.1} =$

80. $\dfrac{5}{0.01} =$

81. $\dfrac{-56}{0.001} =$

82. $\dfrac{-2.3}{0.01} =$

83. $\dfrac{3}{0.1} =$

84. $\dfrac{0.55}{0.01} =$

85. $\dfrac{-31.6}{0.001} =$

86. $\dfrac{0.023}{0.01} =$

87. $\dfrac{15}{0.01} =$

88. $\dfrac{-215}{0.01} =$

89. $\dfrac{-45.6}{0.001} =$

90. $\dfrac{-12.3}{0.01} =$

91. $\dfrac{1}{0.02} =$

92. $\dfrac{-2}{0.03} =$

93. $\dfrac{-4.6}{0.05} =$

94. $\dfrac{-1.3}{0.06} =$

95. $\dfrac{1}{0.25} =$

96. $\dfrac{-2}{0.9} =$

97. $\dfrac{-4.1}{0.2} =$

98. $\dfrac{-1.3}{0.05} =$

99. $\dfrac{1}{0.015} =$

100. $\dfrac{-12}{0.6} =$

101. $\dfrac{-14}{0.003} =$

102. $\dfrac{-0.3}{0.02} =$

103. Write down the number that is 0.2 units on the left of −1: _____

104. Write down the number that is 0.5 units on the left of −2: _____

105. Write down the number that is 0.3 units on the right of −1: _____

106. Write down the number that is 0.4 units on the right of −2: _____

107. Write down the number that is 0.8 units on the left of −9: _____

108. Write down the number that is 0.2 units on the left of 0:_____

109. Write down the number that is 0.9 units on the right of −9:_____

110. Write down the number that is 0.2 units on the right of −5:_____

111. Write down the number that is 0.21 units on the left of −1:_____

112. Write down the number that is 0.51 units on the left of −2:_____

113. Write down the number that is 0.34 units on the right of −1:_____

114. Write down the number that is 0.06 units on the right of −10:_____

115. Write down the number that is 0.11 units on the right of −1:_____

116. Write down the number that is 0.01 units on the right of −2:_____

117. Write down the number that is 0.34 units on the right of 9:_____

118. Write down the number that is 0.06 units on the right of 10:_____

119. Write down the number that is 0.17 units on the right of −9:_____

120. Write down the number that is 0.78 units on the left of −3:_____

121. Write down the number that is 0.01 units on the left of −7:_____

122. Write down the number that is 0.02 units on the right of −1:_____

123. Write down the number that is 0.002 units on the right of −10:_____

124. Write down the number that is 0.111 units on the right of −1:_____

125. Write down the number that is 0.021 units on the right of −2:_____

126. Write down the number that is 0.4 units on the right of 9:_____

127. Write down the number that is 0.03 units on the right of 10:_____

128. Write down the number that is 0.202 units on the right of −9:_____

129. Write down numbers that are very close to 2 on its left: _____ right: _____

130. Write down numbers that are very close to 1 on its left: _____ right: _____

131. Write down numbers that are very close to 0 on its left: _____ right: _____

132. Write down numbers that are very close to −1 on its left: _____ right: _____

133. Write down numbers that are very close to −7 on its left: _____ right: _____

134. Write down numbers that are very close to −12 on its left: _____ right: _____

135. Write down numbers that are very close to –2 on its left: _____ right: _____

136. Write down numbers that are very close to –10 on its left: _____ right: _____

137. Write down numbers that are very close to 9 on its left: _____ right: _____

138. Write down numbers that are very close to 100 on its left: _____ right: _____

139. Write down 2 numbers between 3 and 3.1: _____, _____. Write the same numbers as fractions: _____, _____

140. Write down 2 numbers between 6.2 and 6.3: _____, _____. Write the same numbers as fractions: _____, _____

141. Write down 2 numbers between 6.2 and 6.21: _____, _____. Write the same numbers as fractions: _____, _____

142. Write down 2 numbers between –5.2 and –5.3: _____, _____. Write the same numbers as fractions: _____, _____

143. Write down 2 numbers between 0.25 and 0.251: _____, _____. Write the same numbers as fractions: _____, _____

144. Write down 2 numbers between 1.11 and 1.111: _____, _____. Write the same numbers as fractions: _____, _____

145. Write down 2 numbers between 0.21 and 0.22: _____, _____. Write the same numbers as fractions: _____, _____

146. Write down 2 numbers between 5.99 and 5.999: _____, _____. Write the same numbers as fractions: _____, _____

147. Write down 2 numbers between 6 and 6.01: _____, _____. Write the same numbers as fractions: _____, _____

148. Write the value of each position shown on the number line:

149. Write the value of each position shown on the number line:

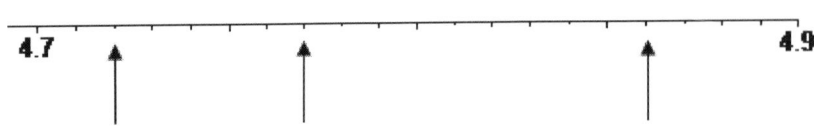

150. Write the value of each position shown on the number line:

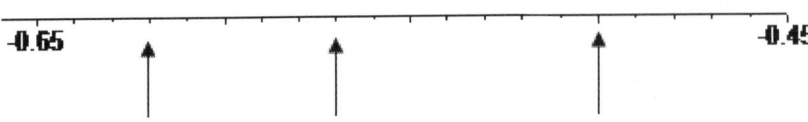

151. Circle the fractions that are greater than 1: $\dfrac{7}{6}, \dfrac{6}{7}, \dfrac{35}{34}, \dfrac{21}{7}, \dfrac{10001}{10000}$

152. A fraction will be greater than 1 if _____

153. Circle the fractions that are greater than 2: $\dfrac{50}{26}, \dfrac{60}{30}, \dfrac{35}{40}, \dfrac{20}{7}, \dfrac{20001}{10000}$

154. A fraction will be greater than 2 if _____

155. Circle the fractions that are greater than 5: $\dfrac{50}{10}, \dfrac{47}{9}, \dfrac{100}{6}, \dfrac{28}{3}, \dfrac{1201}{300}$

156. A fraction will be greater than 5 if _____

157. Circle the fractions that are smaller than $\dfrac{1}{2}$: $\dfrac{1}{3}, \dfrac{2}{3}, \dfrac{4}{9}, \dfrac{28}{29}, \dfrac{34}{60}, \dfrac{23}{51}, \dfrac{17}{32}, \dfrac{34}{67}$

158. A fraction will be smaller than $\dfrac{1}{2}$ if: _____

159. Circle the fractions that are smaller than $\dfrac{1}{3}$: $\dfrac{2}{7}, \dfrac{5}{9}, \dfrac{4}{11}, \dfrac{13}{29}, \dfrac{24}{75}, \dfrac{3}{11}$

160. A fraction will be smaller than $\dfrac{1}{3}$ if: _____

161. Write down the fractions in different ways:

$\dfrac{1}{2} =$ $\dfrac{1}{3} =$ $\dfrac{1}{4} =$ $\dfrac{7}{4} =$ $\dfrac{2}{3} =$ $\dfrac{11}{8} =$

$\dfrac{a}{b} =$ $\dfrac{3a}{a} =$ $\dfrac{a+2}{2+a} =$ $\dfrac{x}{7x} =$ $\dfrac{1+a}{a-1} =$

Fill the blank with: <,> or =:

162. $\dfrac{1}{2} \underline{} \dfrac{1}{3}$

163. $\dfrac{1}{3} \underline{} \dfrac{1}{4}$

164. $\dfrac{2}{5} \underline{} \dfrac{3}{7}$

165. $\dfrac{5}{8} \underline{} \dfrac{7}{11}$

166. $\dfrac{12}{7} \underline{} \dfrac{13}{8}$

167. $\dfrac{21}{8} \underline{} \dfrac{13}{5}$

168. $\dfrac{35}{8} \underline{} \dfrac{17}{4}$

169. $\dfrac{a}{b} \underline{} \dfrac{a+1}{b+1}$

170. $\dfrac{a}{b-1} \underline{} \dfrac{a+1}{b+1}$

171. $\dfrac{1}{n+1} \underline{} \dfrac{1}{n}, n \geq 0$

172. $\dfrac{1}{n^2} \underline{} \dfrac{1}{n}, n \geq 1$

173. $n^2 \underline{} n, 0 \leq n \leq 1$

174. $\dfrac{1}{n^2} \underline{} \dfrac{1}{n}, 0 \leq n \leq 1$

175. $\dfrac{1}{a} \underline{} \dfrac{1}{b}, a < b$

176. Indicate the location of the fractions on the number line: $-\dfrac{7}{6}, -\dfrac{6}{7}, \dfrac{17}{34}, \dfrac{-1}{7}, \dfrac{10001}{5000}$

177. Indicate the location of the fractions on the number line: $-\dfrac{1}{6}, -\dfrac{8}{7}, \dfrac{20}{9}, \dfrac{-10}{20}, \dfrac{99}{50}$

178. Indicate the location of the fractions on the number line: $-\dfrac{4}{5}, -\dfrac{3}{2}, \dfrac{5}{2}, \dfrac{9}{8}, \dfrac{100}{33}$

179. Indicate the location of the fractions on the number line: $-\dfrac{7}{5}, -\dfrac{9}{3}, \dfrac{2}{3}, \dfrac{1}{10}, -\dfrac{66}{32}$

180. Indicate the location of the fractions on the number line: $-\dfrac{7}{8}, -\dfrac{6}{13}, \dfrac{11}{21}, \dfrac{-2}{17}, \dfrac{100}{501}$

181. Indicate the location of the fractions on the number line: $-\dfrac{10}{6}, -\dfrac{8}{7}, \dfrac{181}{90}, \dfrac{-102}{200}, \dfrac{189}{60}$

182. Indicate the location of the fractions on the number line: $-\dfrac{6}{5}, -\dfrac{5}{2}, \dfrac{2}{5}, \dfrac{90}{80}, \dfrac{33}{100}$

183. Indicate the location of the fractions on the number line: $-\dfrac{12}{5}, -\dfrac{6}{3}, \dfrac{11}{6}, \dfrac{11}{10}, -\dfrac{37}{12}$

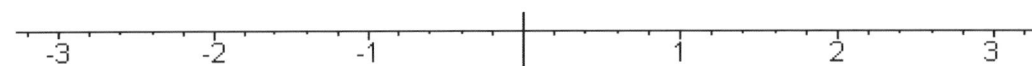

184. Indicate the location of the fractions on the number line: $-\dfrac{10}{4}, -\dfrac{2}{10}, \dfrac{64}{33}, \dfrac{21}{10}, -\dfrac{3}{1}$

Calculate:

185. $1 + \dfrac{2}{3} =$

186. $\dfrac{5}{6} + \dfrac{2}{3} =$

187. $\dfrac{2}{7} - \dfrac{1}{6} =$

188. $5 \cdot \dfrac{3}{8} - \dfrac{2}{12} =$

189. $\left(\dfrac{2}{14} - \dfrac{3}{7}\right) \cdot \dfrac{2}{9} =$

190. $\left(\dfrac{7}{2} - \dfrac{4}{3}\right) \cdot \dfrac{1}{5} =$

191. $\dfrac{5}{6}+\dfrac{2}{3}-6=$

192. $\dfrac{1}{a}+\dfrac{1}{a}=$

193. $\dfrac{1}{d}+d=$

194. $\dfrac{1}{a}+\dfrac{a}{1}=$

195. $\dfrac{1}{b+1}+b=$

196. $\dfrac{a}{b}+\dfrac{1}{b}=$

197. $\dfrac{a}{b}+\dfrac{d}{b}=$

198. $\dfrac{a}{c}+\dfrac{d}{b}=$

199. $\dfrac{a+b}{b}+\dfrac{d}{b}+2=$

200. $\dfrac{\left(\dfrac{a}{b}\right)}{b}=$

201. $\dfrac{a}{\left(\dfrac{a}{b}\right)}=$

202. $\dfrac{\left(\dfrac{b}{a}\right)}{b}=$

203. $\dfrac{\left(\dfrac{b}{a}\right)}{1}=$

204. $\dfrac{\left(\dfrac{1}{a}\right)}{b}=$

205. $\dfrac{\left(\dfrac{b}{1}\right)}{b}=$

206. $\dfrac{1}{\left(\dfrac{a}{b}\right)}=$

207. $\dfrac{\left(\dfrac{a}{b}\right)}{\left(\dfrac{a}{b}\right)}=$

208. $\dfrac{\left(\dfrac{b}{a}\right)}{\left(\dfrac{a}{b}\right)}=$

209. $\dfrac{\left(\dfrac{a}{1}\right)}{\left(\dfrac{a}{b}\right)}=$

210. $\dfrac{\left(\dfrac{a}{b}\right)}{\left(\dfrac{1}{b}\right)}=$

211. $\dfrac{\left(\dfrac{c+1}{d}\right)}{\left(\dfrac{1}{d}+d\right)}=$

212. $\dfrac{1}{\left(\dfrac{1}{d}+d\right)}+d=$

213. $\dfrac{1-d}{(d+2)}+\dfrac{2}{d}=$

214. $\dfrac{1}{d} + \dfrac{2}{d^2} + \dfrac{1}{d^3} =$

215. $\dfrac{2}{3} + \dfrac{3a}{c} - \dfrac{b}{2} =$

216. $\dfrac{\left(\dfrac{4}{b} - \dfrac{a}{7}\right)}{2} =$

217. $\dfrac{a}{c(c+1)} + \dfrac{d}{c+1} =$

218. $\dfrac{2x}{\left(\dfrac{2x+2}{3+x}\right)} + \dfrac{\left(\dfrac{x+1}{x-2}\right)}{x-3} =$

219. $\dfrac{\left(2x + \dfrac{1}{x}\right)}{\left(1 + \dfrac{1}{x}\right)} =$

220. $\dfrac{12}{2a} \times \dfrac{a+1}{6} =$

221. $\dfrac{12}{2a} \div \dfrac{a}{6} =$

222. $3 \times \dfrac{4}{3} =$

223. $3 \div \dfrac{4}{3} =$

224. $12 - \dfrac{4}{3} =$

225. $a \times \dfrac{b}{3c} =$

226. $\dfrac{b}{3a} \div 3a =$

227. $\dfrac{b}{3a} \times 3a =$

228. $\dfrac{\left(\dfrac{1}{3} + \dfrac{2}{5}\right)}{\left(\dfrac{5}{3} - \dfrac{1}{3}\right)} =$

229. $\dfrac{\left(\dfrac{b}{3c}\right)}{2} =$

230. $\dfrac{\left(\dfrac{1}{2}\right)}{2\left(\dfrac{2}{3c}\right)} =$

231. $\dfrac{\left(\dfrac{1}{2}\right)}{2} =$

232. $\dfrac{\left(\dfrac{2}{7}\right)}{3} =$

233. $\dfrac{2}{\left(\dfrac{2}{7}\right)} =$

234. $\dfrac{3}{\left(\dfrac{a}{7}\right)} =$

235. $\dfrac{6}{\left(\dfrac{8}{3}\right)} =$

236. $\dfrac{\left(\dfrac{4}{3}\right)}{\left(\dfrac{3}{4}\right)} =$

237. $\dfrac{\left(\dfrac{2}{3}\right)}{\left(\dfrac{4}{5}\right)} =$

238. $\dfrac{\left(\dfrac{2}{3}\right)}{\left(\dfrac{2}{3}\right)} =$

239. $\left(\dfrac{a}{b}\right)\cdot\left(\dfrac{c}{a}\right) =$

240. $\left(\dfrac{2}{c}\right)\cdot\left(\dfrac{c}{7}\right) =$

241. $\left(\dfrac{b+1}{3}\right)\cdot\left(\dfrac{2}{b}\right) =$

242. $\left(\dfrac{z+1}{z-2}\right)\cdot\left(\dfrac{4}{z+1}\right) =$

243. $\left(\dfrac{3a+6}{5}\right)\cdot\left(\dfrac{1}{a+2}\right) =$

244. $\left(\dfrac{2c-4}{c}\right)\cdot\left(\dfrac{2c}{4c-8}\right) =$

245. $\dfrac{1}{\left(\dfrac{2}{4}\right)}\cdot\left(\dfrac{2}{3}\right) =$

246. $\dfrac{\left(\dfrac{3}{4}\right)}{\left(\dfrac{a}{2}\right)}\cdot\left(\dfrac{2}{3}\right) =$

247. $\dfrac{\left(\dfrac{1}{a}\right)}{\left(\dfrac{2}{a}\right)}+2 =$

248. $\dfrac{\left(x+\dfrac{1}{x}\right)}{\left(1-\dfrac{1}{x}\right)} =$

249. $\dfrac{\left(\dfrac{1}{1+x}+1\right)}{\left(x-\dfrac{2}{x}\right)} =$

250. $\dfrac{\left(\dfrac{x}{3}-2\right)}{\left(2-\dfrac{2+x}{3}\right)} =$

251. $\dfrac{2x}{\left(\dfrac{2}{3+x}\right)}+\dfrac{\left(\dfrac{2}{x}\right)}{x+3} =$

252. $\dfrac{a-b}{\left(1-\dfrac{a}{b}\right)} =$

253. $\dfrac{2}{(1-a)}+\dfrac{2}{a(1-a)} =$

254. $\dfrac{a}{(3+a)^2}+\dfrac{2}{(a+3)} =$

255. $\dfrac{1}{(1-x)^3}+\dfrac{2}{(1-x)^2} =$

256. $\dfrac{1}{(1-x)^3}+\dfrac{2}{x(1-x)^2} =$

257. $\dfrac{1}{(1-x)(2-x)}+\dfrac{2}{x(1-x)^2} =$

258. $\dfrac{2}{(1-x)x}+\dfrac{2}{x^2(1-x)^2} =$

259. $\dfrac{a^2+1}{a} - \dfrac{a+1}{a^2+a} =$

260. $\dfrac{a+x}{x} - \dfrac{y+1}{xy} + \dfrac{2}{y} =$

261. $\dfrac{a+x}{a-x} \div \dfrac{a+x}{x-a} =$

262. $\dfrac{a+x}{a^2-x^2} - \dfrac{a-x}{x-a} =$

263. $\left(\dfrac{2c-4}{c}\right) \div \left(\dfrac{4c^2+16}{c^2}\right) =$

264. $\left(\dfrac{6xy+2}{3y}\right) \div \left(\dfrac{3xy+1}{6y^5}\right) =$

265. $\left(\dfrac{x^2-z^2}{xyz}\right) + \left(\dfrac{z-x^2}{xy}\right) =$

True or False:

266. $\dfrac{a+b}{c} = \dfrac{a}{c} + \dfrac{b}{c}$

267. $\dfrac{a+b}{c+d} = \dfrac{a}{c} + \dfrac{b}{d}$

268. $\dfrac{a+b}{a} = 1 + \dfrac{b}{a}$

269. $\dfrac{a-b}{b-a} = -1$

270. $\dfrac{a}{c+d} = \dfrac{a}{c} + \dfrac{a}{d}$

271. $\dfrac{c-d}{d} = c$

272. $\dfrac{c-d}{d} = -1+c$

273. $\dfrac{ab}{ad} = \dfrac{b}{d}$

274. $\dfrac{a(c-d)}{a} = c-d$

275. $\dfrac{ac-d}{c-d} = a$

276. $\dfrac{2a+d}{d-2a} = -1$

Fill the blank to make the fractions equal:

277. $\dfrac{a}{3} = \dfrac{\;}{6}$

278. $\dfrac{a-b}{4} = \dfrac{\;}{12}$

279. $\dfrac{a}{b} = \dfrac{\;}{2b}$

280. $\dfrac{1}{a} = \dfrac{\;}{3a}$

281. $\dfrac{1}{3} = \dfrac{\;}{\_a}$

282. $\dfrac{a-b}{\;} = 1$

283. $\dfrac{2-a}{\;} = \dfrac{a-2}{2}$

284. $\dfrac{2a}{b} = \dfrac{\;}{4b}$

285. $\dfrac{x^2}{2xy} = \dfrac{\;}{4y^2}$

286. $\dfrac{2a}{7x} = \dfrac{\;}{14x^2}$

1.3. – PERCENTAGES

1. A percentage is _____ we sometimes use _____ or _____ to represent it.

2. Find (write the expression and simplify it to get a final answer):

   a. 1% of 900 = _____
   b. 2% of 900 = _____
   c. 3% of 900 = _____
   d. 10% of 900 = _____
   e. 15% of 900 = _____
   f. 20% of 900 = _____
   g. 25% of 900 = _____
   h. 35% of 900 = _____
   i. 100% of 900 = _____
   j. 101% of 900 = _____
   k. 110% of 900 = _____
   l. 120% of 900 = _____
   m. 125% of 900 = _____
   n. 140% of 900 = _____
   o. 200% of 900 = _____
   p. 300% of 900 = _____

3. Find (write the expression and simplify it to get a final answer):

   a. 1% of 50 = _____
   b. 2% of 50 = _____
   c. 10% of 70 = _____
   d. 15% of 90 = _____
   e. 20% of 110 = _____
   f. 25% of 350 = _____
   g. 35% of 1100 = _____
   h. 100% of 125 = _____
   i. 101% of 520 = _____
   j. 110% of 130 = _____
   k. 120% of 122 = _____
   l. 125% of 250 = _____
   m. 140% of 9100 = _____
   n. 200% of 240 = _____
   o. 300% of 120 = _____
   p. A% of M = _____

4. Johann scored 130 out 200 in a test, find his score in percentage?

5. Given that in a group of 20 students, 3 are taller than 188cm. Write down the percentage of student shorter than 188cm _____

6. Nina scored 70 out 80 in a test, find her score in percentage?

7. Given a square with side x. Inside it a smaller square is drawn with side length of 90% of x. Find the percentage of the area that is shaded and not shaded.

8. Given a square with length side x and a circle inscribed in it. Find the percentage of the area shaded and not shaded.

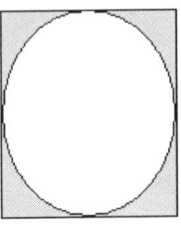

9. Given the following figure. a is 40% of x and b is 40% less of y.

   a. Find the areas of both rectangles in terms of x and y.
   b. Find the percentage of the area shaded and not shaded.

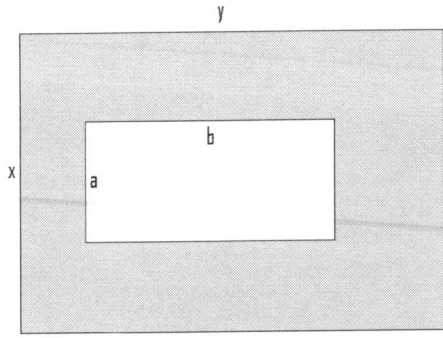

10. In a certain box of cookies there are 80 cookies of 3 colours: white, brown and black. 15% of the cookies are white, 15 cookies are brown and the rest are black.

    a. Find the percentage of brown and black cookies in the box.

    b. Dani ate 2 cookies of each colour; find the new percentages of each kind.

11. Jeff bought a car for 4000$ and sold it for 5000$, Find his benefit in percent.

12. Jessica bought a car for 4000$ and sold it for 3000$, Find her lost in percent.

13. Given the rectangle, write down the percentage of it that is shaded: ____

    Simplify the fraction:

14. Given the following square. Write down the percentage of it that is

    shaded: _____, Simplify the fraction:

15. Given the following circle, find the percentage of the circle that is shaded and not shaded. Write your answer as a fraction, decimal and percentage.

    Shaded: _____   Not Shaded: _____

16. It is known that the area shaded is 30% of 60% of the circle. Find the percentage of the circle that is shaded and not shaded. Write your answer as a fraction, decimal and percentage.

    Shaded: _____   Not Shaded: _____

17. It is known that 20% of 75% of a class of 40 students are going to the cinema. How many are going? Write your answer as a fraction and decimal.

18. It is known that 10% of 40% of a certain amount is 40 euros, find the amount.

19. It is known that 60% of 40% of a certain amount is 20 euros, find the amount.

20. Find 10% of 20% of 30% of 200: _____

21. Find 20% of 30% of 30% of 300: _____

22. Find 80% of 120% of 400: _____

23. Find 90% of 130% of 70% 500: _____

24. It is known that 20% of 20% of a certain amount is 5 euros, find the amount.

25. It is known that 10% of 30% of 5% of a certain amount is 50 euros, find the amount.

26. Given a circle with radius R cm. We know that the area shaded is 20π cm^2 and that 40% of 90% the circle is shaded. Find R in its most simplified form.

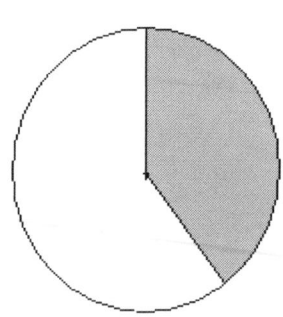

INCREASE OR DECREASE BY A PERCENTAGE

27. The price of a shirt is A $. In case the price increases by:

   a. In case the price increases by 1, state the new price in terms of A _____

   b. In case the price increases by 2%, state the new price in terms of A _____

   c. In case the price increases by 3%, state the new price in terms of A _____

   d. In case the price increases by 5%, state the new price in terms of A _____

   e. In case the price increases by 8%, state the new price in terms of A _____

   f. In case the price increases by 10%, state the new price in terms of A _____

   g. In case the price increases by 18%, state the new price in terms of A _____

   h. In case the price increases by 30%, state the new price in terms of A _____

   i. In case the price increases by 50%, state the new price in terms of A _____

   j. In case the price increases by 58%, state the new price in terms of A _____

   k. In case the price increases by 90%, state the new price in terms of A _____

   l. In case the price increases by 100%, state the new price in terms of A _____

   m. In case the price increases by 101%, state the new price in terms of A _____

   n. In case the price increases by 108%, state the new price in terms of A _____

   o. In case the price increases by 110%, state the new price in terms of A _____

   p. In case the price increases by 200%, state the new price in terms of A _____

   q. In case the price increases by 228%, state the new price in terms of A _____

   r. In case the price increases by 300%, state the new price in terms of A _____

28. The price of a shirt is A $.

   a. In case the price decreases by 1%, state the new price in terms of A _____

   b. In case the price decreases by 2%, state the new price in terms of A _____

   c. In case the price decreases by 3%, state the new price in terms of A _____

   d. In case the price decreases by 5%, state the new price in terms of A _____

   e. In case the price decreases by 8%, state the new price in terms of A _____

f. In case the price decreases by 10%, state the new price in terms of A _____

g. In case the price decreases by 18%, state the new price in terms of A _____

h. In case the price decreases by 30%, state the new price in terms of A _____

i. In case the price decreases by 50%, state the new price in terms of A _____

j. In case the price decreases by 58%, state the new price in terms of A _____

k. In case the price decreases by 90%, state the new price in terms of A _____

l. In case the price decreases by 100%, state the new price in terms of A _____

m. In case the price decreases by 101%, state the new price in terms of A _____

n. In case the price decreases by 110%, state the new price in terms of A _____

29.
   a. To increase an amount by 10% we multiply it by _____
   b. To increase an amount by 25% we multiply it by _____
   c. To increase an amount by 7.2% we multiply it by _____
   d. To decrease an amount by 12% we multiply it by _____
   e. To decrease an amount by 35% we multiply it by _____
   f. To decrease an amount by 5.1% we multiply it by _____
   g. To decrease an amount by 100% we multiply it by _____
   h. To increase an amount by 100% we multiply it by _____
   i. To increase an amount by 200% we multiply it by _____
   j. To increase an amount by M% we multiply it by _____
   k. To decrease an amount by S% we multiply it by _____

30. The price of a shirt is B $. In case the price increases by 10% and then decreases by 10%, state the new price in terms of B _____ and the overall change in the price (as a percentage).

31. The price of a shirt is C $. In case the price increases by 20% and then decreases by 30%, state the new price in terms of C _____ and the overall change in the price (as a percentage).

32. The price of a shirt is D $. In case the price decreases by 20% and then increases by 40%, state the new price in terms of D _____ and the overall change in the price (as a percentage).

33. The price of a shirt is E $. In case the price decreases by 30% and then increases by 50%, state the new price in terms of E _____ and the overall change in the price (as a percentage).

34. The price of a shirt is E $. In case the price increases every month by 4%, write the expression for the price after 80 months: _____

35. The price of a shirt is M$. In case the price decreases every month by 12%, write the expression for the price after 10 months: _____

36. The price of a shirt is M$. In case the price decreases every month by 2.5%, write the expression for the price after 10 months: _____

37. The price of a shirt is M$. The price increases by x% every month. State its price in terms of M and x after n months: _____

BIGGER OR SMALLER BY A PERCENTAGE

38. Find the percentage by which:

   a. 5 is bigger than 4: _____

   b. 4 is smaller than 5: _____

   c. 11 is bigger than 10: _____

   d. 10 is smaller than 11: _____

   e. 51 is bigger than 50: _____

   f. 40 is smaller than 45: _____

   g. A is bigger than B: _____

   h. x is smaller than y: _____

39. Given that the long side of the <u>shaded rectangle</u> is 70% of x and that its short side is 60% of y. Find the percentage of the big rectangle that is shaded.

40. Given that the side length of the square is two thirds of the short side of the rectangle find:

   a. The area of the shapes in terms of x.

      Rectangle: _____

      Square: _____

   b. The percentage of the area of the rectangle that is shaded and not shaded.

c. The percentage by which the <u>area</u> of the square is <u>smaller</u> than the <u>area</u> of the rectangle.

d. The percentage by which the <u>perimeter</u> of the square is <u>smaller</u> than the <u>perimeter</u> of the rectangle.

41. Given the diagram in which a rectangle is located inside a square. The side length of the square is 2x. The rectangle's long side is 80% of the side of the square. The short side of the rectangles is 30% less of the side of the square. Find

   a. The area of the square in terms of x.

   b. The side lengths of the rectangle in terms of x written as a fraction.

   c. The area of the rectangle written as a fraction in terms of x.

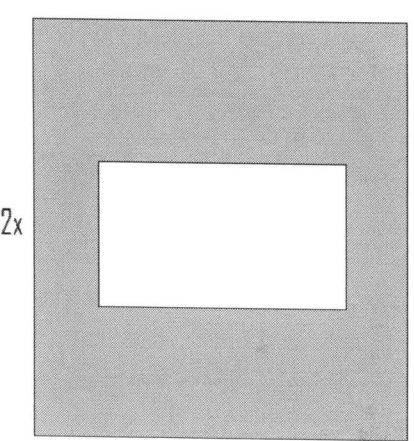

   d. Using the previous parts the percentage of the area that is not shaded.

   e. The percentage by which the <u>area</u> of the square is **bigger** than the <u>area</u> of the rectangle.

   f. The percentage by which the <u>perimeter</u> of the rectangle is **smaller** than the <u>perimeter</u> of the square.

2. Ricardo drives to work 40% less than Rhona. Rhona drives to work 10% more than Alex who drives 400 km per week.

   a. How many km does Rhona drive to work per week?

   b. How many km does Ricardo drive to work per week?

   c. By what percentage does Ricardo drive more or less than Alex?

RATIO AND PROPORTION

42. The ratio between 2 and 5 is the same as between _____ and a 100.

43. The ratio between 3 and 7 is the same as between _____ and 35.

44. The ratio between 2 and 12 is the same as between 6 and _____

45. The ratio 1:3:7 is the same as _____

46. Divide 120 in the ratio 2:3

47. Divide 160 in the ratio 3:4

48. Divide 180 in the ratio 2:3:4

49. Divide 360 in the ratio 2:5:8

50. Divide 30 in the ratio 1:2:3

51. The diagram representing an apartment has the scale 1:50. The dimensions of a bedroom in the diagram are 5 x 8 cm. Find the dimensions, perimeter and area of the bedroom.

52. To make a chocolate cake the ingredients needed are 2 eggs, 1 cup of sugar and 3 cups of flower. Find the ingredients needed to make a cake half as big.

53. In a certain family with 2 children the parents eat twice as much as the kids. The family ordered 600g of Pasta, find the amount of pasta each one of the family members will eat.

54. The scale of a map is 1:800000. Find the real distance represented by:

   a. 1 cm

   b. 9 cm

   c. The distance in the map that represent 10km

   d. The distance in the map that represent 50km

1.4. – PRIME NUMBERS AND FACTORS GCD AND LCM

1. A prime number is: _____

2. Write 5 examples of prime numbers: _____

3. Write 5 examples of numbers that are not prime: _____

4. Write down the prime factors of the following numbers:

   a. 3: _____
   b. 4: _____
   c. 5: _____
   d. 6: _____
   e. 8: _____
   f. 9: _____
   g. 10: _____
   h. 15: _____
   i. 11: _____
   j. 12: _____
   k. 13: _____
   l. 18: _____
   m. 20: _____
   n. 21: _____
   o. 22: _____
   p. 23: _____
   q. 24: _____
   r. 25: _____
   s. 26: _____
   t. 27: _____
   u. 28: _____
   v. 29: _____
   w. 30: _____
   x. 40: _____
   y. 45: _____
   z. 52: _____
   aa. 66: _____
   bb. 70: _____
   cc. 76: _____
   dd. 78: _____
   ee. 80: _____
   ff. 81: _____
   gg. 82: _____
   hh. 83: _____
   ii. 84: _____
   jj. 85: _____
   kk. 88: _____
   ll. 90: _____
   mm. 92: _____
   nn. 100: _____
   oo. 110: _____
   pp. 200: _____
   qq. 210: _____
   rr. 1000: _____
   ss. 550: _____
   tt. 442: _____

Write down 3 multiples of the following numbers:
1. 9: <u>18, 27, 90</u>
2. 5:
3. 2:
4. 23:
5. 25:
6. 20:
7. 10:
8. 150:

GREATEST COMMON DIVISOR (GCD)

Example: Find the Greatest Common Divisor (GCD) of 120 and 80.

Since $\begin{aligned} 120 &= 2^3 \cdot 3 \cdot 5 \\ 80 &= 2^4 \cdot 5 \end{aligned}$ their common divisors are $2^3, 5$ so the GCD is $2^3 \cdot 5 = 40$

5. Find the greatest common divisor of 6 and 8.

6. Find the greatest common divisor of 7 and 9.

7. Find the greatest common divisor of 8 and 12.

8. Find the greatest common divisor of 12 and 10.

9. Find the greatest common divisor of 9 and 15.

10. Find the greatest common divisor of 18 and 20.

11. Find the greatest common divisor of 30 and 25.

12. Find the greatest common divisor of 120 and 20.

13. Find the greatest common divisor of 42 and 14.

14. Find the greatest common divisor of 100 and 13.

15. Find the greatest common divisor of 22 and 20.

16. Find the greatest common divisor of 220 and 310.

17. Find the greatest common divisor of 68 and 90.

18. Find the greatest common divisor of 512 and 360.

19. Find the greatest common divisor of 640 and 312.

LEAST COMMON MULTIPLE (LCM)

Example: Find the Least common multiple (LCM) of 120 and 80.

Since $\begin{array}{l}120 = 2^3 \cdot 3 \cdot 5 \\ 80 = 2^4 \cdot 5\end{array}$ the highest prime factors are $2^4, 3, 5$ so the LCD is $2^4 \cdot 3 \cdot 5 = 240$

20. Find the least common multiple of 6 and 8.

21. Find the least common multiple of 7 and 9.

22. Find the least common multiple of 12 and 8.

23. Find the least common multiple of 15 and 14.

24. Find the least common multiple of 18 and 10.

25. Find the least common multiple of 12 and 10.

26. Find the least common multiple of 120 and 20.

27. Find the least common multiple of 42 and 14.

28. Find the least common multiple of 100 and 13.

29. Find the least common multiple of 22 and 20.

30. Find the least common multiple of 220 and 310.

31. Find the least common multiple of 68 and 90.

32. Find the least common multiple of 512 and 360.

33. Find the least common multiple of 640 and 312.

1.5. – TYPES OF NUMBERS

Natural Numbers (N): $\quad$ N = {__, __, __, __, __ ...}

Integers (Z): $\quad$ Z = {..., __, __, __, __, __, 0, __, __, __, __, __ ...}

Rational Numbers (Q): $\quad$ Q = $\{\frac{a}{b}, a, b \in Z\}$

Numbers that **can** be written as _____ being both the

numerator and the denominator _____.

Examples: $\frac{1}{1}, \frac{2}{3}, \frac{-7}{3}, \frac{4}{-1}, \frac{__}{__}, $ _____, _____ ...

Irrational Numbers (Q'): $\quad$ Q' ≠ $\{\frac{a}{b}, a, b \in Z\}$ Numbers that _____ be written as

fractions, being both the _____ and _____ Integers.

Examples: __, __, __ ...

Real Numbers (R): $\quad$ R = Q + Q' (Rationals and Irrationals)

Represented in a Venn diagram:

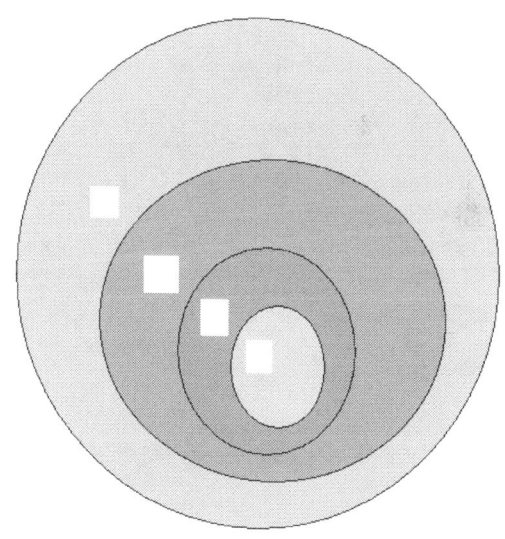

Exercises

1. Natural numbers are contained in the _____ numbers.

2. Integer numbers are contained in the _____ numbers

3. Rational numbers are contained in the _____ numbers.

4. Irrational numbers are located _____.

5. Shade the area in which the irrational numbers are located:

6. True or False:

    a. All Natural numbers are Integers: ____

    b. All Real numbers are Natural: ____

    c. All Rational numbers are Real: ____

    d. All Real numbers are Rational: ____

    e. All Integer numbers are Rational: ____

    f. All Real numbers are Irrational: ____

    g. Some Irrational numbers are Real and some are not: ____

    h. Some Irrational numbers are Integers: ____

    i. Some integers are negative: ____

    j. Some Irrationals are negative: ____

    k. Some Natural numbers are negative: ____

7. Fill the chart with yes or no (follow the example):

Number	Natural	Integer	Rational	Real
-2	no	yes	yes	yes
π				
$-3.121212\ldots$				
-15.16				
$\sqrt{3}$				
$-2\frac{2}{5}$				
$\sqrt[3]{8}$				

8. Fill the numbers column with appropriate numbers and yes or no. Follow the example.

Number	Natural	Integer	Rational	Real
	no	yes		
		no	yes	yes
	yes	yes	yes	
			no	yes
		no	yes	yes
			yes	
	no			
		yes	no	

4. Convert the following numbers into the form: $\dfrac{n}{m}$

1. $0.333\ldots =$

2. $1.111\ldots =$

3. $5.3 =$

4. $5.2828\ldots =$

5. $-2.3535\ldots =$

6. $42.67 =$

7. $12.355355\ldots =$

8. $-31.44 =$

9. 0.125125… =

10. 3.22332233… =

11. 1115.36 =

12. 122.53 =

13. 1.123123… =

14. 1.22565656… =

15. 1.5696969… =

16. 5.540404040… =

5. Given the following diagram:

Write the following numbers in the appropriate location in the diagram:

a. 2.2
b. −5
c. 3
d. $\dfrac{1}{3}$
e. 5
f. −3.3
g. 1.111…
h. $\dfrac{1}{\sqrt{3}}$
i. 2π
j. $1+2\pi$
k. $\sqrt{2}+3$
l. $\dfrac{4}{2}$

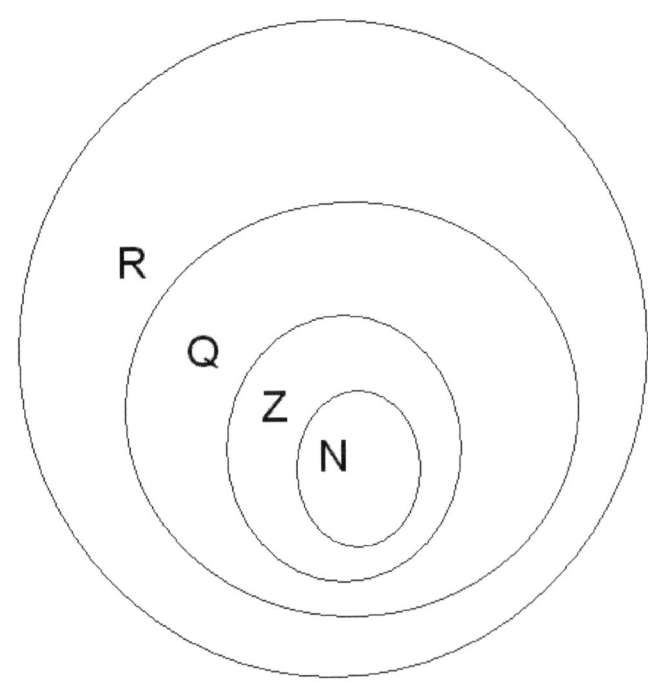

6. Circle the right option. The number –2 is:

    a. Integer and Natural.
    b. Positive
    c. Integer and Rational
    d. Natural and Real
    e. Natural and Rational
    f. None of the above

7. Circle the right option. The number 3.41414141..... is:

    a. Integer and Natural.
    b. Natural
    c. Integer and Real
    d. Rational and Integer
    e. Rational
    f. None of the above

8. Circle the right option. The number 3.41 is:

    a. Integer and Natural.
    b. Integer
    c. Rational and Real
    d. Integer and Real
    e. Rational and negative
    f. None of the above

9. Circle the right option. The number $\sqrt{31}$ is:

    a. Integer and Natural.
    b. Integer
    c. Decimal
    d. Integer and Real
    e. Rational
    f. Irrational

10. Circle the right option. The number 5 is:

    a. Natural.
    b. Integer
    c. Real
    d. Integer and Natural
    e. Rational and Natural
    f. All of the above

1.6. – ROOTS AND RATIONALIZATION

Simplify as much as possible:

1. $\sqrt{0} =$

2. $\sqrt{1} =$

3. $\sqrt{4} =$

4. $\sqrt[3]{8} =$

5. $\sqrt{16} \cdot \sqrt{25} =$

6. $\sqrt[4]{2} \cdot \sqrt[4]{8} =$

7. $\sqrt{-1} =$

8. $\left(\sqrt{4}\right)^2 =$

9. $\left(\sqrt{5}\right)^2 \cdot \left(\sqrt[3]{3}\right)^3 =$

10. $\left(\sqrt{532}\right)^2 =$

11. $\left(\sqrt{a}\right)^2 \left(\sqrt[n]{a}\right)^n =$

12. $\sqrt{0.01} =$

13. $\sqrt{0.25} =$

14. $\sqrt{2.25} =$

15. $\sqrt{\dfrac{a^2}{9}} =$

16. $\sqrt{\dfrac{8}{200}} =$

17. $\sqrt{3} + \sqrt{3} =$

18. $\sqrt{2} + \sqrt{2} + \sqrt{2} =$

19. $\sqrt{2} + \sqrt{8} + \sqrt{2} =$

20. $\sqrt{4} + \sqrt{2} + \sqrt{8} =$

21. $\sqrt{9} + \sqrt{12} + \sqrt{27} =$

22. $\sqrt{50} + \sqrt{75} + \sqrt{12} =$

23. $\sqrt[3]{16} + \sqrt[3]{54} =$

24. $\sqrt[4]{32} - \sqrt[4]{162} =$

25. $\sqrt{27} + \sqrt{81} + \sqrt{48} =$

26. $\sqrt{200} + \sqrt{50} - \sqrt{18} =$

27. $\sqrt{20} + \sqrt{80} - \sqrt{125} =$

28. $\sqrt{10}\sqrt{10} =$

29. $\sqrt[3]{a} \cdot \sqrt[3]{a} \cdot \sqrt[3]{a} =$

30. $\sqrt{3}\sqrt{9}\sqrt{3} =$

31. $\dfrac{\sqrt{200}}{\sqrt{2}} =$

32. $\dfrac{\sqrt{72}}{\sqrt{2}} =$

33. $\dfrac{\sqrt{75}}{\sqrt{5}} =$

34. $\sqrt{3}\dfrac{\sqrt{24}}{\sqrt{2}} =$

35. $\sqrt{a}\sqrt{a} =$

36. $\sqrt{a} + \sqrt{a} =$

Rationalize the denominator:

37. $\dfrac{1}{\sqrt{2}} =$

38. $\dfrac{3}{\sqrt{5}+1} =$

39. $\dfrac{-7}{\sqrt{5}-2} =$

40. $\dfrac{\sqrt{2}+3}{-5} =$

41. $\dfrac{\sqrt{2}+3}{\sqrt{6}-5} =$

42. $\dfrac{\sqrt{2}}{\sqrt{6}+\sqrt{3}} =$

43. $\dfrac{\sqrt{2}-1}{2\sqrt{5}-\sqrt{3}} =$

44. $\dfrac{-1}{2\sqrt{a}+b} =$

45. $\dfrac{3\sqrt{a}-2b}{2\sqrt{a}+\sqrt{b}} =$

Rationalize the numerator:

46. $\dfrac{\sqrt{4}}{\sqrt{5}} =$

47. $\dfrac{3-\sqrt{2}}{\sqrt{5}+1} =$

48. $\dfrac{-7}{\sqrt{5}-2} =$

49. $\dfrac{\sqrt{2}+3}{\sqrt{6}-5} =$

50. $\dfrac{\sqrt{2}}{\sqrt{x}+\sqrt{3}} =$

51. $\dfrac{\sqrt{b}-a}{2\sqrt{a}-\sqrt{3}} =$

52. $\dfrac{-3\sqrt{7}+8}{2\sqrt{5}+7} =$

53. $\dfrac{\sqrt{a}-2\sqrt{b}}{2\sqrt{a}+\sqrt{b}} =$

1.7. – INTERVAL NOTATION AND INEQUALITIES

$x \in (a, b]$ or $\{x \mid a < x \leq b\}$ means x is between a and b, not including a and including b.

Exercises:

1. Represent the following Intervals on the real line:

a. $x \in (2, 5]$

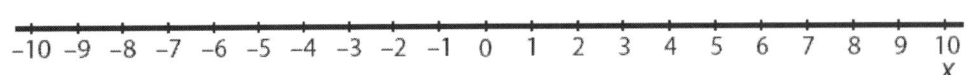

b. $x \in (3, 6)$

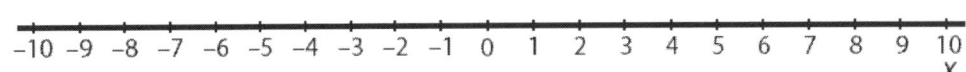

c. $x \in [-5, 9]$

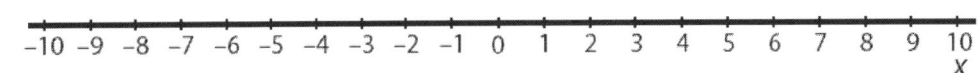

d. $x \in [-8, -1)$

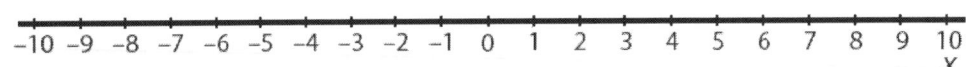

e. $x \in [-\infty, -1)$

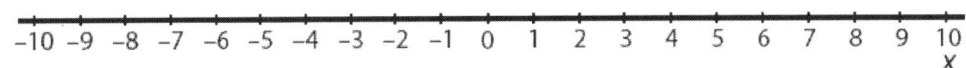

f. $x \in [-\infty, 6]$

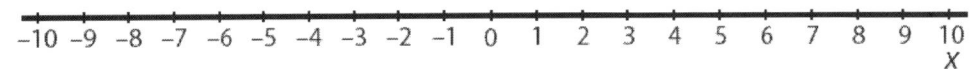

g. $x \in (6, \infty]$

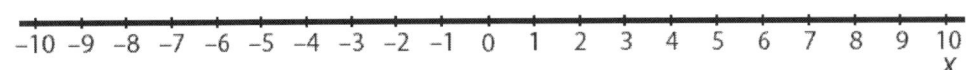

h. $\{x \mid 7 < x < 9\}$

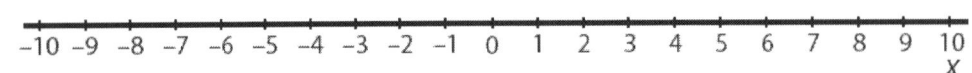

i. $\{x \mid -7 < x < -2\}$

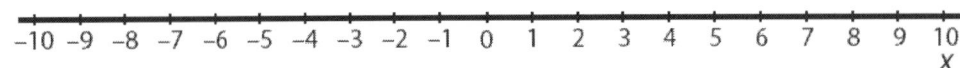

j. $\{x|\ 1 < x < 2\}$

k. $\{x|\ \infty < x < 2\}$

l. $\{x|\ 1 < x < \infty\}$

2. Write each one of the Intervals using all types of notations:

   a. $x \in (4, 5)$

   b. $x \in (-\infty, 5)$

   c. $x \in (4, 5)$

   d. $x \in (3, \infty]$

   e. $x \in\ ]-5, 9]$

   f. $x \in [-8, -1[$

   g. $\{x|\ 7 < x < 9\}$

   h. $\{x|\ -7 < x < -2\}$

3. Solve the following inequalities and shade the solution on the given diagram:

a. $-x \leq 3$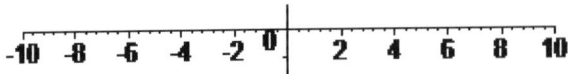

b. $5 - x \leq 2$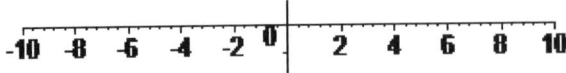

c. $8 - 2x \leq 3$

d. $-2x \leq 4 + x$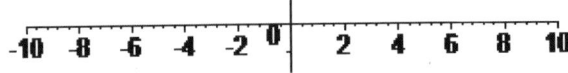

e. $7 + x \leq x + 3$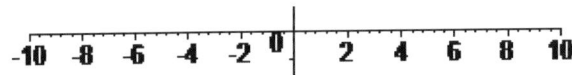

f. $-2x \leq 2x + 1$

h. $-5x + 3 \leq 2x - 1$

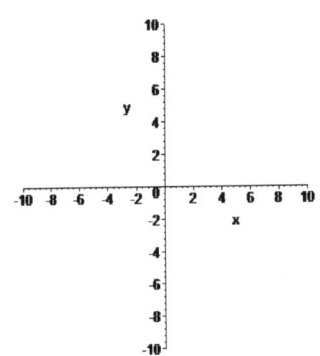
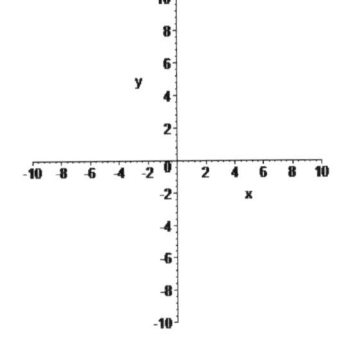

g. $-2x \leq 2x$

i. $7x \leq 4 + 7x + 1$

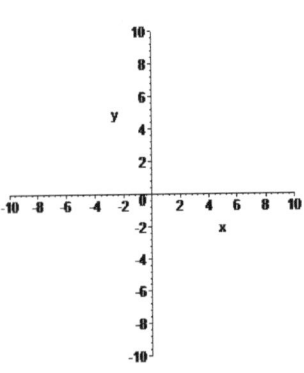

40

j. $\dfrac{x}{2} \leq x+1$

m. $\dfrac{2-x}{3} \leq \dfrac{x}{5} - 3$

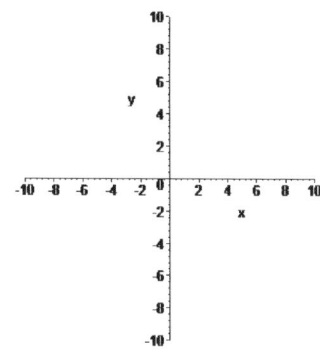
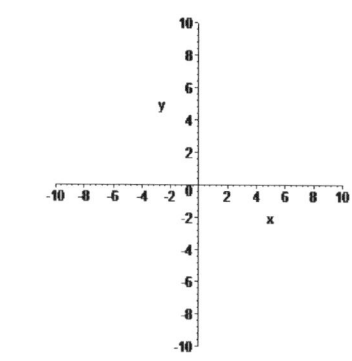

k. $\dfrac{x}{3} \leq \dfrac{x}{6} + 1$

n. $\dfrac{4-2x}{5} \leq \dfrac{2x}{6} - \dfrac{x}{2}$

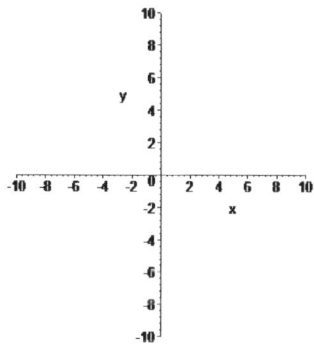
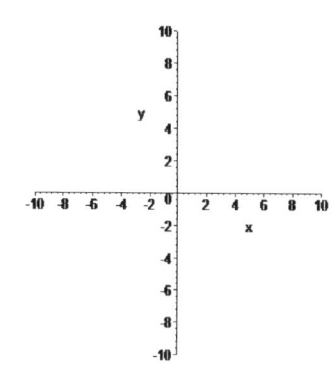

l. $\dfrac{x-4}{6} \leq x-1$

o. $\dfrac{-2x}{5} - 3 \leq \dfrac{x-2}{4} - \dfrac{x-1}{2}$

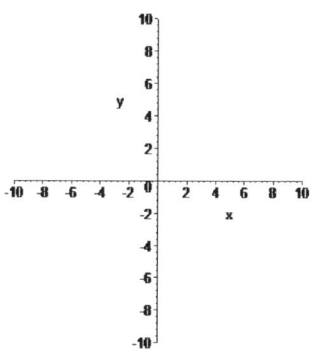
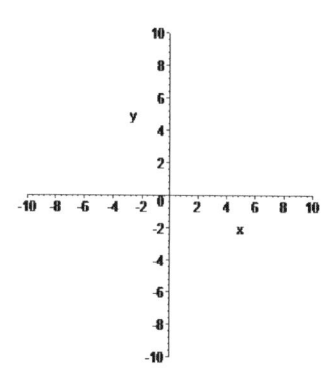

p. $\dfrac{y+4}{6} \leq y-1$

s. $\dfrac{-2y}{5} - 1 \leq y - \dfrac{y-1}{2}$

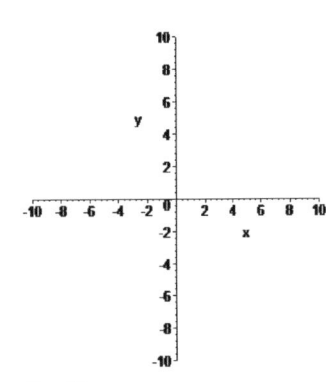
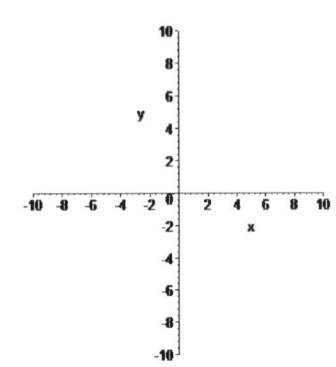

q. $\dfrac{2-2y}{3} \leq \dfrac{y}{4} - 1$

t. $-2 \leq 2x \leq 1$

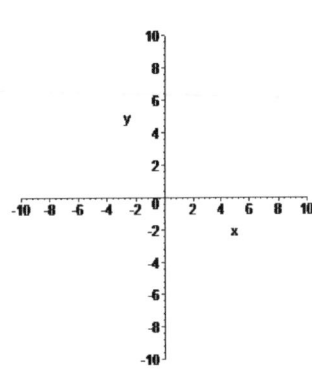
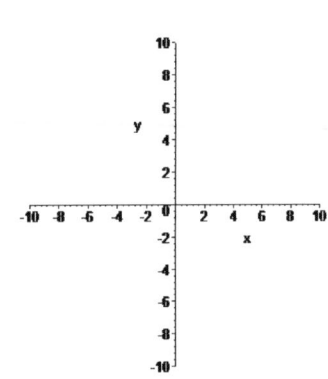

r. $\dfrac{4-y}{5} \leq \dfrac{y}{2} - y$

u. $-8 \leq \dfrac{-6x+3}{4} \leq 7$

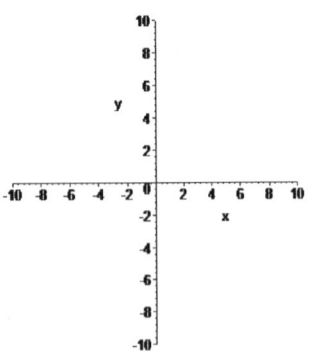
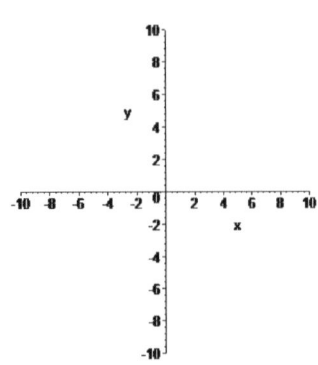

v. $-10 \leq 4y+2 \leq 9$

w. $0 \leq \dfrac{y+2}{3} \leq 2$

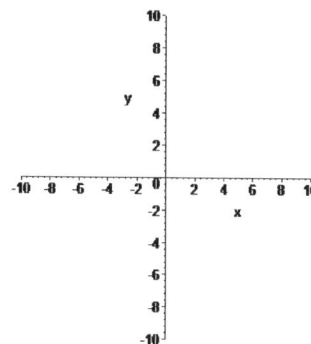

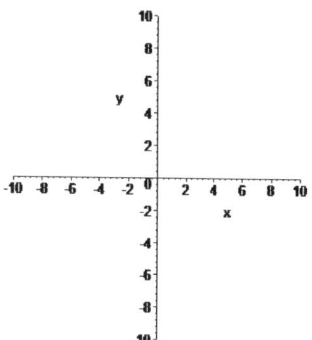

4. Solve the inequalities:

   a. $-2 \leq -\dfrac{5y}{3}+y \leq 0$

   b. $-3 \leq -\dfrac{4x}{3}+x \leq 0$

   c. $-2 \leq -\dfrac{5-y}{3}+\dfrac{y}{2}+1 \leq 1$

   d. $-3 \leq \dfrac{x}{6}-\dfrac{5x}{3} \leq 0$

   e. $-1 \leq \dfrac{x}{8}-\dfrac{5x+1}{2}+\dfrac{x}{4} \leq 1$

   f. $0 \leq \dfrac{x}{6}-\dfrac{5x+2}{3}+\dfrac{x}{4} \leq 2$

5.
   a. Solve the inequality $2x \leq 2$

   b. Solve the inequality $-x < -2$.

   c. Represent both solutions on the real line:

   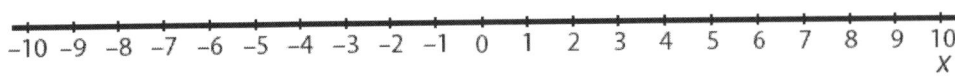

   d. State their intersection: _____.

6.
   a. Solve the inequality $2x - 2 \leq 2$

   b. Solve the inequality $-3x + 1 > -2$.

   c. Represent both solutions on the real line:

   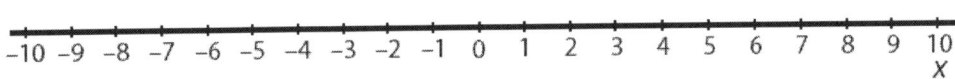

   d. State their intersection: _____.

7.
   a. Solve the inequality $x - 2 \leq -5$

   b. Solve the inequality $-2x + 14 \leq -2$.

   c. Represent both solutions on the real line:

   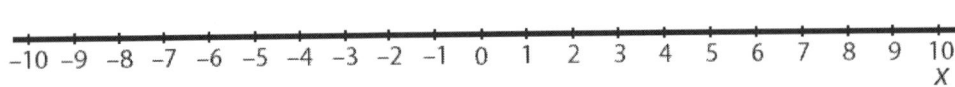

   d. State their intersection: _____

44

8.
   a. Solve the inequality $3x - 7 \leq 2$

   b. Solve the inequality $-x < -2$.

   c. Represent both solutions on the real line:

   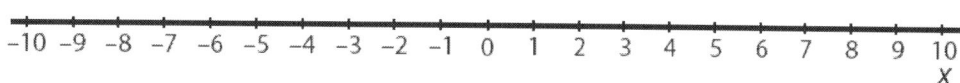

   d. State their intersection: _____.

9.
   a. Solve the inequality $5x - 2 \leq 2$

   b. Solve the inequality $-2x + 1 > -2$.

   c. Represent both solutions on the real line:

   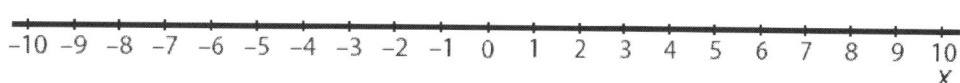

   d. State their intersection: _____.

10.
   a. Solve the inequality $5x - 2 \leq -12$

   b. Solve the inequality $-2x - 3 \leq -2$.

   c. Represent both solutions on the real line:

   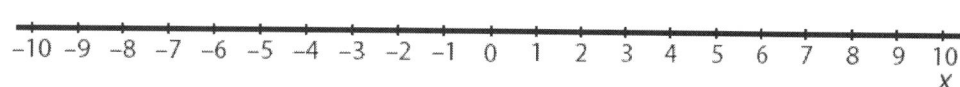

   d. State their intersection: _____

1.8. – EXPONENTS

Product:

$a^0 = \_\_$ $a^1 = \_\_$ $a^2 = \_\_ \times \_\_$
$a^3 = \_\_ \times \_\_ \times \_\_$
$a^3 a^2 = _____ = \_\_$

$$a^m a^n = _____$$

Division:

$\dfrac{a^5}{a^3} = \dfrac{_____}{_____} = \dfrac{\_\_\_\_}{\_\_} = \_\_$

$\dfrac{a^2}{a^5} = \dfrac{_____}{_____} = \dfrac{\_\_\_\_}{\_\_} = \_\_$

$$\dfrac{a^m}{a^n} = _____$$

Power:

$(a^2)^3 = _____ = \_\_$

$\left(\dfrac{a^2}{b}\right)^3 = \dfrac{_____}{_____} = \dfrac{\_\_\_\_}{\_\_}$

$$(a^m)^n = \_\_\_$$

$$\left(\dfrac{a^m}{b^k}\right)^n = \dfrac{\_\_\_\_}{\_\_\_\_}$$

Radicals:

$(a^3)^{\frac{1}{2}} = \_\_\_ = \_\_\_$
$(a^4)^{\frac{1}{7}} = \_\_\_ = \_\_\_$

$$(a^m)^{\frac{1}{n}} = \_\_\_ = \_\_\_$$

Exercises

Write in all possible forms and evaluate without using a calculator (follow example):

1. $4^{-1} = \dfrac{1}{4} = 0.25$
2. $10^0 =$
3. $10^1 =$
4. $10^3 =$
5. $10^{-1} =$
6. $10^{-2} =$
7. $10^{-3} =$
8. $10^{-4} =$
9. $2^0 =$
10. $2^1 =$
11. $2^{-1} =$
12. $2^{-2} =$
13. $2^{-3} =$
14. $2^{-4} =$
15. $(-1)^0 =$
16. $-1^0 =$
17. $(-1)^1 =$
18. $-1^1 =$
19. $(-1)^{-1} =$
20. $-1^2 =$

21. $(-1)^2 =$

22. $-1^2 =$

23. $(-1)^{-2} =$

24. $-1^{-2} =$

25. $(-3)^0 =$

26. $(-3)^1 =$

27. $-3^1 =$

28. $(-3)^2 =$

29. $-3^2 =$

30. $(-3)^{-1} =$

31. $-3^{-1} =$

32. $(-3)^{-2} =$

33. $-3^{-2} =$

34. $9^{\frac{1}{2}} =$

35. $4^{\frac{1}{2}} =$

36. $16^{-\frac{1}{2}} =$

37. $8^{-\frac{2}{3}} =$

38. $27^{-\frac{4}{3}} =$

39. $125^{\frac{1}{3}} =$

40. $16^{\frac{3}{4}} =$

41. $(3^{-1})^2 =$

42. $(-8^{-3})^{\frac{2}{3}} =$

43. $(-27^{-1})^{\frac{2}{3}} =$

44. $(16^{-1})^{-\frac{3}{2}} =$

45. $\left(\frac{1}{2}\right)^0 =$

46. $\left(\frac{1}{2}\right)^1 =$

47. $\left(\frac{1}{2}\right)^{-1} =$

48. $\left(\frac{1}{2}\right)^2 =$

49. $\left(\frac{1}{2}\right)^{-2} =$

50. $\left(\frac{3}{5}\right)^0 =$

51. $\left(\frac{3}{4}\right)^1 =$

52. $\left(\frac{2}{5}\right)^{-1} =$

53. $\left(\frac{5}{11}\right)^2 =$

54. $\left(\frac{a}{b}\right)^{-1} =$

55. $\left(\frac{1}{b}\right)^{-1} =$

56. $b^{-1} =$

57. $\left(\frac{-11}{2}\right)^{-2} =$

58. $\left(\frac{3}{-2}\right)^1 =$

59. $\left(\frac{-12}{\sqrt{2}}\right)^{-1} =$

60. $\left(\frac{5\sqrt{2}}{11}\right)^2 =$

61. $\left(\frac{-2\sqrt{5}}{2}\right)^{-2} =$

62. $\left(\frac{3+5\sqrt{2}}{-2}\right)^2 =$

63. $\left(\dfrac{-12}{2-\sqrt{2}}\right)^{-2} =$

64. $\left(\dfrac{5+\sqrt{2}}{11}\right)^{2} =$

65. $\left(\dfrac{-2-\sqrt{5}}{2+\sqrt{2}}\right)^{-2} =$

66. $\left(\dfrac{-27}{8}\right)^{\frac{2}{3}} =$

67. $\left(\dfrac{16}{9}\right)^{\frac{3}{4}} =$

68. $\left(\dfrac{1}{2}\right)^{\frac{3}{2}} =$

69. $\left(\dfrac{9}{16}\right)^{\frac{1}{2}} =$

70. $\left(\dfrac{8}{27}\right)^{-\frac{1}{3}} =$

71. $a^{-2} =$

72. $a^{-\frac{1}{2}} =$

73. $a^{-\frac{2}{7}} =$

74. $5^{27} 5^{-29} =$

75. $4^{27} 2^{-49} =$

76. $9^{12} 3^{-20} =$

77. $a^{7} a^{-9} =$

78. $(-125)^{\frac{2}{3}} =$

79. $\dfrac{5^{10}}{5^{2}} =$

80. $\dfrac{3^{10}}{9^{2}} 3^{-2} =$

81. $\dfrac{3^{1}}{9^{\frac{1}{2}}} 3^{-\frac{1}{2}} =$

82. $\dfrac{\sqrt{2}\cdot 4^{2}}{2^{\frac{3}{4}}} 2^{-\frac{1}{2}} =$

83. $\dfrac{a^{-1}}{a^{-2}} =$

84. $\sqrt{\dfrac{a^{-10}}{a^{-12}}} =$

85. $\sqrt{\sqrt{a}} =$

86. $\sqrt{a\sqrt{a}} =$

87. $a\sqrt{\sqrt[3]{a}} =$

88. $\dfrac{1}{\sqrt[4]{\sqrt{a}}} =$

89. $\sqrt{\sqrt{\sqrt[7]{a^{2}}}} =$

90. $\sqrt[3]{\sqrt{a\sqrt{a^{2}}}} =$

91. $\dfrac{2\sqrt{a}}{\sqrt{2a}} =$

92. $\dfrac{\sqrt{a}}{\sqrt[3]{\sqrt{a}}} =$

93. $\dfrac{a\sqrt{a}}{\sqrt[5]{\sqrt{a}}} =$

94. $\dfrac{\sqrt{8}\sqrt{a}}{\sqrt{2a}} =$

95. $\sqrt{\dfrac{\sqrt{a}a^{-1}}{a\sqrt{a^{-2}}}} =$

96. $\dfrac{a}{\sqrt{2a^{-1}}} =$

97. $\dfrac{\sqrt{\dfrac{1}{a}}}{\sqrt{aa^{-2}}} =$

98. $\left(\dfrac{2}{5}\right)^3 \times \left(\dfrac{5}{3}\right)^3 =$

99. $\left(\dfrac{4}{7}\right)^2 \div \left(\dfrac{9}{7}\right)^2 =$

100. $\sqrt{\left(\dfrac{7}{5}\right)^7 \div \left(\dfrac{49}{125}\right)^3} =$

101. $\left(\dfrac{2}{5}\right)^3 \cdot \left(\dfrac{3}{5}\right)^{-4} =$

102. $\left(\dfrac{4^2}{5^{-1}}\right)^3 \cdot \left(\dfrac{25^{-1}}{64}\right)^2 =$

103. $\left(\dfrac{3^{-5}}{4^2}\right)^2 \div \left(\dfrac{9^{-2}}{2^3}\right)^3 =$

104. $\left(\dfrac{5^4}{7^{-3}}\right)^2 \div \left(\dfrac{25^{-1}}{49}\right)^{-3} =$

105. $\sqrt[3]{\left(\dfrac{3}{4}\right)^5 \div \left(\dfrac{9}{64}\right)^2} =$

106. $\left(\dfrac{2^{-3}}{3^{-2}}\right)^3 \cdot \left(\dfrac{4}{27}\right)^2 =$

107. $2^{-1} + 2 =$

108. $3^{-1} - 3^{-2} =$

109. $5^{-1} - 5^{-2} =$

110. $3^{-3} + 2^{-2} =$

111. $3^{-2} + 4^{-2} =$

112. $7^{-2} + 2^{-2} =$

113. $8^{-2} - 3^{-2} =$

114. $7^{-2} - 2^{-3} =$

115. $a^{-1} + a^{-1} =$

116. $ba^{-1} + a^{-1} =$

117. $2x^{-1} + x^{-2} =$

118. $a^{-1} - ba^{-1} =$

119. $(ba)^{-1} + a^{-1} =$

120. $\dfrac{1}{x} + x^{-2} =$

121. $ba^{-1} + (ba)^{-1} =$

122. $\dfrac{a+a}{3a} =$

123. $\dfrac{2a+a}{5\sqrt{a}} =$

124. $\dfrac{a^2 + a^3}{2a} =$

125. $\dfrac{4b^{-1}a^2}{2ba^{-1}} =$

126. $\dfrac{4b^{-3}}{\sqrt{2b}} =$

127. $\dfrac{9b^{-\frac{1}{2}}a^2}{27^{-1}b^{-1}a} =$

128. $\dfrac{4b^{-1}a^5 a^2}{8ba^{-1}} =$

129. $\dfrac{\sqrt[4]{a^2} + \sqrt{a}}{\sqrt{2a}} =$

130. $\dfrac{b\sqrt[3]{a} + ba^{\frac{1}{3}}}{a\sqrt{b}} =$

131. $\dfrac{3^{-2}}{9^{\frac{2}{3}}} 27^{\frac{5}{4}} =$

132. $\dfrac{4^{-4}\sqrt{2}}{8^{-\frac{2}{3}}} 16^{\frac{3}{4}} =$

133. $\sqrt{5}\, \dfrac{25^2 5^{-1}}{25^{\frac{4}{3}}} 5^{\frac{1}{4}} \sqrt[3]{5} =$

134. $\dfrac{4^{-2} 2^{-4}}{16^2 (\sqrt[6]{16^4})} 8^{\frac{1}{4}} 2^{-1} =$

135. $x\sqrt{x}\sqrt{3} =$

136. $x\sqrt{x} + \sqrt{2x} =$

137. $\dfrac{1}{x\sqrt{x}} =$

138. $\dfrac{x\sqrt[3]{x}}{\sqrt{x}} =$

139. $\dfrac{\sqrt{2x}}{x\sqrt{4x}} =$

140. $\dfrac{\sqrt{3x}}{x + x^2} =$

141. $\dfrac{\sqrt{3x}}{\sqrt[3]{3x^2}} =$

142. $\dfrac{\sqrt{25x^2}}{\sqrt[3]{5x^3}} =$

143. $s^n s^{2n} s^2 =$

144. $a^{2k} b a^3 b^{2k} a =$

145. $\dfrac{3^n}{9^n} 27^n =$

146. $\dfrac{3^{2n+1}}{81^{n-2}} 27^{2n} =$

147. $\dfrac{6^n}{8^{2n}} 24^{3n} =$

148. $\dfrac{2^n}{8^{n+1}} 16^{n-2} =$

149. $\dfrac{5^{-n}}{125^{2n-2}} 5^{-n+2} =$

150. $\dfrac{12^{2n+1}}{48^{3n-1}} \div 36^{4n} =$

151. $\dfrac{x^{-n}}{x^{2n-2}} x^{-n+5} =$

152. $\dfrac{2x^{-n+1}}{2^2 x^{3n+2}} x^{n+5} =$

153. $\dfrac{2yx^{-2n+3}}{2^5 y^{-1} x^{-4n+2}} x^{-2n+1} =$

154. $\dfrac{4^2 y^2 x^{-3} z}{2^2 xz^2 y^{-1} x} x^{-2} z^2 =$

155. $\dfrac{4^2 y^2 (x^{-2} z^2)^{-2}}{(2^2 x)^3 z^2 y^{-1} x} x^{-2} z^2 =$

156. $\dfrac{4^{-2} y^3 (x^{-2} z^3)^{-1}}{(2^{-3} x)^{-3} z^{-2} y^{-1} x} xz^2 =$

157. $\left(\dfrac{a}{b^2}\right)^2 \div \left(\dfrac{a^{-1}}{b^3}\right)^{-3} \cdot \left(\dfrac{1}{b}\right)^3 =$

158. $\left(\dfrac{ab}{b^2}\right)^{-2} \div \left(\dfrac{(2ba)^{-1}}{b^3}\right)^{-3} \cdot \left(\dfrac{2}{b}\right)^3 =$

159. $\dfrac{a^{-2} b^n (a^{-2n} b^3)^{-1}}{(b^{-3n} a)^3 \sqrt{ab^{-1}}} =$

160. $\dfrac{a^{-2} b^n (a^{-2n} b^2)^n}{(b^{-3n} a)^n a^{-2n} b^n} =$

161. $\dfrac{3^n a^{-2} b^n (a^{-2n} b^3)^{n+1}}{(9^n b^{-2n} a)^n a^{-2n} b^{n+2}} =$

162. $\dfrac{3^n + 3^{n+1}}{3^{n-1}} =$

163. $\dfrac{4^n + 4^{n-1}}{2^{n-2}} =$

164. $\dfrac{7^{2n} + 7^{2n-1}}{7^{2n-2}} =$

165. $\dfrac{7^{3n-1} - 7^{3n}}{7^{2n-2}} =$

166. $\dfrac{3^n + 3^{n+1}}{3^{n-1} + 3^n} =$

167. $\dfrac{2^n + 2^{n-1}}{2^{n-2} + 2^{n-1}} =$

1.9. – EQUATIONS

1st Degree Equations

1. $\dfrac{x}{12} = 5$

2. $\dfrac{x}{7} + 2 = 5$

3. $\dfrac{2x}{7} + 2 = 5 - 3x$

4. $\dfrac{2x}{7} + \dfrac{2}{5} = -2x + 1$

5. $\dfrac{2x-1}{x} = 3$

6. $\dfrac{x+2}{2x} = 5$

7. $\dfrac{x-2}{2x-1} = 6$

8. $\dfrac{2x-2}{x+1} = -2$

9. $\dfrac{2x}{7} + 1 = \dfrac{-5x}{7}$

10. $\dfrac{2x}{7} + 4 = \dfrac{3x}{2}$

11. $\dfrac{2}{x} - 3 = \dfrac{3}{2x}$

12. $\dfrac{2}{x-2} - 3 = \dfrac{3}{x-2}$

13. $\dfrac{-2}{x} = \dfrac{3}{x-2}$

14. $\dfrac{4}{x+1} = \dfrac{4}{x+2}$

15. $\dfrac{2}{x+1} = \dfrac{4}{x+2}$

16. $-\dfrac{2}{2x+1} - 2 = \dfrac{4}{2x+1}$

17. $\dfrac{x}{2} - \dfrac{x}{5} = 3$

18. $\dfrac{2}{x} + \dfrac{3}{5} = 3$

19. $\dfrac{2x-7}{2} - \dfrac{3x}{5} = x$

20. $1 - \dfrac{1}{x} = 7 - \dfrac{3x+1}{x}$

21. $3 - \dfrac{2x}{x-2} = 7 - \dfrac{2x+1}{x-2}$

22. $\dfrac{2-x}{x-2} = 1$

23. $\dfrac{2-x}{x-2} = -1$

24. $\dfrac{5-7x}{3x-2} = -1 + \dfrac{5}{3x-2}$

25. $\dfrac{15-x}{3-x} = 7 - \dfrac{5x}{3-x}$

26. Write an equation whose solution is $\dfrac{2}{3}$

Isolate x

1. $\dfrac{4}{x} = \dfrac{a}{x+6}$

2. $\dfrac{14}{x+2} = \dfrac{a}{x+2} - a$

3. $\dfrac{2}{x+3} - a = \dfrac{a+b}{x+3}$

4. $\dfrac{5}{2x+1} - 3a = \dfrac{b}{2x+1}$

5. $\dfrac{-2x}{a+3} = \dfrac{x+2}{2a-1}$

6. $\dfrac{-5x+1}{2a} = \dfrac{bx}{3a+2}$

7. $\dfrac{a}{x+2} = \dfrac{b}{x+2} - b + 1$

8. $\dfrac{b}{2x-4} - 3 = \dfrac{b}{2x-4} - b + 1$

9. $\dfrac{1}{ax+2} = \dfrac{b}{x+a}$

10. $\dfrac{1}{ax+2} = \dfrac{b}{ax+2} - 3$

11. $3\dfrac{x}{ax+2} = 3$

12. $-3\dfrac{2x}{ax+3} = b$

13. $\dfrac{2x-3}{2ax+5} = -3b$

14. $\dfrac{x}{ax+2} = \dfrac{2}{a} - 3$

15. $\dfrac{bx}{x+2} = 3 - b$

16. $\dfrac{b+x}{x-3} = \dfrac{b}{x-3} + a$

17. $\dfrac{bx}{a} = 2x + 8$

18. $\dfrac{ax+b}{dx+2} = c - g$

19. $\dfrac{1}{x+2} + \dfrac{1}{b} = 2$

20. $\dfrac{1-a}{x} + \dfrac{2a}{x} = 2b$

21. $x - \dfrac{2+ax}{b} = 2x + 3$

22. $\dfrac{7-2ax}{x+1} = 2 + b$

23. $\dfrac{3-2x}{2x-3} = a$

24. $\dfrac{2}{1-x} = \dfrac{2a}{x-1} - a$

25. $\dfrac{3}{a-2x} = \dfrac{b}{2x-a} - c$

26. Complete the RHS of the equation so its solution is a

$\dfrac{x+1}{xa} - 1 = $ _____

55

Quadratic equations

a. Solve the following equations using the "complete the square method".
b. Check your answers using the quadratic formula.
c. Write the factorized expression.

1. $x^2 - 4x + 1 = 3$

2. $x^2 - 4x + 1 = -3$

3. $x^2 - 4x + 1 = -13$

4. $x^2 + 6x + 2 = 2$

5. $x^2 + 6x + 2 = -10$

6. $x^2 + 8x + 3 = -10$

7. $x^2 - 12x - 2 = 3$

8. $x^2 - 2x - 5 = 3$

9. $x^2 - 3x - 5 = 3$

10. $x^2 - 4x - 5 = 3$

11. $x^2 - 3x - 3 = -3$

12. $x^2 - 3x - 4 = -1$

13. $x^2 - 7x - 5 = 3$

14. $x^2 + x - 3 = 2$

15. $x^2 - 2x + 4 = 5$

16. $x^2 + 3x - 1 = 3$

17. $x^2 + 7x - 3 = 2$

18. $x^2 + 8x = 0$

19. $x^2 - 7x =$

20. $-x^2 + 10x + 4 = -1$

21. $2x^2 - 10x - 2 = 0$

22. $3x^2 - 9x - 6 = 0$

23. $-4x^2 - 2x - 6 = 1$

24. $2x^2 - x - 1 = 2$

25. $-5x^2 + 2x - 11 = -2$

26. $-2x^2 - 2x = 0$

27. $4x^2 - 2x = 0$

28. $-2x^2 - 3 = -5$

29. $6x^2 - 7x = 0$

30. $2x^2 - 6x = 0$

31. Write a quadratic equation whose solutions are $\dfrac{1}{2}$ and b

Rational equations 2nd degree

1. $\dfrac{3}{x^2-4}=2$

2. $\dfrac{2}{x^2-2x+1}=1$

3. $-\dfrac{2}{x^2-2x+3}=1$

4. $\dfrac{x}{x^2-4}=2$

5. $\dfrac{x}{x-4}=5$

6. $\dfrac{x^2}{x^2-4x}=2$

7. $\dfrac{x^2-1}{x-5}=2$

8. $\dfrac{x}{x-4}+\dfrac{2}{x-4}=5$

9. $\dfrac{x}{x-4}+\dfrac{2}{x+3}=-2$

10. $\dfrac{x-1}{2x-2}-\dfrac{2x-1}{x+3}=3$

11. $\dfrac{x}{3x+2}-\dfrac{2x-1}{2x+3}=7$

12. $\dfrac{1}{x}+\dfrac{2}{x^2}=3$

13. $\dfrac{2}{x^3} - \dfrac{3}{x^2} = -\dfrac{1}{x}$

14. $\dfrac{1}{x-1} + \dfrac{2}{x^2-1} = 2$

15. $\dfrac{1}{x-3} - \dfrac{2}{x^2-9} = 4$

16. $\dfrac{5}{x-2} - \dfrac{3}{x^2-4} = -2$

17. $\dfrac{2}{x^n} - \dfrac{3}{x^{n+1}} = 5$

18. $\dfrac{3}{25-x^2} - \dfrac{4}{5-x} = 1$

19. Write a rational equation that has 3 as a solution. Solve the equation to check for other solutions.

20. Write a rational equation that has $\dfrac{1}{5}$ as a solution. Solve the equation to check for other solutions.

Radical Equations

1. $\sqrt{3} = \sqrt{x}$ $x =$

2. $3 = \sqrt{x}$ $x =$

3. $1 = \sqrt{-2x}$ $x =$

4. $\dfrac{2}{\sqrt{x}} = 1 + x$

5. $\sqrt{8x + 2} = 0$

6. $\sqrt{5x - 2} = 6$

7. $\sqrt{5x^2 - 2} = 3$

8. $\sqrt{x^2 + 1} = -2$

9. $\sqrt{x^2 - 2} + 4 = -2$

10. $\sqrt{2x^2 - 2} + 4x = -2$

11. $\sqrt{2x - 2} + 3x + 2 = -2$

12. $\sqrt{x + 1} + \sqrt{x + 3} = 2$

13. $\sqrt{x - 1} + \sqrt{x + 3} = 2$

14. $\sqrt{x - 3} + \sqrt{x + 3} = 3$

15. $\sqrt{5x + 1} - \sqrt{3x - 3} = 2$

16. $\sqrt{8x + 2} - \sqrt{3x - 3} = 0$

17. $\sqrt{x - 1} + \sqrt{x + 2} = -2$

18. $\dfrac{12}{\sqrt{x}} = 8 - \sqrt{x}$

19. $\sqrt{x + 9} = x - \sqrt{2 + x}$

Higher degree simple equations

1. $x^4 - 2x^2 = 0$

2. $10(2x - 3)(x^2 - 3)(x + 5)(x^3 + 2) = 0$

3. $(2x - 3)(x - 3) = 1$

4. $(6x - 7)(3x^2 - 5)(2x + 7)(2x^5 - 64)(4x^4 + 5) = 0$

5. $3x^5 - x^2 = 0$

6. $100(x - 2)^{100}(x^2 - 5)^{10} = 0$

7. $x^6 - 32x = 0$

8. $x^6 - 2x^5 + x^4 = 0$

9. $x^3 - 4x^2 + 3x = 0$

10. $2x^3 - 5x = 0$

11. $2x^3 - x^2 = 0$

12. $ax^4 - 3x = 0$

13. $ax^5 - x^2 = 0$

14. $a(x - a)^{10}(x^2 - a)^{12}(x^3 - a)^{12} = 0$

15. $x^4 - 5x^2 + 3 = -1$

16. $x^4 - 10x^2 + 3 = -6$

17. $x^6 + 3x^3 - 10 = 0$

18. $x^8 = -2x^4 - 1$

19. $x^4 - 13x^2 + 36 = 0$

20. $x^5 - 15x^3 + 54x = 0$

21. $x^5 + x^3 - 6x = 0$

22. $x^4 = 6x^2 - 5$

Rational exponent equations

1. $x^{\frac{1}{2}} = 2$

2. $x^{-1} + x^0 = a$

3. $x^{-2} = 0$

4. $2x^{\frac{2}{3}} = 3$

5. $3x^{-\frac{1}{2}} = 2$

6. $3x^{-\frac{1}{2}} = 0$

7. $ax^{-\frac{3}{7}} = 0$

8. $3x^{-\frac{6}{7}} = -2$

9. $x + x^{-\frac{1}{2}} = 0$

10. $2x - x^{\frac{2}{5}} = 0$

11. $x^{\frac{1}{3}} + 1 = 0$

12. $3x^{\frac{1}{2}} - x^2 = 0$

13. $8x^{-2} + x^{-1} = 2$

14. $5x^{\frac{4}{3}} = -1$

15. $3x^{-\frac{3}{4}} = -2$

16. $x - 2x^{\frac{2}{3}} = 0$

17. $2x^2 - x^{-\frac{3}{2}} = 0$

18. $3x^{-2} = -5$

19. $x^{\frac{1}{2}} - 2x^{\frac{1}{6}} = 0$

20. $4x^{\frac{1}{4}} - 2x^{\frac{1}{2}} = 0$

Exponential equations

1. $2^x = 2$

2. $2^{x+2} = 2^2$

3. $\left(\dfrac{1}{32}\right) 2^{3x+4} = 4$

4. $2^{-4x+1} = 8$

5. $3^{-5x+3} = 9$

6. $\left(\dfrac{1}{4}\right)^{x+2} = \dfrac{1}{16}$

7. $2^{x+2} = \dfrac{-1}{16}$

8. $2^{-2x+1} = 8^x$

9. $\left(\dfrac{1}{3}\right)^{4x^2-1} = 9^{2x}$

10. $\left(\dfrac{1}{125}\right)5^{x-1} = 1$

11. $3^{2x-5} = \dfrac{1}{3}$

12. $3^{2x^2-5} = \dfrac{1}{27}$

13. $\left(\dfrac{1}{5}\right)^{x-1} = -1$

14. $5^{x-1} = 5^{x(x-1)}$

15. $6^{x^2-8} = 6$

16. $5^{x-1} = \dfrac{1}{125}$

17. $\left(\dfrac{1}{36}\right)^{2x-3} = \dfrac{1}{6}$

18. $6^{2x-3} = -\dfrac{3}{4}$

19. $2^x = 3$

20. $5^x = 3$

21. $1^x = 2$

22. $2^x = -2$

23. $4^x = (0.5)^{x-2}$

24. $1000^{2x-1} = (0.01)^{3x-2}$

25. $\dfrac{1}{5^x - 4} = 1$

26. $\dfrac{1}{5^x - 24} = 1$

27. $\dfrac{1}{5^{3x} - 24} = 1$

28. $\dfrac{2}{2^x - 7} = 2$

29. $\dfrac{125}{2^{\frac{x}{3}} - 7} = 5$

30. $6^x + 6^{x+1} = \dfrac{7}{6}$

31. $5^x + 5^{x+1} + 5^{x-1} = \dfrac{31}{5}$

32. $7^{x-1} + 7^{x-2} = \dfrac{8}{49}$

33. $7^{x-1} + 7^{x-2} = \dfrac{8}{7}$

34. $2^x + 2^{x-1} + 2^{x+2} = 11$

35. $2^x + 2^{x-1} + 2^{x+2} = 22$

36. $5^{2x} - 6 \times 5^x = -5$

37. $3^{2x} - 4 \times 3^x - 2 = -5$

38. $5^{2x} + 4 \times 5^x - 10 = -5$

39. $8^{2x} - 9 \times 8^x + 8 = 0$

40. $2 \times 8^{2x} - 18 \times 8^x + 10 = -6$

41. $3^{2x+1} - 3^{x+2} + 81 = 0$

42. $5^{2x-1} - 6 \times 5^{x-1} = -1$

43. $3^{2x+2} - 4 \times 3^{x+2} + 27 = 0$

Systems of equations

1. One equation with 1 variable may have _____ or _____ solutions. Give examples:

2. One equation with 2 two variable may have _____ or _____ or _____ solutions. Give examples:

3. Equations of the first degree are equations in which _____
   Give examples with 1, 2 and 3 variables:

4. Equations of the 2nd degree are equations in which _____
   Give examples with 1 and 2 variables:

5. The solution to one equation of the first degree with 2 two variable, graphically speaking, is a _____. The collection of points will form a _____.

6. Write a system of equations whose only solution is $x = 1, y = 2$.

7. Write a system of equations whose only solution is $x = 0, y = -\frac{1}{2}$.

8. Write a system of equations whose only solution is $x = -3, y = -\frac{3}{2}$.

9. Write a system of equations whose only solution is $x = 15, y = -6$.

10. Given the equations I) $2x + y = 3$, II) $2y - x = 4$

   a. Write a few solutions to the equations

   I) _____

   II) _____

   b. Show the solutions on the graph.

   c. Draw a conclusion:

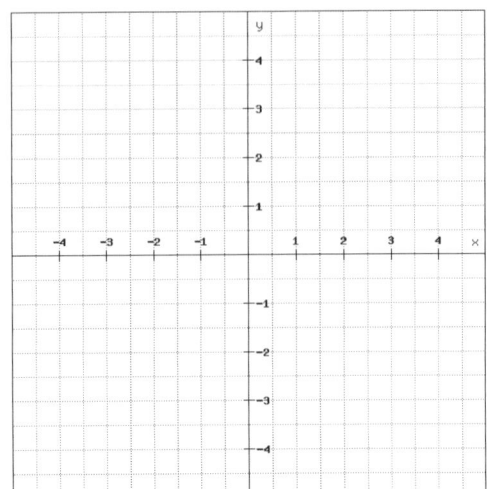

11. Given the equations I) $4x + 2y = 3$, II) $y + 2x = 8$

   a. Write a few solutions to the equations

   I) _____

   II) _____

   b. Show the solutions on the graph.
   c. Draw a conclusion:

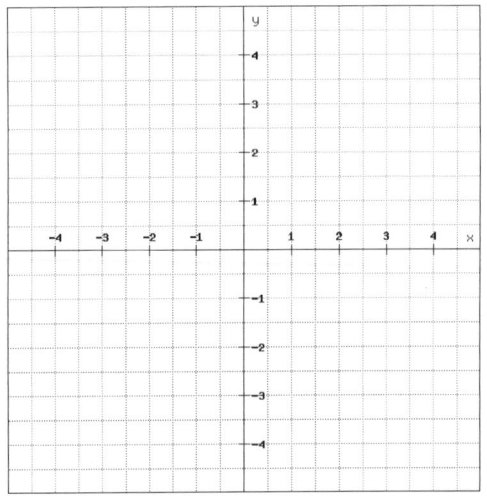

12. Given the equations I) $6x - 2y = 2$, II) $y - 3x = -1$

   a. Write a few solutions to the equations

   I) _____

   II) _____

   b. Show the solutions on the graph.
   c. Draw a conclusion:

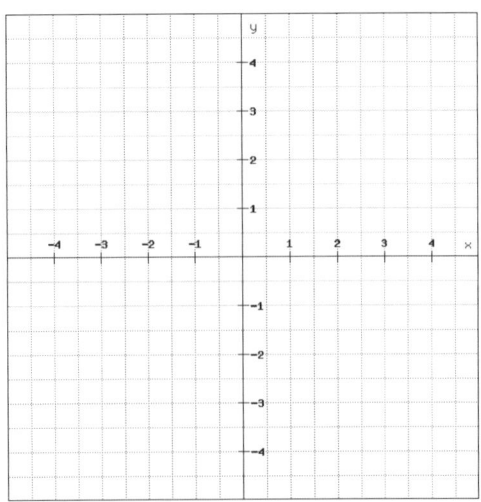

Solve:

13. $\begin{aligned} 5x+1 &= 2y \\ 4y+x-3 &= 0 \end{aligned}$

18. $\begin{aligned} 5x+1 &= 2y \\ 10y-25x &= 10 \end{aligned}$

14. $\begin{aligned} 5x+3y &= 2-2y \\ -y+2x-5 &= 0 \end{aligned}$

19. $\begin{aligned} 2x+1 &= 2y \\ -4y+4x+2 &= 0 \end{aligned}$

15. $\begin{aligned} 5x &= 2y \\ -y+2x &= 0 \end{aligned}$

20. $\begin{aligned} x+1 &= 2y \\ 4y-2x-3 &= 0 \end{aligned}$

16. $\begin{aligned} x &= 2y-7 \\ 4y-2x &= 0 \end{aligned}$

21. $\begin{aligned} 4x &= y \\ 3y-12x &= 0 \end{aligned}$

17. $\begin{aligned} -5x+1 &= 2y \\ -4y+x-3 &= x \end{aligned}$

22. $\begin{aligned} 2x+7y &= 4 \\ 3y-5x-3 &= 0 \end{aligned}$

23. $\dfrac{x}{2} - 1 = 5y$
   $3y + x - 2 = 0$

24. $\dfrac{x}{5} + 1 = 2y$
   $\dfrac{y}{3} + \dfrac{x}{2} - 3 = 0$

25. $\dfrac{x}{5} + 2 = 6y$
   $-3y + \dfrac{x}{10} + 1 = 0$

26. $x = 2y$
   $-y + x^2 - 5 = 0$

27. $x = 1 - y$
   $-y + x^2 - 5 = 0$

28. $x = 1 - y^2$
   $-y^2 + x^2 - 5 = 0$

1.10. – EXPANDING AND FACTORING

Expand:

1. $(x+1)^2 =$
2. $(x-1)^2 =$
3. $(x+2)^2 =$
4. $(x-2)^2 =$
5. $(a+b)^2 =$
6. $(a-b)^2 =$
7. $(2a+b)^2 =$
8. $(a-3b)^2 =$
9. $(2x+3)^2 =$
10. $(4-x)^2 =$
11. $(x+2)(x-3) =$
12. $(x-2)(x+2) =$
13. $(3+x)(x-7) =$
14. $(2x+2)(x-5) =$
15. $(3x-1)(x+2) =$
16. $(x+4)(x^2-4x+3) =$
17. $(x+6)(x^5-6x^2-3x+1) =$
18. $(x-a)(x+2a+b) =$
19. $(\sqrt{a}-\sqrt{b})(\sqrt{a}+\sqrt{b}) =$
20. $(2x-3c)(2x+3c-1) =$
21. $x(x+8)^2 =$
22. $(x-6)^2 3x =$
23. $2-(x+1)^2 =$
24. $(x+3)^2 - (x+2)^2 =$
25. $(x-2)^2 + (x+2)^2 =$
26. $(x-\sqrt{2})^2 =$
27. $(x-\sqrt{2})(x+\sqrt{2}) =$
28. $5(x-\sqrt{a})(x+\sqrt{a}) =$
29. $(\sqrt{a}-\sqrt{b})^2 =$
30. $2(x-\sqrt{10})(x+\sqrt{10}) =$
31. $(x-\dfrac{2}{x})^2 =$
32. $(x-\dfrac{2}{\sqrt{x}})^2 =$
33. $(3x-\dfrac{2}{3\sqrt{x}})^2 =$
34. $2(\sqrt{a}-\dfrac{1}{\sqrt{a}})^2 =$
35. $(\sqrt{a}-\dfrac{1}{\sqrt{a}})(-\sqrt{a}-\dfrac{1}{\sqrt{a}}) =$
36. $(2^x+2^{-x})^2 =$
37. $(4^{2x}+2^{-x})^2 =$
38. $(3^{2x}+3^{-2x})^2 =$

39. $(7^x - 7)^2 =$

40. $(a^{nx} - b^{nx})^2 =$

41. $(x^2 - y^2)(x^2 + y^2) =$

42. $(x^3 - y^3)(x^3 + y^3) =$

43. $(x^n - y^n)(x^n + y^n) =$

44. $(a^x - b^x)^2 =$

45. $(a^{mx} - a^{-mx})^2 =$

46. $(a^{mx} - a^{-mx})(a^{mx} + a^{-mx}) =$

Given the following polynomials, obtain the maximum possible common factor:

1. $x - ax =$
2. $3x - x - ax =$
3. $-x + ax =$
4. $xy + 2x =$
5. $8xy - 2y =$
6. $-6x + 12xy =$
7. $12xyz + 2xy =$
8. $14xy - 2yz =$
9. $12xz + 14xyz =$
10. $xy + 4y^2 + 5y =$
11. $z - 4z^2 + 8zy =$
12. $-8x^3 - 4xyz =$
13. $-6x^4 + x^2y^2 + x^2 =$

14. $-9x^7y^3 + 3x^3y =$
15. $-90x^{10}y^5 - 3x^3y^4 =$
16. $-80x^4y^6z^8 + 8x^{12}y^4z^6 =$
17. $xyz + 2x^2y^2z^2 + 3x^3y^3z^3 =$
18. $10x^3y^2z^4 + 2x^2y^6z^4 - 5x^2y^4z^2 =$
19. $20x^{30}y^{20}z^{40} - 2x^{20}y^{60}z^{40} - 2x^{20}y^{40}z^{20} =$
20. $ax^m + x^m =$
21. $ax^{m+1} + x^m =$
22. $ax^m + x^{m-1} =$
23. $ax^m - x =$
24. $-ax^m - x^{2m} =$
25. $z^{n+1} - z^{n+2} =$
26. $ax^{m+2} + x^{m-1} =$

Given the following polynomials factor, if possible.

1. $x^2 - 6x + 9 =$
2. $x^2 - 5x + 6 =$
3. $x^2 + 4x + 10 =$
4. $-x^2 - x + 6 =$
5. $x^2 + x - 6 =$
6. $x^2 + 5x + 6 =$
7. $-x^2 + 7x - 10 =$

8. $x^2 - 6x + 12 =$
9. $x^2 + 3x + 2 =$
10. $x^2 - x - 2 =$
11. $-x^2 + 4x =$
12. $-x^2 + 4x - 10 =$
13. $x^2 + x - 2 =$
14. $x^2 + 3x + 7 =$

74

15. $x^2 - 3x + 2 =$
16. $x^2 - x + 7 =$
17. $x^2 + 5x + 9 =$
18. $-x^2 - 5x + 6 =$
19. $x^2 - 2xa + a^2 =$
20. $x^2 - a^2 =$
21. $c^2 - a^2 =$
22. $x^2 - x =$
23. $2x^2 - x =$
24. $2x^2 + 3x =$
25. $x^2 + 5x =$
26. $x^2 - 7x + 12 =$
27. $2x^2 - 4x =$
28. $x^2 - 7x + 10 =$
29. $x^2 - 7x + 6 =$
30. $x^2 - x - 12 =$
31. $x^2 + x - 12 =$
32. $x^2 - 3x - 10 =$
33. $x^2 - 8x - 9 =$
34. $x^2 - 1 =$
35. $x^2 + 1 =$
36. $x^2 - 2 =$
37. $x^2 - 3 =$
38. $x^2 - 4 =$
39. $-x^2 + 1 =$
40. $-x^2 + 2 =$
41. $-x^2 + 3 =$
42. $-x^2 + 4 =$
43. $-x^2 + 13 =$

44. $-x^2 + 49 =$
45. $2x^2 - 72 =$
46. $-x^2 - 2 =$
47. $5x^2 - 125 =$
48. $-x^2 + 81 =$
49. $-3x^2 + 27 =$
50. $2x^2 - 6 =$
51. $3x^2 - 1 =$
52. $-2x^2 - 3 =$
53. $5x^2 - 6 =$
54. $4x^2 - 2 =$
55. $-8x^2 - 1 =$
56. $x^2 - b =$
57. $ax^2 - b =$
58. $-ax^2 + b =$
59. $2x^2 - 4x + 2 =$
60. $3x^2 - 3x - 18 =$
61. $-4x^2 + 20x + 24 =$
62. $7x^2 + 7x - 630 =$
63. $-5x^2 + 10x + 75 =$
64. $3x^2 - 12x - 63 =$
65. $2x^2 + 2x - 112 =$
66. $2x^2 - 12x - 14 =$
67. $-5x^2 + 15x + 90 =$
68. $-3x^2 - 12x - 12 =$
69. $-2x^2 - 26x - 84 =$
70. $6x^2 + 48x + 72 =$

Given the following polynomials, complete the square.

1. $x^2 - 6x + 9 =$

2. $x^2 - 5x + 6 =$

3. $x^2 + 4x + 10 =$

4. $-x^2 - x + 6 =$

5. $x^2 + x - 6 =$

6. $x^2 + 5x + 6 =$

7. $-x^2 + 7x - 10 =$

8. $x^2 - 6x + 12 =$

9. $x^2 + 3x + 2 =$

10. $x^2 - x - 2 =$

11. $-x^2 + 4x =$

12. $-x^2 + 4x - 10 =$

13. $x^2 + x - 2 =$

14. $x^2 + 3x + 7 =$

15. $2x^2 - 4x + 2 =$

16. $3x^2 - 3x - 6 =$

17. $-4x^2 + 20x - 24 =$

18. $7x^2 - 7x - 630 =$

19. $-5x^2 + 10x + 75 =$

20. $3x^2 - 12x - 63 =$

21. $2x^2 + 2x - 112 =$

22. $2x^2 - 12x - 14 =$

23. $-5x^2 + 15x + 90 =$

24. $-3x^2 - 12x - 12 =$

25. $-2x^2 - 26x - 84 =$

26. $6x^2 + 48x + 72 =$

Factor and simplify:

1. $\dfrac{x^2-6x+9}{x^2-7x+12}=$

2. $\dfrac{x^2-5x+6}{x^2+x-6}=$

3. $\dfrac{x^2-9}{x^2-7x+12}=$

4. $\dfrac{x^2-1}{x^2-2x+1}=$

5. $\dfrac{x^2-6x+8}{x^2-4x+4}=$

6. $\dfrac{x^2-16}{x^2+5x+4}=$

7. $\dfrac{x^2-x-2}{x^2+6x+5}=$

8. $\dfrac{3x+9}{x^2-9}=$

9. $\dfrac{x^2-6x}{x^2-7x+6}=$

10. $\dfrac{x^2-x}{x^2+x-2}=$

11. $\dfrac{x^2-4}{x^2+x-2}=$

12. $\dfrac{4-x}{x-4}=$

13. $\dfrac{x^2-x}{1-x}=$

14. $\dfrac{2x-1}{4x^2-4x+1}=$

15. $\dfrac{x^2-2x}{x^2-4}=$

16. $\dfrac{4x^2+4x+1}{2x^2+5x+2}=$

17. $\dfrac{3x^2+4x+1}{9x^2-1}=$

18. $\dfrac{4x^2+4x-3}{2x^2-13x+15}=$

19. $\dfrac{4x^2+4x-3}{2x^2+13x+15}=$

20. $\dfrac{5x^2-12x+4}{10x^2+16x-8}=$

1.11. – EVALUATING EXPRESSIONS

Evaluate the expression given the value of x:

1. $x = 3$, $x^2 + x =$

2. $x = -3$, $x^2 + x =$

3. $x = -2$, $2x^2 + 3x =$

4. $x = -2$, $x^{-1} =$

5. $x = -2$, $x^3 =$

6. $x = -3$, $x^{-3} =$

7. $x = -9$, $2x^{-2} =$

8. $x = 4$, $x^{-2} + x =$

9. $x = -2$, $2x^2 + \dfrac{x}{2} =$

10. $x = -2$, $\dfrac{1}{x} + \dfrac{x}{2} =$

11. $x = 4$, $\dfrac{1}{x-3} + \dfrac{x}{2} =$

12. $x = 10$, $\dfrac{10}{x-5} + \dfrac{x-2}{2} =$

13. $x = -1$, $5x^{-3} + 2x^{-1} + 1 =$

14. $x = 3$, $x^{-2} + x + x^2 =$

15. $x = 2$, $x^{-3} + x^{-2} + x^{-1} + x^0 =$

16. $x = 2$, $2x^{-2} \cdot x^{-1} =$

17. $x = -1$, $x^{-200} - 2x^{501} =$

18. $x = -5$, $5x^{-2} - x^2 =$

19. $x = -2$, $2^x =$

20. $x = -2$, $3^x =$

21. $x = -2$, $2^{2x+1} =$

22. $x = -1$, $2^{3x-1} =$

23. $x = 2$, $2^{\frac{3}{x}} =$

24. $x = -\dfrac{1}{2}$, $4^x =$

25. $x = -\dfrac{2}{3}$, $8^x =$

1.12. – EQUATIONS/INEQUALITIES WITH ABSOLUTE VALUE

1. $|-3|=$ $|3|=$ $|-3+3|=$ $|-3-3|=$

2. $|-3|+3=$ $|3|-4=$ $|-3+5|+2=$ $|-3-3|-3=$

3. $|1-3+|-2||=$

5. $|-2-23|-|-12|=$

4. $|-2-3|+|-2|=$

6. $2|1-3+|-2|+1|-2=$

7. $|-2-3||-2|=$

8. $-|-12-3|-|-2-1|=$

9. $5-|12-3+|1-2||-|-12-10|+1=$

10. $|2-|-12-3|-|-2-1||=$

11. $|x|-2|x|=$

12. $|x||x|=$

13. An absolute value of a number represents its _____

14. $|x|=|-x|$ True / False, if false write down an example to show it

15. $|x+y|=|x|+|y|$ True / False, if false write down an example to show it

16. $-|x|$ is _____ number

17. If $x=|x|$ it means x is _____

18. If $x=-|x|$ it means x is _____

19. If x is a negative number than $-x=|x|$ True / False

20. If x is a positive number than $x=|x|$ True / False

Assuming $a \geq 0$ the following is satisfied:

I. $|x| = a$ $x = a$ OR $x = -a$
II. $|x| > a$ $x > a$ OR $x < -a$ equivalent to $x \in (-\infty, -a) \cup (a, \infty)$
III. $|x| < a$ $-a < x < a$ equivalent to $x > -a$ and $x < a$ equivalent to $x \in (-a, a)$

1. $|2x| = 5$

2. $|x| = 7$

3. $|4x| = 8$

4. $|x| = -5$

5. $|2x| = 0$

6. $|2x| = -1$

7. $|2x| = 15$

8. $|2x| < 5$

9. $|x| > 7$

10. $|4x| < 8$

11. $|x| < -5$

12. $|3x| < 0$

13. $|6x| > -1$

14. $|5x| > 0$

15. $|3x| \leq 6$

16. $|x| \geq 7$

17. $|4x| \leq 2$

18. $|x| \leq -5$

19. $|2x| < 0$

20. $|2x| \geq -1$

21. $|x| \geq 0$

22. $|2+x| = 5$

23. $|-x| = 7$

24. $|4 - x| = 8$

25. $|3 - 2x| = -5$

26. $|2 - 3x| = 0$

27. $|2 + x| = -1$

28. $|2x + 3| = 15$

29. $|4 - 2x| < 5$

30. $|-x| > 7$

31. $|4 + 2x| < 8$

32. $|x| < -5$

33. $|3 + x| < 0$

34. $|6 - 2x| > -1$

35. $|5 + x| > 0$

36. $|1 - 3x| \leq 6$

37. $|1 + x| \geq 7$

38. $|4 + x| \leq 2$

39. $|3 + 2x| \leq -5$

40. $|2 + 3x| < 0$

41. $|7 - 6x| \geq -1$

42. $|1 - x| \geq 0$

43. $|2x + 1| + 3 = 5$

44. $|7x + 21| - 5 = -5$

45. $2 - |5 - 8x| = 15$

46. $|4x + 2| = -5$

47. $|8x + 12| = 100$

48. $|2x + 1| < 2$

49. $|8 - 2x + 1| > 6$

50. $|5x - 21| + 3 > 0$

51. $|5x - 21| \geq 0$

52. $|8x + 11| - 1 > -2$

53. $|91x + 61| < -2$

54. $|8 - 3x| > 8$

55. $|18 - 6x| + 1 > 3$

56. $|1 - 6x| - 2 < 7$

57. $|8 - 5x| \leq 0$

58. $|5x - 21| > 1$

59. $|x + 11| + 1 = 5$

60. $|x + 3| - 2 \leq 5$

61. $|x + 11| = -15$

62. $|2x + 11| + 2 < 15$

63. $|3x + 11| = x$

64. $|x + 2| = 5 - x$

65. $|3x + 1| < 5x$

66. $|x - 4| = 3x$

67. $|2x - 6| \leq 5 + 2x$

68. $|2x + 4| < 2 - 3x$

69. $|2x - 2| > 11 - 2x$

70. $|7x - 16| + x = 5 + 12x$

71. $|2x - 6| - 2 = 21$

72. $|2x - 6| \geq 4$

73. $|3x - 6| + 1 > -4$

74. $|4x - 6| - 4 < -4x$

75. $|\frac{1}{2}x - 4 + x| \leq 1 + x$

76. $|2x + \frac{1}{2}| > 2 - 3x$

77. $|2x - \frac{1}{2}| = 1 - 2x$

78. $|\frac{x}{2} - 7| \leq 3 + 2x$

79. $|\frac{x}{2} + 2| = 1 - x$

1.13. – LOGARITHMS AND LOGARITHMIC EQUATIONS

Definition of logarithms: $\quad b^c = a \Leftrightarrow \log_b(a) = c \quad\quad 1 \neq b > 0$

1. Complete the table and find x if possible:

Exponential Form	Logarithmic Form
$5^3 = 125$	
	$\log_6 36 = 2$
	$\log_x 64 = 2$
$x^3 = 27$	
	$\log_3(x+1) = 2$
$e^x = 9$	
	$\ln x = \log_e x = 2$
$e^{2x-1} = 17$	
	$\ln(3x+2) = \log_e(3x+2) = 2$
$4^x = 9$	
	$\log_6 x = 2$
$2^x = e$	
	$\ln(x^2) = \log_e(x^2) = 4$
	$\log 0.001 = x$
$10^x = 200$	
	$\log_3 \dfrac{1}{9} = -2$
	$\log_2 0.5 = x$

Logarithms were "invented" in order to solve equations in which: _____

Properties of logarithms:
  I. **Product Rule:** $Log_b(MN) = Log_b(M) + Log_b(N)$, M, N, b positive, b≠1
  II. **Quotient Rule:** $Log_b(\frac{M}{N}) = Log_b(M) - Log_b(N)$, M, N, b positive, b≠1
  III. **Power Rule:** $Log_b(M^p) = pLog_b(M)$, M, b positive, b≠1
  IV. $a^{\log_a(x)} = x$

Evaluate:

1. $Log_2(2) =$
2. $Log_2(4) =$
3. $Log_2(8) =$
4. $Log_2(16) =$
5. $Log_2(32) =$
6. $Log_2(2^n) =$
7. $Log_5(25) =$
8. $Log_5(125) =$
9. $Log_5(625) =$
10. $Log_3(3) =$
11. $Log_5(0) =$
12. $Log_5(1) =$
13. $Log_a(1) =$
14. $Log_2(-3) =$
15. $Log_2(\frac{1}{8}) =$
16. $Log_7(\frac{1}{49}) =$
17. $Log_4(32) =$
18. $Log_8(32) =$
19. $Log_{\frac{1}{2}}(4) =$
20. $Log_{\frac{1}{2}}(16) =$
21. $Log_{\frac{1}{3}}(81) =$
22. $Log_{\frac{1}{2}}(8) =$
23. $Log_{\frac{1}{2}}(-8) =$
24. $Log_{\frac{1}{3}}(\frac{1}{9}) =$
25. $Log_{\frac{1}{5}}(\frac{1}{125}) =$
26. $Log_1(8) =$
27. $Log_2(\frac{1}{\sqrt{8}}) =$
28. $Log_2(\sqrt[3]{32}) =$
29. $Log_3(\sqrt[3]{81}) =$
30. $Log_{\sqrt[5]{8}}(\sqrt[5]{8}) =$
31. $Log_{\frac{1}{2}}(\sqrt[5]{16}) =$
32. $Log_{17}(\frac{17}{17^{\frac{1}{3}}}\sqrt[5]{17}) =$
33. $Log(\sqrt{10}) =$
34. $Log(\sqrt[3]{10}) =$
35. $Log(\sqrt[7]{100}) =$
36. $Log(\sqrt[3]{10000}) =$
37. $Log(10^{-19}) =$

38. $Log(50) - Log(5) =$

39. $Log(25) + Log(4) =$

40. $Log_3(45) - Log_3(5) =$

41. $Log_6(18) + Log_6(2) =$

42. $Log_a(a) + Log_a(a^2) =$

43. $Log_a(a) + Log_a(\frac{1}{a}) =$

44. $Log_a(\frac{1}{a}) - Log_a(a) =$

45. $\dfrac{Log_a(a)}{Log_a(2a)} =$

46. $Log_a(a^x) =$

47. $Log_a(a^{2x-3}) =$

48. $Log_e(e) =$

49. $Ln(e) =$

50. $Ln(e^2) =$

51. $Ln(e^{\frac{1}{2}}) =$

52. $Ln(e^{\frac{2}{5}}) =$

53. $Ln(e\sqrt[3]{e^4}) =$

54. $Ln(1) =$

55. $Ln(0) =$

56. $Ln(e^0) =$

57. $Ln(e^n) =$

58. $Ln(\frac{1}{\sqrt{e}}) =$

59. $Ln(\frac{1}{\sqrt[3]{e^2}}) =$

60. $Log_\pi(\frac{1}{\pi^4}) =$

61. $Log_\pi(\frac{1}{\sqrt{\pi^5}}) =$

62. $Log_a(\frac{1}{\sqrt[3]{a^2}}) =$

63. $\dfrac{Ln(e^{-1})}{Log_{12}(\sqrt{12})} =$

64. $\dfrac{Ln(\sqrt{e})}{Log_2(40) - Log_2(5)} =$

65. $\dfrac{Log(500) - Log(5)}{Log_7(98) - Log_7(2)} =$

66. $\dfrac{Ln(a) + Ln(\frac{e}{a})}{Log_{12}(288) - Log_{12}(2)} =$

67. $\dfrac{\left(\dfrac{1}{\log(100)}\right)}{Log_a(2a) - Log_a(2a^2)} =$

68. $Log_2(3b) - Log_2(3b^2) - Log_2(\frac{1}{8b}) =$

69. $Log_b(b-1) - Log_b(1-b^2) + Log_b(b+1) =$

70. $10^{Log(100)} =$

71. $3^{Log_3(9)} =$

72. $3^{Log_3(\frac{1}{27})} =$

73. $9^{Log_3(\frac{1}{81})} =$

74. $32^{Log_2(\sqrt{2})} =$

75. $a^{3Log_a(\sqrt{b})} =$

13. $Log_3(\frac{2}{3}) =$

14. $Log_5(\frac{2}{\sqrt{5}}) =$

15. Simplify:

    a. $\log_x b \cdot \log_b x = $ ___

    b. $\log_x q \cdot \log_q r \cdot \log_r x = $ ___

Logarithmic Equations

1. $Log_4(x) = 2$

2. $Log_{\frac{1}{3}}(x) = 4$

3. $Log_4(x) = 4$

4. $Log_4(x) + Log_4(x) = 4$

5. $Log_{10}(2x+1) = 2$

6. $Log_6(4x^2 - 6) = 2$

7. $Log_2(64) = x$

8. $Log_2(x+2) + Log_2(x) = 0$

9. $Log_5(5x+5) - Log_5(x+1) = 1$

10. $Log_2(x-1) - Log_2(x) = -1$

11. $3^x = 81$

12. $3^{2x} = \sqrt{27}$

13. $2^{5x+2} = \dfrac{1}{\sqrt[3]{\sqrt{32}}}$

14. $Ln(x) = 2.7$

15. $Ln(x+1) = 1.86$

16. $e^x = 3$

17. $e^x = \sqrt{e}$

18. $Log_b(81) = 4$

19. $e^{-2x} = 4.12$

20. $Log_3(x) = Log_3(7) + Log_3(3)$

21. $Log_3(x^2 - 5) = Log_3(12) - Log_3(3)$

22. $5 \cdot 9^x = 10$

23. $10e^{4x+1} = 20$

24. $3^t = 2 \cdot 5^{2t}$

25. $3^{t+1} = 4 \cdot 6^{2t-3}$

26. $3 \cdot 2^t = 5 \cdot 6^{2t-3}$

27. $2 \cdot e^t = 8 \cdot 7^{2t-3}$

28. $b^t = c \cdot d^{2t}$

29. $a \cdot b^t = c \cdot d^{2t}$

30. $e^t + e^t = 2$

31. $e^{2t} + e^{2t} = 3$

32. $Ln(x) = 2$

33. $Ln(x^2) = 2$

34. $Ln(x^2 - 1) = 2$

35. $Ln(x+1) - Ln(2x) = -1$

36. $Ln(x^2 + 1) = 1$

37. $Log_{10}(x^2 + 19) = 2$

38. $Ln(x-2) + Ln(2x-5) = 0$

39. $Log(x+9) + Log(x) = 1$

40. $Log_2(\frac{1}{x}) - Log_2(4x+2) = -1$

41. $Log_5(1+\frac{1}{x}) + Log_5(\frac{5}{4x}) = 2$

42. Given the equation: $Log_3(\frac{x}{2}) - Log_9(x+9) = \frac{1}{2}$

   a. Change the base of the second logarithm to 3.

   b. Simplify the denominator of the second logarithm after the change of base.

   c. Solve the equation.

43. $Log_2(\frac{x}{3}) - Log_4(x+2) = -\frac{1}{2}$

44. $Log(x) + Log_2(x-2) = 4$

45. $Log_2(x) + 2Log_3(x+1) = 3$

46. $Log_2(\frac{1}{x}) - 2Log_2(x) = 3$

47. $Log_2(x) - Log_3(x) = Log_3(x)$

48. $Log_2(x) - 2Log_x(2) = 0$

49. $Log_2(x) - 2Log_x(2) = 1$

50. $Log_2(x) - Log_x(3) = 0$

1.14. – SEQUENCES AND SERIES

Given The following sequences, write the first 3 terms and the term in the 20th position. If possible identify the pattern using text (follow example):

1. $a_n = 3n$ $\quad a_1 = 3 \quad a_2 = 6 \quad a_3 = 9 \quad a_{20} = 60$ Pattern: __add 3__

2. $a_n = 3n + 1$ $\quad a_1 = \quad a_2 = \quad a_3 = \quad a_{20} =$ Pattern: _____

3. $a_n = 3n - 5$ $\quad a_1 = \quad a_2 = \quad a_3 = \quad a_{20} =$ Pattern: _____

4. $a_n = 2n + 1$ $\quad a_1 = \quad a_2 = \quad a_3 = \quad a_{20} =$ Pattern: _____

5. $a_n = 2n$ $\quad a_1 = \quad a_2 = \quad a_3 = \quad a_{20} =$ Pattern: _____

6. $a_n = 2n - 4$ $\quad a_1 = \quad a_2 = \quad a_3 = \quad a_{20} =$ Pattern: _____

7. $a_n = -4n$ $\quad a_1 = \quad a_2 = \quad a_3 = \quad a_{20} =$ Pattern: _____

8. $a_n = -4n + 10$ $\quad a_1 = \quad a_2 = \quad a_3 = \quad a_{20} =$ Pattern: _____

9. $a_n = -4n - 6$ $\quad a_1 = \quad a_2 = \quad a_3 = \quad a_{20} =$ Pattern: _____

10. $a_n = \dfrac{n}{3}$ $\quad a_1 = \quad a_2 = \quad a_3 = \quad a_{20} =$ Pattern: _____

11. $a_n = \dfrac{n}{2}$ $\quad a_1 = \quad a_2 = \quad a_3 = \quad a_{20} =$ Pattern: _____

12. $a_n = \dfrac{2n}{5} + 1$ $\quad a_1 = \quad a_2 = \quad a_3 = \quad a_{20} =$ Pattern: _____

13. $a_n = \dfrac{-3n}{7} + 5$ $\quad a_1 = \quad a_2 = \quad a_3 = \quad a_{20} =$ Pattern: _____

14. $a_n = \dfrac{n}{9} - 5$ $\quad a_1 = \quad a_2 = \quad a_3 = \quad a_{20} =$ Pattern: _____

15. $a_n = \dfrac{n}{10} - 1$ $\quad a_1 = \quad a_2 = \quad a_3 = \quad a_{20} =$ Pattern: _____

16. $a_n = \dfrac{3n}{4} + 2$ $\quad a_1 = \quad a_2 = \quad a_3 = \quad a_{20} =$ Pattern: _____

17. $a_n = n^2$ $\quad a_1 = \quad a_2 = \quad a_3 = \quad a_{20} =$ Pattern: _____

18. $a_n = n^3$ $\quad a_1 = \quad a_2 = \quad a_3 = \quad a_{20} =$ Pattern: _____

19. $a_n = 2^n$ $\quad a_1 = \quad a_2 = \quad a_3 = \quad a_{20} =$ Pattern: _____

20. $a_n = -2^n$ $\quad a_1 = \quad a_2 = \quad a_3 = \quad a_{20} =$ Pattern: _____

21. $a_n = 2^{-n}$ $\quad a_1 = \quad a_2 = \quad a_3 = \quad a_{20} =$ Pattern: _____

22. $a_n = -2^{-n}$ $a_1=$ $a_2=$ $a_3=$ $a_{20}=$ Pattern: _____

23. $a_n = (-2)^n$ $a_1=$ $a_2=$ $a_3=$ $a_{20}=$ Pattern: _____

24. $a_n = 2^{n-1}$ $a_1=$ $a_2=$ $a_3=$ $a_{20}=$ Pattern: _____

25. $a_n = 2^{n+2}$ $a_1=$ $a_2=$ $a_3=$ $a_{20}=$ Pattern: _____

26. $a_n = 3 \times 2^n$ $a_1=$ $a_2=$ $a_3=$ $a_{20}=$ Pattern: _____

27. $a_n = -5 \times 2^{n-1}$ $a_1=$ $a_2=$ $a_3=$ $a_{20}=$ Pattern: _____

28. $a_n = 5 \times 2^{1-n}$ $a_1=$ $a_2=$ $a_3=$ $a_{20}=$ Pattern: _____

29. $a_n = (-3)^{2-n}$ $a_1=$ $a_2=$ $a_3=$ $a_{20}=$ Pattern: _____

30. $a_n = 2 \times (-3)^n$ $a_1=$ $a_2=$ $a_3=$ $a_{20}=$ Pattern: _____

31. $a_n = 2 \times (-5)^{n-1}$ $a_1=$ $a_2=$ $a_3=$ $a_{20}=$ Pattern: _____

32. $a_n = (-3)^{n+1}$ $a_1=$ $a_2=$ $a_3=$ $a_{20}=$ Pattern: _____

33. $a_n = 1 + 5^{n-2}$ $a_1=$ $a_2=$ $a_3=$ $a_{20}=$ Pattern: _____

34. $a_n = 3 \times 2^n$ $a_1=$ $a_2=$ $a_3=$ $a_{20}=$ Pattern: _____

35. $a_n = -5 \times 2^{n-1}$ $a_1=$ $a_2=$ $a_3=$ $a_{20}=$ Pattern: _____

36. $a_n = 2 \times 3^n$ $a_1=$ $a_2=$ $a_3=$ $a_{20}=$ Pattern: _____

37. $a_n = 5^{n-2} + 3$ $a_1=$ $a_2=$ $a_3=$ $a_{20}=$ Pattern: _____

38. $a_n - (-3)^n$ $a_1=$ $a_2=$ $a_3=$ $a_{20}=$ Pattern: _____

39. $a_n = 2 \times (-3)^n$ $a_1=$ $a_2=$ $a_3=$ $a_{20}=$ Pattern: _____

40. $a_n = 2 \times (-5)^{n-1}$ $a_1=$ $a_2=$ $a_3=$ $a_{20}=$ Pattern: _____

41. $a_n = (-3)^{n+1}$ $a_1=$ $a_2=$ $a_3=$ $a_{20}=$ Pattern: _____

42. $a_n = 1 + 5^{n-2}$ $a_1=$ $a_2=$ $a_3=$ $a_{20}=$ Pattern: _____

43. The sequences in which the pattern is add/subtract a number are called _____

44. The sequences in which the pattern is multiply/divide (pay attention that dividing by a is the same as multiplying by ____) a number are called _____

45. $a_n = 2a_{n-1}$ $a_1=1$ $a_2=$ $a_3=$ $a_{20}=$ Pattern: _____

46. $a_{n+2} = a_n + a_{n+1}$ $a_1=1$ $a_2=1$ $a_3=$ $a_{20}=$ Pattern: _____

47. In the last 2 sequences the terms are given in terms of _____

48. (T/F) Arithmetic and Geometric sequences are most of the sequences that exist.

49. The terms in a convergent geometric sequence tend to _____, in a none–convergent sequence the terms tend to _____ or _____.

50. Give an example of a convergent geometric sequence:

51. Give an example of a divergent geometric sequence:

52. Give an example of a alternating convergent geometric sequence:

53. Give an example of a none alternating divergent geometric sequence:

54. A convergent geometric sequence is a sequence in which r is _____.

Arithmetic sequence (Pattern – Add a constant):

General term: $a_n = a_1 + (n-1)d$

Sum: $S_n = \dfrac{n}{2}(2a_1 + (n-1)d)$

Geometric Sequence (Pattern – multiply by a constant):

General term: $a_n = a_1 r^{n-1}$

Sum: $S_n = \dfrac{a(r^n - 1)}{r - 1}$

Convergent geometric sequence ($-1 < r < 1$): $S_\infty = \dfrac{a_1}{1-r}$

Example:

3, 7, 11, 15…
Arithmetic sequence.
Pattern: add 4.
General term: $a_n = 3 + (n-1)4$
General term can be written also like this: $a_n = -1 + 4n = 4n - 1$

Given the following sequences:

a. For each one write: arithmetic, geometric convergent, geometric divergent or neither, the <u>next term</u> and their <u>general term</u> (in case they are geometric or arithmetic only).

b. Try to write the general term of the other sequences as well.

55. 1, 2, 3, 4, ___ ...

56. 1, 2, 4, 8, ___ ...

57. 1, 3, 5, 7, ___ ...

58. 1, 3, 9, 27, ___ ...

59. 4, 6, 9, 13,5, ___ ...

60. 4, 1, –2, –5, ___ ...

61. 5, 0, –4, –7, ___ ...

62. 10, 1000, 100000, ___ ...

63. 30, 10, $\dfrac{10}{3}$, $\dfrac{10}{9}$, ___ ...

64. 2, 10, 50, 250, ___ ...

65. 2, 102, 202, 302, ___ ...

66. 1, –1, 1, –1, ____

67. –2, 2, –2, 2, ___ ...

68. 3, –6, 12, –24, ___ ...

69. –8, 4, –2, 1, ___ ...

70. 5, 1, $\frac{1}{5}$, $\frac{1}{25}$, ___ ...

71. 100, 10, 1, $\frac{1}{10}$, ___ ...

72. $\frac{3}{4}$, $\frac{3}{8}$, $\frac{3}{16}$, ___ ...

73. 12, 11, 10, 9, ___ ...

74. $\frac{4}{9}$, $\frac{5}{9}$, $\frac{6}{9}$, ___ ...

75. 9, 8, 6, 5, 3, 2, ___ ...

76. 5, 9, 13, ___ ...

77. 1, $\frac{3}{2}$, $\frac{9}{4}$, $\frac{27}{8}$, ___ ...

78. 5, $-\frac{5}{3}$, $\frac{5}{9}$, $-\frac{5}{27}$, ___ ...

79. –1, –2, –3, ___ …

80. –2, 4, –8, ___ …

81. 70, 20, $\dfrac{40}{7}$, ___ …

82. 100, 10, 1, ___ …

83. 100, –10, 1, $\dfrac{-1}{10}$, ___ …

84. 3, 24, 192, ___ …

85. 90, 9, $\dfrac{9}{10}$, ___ …

86. $\dfrac{3}{2}$, $\dfrac{4}{3}$, $\dfrac{5}{4}$, ___ …

87. $\dfrac{40}{3}$, $\dfrac{20}{6}$, $\dfrac{10}{12}$, $\dfrac{5}{24}$, ___ …

88. $\dfrac{2}{3}$, $-\dfrac{4}{9}$, $\dfrac{8}{27}$, $-\dfrac{16}{81}$, ___ …

89. $-\dfrac{1}{2}$, $-\dfrac{1}{4}$, $-\dfrac{1}{8}$, $-\dfrac{1}{16}$, ___ …

90. $\dfrac{1}{7}$, $-\dfrac{1}{14}$, $\dfrac{1}{21}$, $-\dfrac{1}{28}$, ___ …

91. 8, 5, 3, 0, ___ ...

92. $3, \dfrac{3}{4}, \dfrac{3}{16}, $ ___ ...

93. $81, -9, 1, -\dfrac{1}{9},$ ___ ...

94. 2, –10, 50, ___ ...

In each one of the following sequences find the term indicated:

95. 1, 4, 7... (a_{31})

96. –8, –5, –2... (a_{37})

97. 4, –8, 16... (a_{15})

98. 32, –8, 2... (a_{11})

99. 68, –34, 17... (a_9)

100. 3, 14, 25... (a_9)

101. –4000, 1000, –250,... (a_7)

102. ln(200), ln(100), ln(50)... (a_7)

103. The 4th term of a geometric sequence is 3, the 6th term is $\frac{27}{4}$.

    a. Find the ratio of the sequence.
    b. Is this sequence convergent? Explain
    c. Find a_1
    d. Find a_{12}
    e. Sum the first 15 terms.

104. The 2nd term of a arithmetic sequence is –2, the 6th term is –4.

    a. Find the difference of the sequence.
    b. Find a_1
    c. Find a_{12}
    d. Sum the first 50 terms.

105. The 10th term of a geometric sequence is 5, the 14th term is $\dfrac{80}{81}$

    a. Find the ratio of the sequence.
    b. Is this sequence convergent? Explain
    c. Find a_1
    d. Find a_7
    e. Sum the first 10 terms.
    f. Sum all the terms of the sequence.

106. The 7th term of a arithmetic sequence is 120, the 16th term is 201.

    a. Find the difference of the sequence.
    b. Find a_1
    c. Find a_{12}
    d. Sum the first 50 terms.

107. All the terms in a geometric sequence are positive. The first term is 7 and the 3rd term is 28.

   a. Find the common ratio.
   b. Find the sum of the first 14 terms.

108. The fifth term of an arithmetic sequence is –20 and the twelfth term is –44.

   a. Find the common difference.
   b. Find the first term of the sequence.
   c. Calculate the eighty–seventh term.
   d. Calculate the sum of the first 150 terms.

109. Sum the following sequences:

   a. $3 + 6 + 9 + 12 + \ldots + 69 =$

   b. $6 + 14 + 22 + 30 + \ldots + 54 =$

   c. $5 + \dfrac{5}{3} + \dfrac{5}{9} + \ldots =$

   d. $1 + 2 + 3 + 4 + \ldots + 158 =$

   e. $9 + 18 + 27 + 36 + \ldots + 900 =$

   f. $80 + 20 + 5 + \ldots$

g. $100 + 97 + 94 + \ldots + 19 =$

h. $18 + 6 + 2 + \ldots =$

i. $\dfrac{2}{5} + \dfrac{6}{10} + \dfrac{18}{20} + \ldots + \dfrac{243}{80}$

j. $\dfrac{1}{3} + \dfrac{2}{9} + \dfrac{4}{27} + \ldots =$

k. $12 + 7 + 2 + \ldots - 98 =$

l. $100 + 150 + 200 + \ldots + 1000 =$

110. Consider the arithmetic series $-6 + 1 + 8 + 15 + \ldots$

Find the least number of terms so that the sum of the series is greater than 10000.

111. In a theatre there are 20 seats in the first row, 23 in the 2nd, 26 in the 3rd etc. There are 40 rows in the theatre. Find the total number of seats available.

112. A ball bounces on the floor. It is released from a height of 160 cm. After the 1st bounce it reaches a height of 120 cm and 90 cm after the 2nd. If the patterns continue find:

    a. The height the ball will reach after the 6th bounce.
    b. The total distance the ball passed after a long period o time.

113. In a certain forest the current population of rabbits is 200 objects. It is know that the population increases by 20% every year.

    a. Find the population of rabbits after a year.
    b. Find the population of rabbits after 2 years.
    c. What kind of a sequence is it? State the expression for the population after n years.
    d. Find the total number of rabbits after 10 years (assuming none has died).

114. In a research it was observed that the number of defective products produced by a machine per year decreases by 10% every year (due to technological improvements). In a certain year the machine made 300 products.

   a. Find the number of defective products produced a year later.
   b. Find the number of defective products produced 2 years later.
   c. What kind of a sequence is it? State the expression for the number of errors committed after n years.
   d. Find the total number of bad products produced in the first 8 years.

115. In a certain company the pay scale follows a pattern of an arithmetic sequence (every year). This means:

   a. The salary increases by a certain % every year (True/False), explain.

   b. The salary increases by a certain amount every year (True/False), explain

116. Given the sequence: $a, a^2, a^3 ...$

    a. This is a _____ sequence.
    b. Write down its general term, simplified.
    c. It is known that the infinite sequence adds up to 10, find a.

117. Given the sequence: $a^{-2}, a^{-3}, a^{-4} ...$

    a. This is a _____ sequence.
    b. Write down its general term, simplified.
    c. It is known that the infinite sequence adds up to $\frac{1}{2}$, find a.

COMPOUND INTEREST

1. 1200$ are put in account that gives 2% per year. Calculate the amount of money in the account after:

    a. 1 year.

    b. 2 years.

2. To increase an amount A by 5% it should be multiplied by _____.

3. To increase an amount A by 56% it should be multiplied by _____.

4. To decrease an amount A by 5% it should be multiplied by _____.

5. To increase an amount A by 15% it should be multiplied by _____.

6. To decrease an amount A by 12% it should be multiplied by _____.

7. To increase an amount A by 230% it should be multiplied by _____.

8. 1000$ are put in account that takes 5% commission per year. Calculate the amount of money in the account after:

    a. 1 year.

    b. 2 years.

9. 2000$ are being put in a deposit that pays 5% (per year).

   a. Fill the table:

Number of Years	Interest earned at the end of the year	Amount in deposit ($)
0		2000
1	$\frac{5}{100} \cdot 2000 = 100$	2100
2	$\frac{5}{100} \cdot 2100 = 105$	2205
3	$\frac{5}{100} \cdot 2205 = 110.25$	
4		
5		

   b. Observe the numbers in the compound interest column: 2000, 2100, 2205... What kind of a sequence is that? Write its general term.

   c. How much money will be in the account after 20 years?

   d. Discuss the meaning of writing $a_n = a_1 r^{n-1}$ or writing $a_n = a_0 r^n$. Use the exercise as an example.

10. A loan of 1200$ is made at 12% per year compounded semiannually, over 5 years the debt will grow to:

    a. $1200(1 + 0.12)^5$
    b. $1200(1 + 0.06)^{10}$
    c. $1200(1 + 0.6)^{10}$
    d. $1200(1 + 0.06)^5$
    e. $1200(1 + 0.12)^{10}$

11. A loan of 23200$ is made at 7% per year compounded quarterly, over 6 years the debt will grow to:

    a. $23200(1 + 0.7)^{24}$
    b. $23200(1 + 0.07)^6$
    c. $23200(1 + 0.7)^{24}$
    d. $23200(1 + 0.07)^{24}$
    e. $23200(1 + 0.07)^{12}$

12. A loan of 20$ is made at 14% per year compounded monthly, over 8 years the debt will grow to:

    a. $20(1 + 0.14)^{80}$
    b. $20(1 + 0.01)^{96}$
    c. $20(1 + 0.014)^{96}$
    d. $20(1 + 0.01)^{12}$
    e. $20(1 + 0.07)^{12}$

13. A loan of X$ is made at 8% per year compounded every 4 months, over 5 years the debt will grow to:

    a. $X(1 + 0.08)^4$
    b. $X(1 + 0.02)^5$
    c. $X(1 + 0.08)^{15}$
    d. $X(1 + 0.02)^{15}$
    e. $X(1 + 0.8)^{15}$

14. A loan of X$ is made at i% per year compounded every m months, over n years the debt will grow to:

$$Debt = \underline{}(1 + \underline{})^{\underline{}}$$

15. Calculate the total amount owing after two years on a loan of 1500$ if the interest rate is 11% compounded

    a. Annually

    b. Semiannually

    c. Quarterly

    d. Monthly

16. How much will a client have to repay on a loan of 800$ after 2 years, if the 12% interest is compounded annually.

17. Find the compound interest **earned** by the deposit. Round to the nearest cent. $3000 at 12% compounded semiannually for 10 years

18. How many years will it take to a 100$ to double assuming interest rate is 6%. Compounded semiannually.

19. How many years will it take to a X$ to triple assuming interest rate is 7%. Compounded quarterly

20. Find the interest rate given to a certain person in case he made a deposit of 1000$ and obtained 1200$ after 3 years, compounded monthly.

21. Find the interest rate given to a certain person in case he made a deposit of 2500$ and obtained 3000$ after 10 years, compounded yearly.

SIGMA NOTATION

1. The sum $\sum_{k=2}^{4} 2^k$ is equal to which of the following?
   a. $2^1 + 2^2 + 2^3 + 2^4$
   b. $2^2 + 2^4$
   c. $2^2 + 3^3 + 4^4$
   d. $2^2 + 2^3 + 2^4$

2. The sum $\dfrac{1}{4}\sum_{m=2}^{4} x_m$ is equal to which of the following?
   a. $\dfrac{1}{4}x_2 + \dfrac{1}{4}x_3 + \dfrac{1}{4}x_4$
   b. $\dfrac{1}{4}x_2 + x_3 + x_4$
   c. $\dfrac{1}{2}x_2 + \dfrac{1}{3}x_3 + \dfrac{1}{4}x_4$
   d. $\dfrac{1}{4}(2+3+4)$

3. The sum $\sum_{j=4}^{n} \dfrac{j}{j+1}$ is equal to which of the following?
   a. $\dfrac{1}{2} + \dfrac{3}{4} + \dfrac{5}{6} + \ldots + \dfrac{n}{n+1}$
   b. $\dfrac{1}{2} + \dfrac{2}{3} + \dfrac{3}{4} + \ldots + \dfrac{n}{n+1}$
   c. $\dfrac{4}{5} + \dfrac{5}{6} + \dfrac{6}{7} + \ldots + \dfrac{n}{n+1}$
   d. $\dfrac{4}{5} + \dfrac{5}{6} + \dfrac{6}{7} + \ldots + \dfrac{n+4}{n+5}$

4. Write out fully what is meant by
   a. $\sum_{i=4}^{i=6} 2i - 1 =$
   b. $\sum_{i=2}^{i=5} \dfrac{i}{i^2 + 1} =$
   c. $\sum_{i=4}^{i=6} (2i - 3)^2 =$
   d. $\sum_{k=3}^{i=7} (2^k + \sqrt{k}) =$
   e. $\sum_{i=1}^{i=4} (-1)^i \times 3^{2i}$

5. Write each series using sigma notation:

   a. $4 + 9 + 16 + 25 + 36 + 49 + 64 + 81 = \sum_{i=\_\_}^{i=\_\_}$ _____

   b. $5 + 9 + 13 + 17 + 21 + 25 + 29 + 33\ldots = \sum_{i=\_\_}^{i=\_\_}$ _____

   c. $1 - \dfrac{1}{3} + \dfrac{1}{9} - \dfrac{1}{27} + \dfrac{1}{81} - \dfrac{1}{243} = \sum_{i=\_\_}^{i=\_\_}$ _____

6. Use sigma notation to represent $3 + 6 + 9 + 12 + \ldots$ for 28 terms. Sum the terms.

   $\sum_{i=\_\_}^{i=\_\_}$ _____

7. Use sigma notation to represent $-3 + 6 - 12 + 24 - 48 + \ldots$ for 35 terms. Sum the terms.

   $\sum_{i=\_\_}^{i=\_\_}$ _____

8. Use sigma notation to represent: $8.3 + 8.1 + 7.9 + 7.7 + \ldots + 0.9$. Sum the terms

   $\sum_{i=\_\_}^{i=\_\_}$ _____

9. Use sigma notation to represent: $12 + 9 + 3 + \ldots -120$. Sum the terms

   $\sum_{i=\_\_}^{i=\_\_}$ _____

10. An infinite geometric series is given by $\sum_{i=1}^{\infty} 2(1-x)^i$

   a. Find the value of x for which the series has a finite sum

   b. When x = 0.5, find the minimum number of terms needed to give a sum which is greater than 1.9

11. Given the sequence x, x^2, x^3...

   a. Use sigma notation to represent the sum of its first 10 terms.

   b. Assuming its infinite and that its sum is 5 find x and write down the first three terms of the sequence.

1.17. – SIGNIFICANT FIGURES

Whenever a measurement is performed an error is committed. Significant figures in a measurement include all of the digits that are known precisely plus one last digit that is estimated. The error can be caused by insufficient precision of the measuring device used, by the person doing the measurement, etc. Communicating our uncertainty in a measurement is as important as the measurement itself. The following rules help us to communicate our measurements better.

1. Non – zero digits are always significant: 2<u>03</u>.2<u>3</u>0002

2. All **final zeros** after the decimal point are significant: 2.745<u>0</u> ; 0.142<u>0</u>

3. <u>Zeros between</u> two other significant digits are <u>always significant</u>: 7<u>0</u>.0 ; 1<u>00</u>2 ; 9.<u>00</u>0

4. Zeros used only for spacing the decimal point are **not** significant: 1<u>00</u> ; 0.<u>00</u>078

5. On adding or subtracting, the answer is rounded to the <u>same number of</u> _____ as the measurement with the <u>least number</u> of decimal places.

6. On multiplying or dividing two numbers, the answer is rounded off to the number of _____ in the <u>least precise term used in the calculation</u>

Determine the number of significant digits in each of the following:

1. 273.20 cm _____
2. 4513.01 L _____
3. 2.00011 km _____
4. 0.0001010450 sec _____
5. 4.75 kg _____
6. 1.0 _____
7. 10.0 _____
8. 300 _____
9. 101 _____
10. 10 _____
11. 1.0 _____
12. 9.401°C _____
13. 0.2 ml _____
14. 310 kg _____
15. 200.103 mm _____
16. 704000 h _____

Answer using proper number of significant figures:

11. 3.414 s + 10.02 s + 58.325 s + 0.00098 s = __71.76 s__

12. 2.326 h – 0.10408 h = __2.222 h__

13. 10.19 m x 0.013 m = __0.13 m²__

14. 140.01 cm x 26.042 cm x 0.0159 cm = __58.0 cm³__

15. 80.23 m / 2.4 s = __33 m/s__

16. 4.301 kg / 1.9 cm³ = __2.3 kg/cm³__

17. An experiment involves the following substances:

    85.238 g of Iron, 32.1 g of Water, 0.0026 g of Oil, 7.13 g of Glass

    a. How many significant digits are there in each measurement?
    b. What is the total mass of substances in this experiment?
    c. How many significant digits are there in the answer to part b?

18. A certain living room was measured to be 12.412m long and 5.212m wide. Determine:

   a. The area of the living room to the correct number of decimal places.

   b. The area of the living room to 3 significant figures.

   c. The area of the living room to 4 significant figures.

   d. The area of the living room to 1 decimal place.

   e. The perimeter of the living room to the correct number of decimal places.

   f. The perimeter of the living room to 3 significant figures.

   g. The perimeter of the living room to 4 significant figures.

   h. The perimeter of the living room to 1 decimal place.

19. The length of a certain object was measured to be 17.40 mm. After a certain process it was measured to be 9.0 mm.

   a. Which measurement is more precise, before or after the process? Explain.
   b. What length was lost during the process?

1.16. – SCIENTIFIC NOTATION

1. How many significant figures does the measurement of 200 mm have? _____ However, what if whoever performed the measurement was accurate to within 1 mm?

2. Reporting the value as 200.0 suddenly turns the term having one significant digit into a term having _____.

3. The solution to this problem is called "scientific notation". In this case the solution to the problem would be: _____. With this notation, it is clear that three significant digits are intended.

4. Typically a _____ is placed to the left of the decimal, and this number is then multiplied by the appropriate _____. Our experimenter could report the measured quantity as 10.0×10^1 mm, but the first version is more common.

Write the following numbers in scientific notation and indicate the number of significant figures, later write with 3 significant figures:

1. 1026.90 = _____ 3S.F. _____

2. 0.03045 = _____ 3S.F. _____

3. 12,000 = _____ 3S.F. _____

4. 0.00690 = _____ 3S.F. _____

Write In scientific notation (use appropriate number of significant figures):

5. 0.11 = _____

6. 0.015 = _____

7. 0.0071 = _____

8. 0.0000001 = _____

9. 1.2 = _____

10. 1.02 = _____

11. 0.3 = _____

12. 0.00004 = _____

13. 0.06023 = _____

14. 0.000345 = _____

15. 0.00155 = _____

16. 0.0000204 = _____

17. 100 = _____

18. 10100 = _____

19. 11.0 = _____

20. 200 = _____

21. 201 = _____

22. 10.00 = _____

23. 101.0 = _____

24. 1.200 = _____

25. 1500 = _____

26. 2000 = _____

27. 51223 = _____

28. 100.80 = _____

29. 209.1 = _____

30. 24.18 = _____

31. 5500 = _____

32. 766600 = _____

33. 54000 = _____

34. 44500 = _____

35. 65000 = _____

36. 0.00545 = _____

37. 0.001545 = _____

38. 0.00020545 = _____

39. 0.050425 = _____

40. 0.0050545 = _____

41. 70000 = _____

Calculate giving your answers in scientific notation with the proper number of significant figures.

42. $(9.9 \cdot 10^{-8}) / (3.30 \cdot 10^{-4}) =$ _____

43. $(1.56 \cdot 10^{-7}) + (2.43 \cdot 10^{-8}) =$ _____

44. $(7.4 \cdot 10^{10}) / (3.7 \cdot 10^{3}) =$ _____

45. $(2.5 \cdot 10^{-8}) \cdot (3.0 \cdot 10^{-7}) =$ _____

46. $(2.67 \cdot 10^{-3}) - (9.5 \cdot 10^{-4}) =$ _____

47. $(2.3 \cdot 10^{-4}) \cdot (2.0 \cdot 10^{-3}) =$ _____

CHAPTER 2 - GEOMETRY

2.1. – GEOMETRY

ANGLES

1. An angle is the figure formed by _____ lines that start at a common point.

    For example:

    We say that the following angle has a size of _____ degrees or ____°

2. Use the following square to sketch an angle of 45° degrees:

POINTS

3. Indicate the following points on the plane: A(1,5), B(–1, 4), C(–3, –7), D(6,–5), E(–1, –1), F(2, 0), G(0,–4), H(–4, 0)

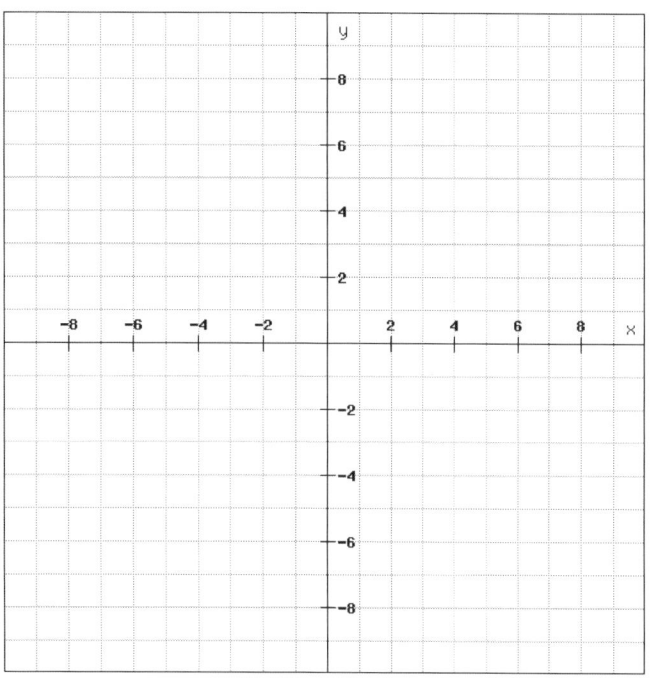

LINES

4. Indicate the following points on the plane: A(0,0), B(1, 1), C(–2, –2), D(6,6)

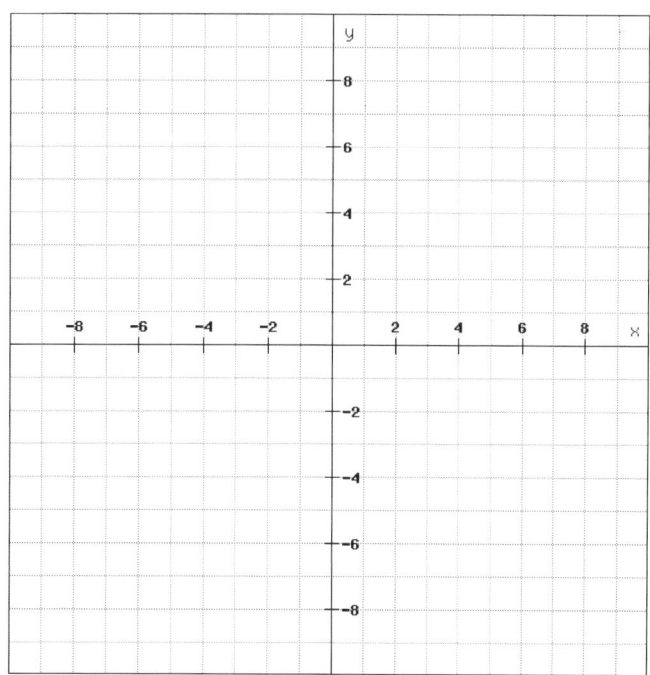

   a. What do these points have in common?

   b. Could you describe all the points that satisfy this property? How?

5. Indicate the following points on the plane: A(0,0), B(1, 2), C(–2, –4), D(4,8)

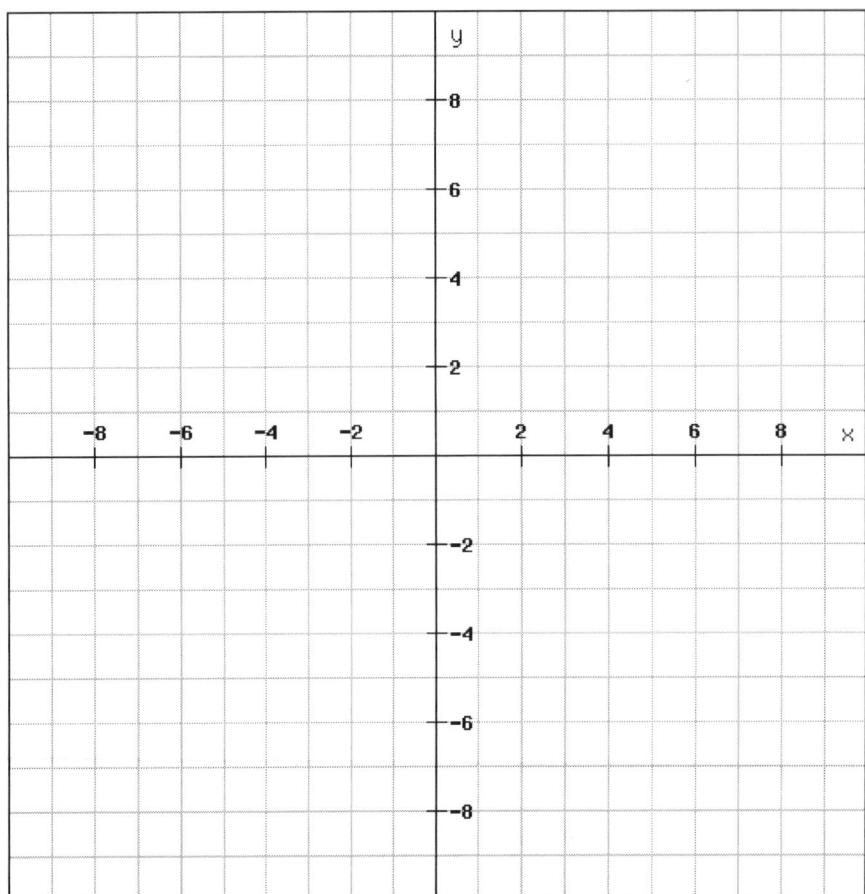

a. What do these points have in common? Use a ruler to draw the line that connects them.

b. Could you describe all the points that satisfy this property? How?

c. On the same graph sketch the following points E(0,1), F(1, 3), G(–2, –3), H(4,9)

d. What do these points have in common? Use a ruler to draw the line that connects them. What is the relation between this line and the previous line?

6. Indicate the following points on the plane: A(0, –2), B(1, 1), C(2, 4), D(–2,–8)

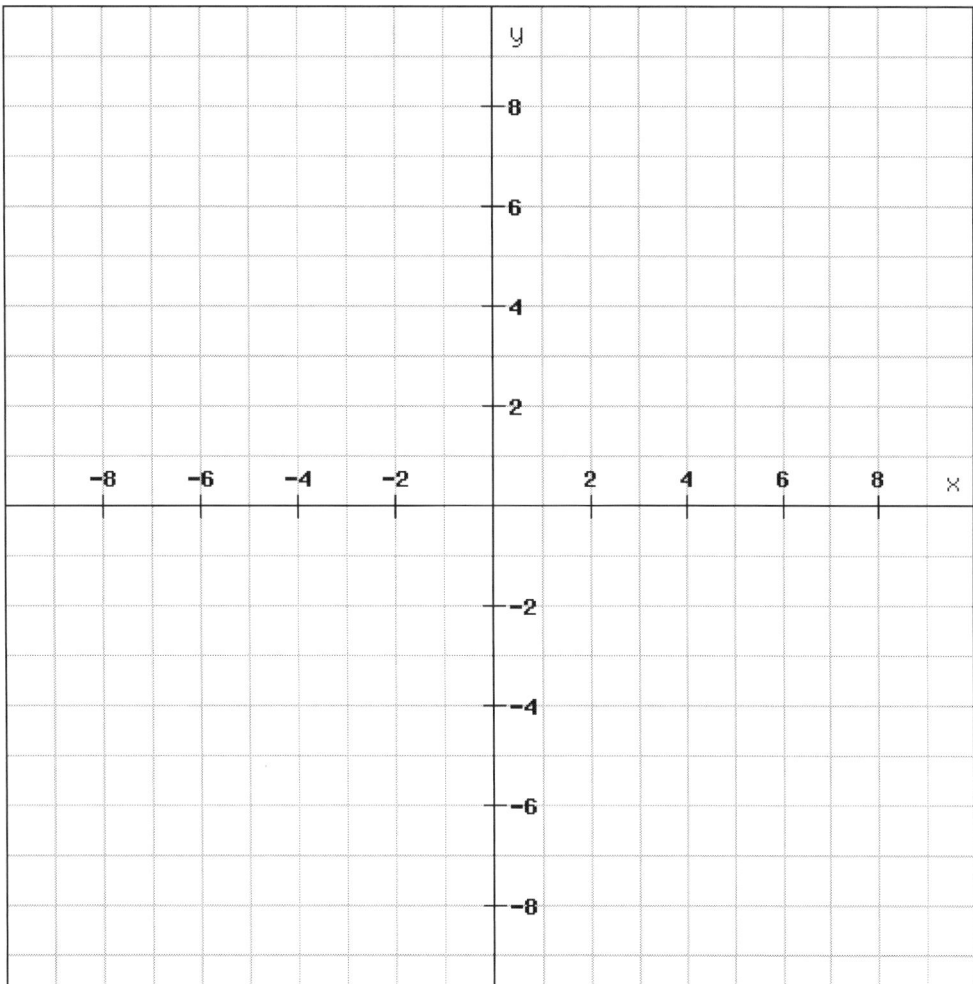

a. What do these points have in common? Use a ruler to draw the line that connects them.

b. Could you describe all the points that satisfy this property? How?

c. On the same graph sketch the following points E(0,1), F(1, 4), G(–2, –5), H(2, 7)

d. What do these points have in common? Use a ruler to draw the line that connects them. What is the relation between this line and the previous line?

SQUARES, RECTANGLES AND TRIANGLES

7. Indicate the following points on the plane: A(0, 6), B(6, 0), C(0, 0)

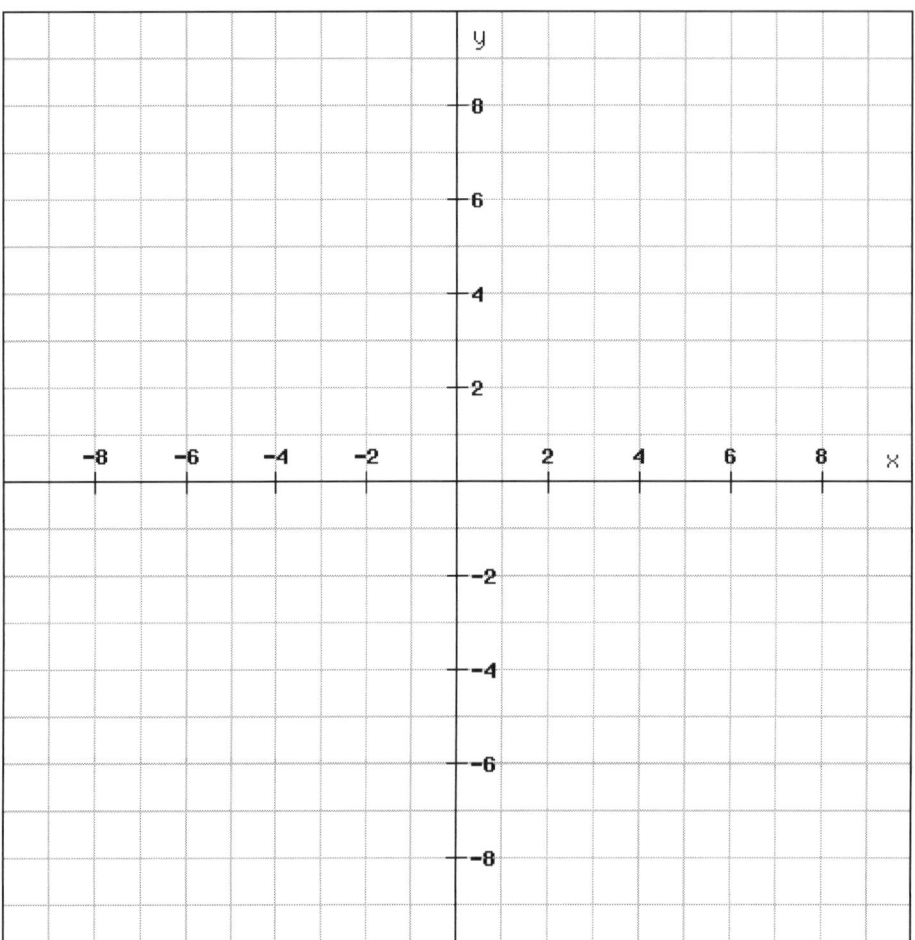

    a. Use a ruler to draw the line that connects each pair of points to form a triangle.

    b. Find all the angles of the triangles you can.

    c. This kind of triangle is called _____ and _____

    d. Write down the lengths of the 2 equal sides: _____

    e. Write down the Pythagorean Theorem: _____.

    This theorem is only true in _____ triangles.

    f. Use P. Theorem to find the length of the third side of the triangle.

    g. Add the point D(6, 6) to the graph. The form ABCD is a _____. The area of this shape is _____

    h. Use the area of the square to find the area of the triangle.

8. Indicate the following points on the plane: A(–4, 0), B(2, 6), C(8, 0)

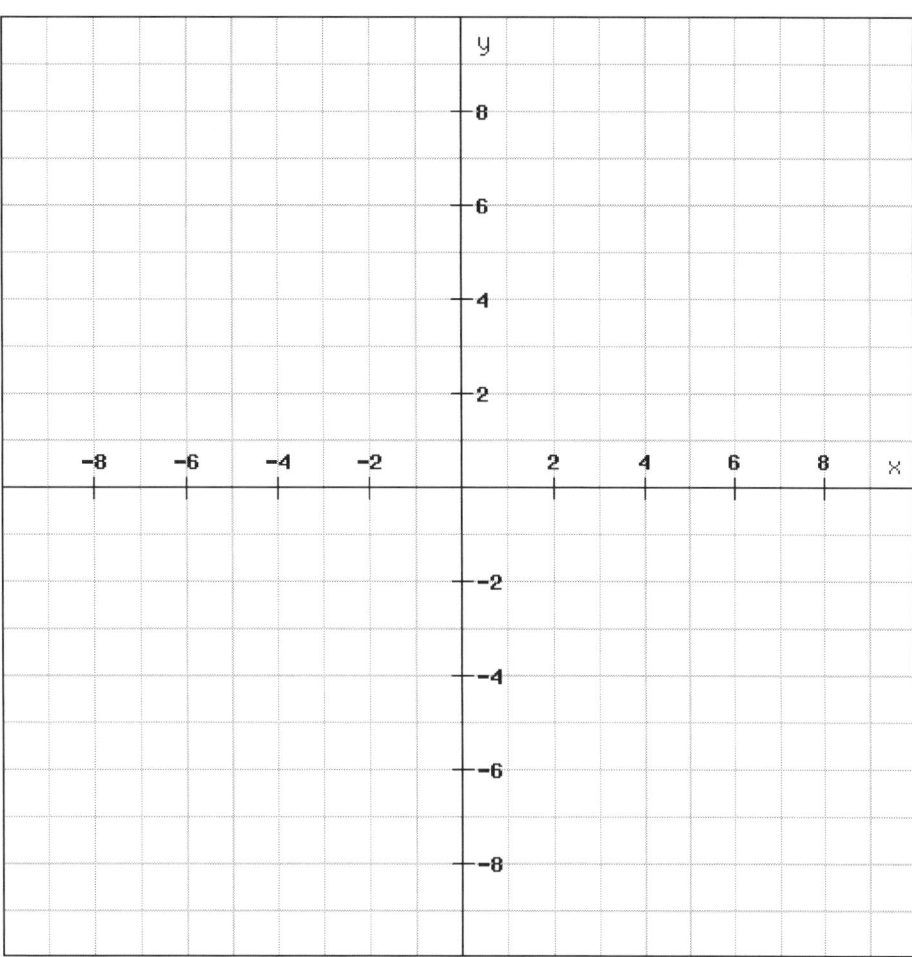

a. Use a ruler to draw the line that connects each pair of points to form a triangle.

b. This kind of triangle is called _____

c. Write down the Pythagorean Theorem: _____.

   This theorem is only true in _____ triangles.

d. Add the point D (2, 0) to the graph. The triangle ABD is _____.

e. The length of AD is _____. The Length of BD is _____. Use P. Theorem to find the length of AB.

f. In consequence state the length of BC: _____.

g. The perimeter of the triangle ABC is _____

h. Add the point E (–4, 6) to the graph. The shape AEBD is a _____. The area of this shape is ___. Use this area to find the area of the triangle ABD and ABC.

131

9. Indicate the following points on the plane: A(–6, 0), B(3, 6), C(5, 0)

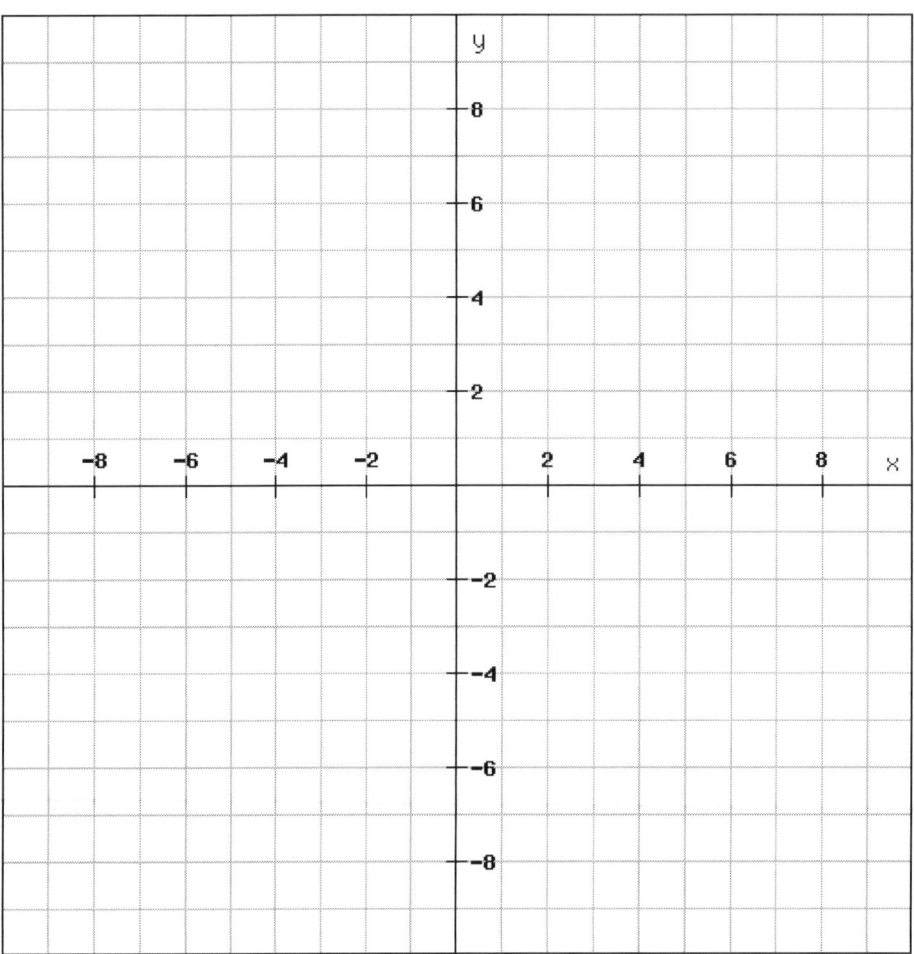

a. Use a ruler to draw the line that connects each pair of points to form a triangle.

b. Is this triangle isosceles or right angled?

c. Add the points D (–6, 6) and E (5, 6) to the graph. The shape ADEC is a _____

    The area of this shape is _____.

d. Add the point F (3, 0) to graph and use the corresponding theorem to find the

    length of AB: _____ and BC _____.

e. The perimeter of the triangle ABC is _____

f. The line BF is called the _____ of the triangle.

g. Every triangle has ___ heights. A height is a lines that starts at a _____

    and ends at _____ forming an angle of _____ with it.

h. Find the area of the triangles ABF, FBC and ABC.

10. Indicate the following points on the plane: A (–5, 0), B (5, 0), C (0, $\sqrt{75}$)

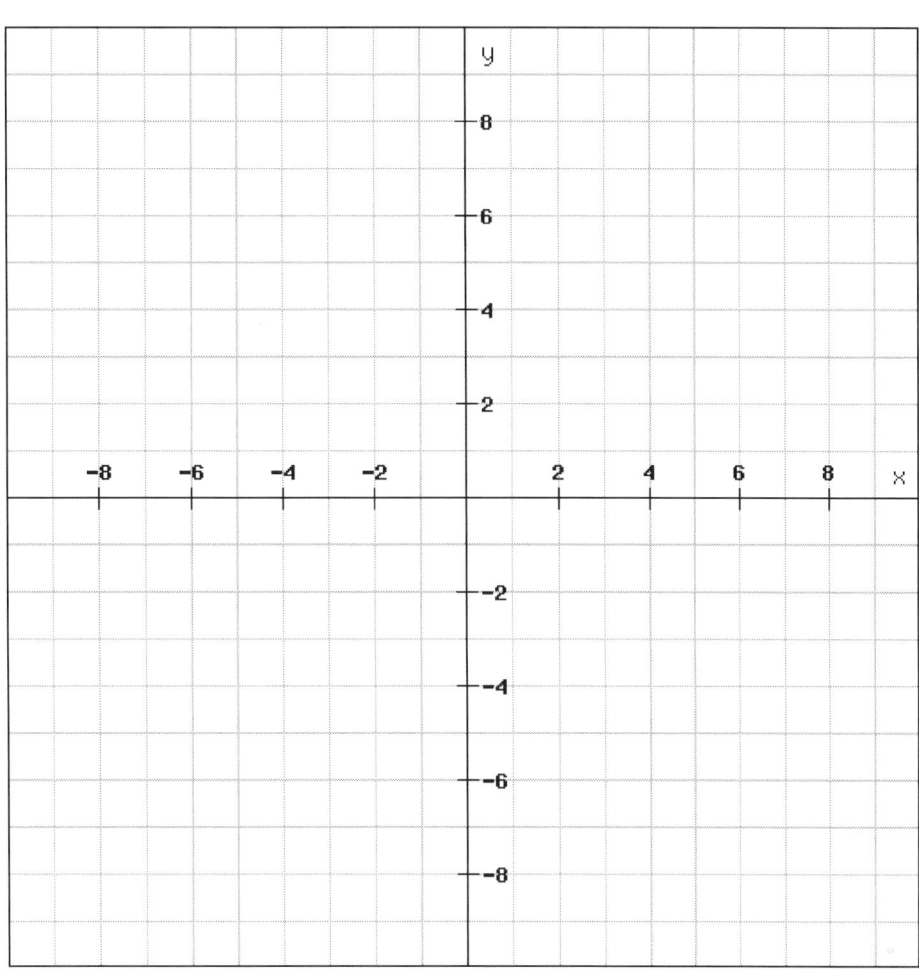

a. Use a ruler to draw the line that connects each pair of points to form a triangle.

b. Add the points D (0, 0) to the graph and use the corresponding theorem to find length of AB: _____ and BC _____.

c. What kind of triangle is this? _____

d. What can you say about the angles of this triangle?

e. The perimeter of the triangle ABC is _____

f. Find the area of the triangle ABC.

11. Define and sketch an example, include all the known angles and lengths of sides in your example.

   a. Equilateral triangle:

   b. Isosceles triangle:

   c. Right angled triangle:

   d. Right angled and isosceles triangle:

12. Given the following triangle, sketch all the altitudes in the triangle.

    An altitude is: _____. The point where they meet is called "orthocenter".

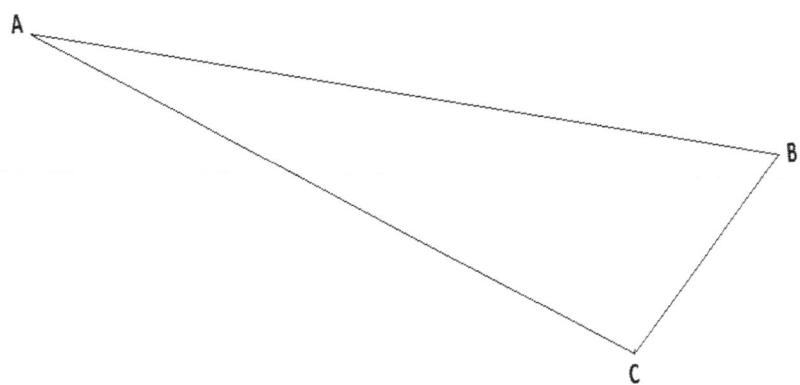

13. Given the following triangle, Sketch all the perpendicular bisectors in the triangle. The point where they meet is called circumcenter, it is the centre of

    _____

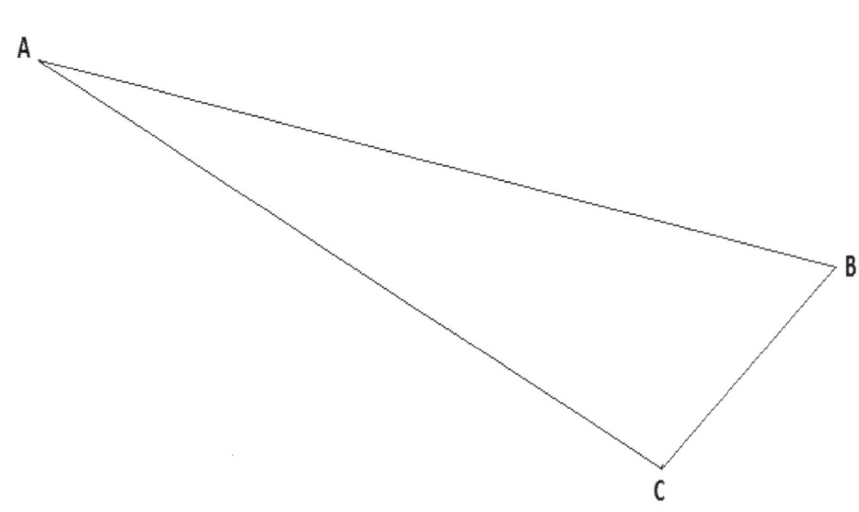

14. Given the following triangle, Sketch all the angle bisectors in the triangle. The point where they meet is called incenter, it is the centre of _____

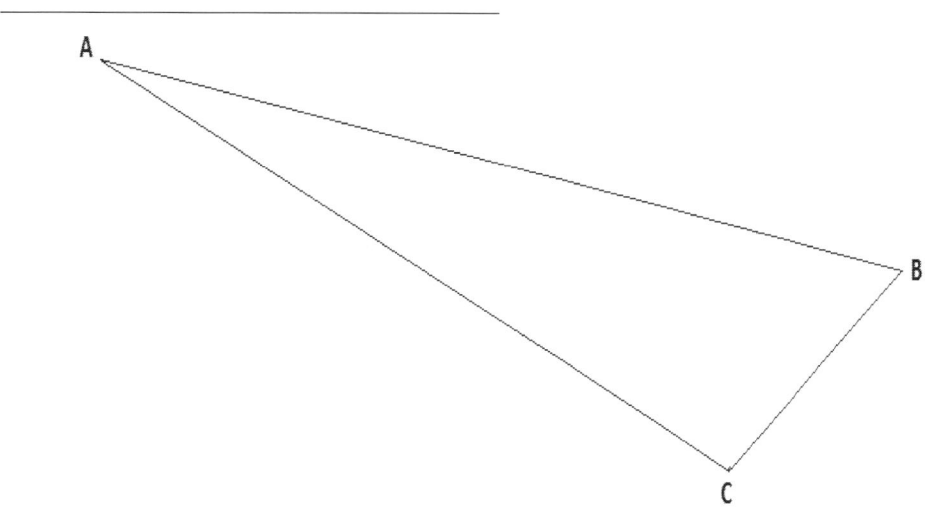

15. Given the following triangle, Sketch all the medians in the triangle. The point where they meet is called centroid. If the centroid is M then the following relations are satisfied (complete):

$$AM = \frac{2}{3} AD \qquad BM = \qquad CM =$$

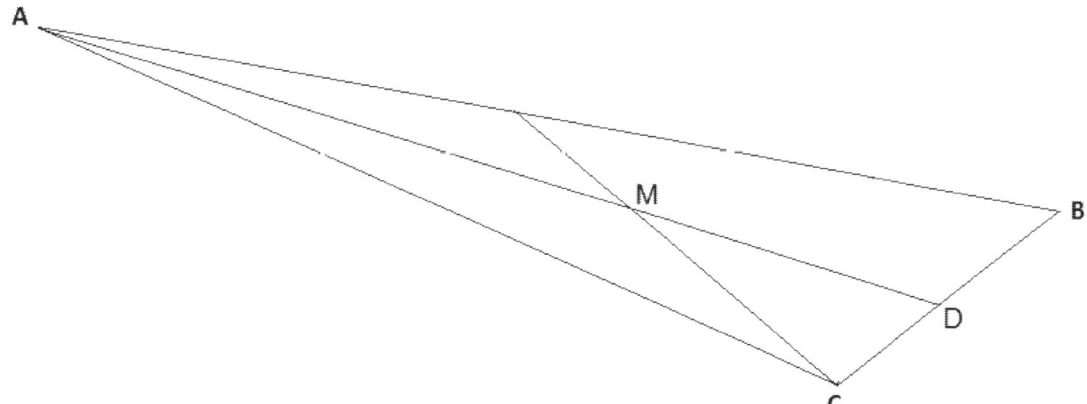

16. Given the following triangle, it is known that AB = 10cm, AD = 7cm and DC = 4cm. Angle CDB = 90°. Find:

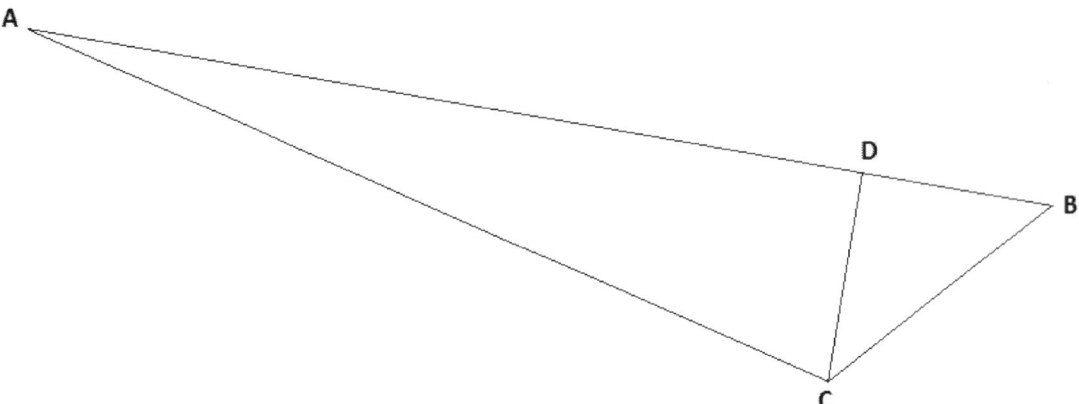

   a. The lengths of BC and AC.
   b. The area of ABC.
   c. The perimeter of ABC

17. Given the following triangle, it is known that AC = 13cm, DB = 4cm and DC = 5cm. Angle CDB = 90°. Find:

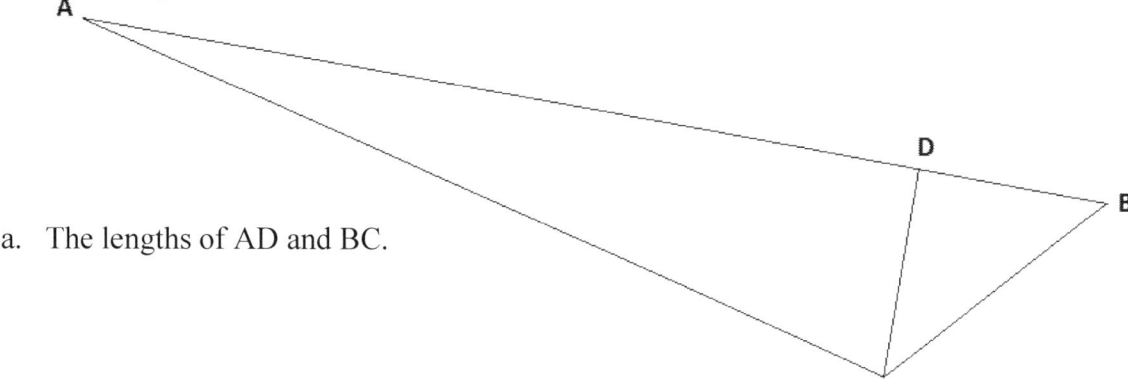

   a. The lengths of AD and BC.

   b. The area of DCB.

   c. The perimeter of ABC

18. Given the following triangle, it is known that AC = 20cm, DB = 10cm and DC = 11 cm. Angle CDB = 90° and angle CEA = 90°. Find:

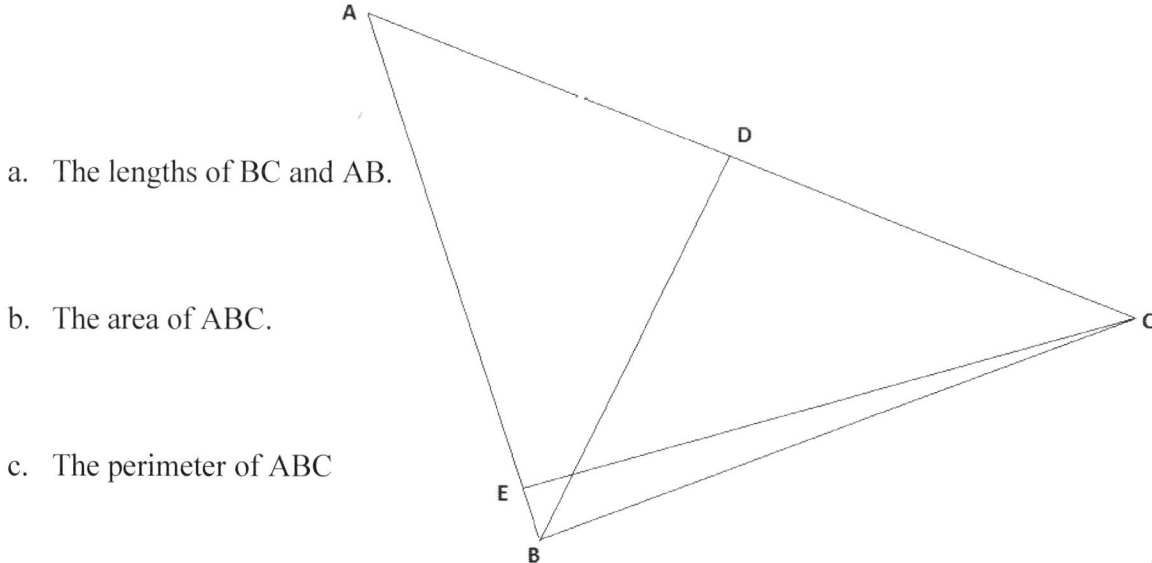

   a. The lengths of BC and AB.

   b. The area of ABC.

   c. The perimeter of ABC

   d. What do EC and BD have in common?

   e. The lengths of EC, EB and AE

137

19. Given a right angled isosceles triangle whose longest side is 10 cm long.

   a. Sketch the triangle.
   b. Find the perimeter of the triangle.
   c. Find the area of the triangle.

20. Given a right angled isosceles triangle whose smallest side is X cm long.

   a. Sketch the triangle.
   b. Find the perimeter of the triangle in terms of X.
   c. Find the area of the triangle in terms of X.

SIMILAR TRIANGLES

21. 2 triangles are similar if all of their angles are _____

22. 2 triangles are similar if <u>any</u> of the following is satisfied:

   a. 2 of their angles are _____. Sketch an example:

   b. 2 of their sides are _____ and the angles between them are _____. Sketch an example:

   c. All the sides are _____. Sketch an example:

23. All right angled triangles are similar True / False. Sketch an example to show answer:

24. Determine if the following pair of triangles are similar, give a reason:

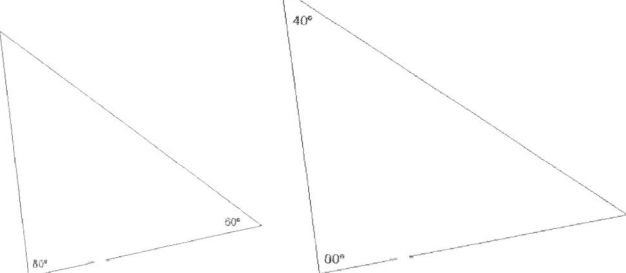

25. Determine if the following pair of triangles are similar, give a reason:

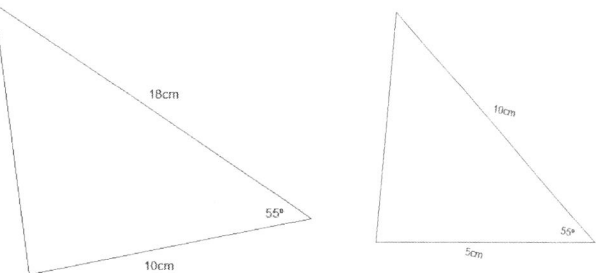

26. Determine if the following pair of triangles are similar, give a reason:

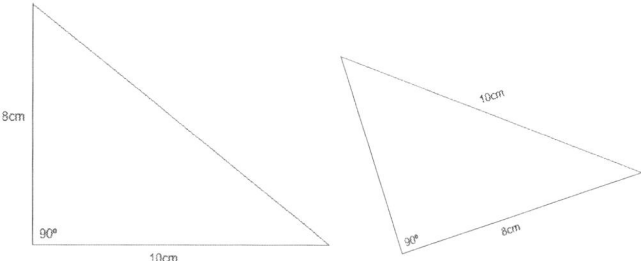

27. Determine if the following pair of triangles are similar, give a reason:

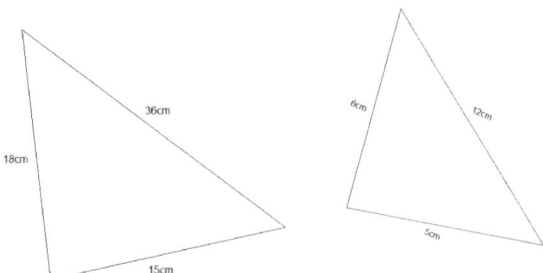

28. Determine if the following pair of triangles are similar, give a reason:

29. Determine if the following pair of triangles are similar, give a reason:

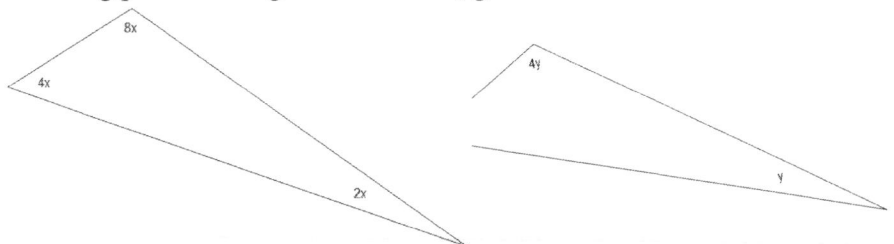

30. Given that $AB \parallel CD$, determine if the triangles ABE and CED are similar, give a reason:

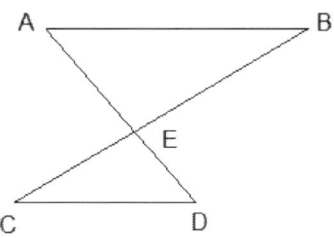

31. Given that $BC \parallel DE$, determine if the triangles ABC and ADE are similar, give a reason:

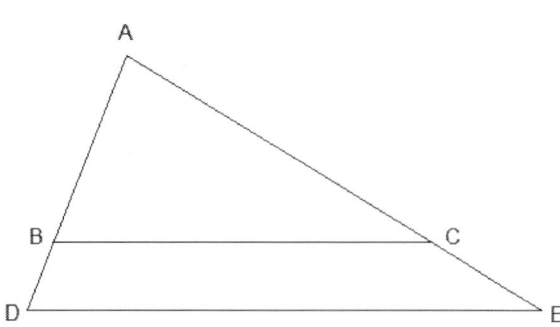

32. The shadow of a man formed by a street light on the ground is equal to twice its height. If the man is 10m away from the street light and his height is 1.80m, how high is the street light?

33. Given that $AB \parallel CD$, find ED:

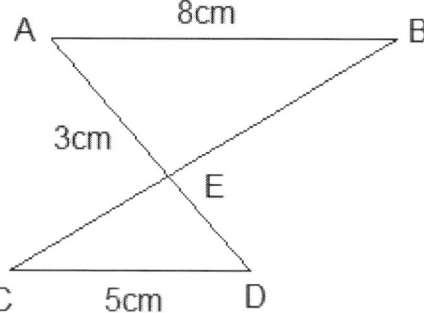

34. In the following triangle the tangle BAC is a right angle. AD is a height from A to the BC. Show that triangles ABC, ADB and ADC are all similar. If BC = 10cm and AD = 2DC find the perimeter and area of ABD.

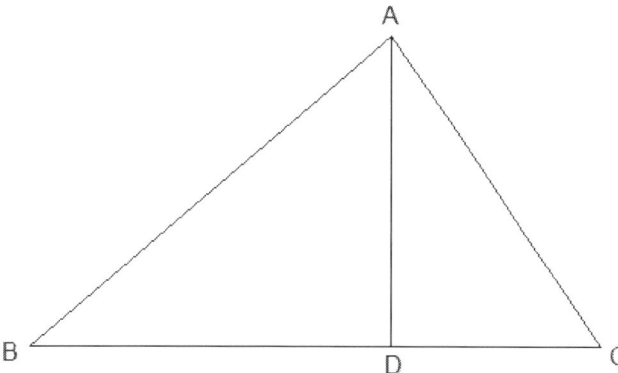

35. The following triangle AB = AC. AD is a height from A to the BC. Show that triangles ABD and ACD are similar. If BD = x and 2AB = 3AD, find the perimeter and area of ABC in terms of x.

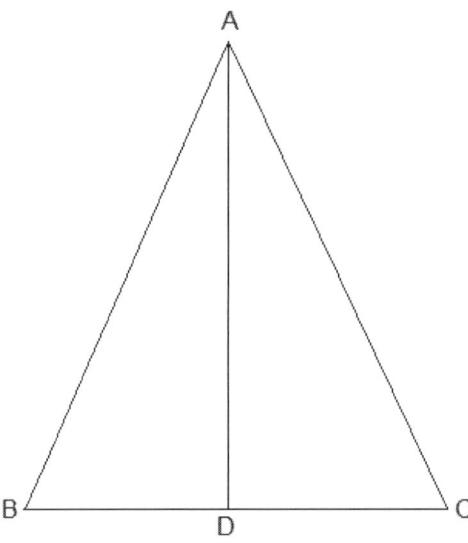

36. Given the facade of a certain house, it is known that AC = 4m, CD = 2AC, CE = 7m DE = 3m. ABCD is a rectangle.
Find:

a. The height of the house above ground (help: lower a height from E).

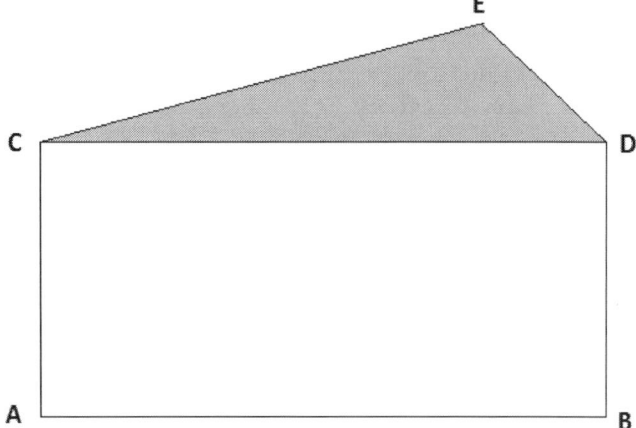

b. The area of the entire facade.

DISTANCE AND MIDPOINT

37. Indicate the following points on the plane: A(2,3), B(6, 9), C(–3, –7), D(6,–5)

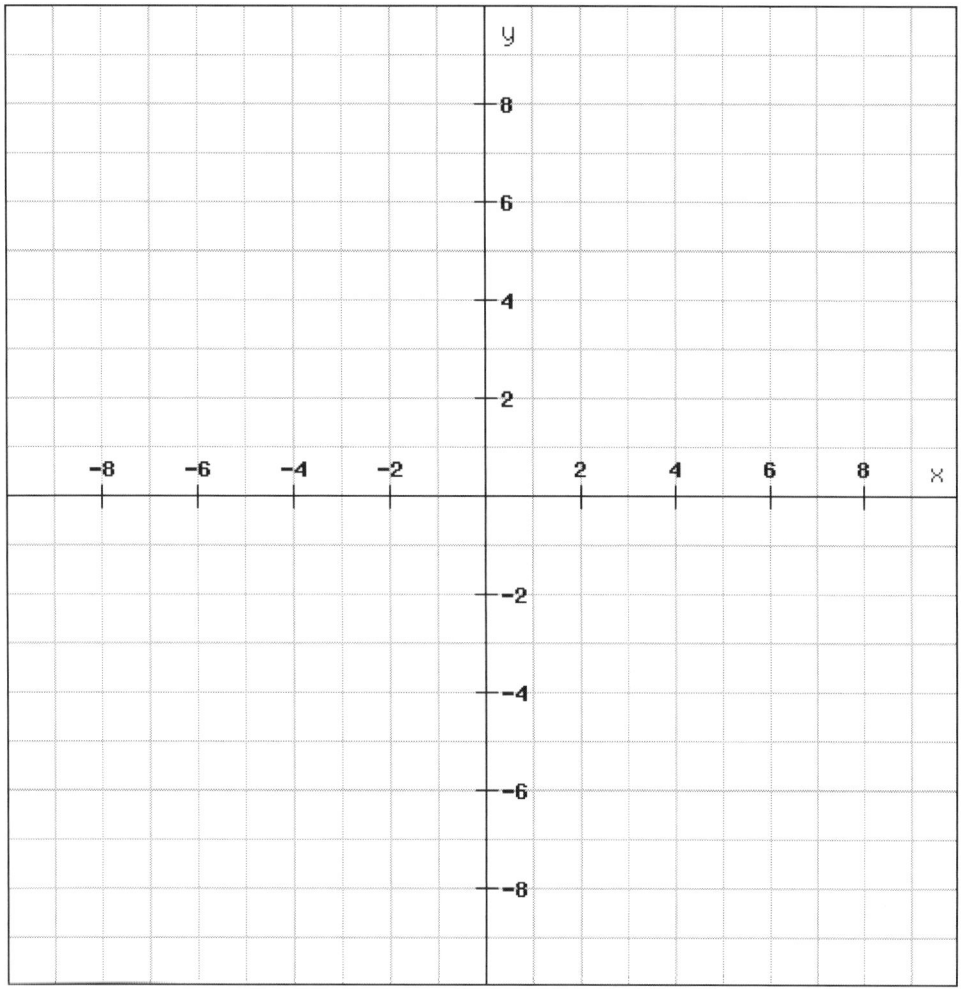

a. Add the point (6, 3) and use Pythagorean Theorem to find the distance between the points A and B.

b. Add the point (–3,–5) and use Pythagorean Theorem to find the distance between the points C and D.

c. Find the distance AC

d. Find the midpoint between AB (help: the midpoint x coordinate is the "average" of the x coordinates and the y coordinate is the "average" of the y coordinates)

e. Find the midpoint between CD

f. Find the midpoint between AC

38. Find the distance between (1, 3) and (7, -3), find the mid point.

39. Find the distance between (-5, -4) and (2, -9), find the mid point.

40. Find a point whose distance to the point (2, 1) is 7.

41. Find a point whose distance to the point (-4, 2) is 3, can you draw a conclusion about such points in general?

42. The midpoint between the points (a, 5) and (-2, b) is (0, 0) find a and b.

43. Given that AB = BC = CD and A, B, C and D are aligned. Point A is (2, 4) and point D is (10, 10). Find points B and C.

44. Given that the distance AB = BC = CD. Point A is (-4, 8) and point B is (-2, 1). Find points C and D.

144

CIRCLES

45. Given the following circle:

    a. Sketch a diameter.
    b. Sketch a radius.
    c. The diameter is _____ the radius
    d. Sketch a chord smaller than the diameter
    e. Sketch a chord smaller than the radius

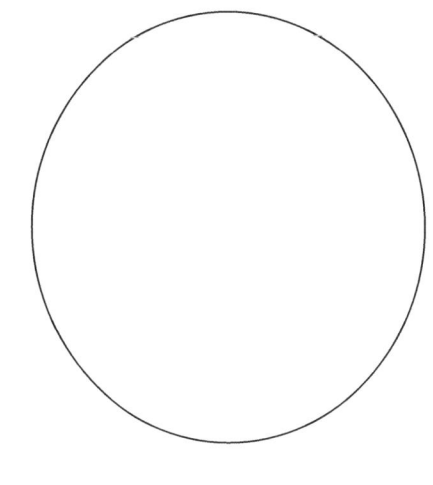

46. Given the following circle:

    a. Sketch a 60° angle.
    b. Show the corresponding minor arc/major arc
    c. Choose 3 points on the circle, connect them with chords. The triangle formed is inscribed in the circle. The circle is circumscribed about the triangle.
    d. Chords that are at the same distance from the centre are _____

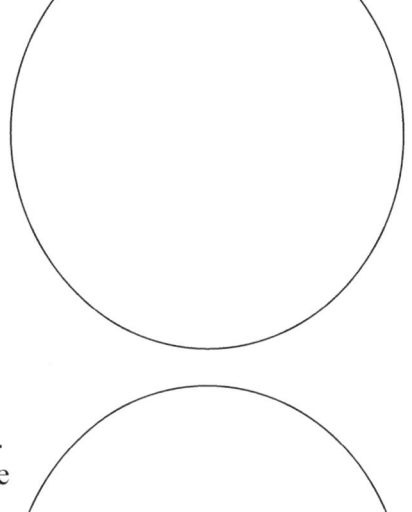

47. Given the following circle:

    a. Choose 3 points on the circle, name them A, B and C. Sketch AB and BC. The angle ABC is inscribed in the circle.
    b. Choose a 4th point on the circle, name it D. Sketch AD and CD. The angle ADC is inscribed in the circle.
    c. What is your conclusion?

48. Given the following circle:

    a. Choose 3 points on the circle, name them A, B and C. Sketch AB and BC. The angle ABC is inscribed in the circle.
    b. Sketch the center of the circle; name it O. Sketch AO and CO. The angle AOC is inscribed in the circle.
    c. What is your conclusion?

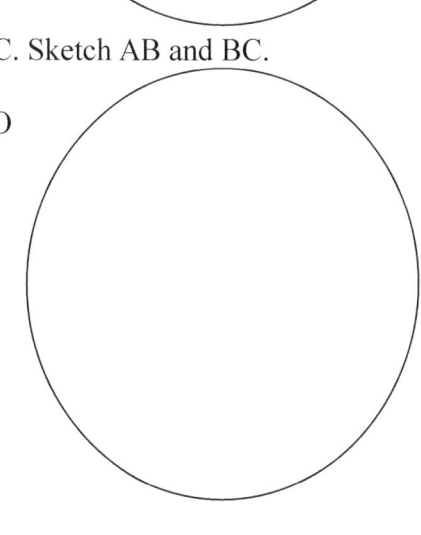

49. Given the following circle:

   a. Sketch the diameter of the circle; name it AC. Sketch a 3rd point B. Connect AB, AC and BC. The angle ABC is inscribed in the circle. Its size is: _____
   b. Choose a 4th point on the circle; name it D. Connect AD, DC. The angle ADC is inscribed in the circle. Its size is:

   _____
   c. What is your conclusion?

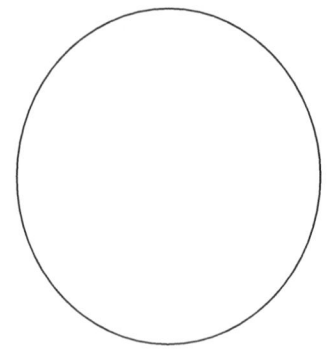

50. Given the following circle:

   Sketch the diameter of the circle; name it AC. Sketch a 3rd point B. Connect AB, AC and BC. Given that the radius of the circle is 1cm and AB = 1cm find the perimeter of ABC.

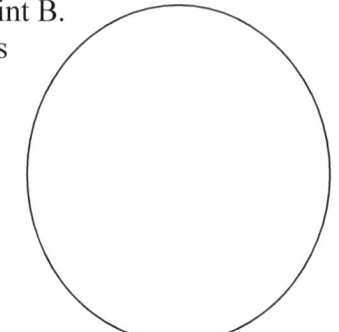

51. Sketch a chord whose length is half of the diameter. In case the radius is 2cm find the area and perimeter of the triangle formed by connecting the center of the circle with the ends of the chord.

52. Given a circle with radius R, find

   The Perimeter of the circle: _____

   The Area of the circle: _____

53. Given a circle with radius $\frac{4}{\pi}$ cm, find

   The Perimeter of the circle: _____

   The Area of the circle: _____

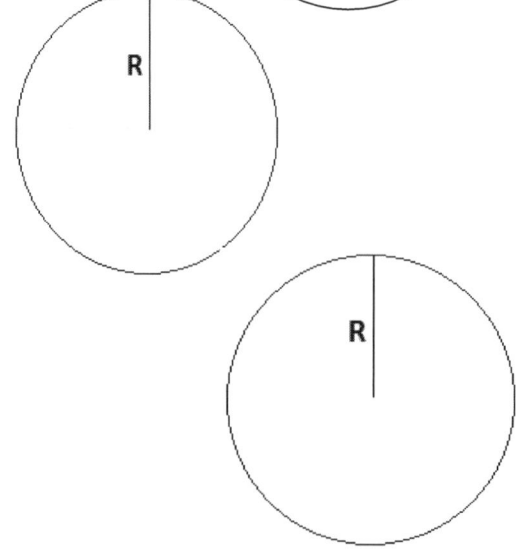

146

54. Given a circle with perimeter 20π cm, find

   The radius of the circle: _____

   The Area of the circle: _____

55. Given a circle with area 16π cm^2, find

   The radius of the circle: _____

   The perimeter of the circle: _____

56. Shade 10% of the figure, find the corresponding angle. The length
    Of an arc in a circle is L = _____

57. Given that R = 5 cm. Shade 20% of the figure, find the corresponding angle and
    the area shaded. Find the perimeter of the shaded area.

58. Given that R = 15 cm. Shade 30% of the figure, write the corresponding angle and find the area shaded. Find the perimeter of the shaded area.

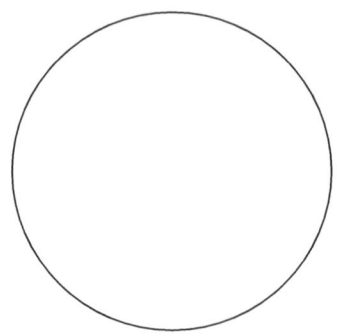

59. Given a circle with radius 10cm:

   a. Find the <u>percentage</u> of the area shaded.
   b. Find the <u>size</u> of the shaded area.
   c. Find the <u>perimeter</u> of the shaded area.

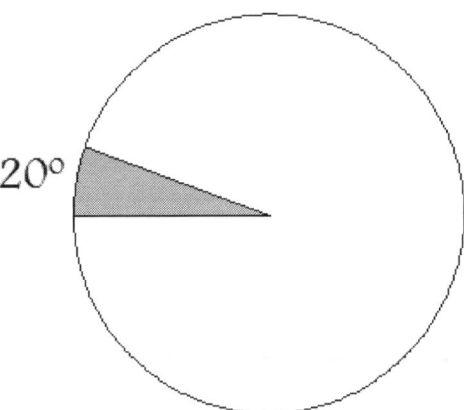

60. Given a circle with radius 10cm:

   a. Find the <u>percentage</u> of the shaded area of the total area of the circle in terms of the angel x.
   b. Find the <u>size</u> of the shaded area in terms of x.
   c. Find the <u>perimeter</u> of the shaded area in terms of x.

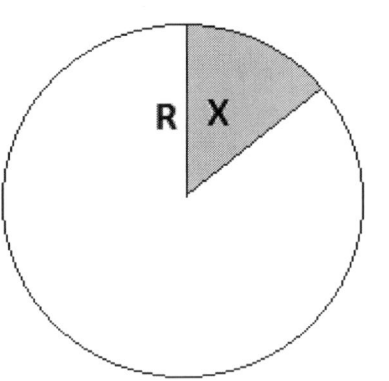

61. The length of the perimeter of a circle with radius r is _____. The length of the arc that corresponds an angle x° is _____. In case the angle x is measured in radians it would be _____.

The area of a circle with radius r is _____. The area of the sector that corresponds an angle x° is _____. In case the angle x is measured in radians it would be _____.

62. Given the circle with r = 2cm :

   a. Show the arc corresponding an angle of 45°.
   b. Calculate its length.
   c. Shade the corresponding sector area.
   d. Calculate it.

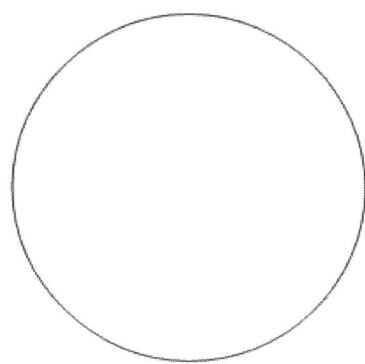

63. Given the circle with r = 3.2m:

   a. Show the arc corresponding an angle of 20°.
   b. Calculate its length.
   c. Shade the corresponding sector area.
   d. Calculate it.

64. Given the circle with r = 3m:

   a. Show the arc corresponding an angle of $\frac{\pi}{10} rad$.
   b. Calculate its length.
   c. Calculate its perimeter.
   d. Shade the corresponding sector area.
   e. Calculate it.

65. Given the circle with r = 6m:

   a. Show the arc corresponding an angle of 1 radian.
   b. Calculate its length.
   c. Shade the corresponding sector area.
   d. Calculate it.

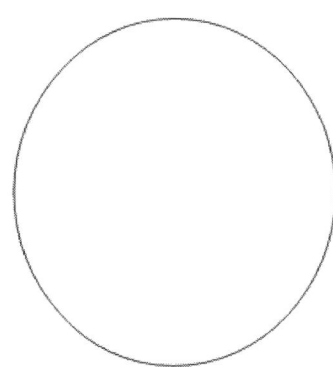

66. Given the following concentric circles with radii 3 cm and 5 cm correspondingly. Find the shaded area.

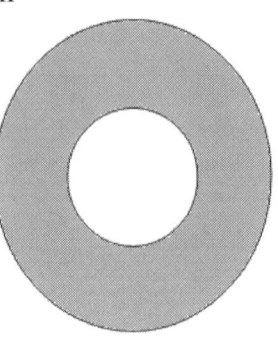

67. Given the following concentric circles with radii 10m and 14m correspondingly. Calculate the shaded area.

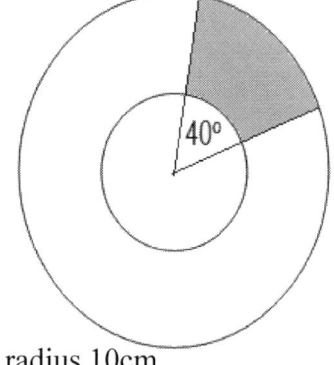

68. Given the following circle, AB is a chord on a circle with radius 10cm. Calculate the shaded area.

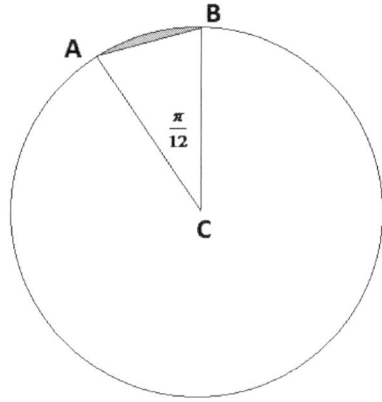

69. Given a circle with radius 8 cm. The segments AB and AC are tangent to the circle. Find the shaded area.

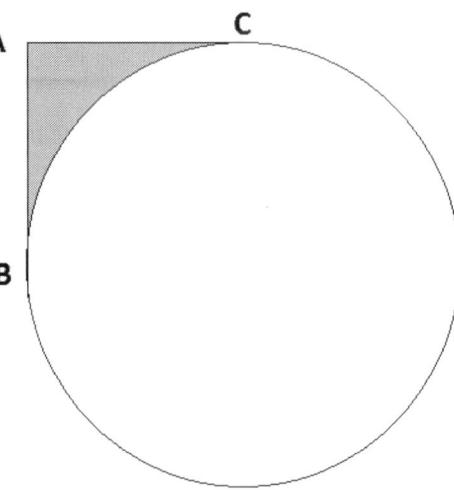

150

70. Given a circle with radius 10cm in which a square is circumscribed

   a. Find the length of the side of the square.
   b. Find the area of the square.
   c. Find the area of the circle
   d. Find the percentage of the area of the circle that the square occupies.

71. Given a circle with radius 10cm circumscribed in a square:

   a. Find the length of the side of the square.
   b. Find the area of the square.
   c. Find the area of the circle
   d. Find the percentage of the area of the square that the circle occupies.

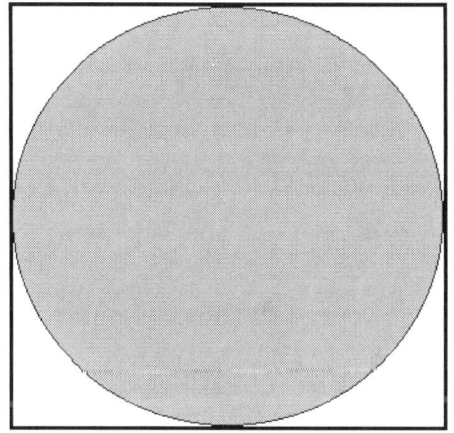

72. On the following diagram sketch the following directions:

   a. N
   b. N30°E
   c. N45°E
   d. E45°N
   e. S10°W
   f. W80°S
   g. W20°N
   h. N30°W

   State a conclusion about the "uniqueness" of a direction.

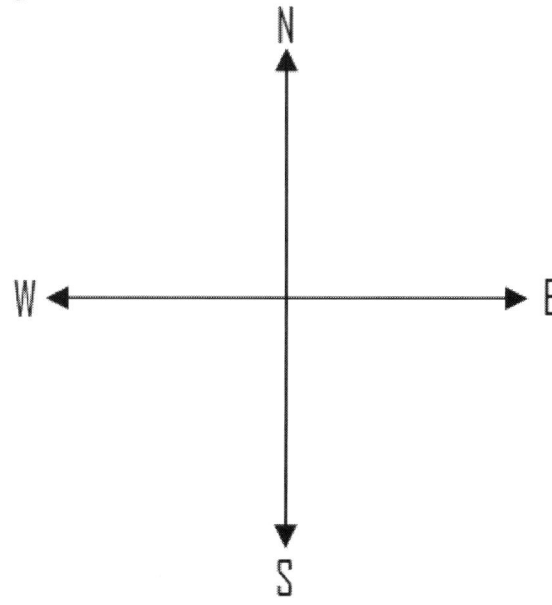

151

73. Given the following table, fill the blank using a, b, c, d, h, r

	Shape	Area	Perimeter
Square		a^2	$4a$
Rectangle		$a \cdot b$	$2(a+b)$
Parallelogram		$a \cdot h$	$2(a+b)$
Isosceles Trapezoid		$\dfrac{(a+c)h}{2}$	$a+c+2b$
Trapezoid		$\dfrac{(a+b)h}{2}$	$a+b+c+d$
Rhombus		$\dfrac{d \cdot r}{2}$	$4a$
Kite		$\dfrac{d \cdot r}{2}$	$2(a+b)$

74. Given the following quadrilaterals. Write the name of each one of them:

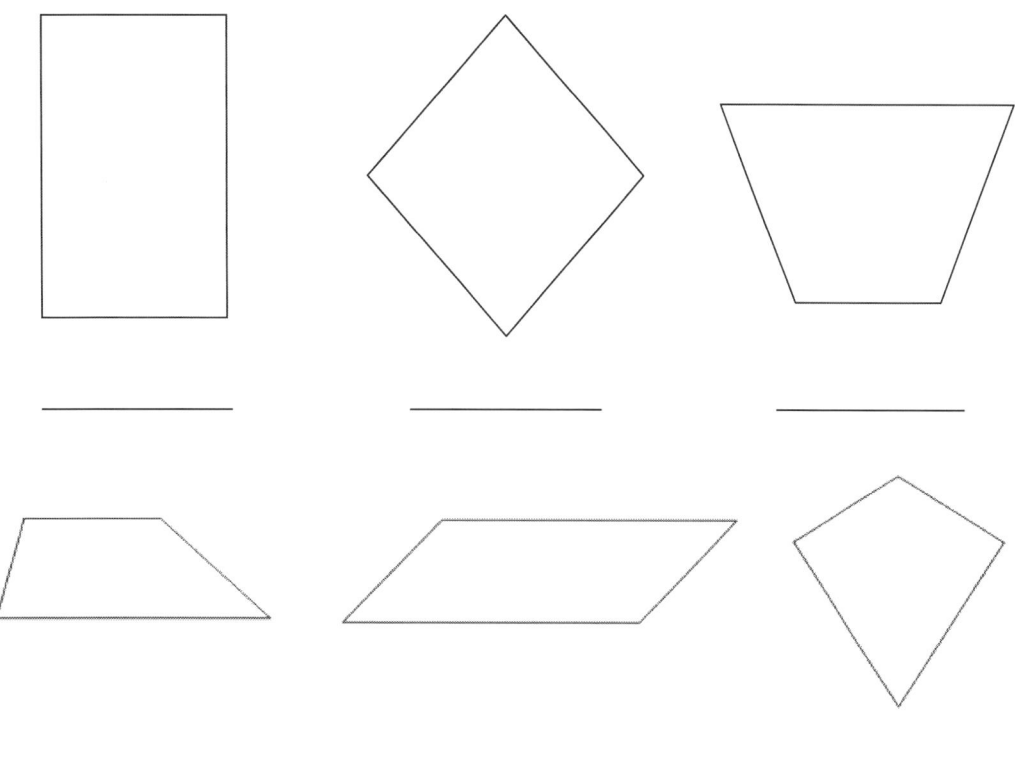

75. Given the following table, fill the blanks with yes or no.

	Shape (sketch)	Only 1 pair of parallel sides	2 pairs of parallel sides	1 pair of equal sides	2 pairs of equal sides	4 equal sides
Square						
Rectangle						
Parallelogram						
Isosceles Trapezoid						
Trapezpezoid						
Rhombus						
Kite						

76. True or False

    a. A square is also a parallelogram   True / False

    b. A square is also a rectangle   True / False

    c. A square is also a trapezoid   True / False

    d. A parallelogram is also a square   True / False

    e. A rectangle is also a square   True / False

    f. A rhombus is always a parallelogram   True / False

    g. A parallelogram is always r rhombus   True / False

    h. A parallelogram is sometimes a rhombus   True / False

    i. A rhombus is always a kite   True / False

    j. All the shapes above mentioned are quadrilaterals   True / False

77. Given the following table, fill the blanks with yes or no.

	Shape (Sketch diagonals as well)	Diagonals are perpendicular	Diagonals are equal	Diagonals bisect angle	Diagonals bisect each other
Square					
Rectangle					
Paralleogram					
Isosceles Trapezoid					
Trapezpezoid					
Rhombus					
Kite					

78. Given the following table, fill the blanks

	Shape	Surface Area	Volume
Cuboid (Rectangular Prism)			
Pyramid (Square based)			
Sphere			
Cylinder			
Cone			

79. Given the following table, fill the blanks

	Shape	Surface Area	Volume
Triangular prism			
Triangle based Pyramid (Tetrahedron)			

80. Find the volume and surface area of a sphere with radius 10cm.

81. Find the volume and surface area of a sphere with radius 0.4m.

82. Find the volume of a square based pyramid with base length $2x$ cm and height is x cm.

83. Find the volume and surface area of a square based cuboid whose base length is 15 cm and height 0.1m

84. Find the volume and surface area of a cone with radius 0.4m and height 2m.

85. Find the volume and surface area of a cylinder with radius 0.4m and height 2m.

156

2.2. – GEOMETRIC TRANSOFRMATIONS

1. Indicate the following points on the plane: A(0,0), B(–1,6), C(4,2). Connect them to form a triangle.

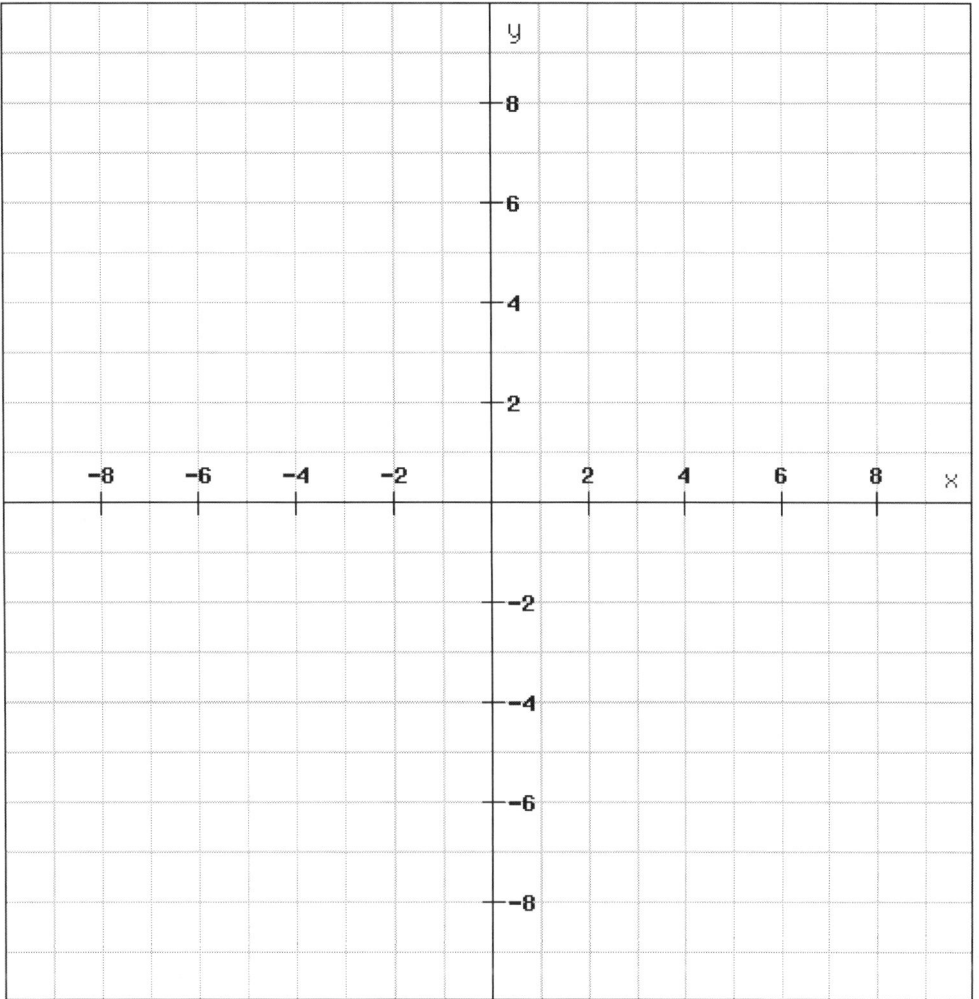

   a. Indicate the following points on the plane: A'(0,–3), B'(–1,3), C'(4,–1), Connect them to form a triangle.

   b. What can you say about the location of the 2nd triangle in comparison to the first one?

   c. This is a _____ translation.

2. Indicate the following points on the plane: A(0,0), B(–1,6), C(4,2). Connect them to form a triangle.

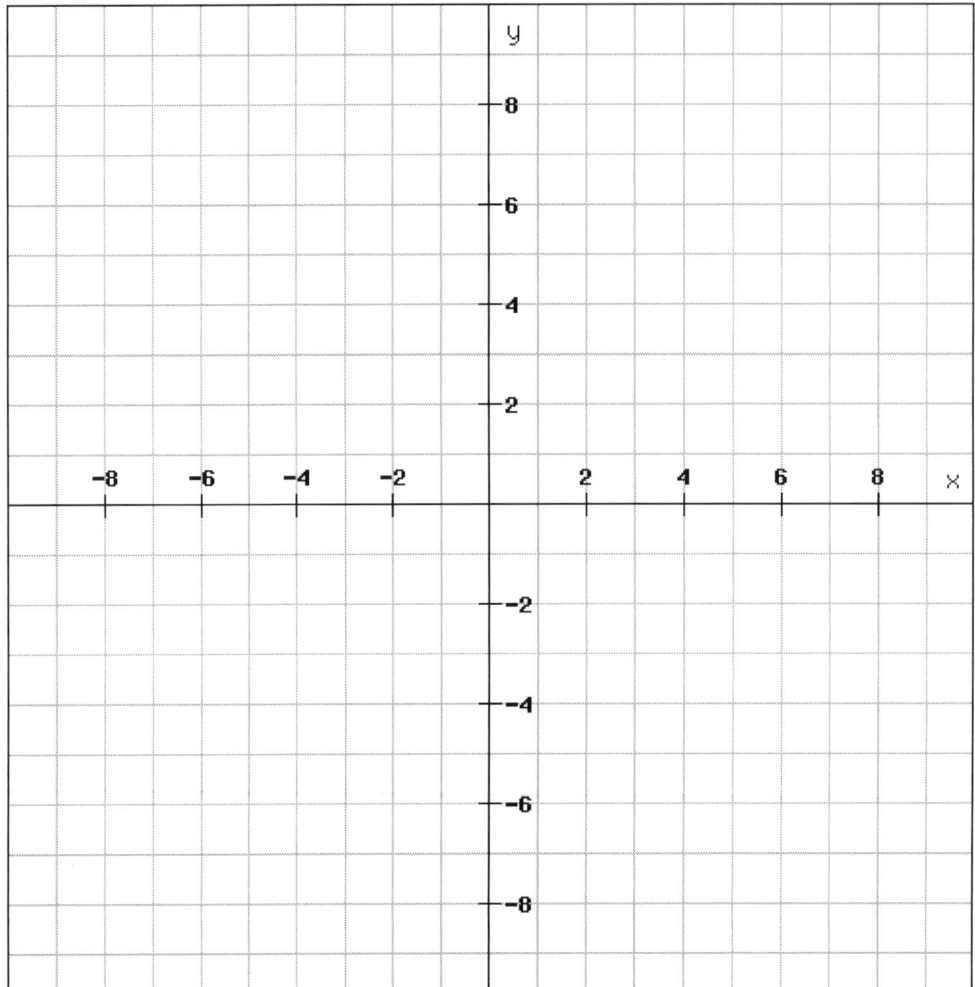

a. Indicate the following points on the plane: A'(4,0), B'(3,6), C'(8,2), Connect them to form a triangle.

b. What can you say about the location of the 2nd triangle in comparison to the first one?

c. This is a _____ translation.

3. Indicate the following points on the plane: A(0,0), B(–1,6), C(4,2). Connect them to form a triangle.

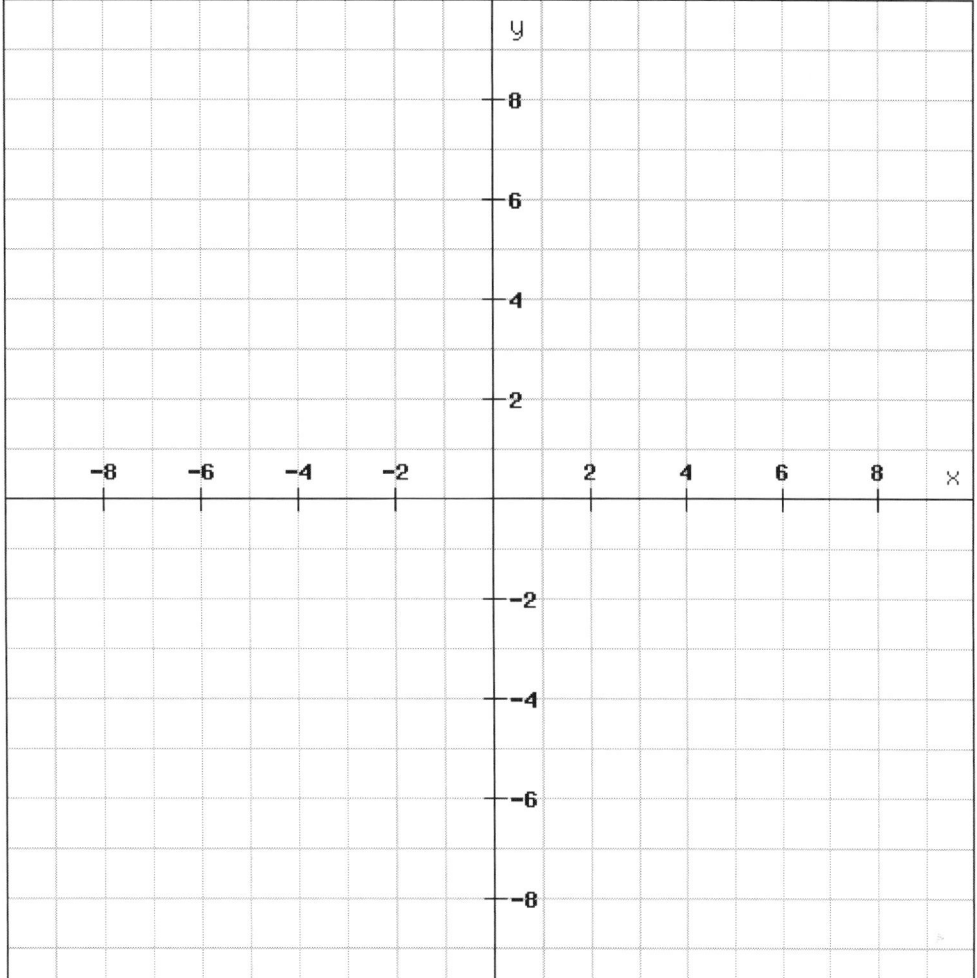

a. Indicate the following points on the plane: A'(–2,–3), B'(–3,3), C'(2,–1), Connect them to form a triangle.

b. What can you say about the location of the 2nd triangle in comparison to the first one?

c. This is a _____ and _____ translations.

4. Indicate the following points on the plane: A(1,0), B(–2,6), C(6,3). Connect them to form a triangle.

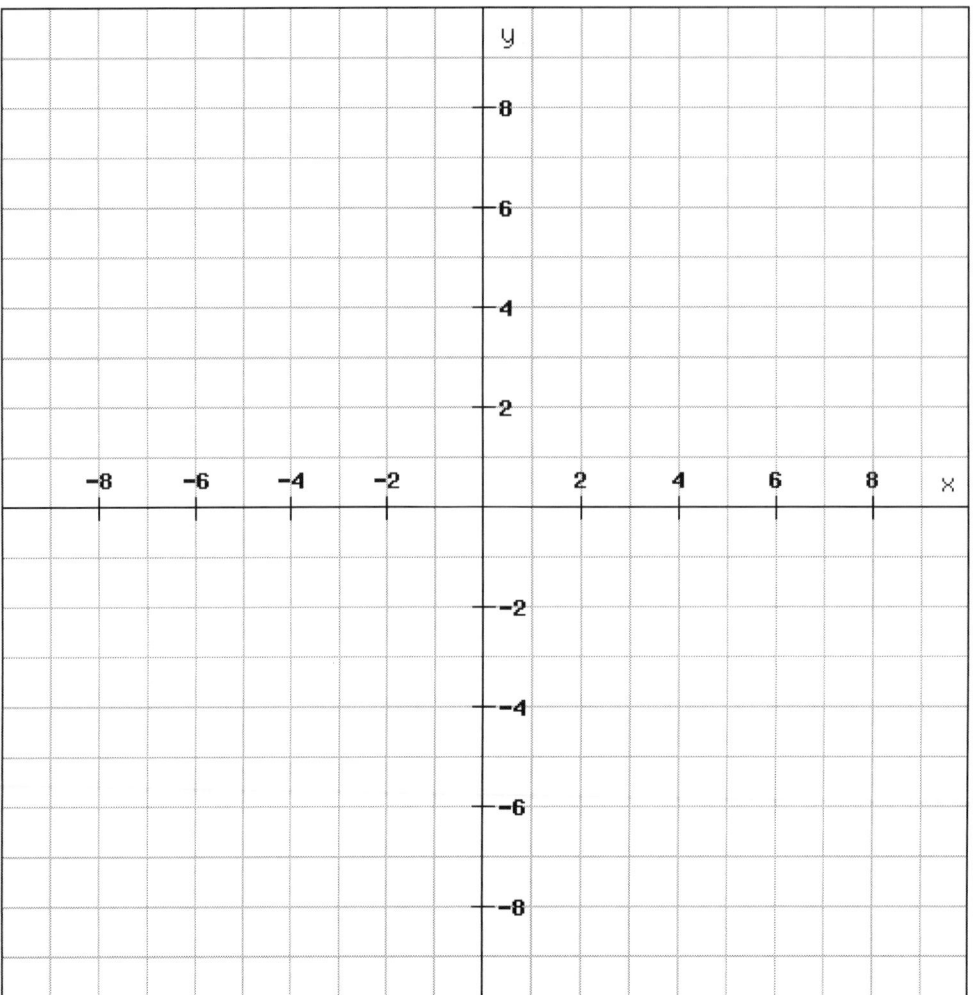

a. Indicate the following points on the plane: A'(–1,0), B'(2,6), C'(–6,3), Connect them to form a triangle.

b. What can you say about the location of the 2nd triangle in comparison to the first one?

c. This is a _____ across the y axis.

d. On changing x into ____ we are generating a _____ across the _____

5. Indicate the following points on the plane: A(1,1), B(–2,6), C(6,3). Connect them to form a triangle.

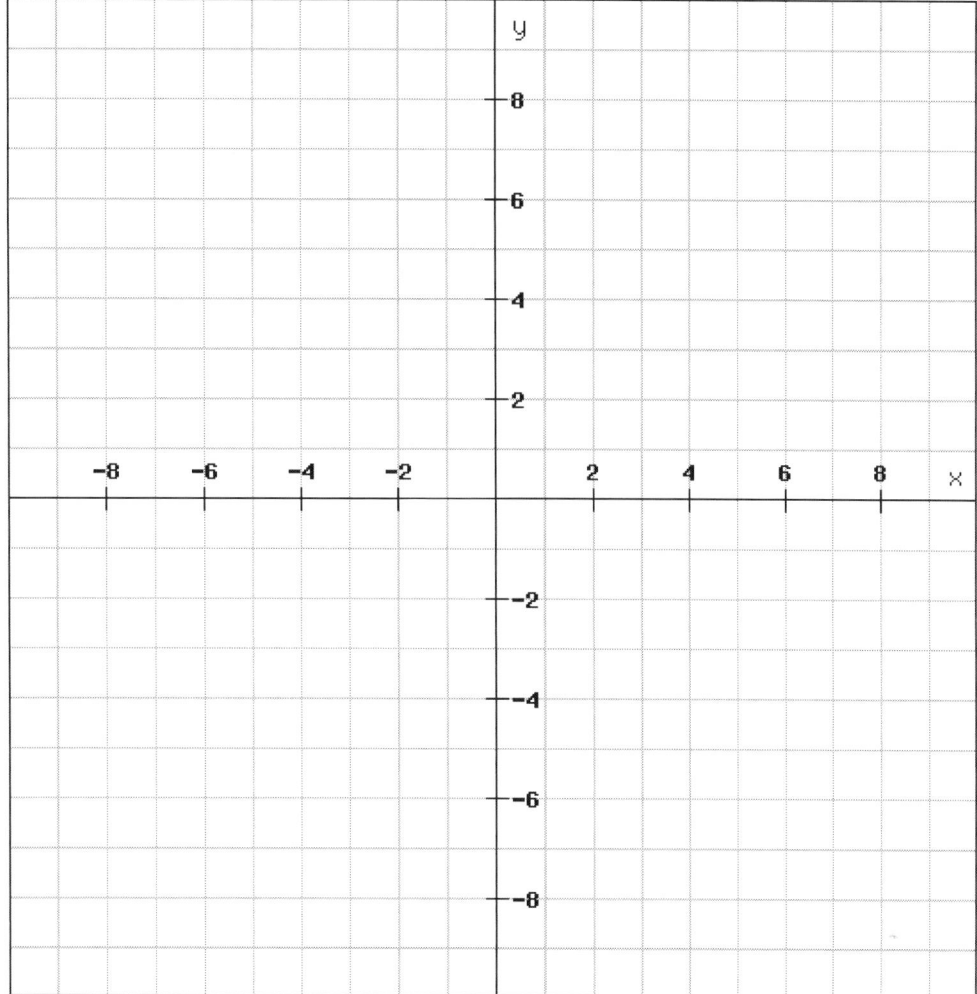

a. Indicate the following points on the plane: A'(1,–1), B'(–2,–6), C'(6,–3), Connect them to form a triangle.

b. What can you say about the location of the 2nd triangle in comparison to the first one?

c. This is a _____ across the x axis.

d. On changing y into ____ we are generating a _____ across the _____

6. Indicate the following points on the plane: A(–4,0), B(0,4), C(4,0), D(0, –4). Connect them to form a square.

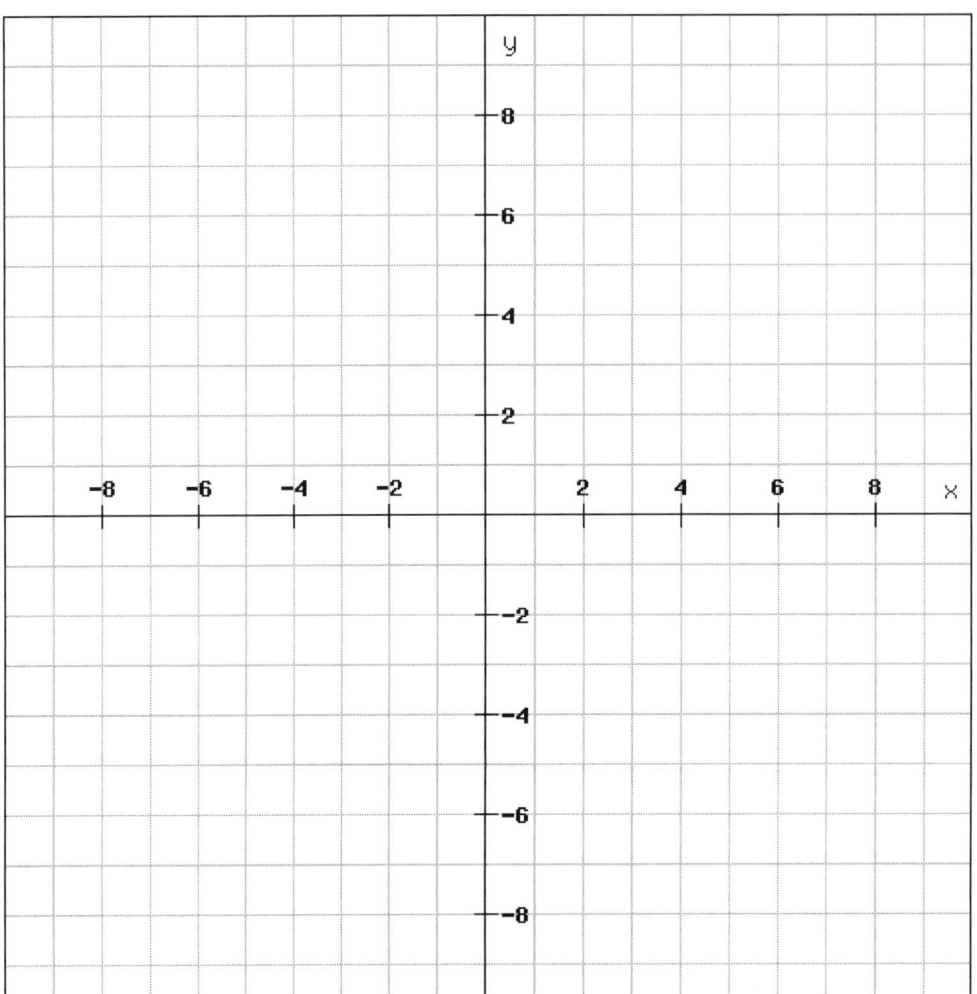

a. Indicate the following points on the plane: $\sqrt{8} \approx 2.83$

   A'$(-\sqrt{8}, \sqrt{8})$, B'$(\sqrt{8}, \sqrt{8})$, C'$(\sqrt{8}, -\sqrt{8})$, D'$(-\sqrt{8}, -\sqrt{8})$ Connect them to form a square.

b. What can you say about the location of the 2nd square in comparison to the first one?

c. This is a _____ of _____ degrees.

d. Write down the coordinates of a square that is a rotation of 90° of the first one:

   A'' = (__, __), B'' = (__, __), C'' = (__, __), D'' = (__, __)

   Conclusions?

7. Indicate the following points on the plane: A(–5,0), B(5,0). Given also the point C(0,a)

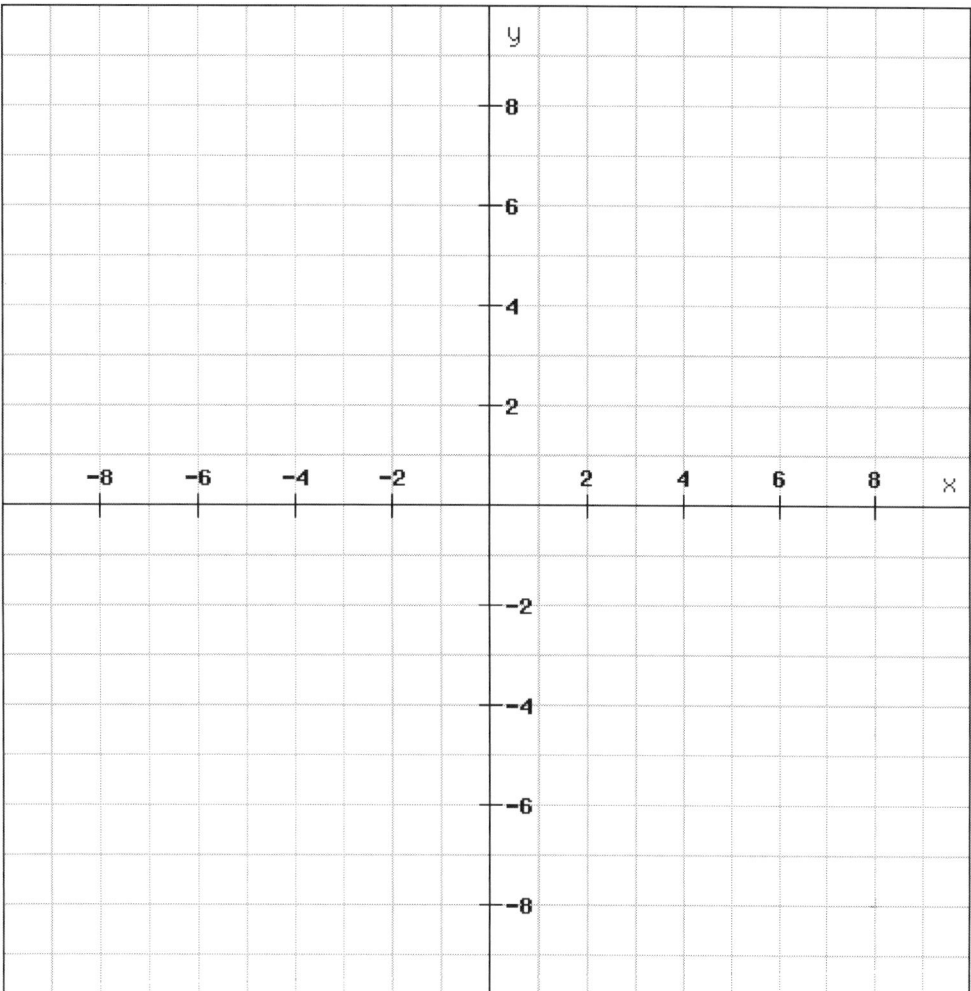

a. Show that the value of *a* in order to create an equilateral triangle is: $\sqrt{75}$
b. Write down the coordinates of the new points after translating the triangle 3 units left and 1 down.

   A' = (__,__), B' = (__,__), C' = (__,__)

c. Write down the coordinates of the new points after rotation the triangle 30° clockwise.

   A'' = (__,__), B'' = (__,__), C'' = (__,__)

d. Write down the coordinates of the new points after rotation the triangle 60° clockwise.

   A''' = (__,__), B''' = (__,__), C''' = (__,__)

8. Indicate the following points on the plane: A(1,0), B(–2,5), C(4,3). Connect them to form a triangle.

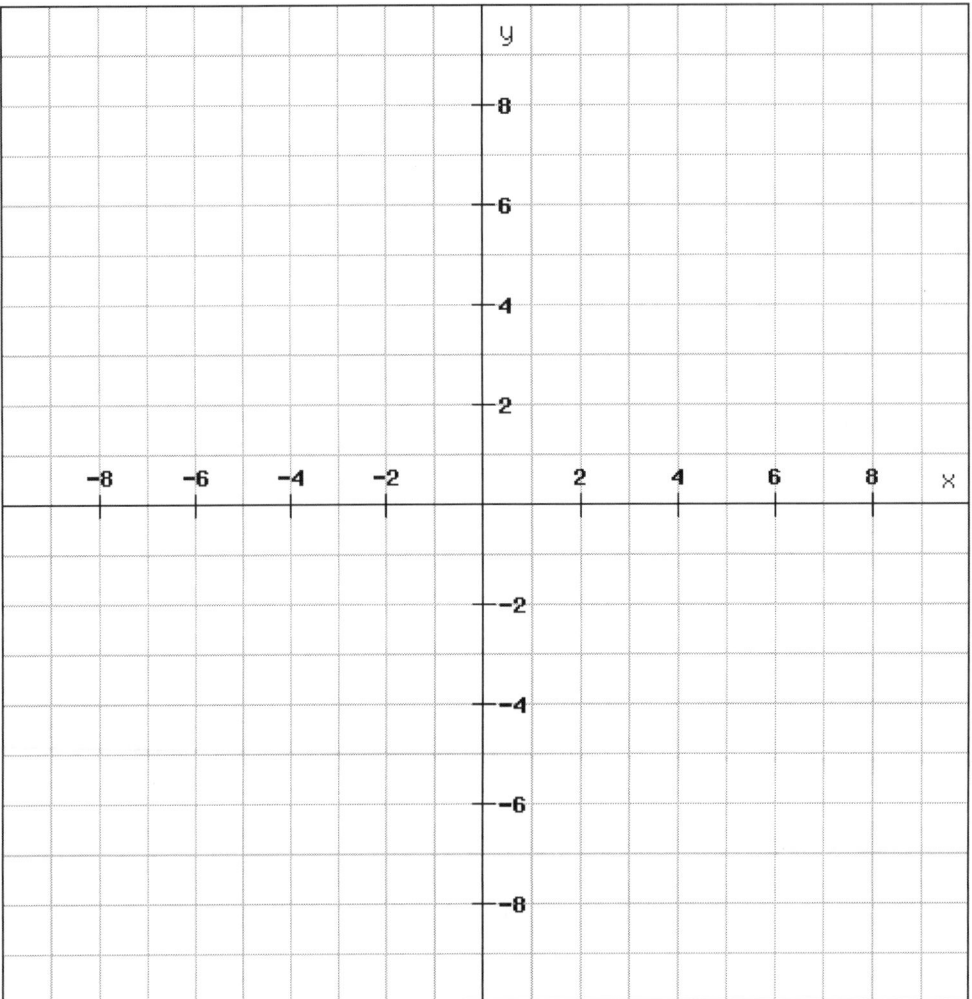

a. Indicate the following points on the plane: A'(2,0), B'(–4,10), C'(8,6), Connect them to form a triangle.

b. What can you say about the 2nd triangle in comparison to the first one?

c. This is a _____ factor ____

d. Indicate the following points on the plane: A'(0.5,0), B'(–1,2.5), C'(2,1.5), Connect them to form a triangle.

e. What can you say about the 2nd triangle in comparison to the first one?

f. This is a _____ factor ____

g. When making all sides of a shape bigger or smaller using the same factor the shape remains _____ to the original one.

164

9. Indicate the following points on the plane: A(0,0), B(2, 0), C(0,–3). Connect them to form a triangle.

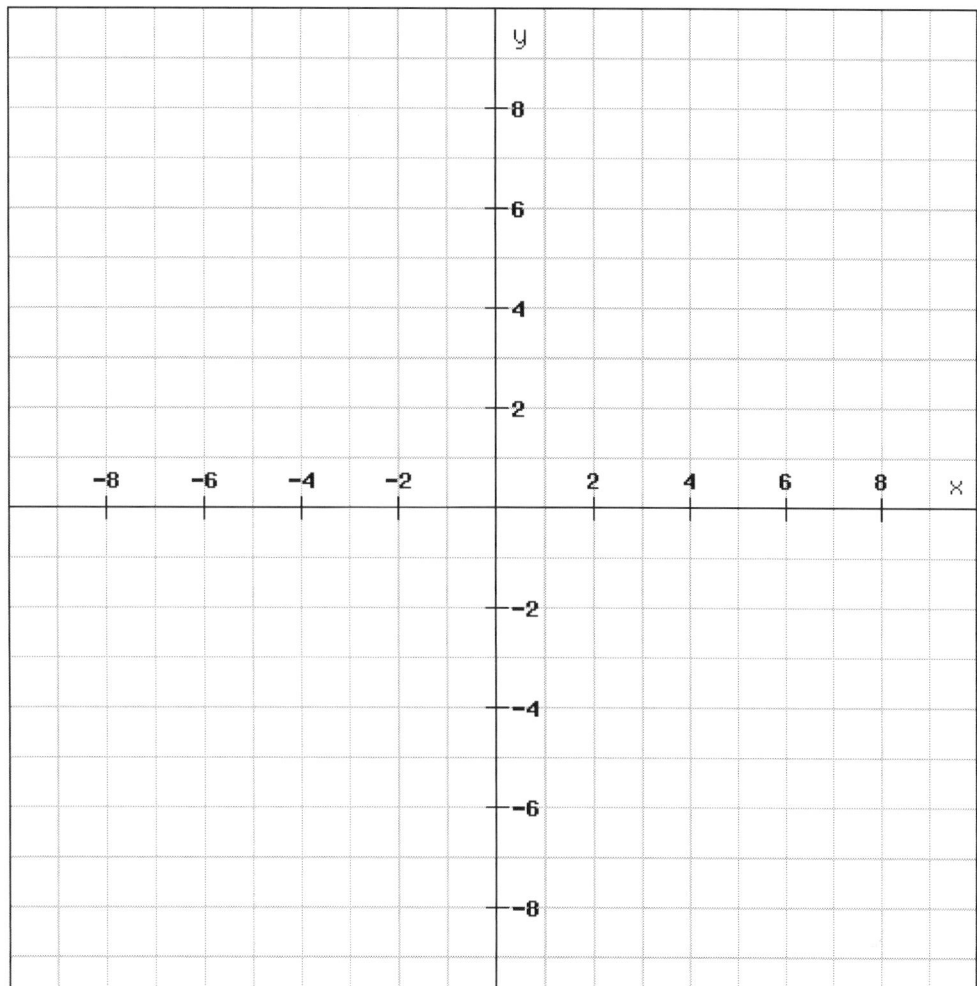

    a. Indicate the points of he triangle formed if we enlarge this triangle by 3.

       A' = (__, __), B' = (__, __), C' = (__, __)

    b. Find the relations:

$$\frac{A'B'}{AB} = \qquad \frac{A'C'}{AC} = \qquad \frac{B'C'}{BC} =$$

10. Given a triangle ABC whose sides are 3, 4 and 5 cm long.

    a. Is his a right angled triangle?
    b. Find the sides of another triangle whose sides are half the length of the sides of ABC. Is this triangle right angled?

11. Given a triangle ABC whose sides are 2, 4 and x cm long. A similar triangle has sides y, 6 and z correspondingly.

    a. Find y
    b. Find $\dfrac{z}{x}$
    c. Is it possible to find a value for x so that ABC will be right angled? If yes, find it (all possibilities).
    d. Find z in that case(s)

166

12. Given a rectangle ABCD whose sides are 5, and x cm long. A similar rectangle has sides y and 12 cm correspondingly. The perimeter of the 1st rectangle is 8 units longer than the perimeter of the 2nd one.

    a. Find x and y

    b. Find the area of the rectangles A_1 and A_2.

    c. Find the quotient $\dfrac{A_2}{A_1}$, conclusions?

13. Given that the area of a square is 16 times as big as the area of a different square. Find the ratio between the sides of the squares.

14. Explain the meaning of the operation "Zooming in/out" frequently used in digital imaging.

CHAPTER 3 – FUNCTIONS

3.1. – INTRODUCTION TO FUNCTIONS

1. Write the definition of a function in your own words:

2. Write 2 examples of relations that <u>are</u> functions:

3. The independent variable is usually represented in the _____

4. The dependent variable is usually represented in the _____

5. Draw a sketch of the functions that describe those relations. Can you write the mathematical expression to describe them?

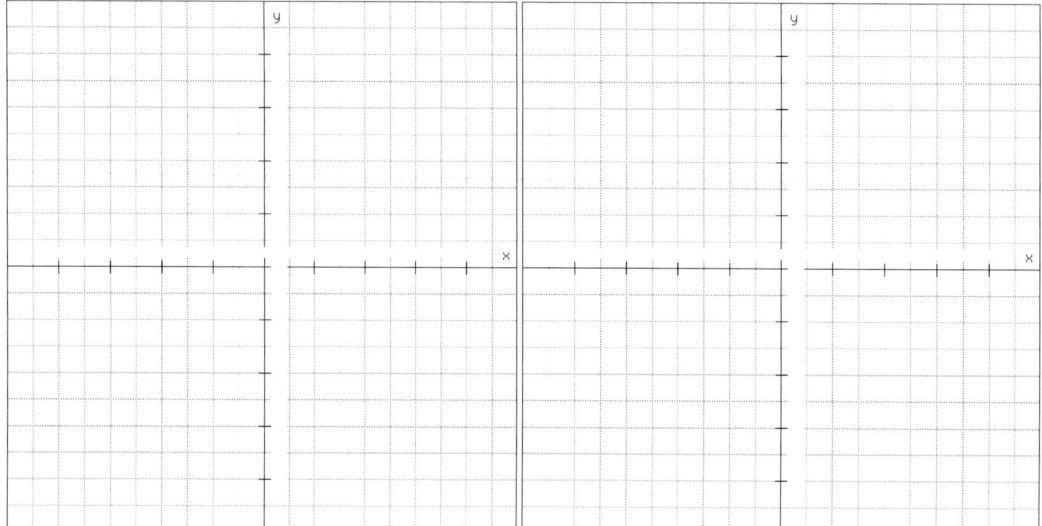

6. Write 2 examples of relations that <u>are not</u> functions:

7. Which one of the following graphs cannot represent function:

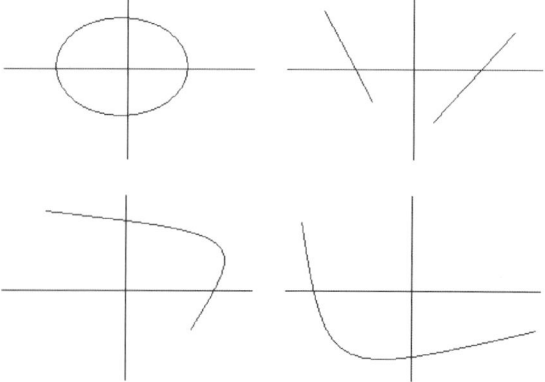

8. Draw an example of a curve that is not a function:

9. Draw an example of a curve that is a function:

10. The domain of a function is the: _____

11. The Range of a function is the: _____

12. Out of the following relations circle the ones that are functions:

    a. Person's name → Person's age
    b. City → Number of habitants
    c. City → Names of habitants
    d. Family → Home Address
    e. Satellite's name → Position of satellite
    f. Time → Position of object
    g. One → One
    h. One → Many
    i. Many → One

13. Given the Height – age curve for a human. Sketch an approximate graph:

    a. Height(0) = _____, it is the

       height of _____

    b. Height(t) = 100cm. t = ___

    c. State its domain:

       _____

    d. State its range:

       _____

    Height (cm)

    Age (years)

169

14. Given the following function that describes the temperature in C° as a function of time (t = 0 corresponds to midnight):

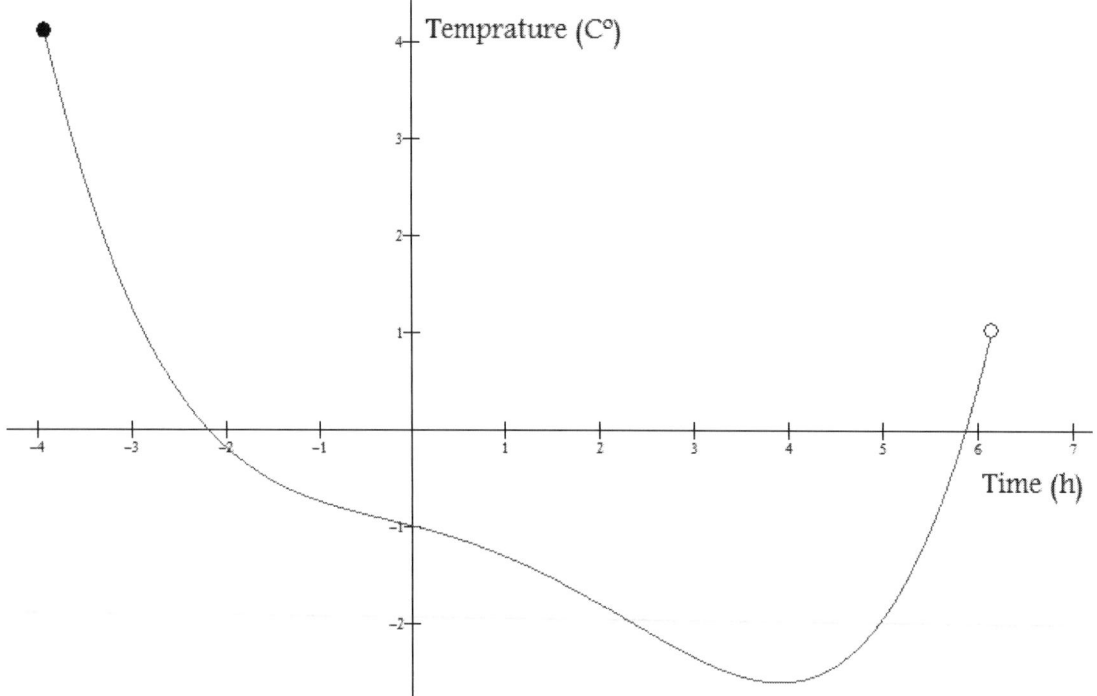

a. f(0) = _____

b. f(2) = _____ = f(__)

c. f(7) = _____

d. f(x) = 3, __x = _____

e. f(x) = 0, __x = _____

f. f(x) = –2 , __x = _____

g. State its domain: _____

h. State its range: _____

i. Is this function one to one? One to many? Explain.

15. Given the function the describes the change in the benefit (%) given by a certain stock:

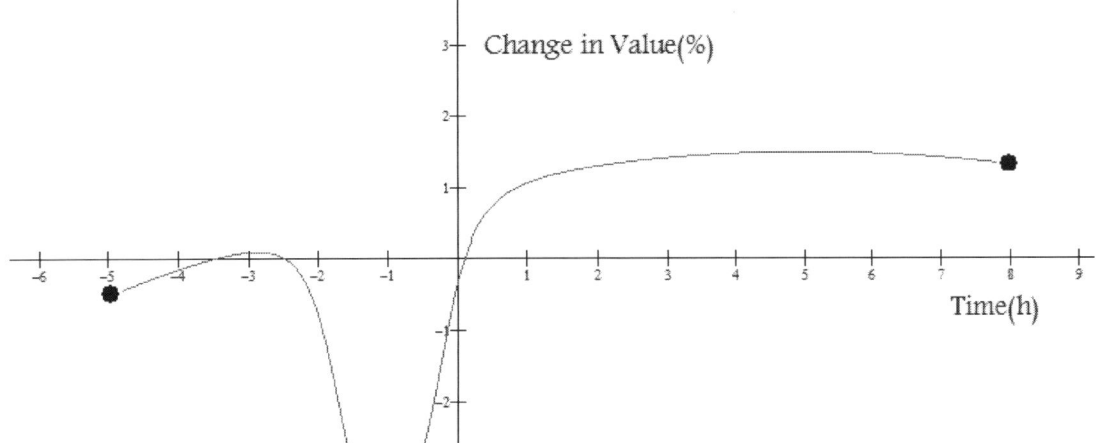

a. f(x) = 0, _x = _____

b. f(0) = _____ = f(__)

c. f(−5) = _____

d. f(1) = _____

e. f(−2) = _____ = f(__)

f. f(3) = _____

g. f(x) = −2, _x = _____

h. Is f(−2) < 0 ?

i. Is f(−2) < f(−1) ?

j. State its domain: _____

k. State its range: _____

l. Where is the function increasing? _____

m. Where is the function decreasing? _____

n. Where is the function stationary? _____

o. Is this function one to one? One to many? Explain.

16. Given the following function:

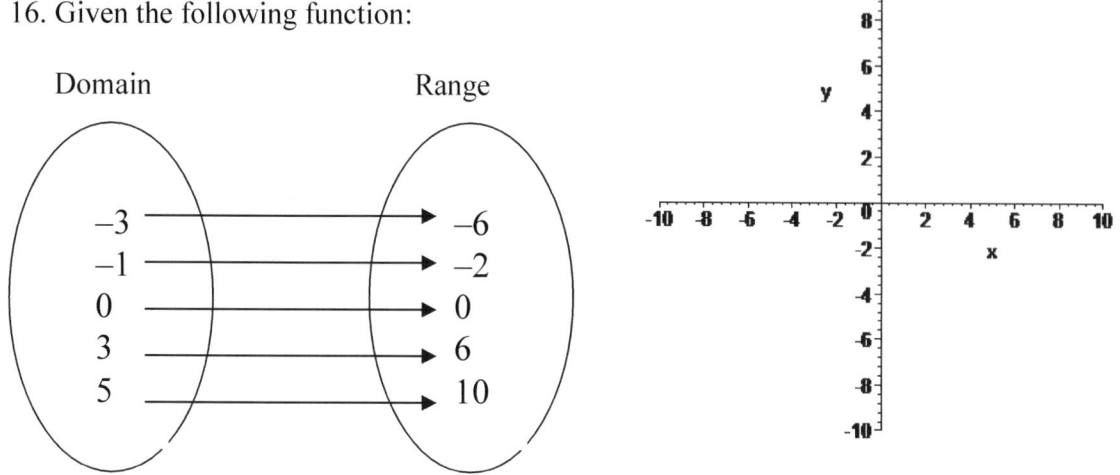

a. What are the allowed values for the independent variable (The domain)?

b. What are the allowed values for the dependent variable (The range)?

c. Sketch the function on the graph.

d. Can you write a mathematical expression to express this function?

17. Given the following function:

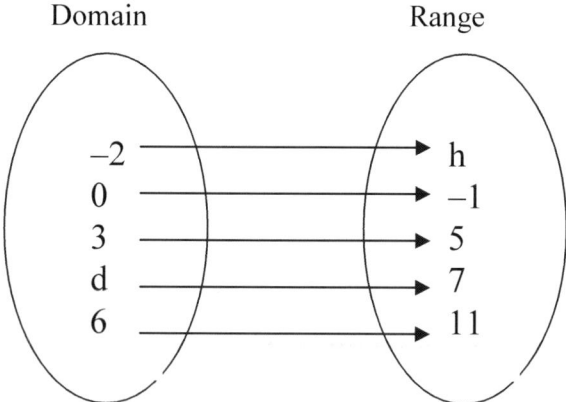

a. Can you write a mathematical expression to express this function?

b. Find h. Find d.

172

18. Use the graph of the gasoline consumption of a truck to answer:

   a. $f(0) = $ ____
   b. $f(50) = $ ____
   c. $f(5) = $ ____
   d. For what values of x is $f(x) = 12$
   e. Is $f(60) > f(70)$?
   f. For what values of x is $f(x) > 15$?
   g. At what positive speed is the consumption of gasoline minimum?
   h. Where is the function increasing? _____
   i. Where is the function decreasing? _____
   j. Where is the function stationary? _____

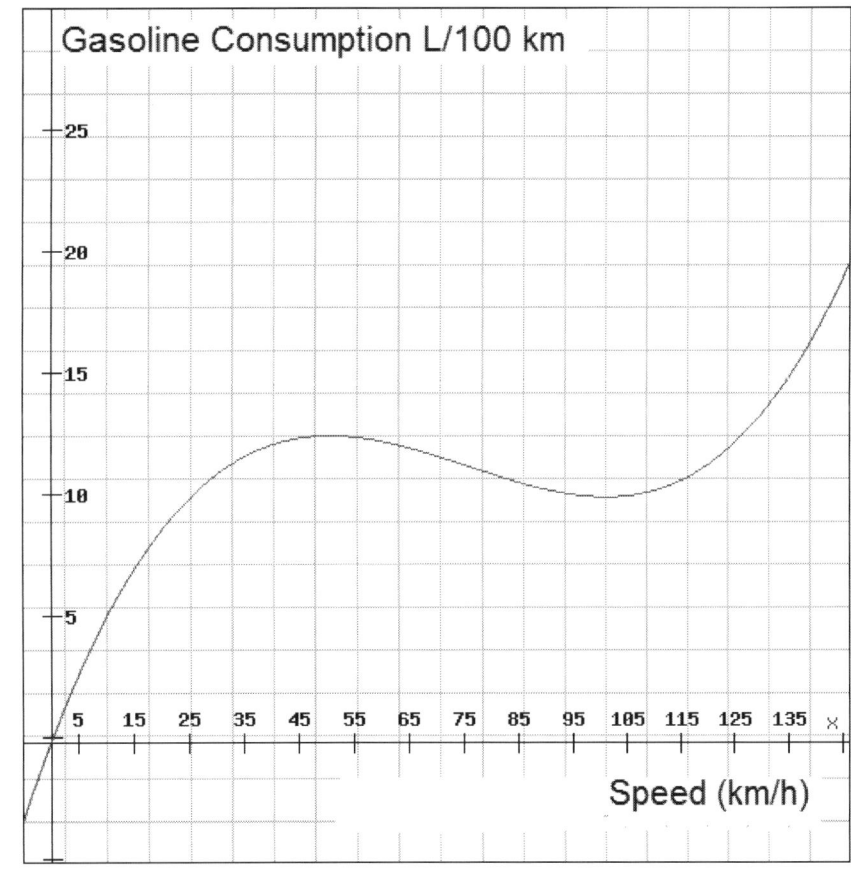

19. Functions can be represented using: _____ or _____ .

20. The following graph describes the concentration of a drug injected into the blood as a function of the time (in minutes) since the injection. $t = 0$ corresponds to the time of injection.

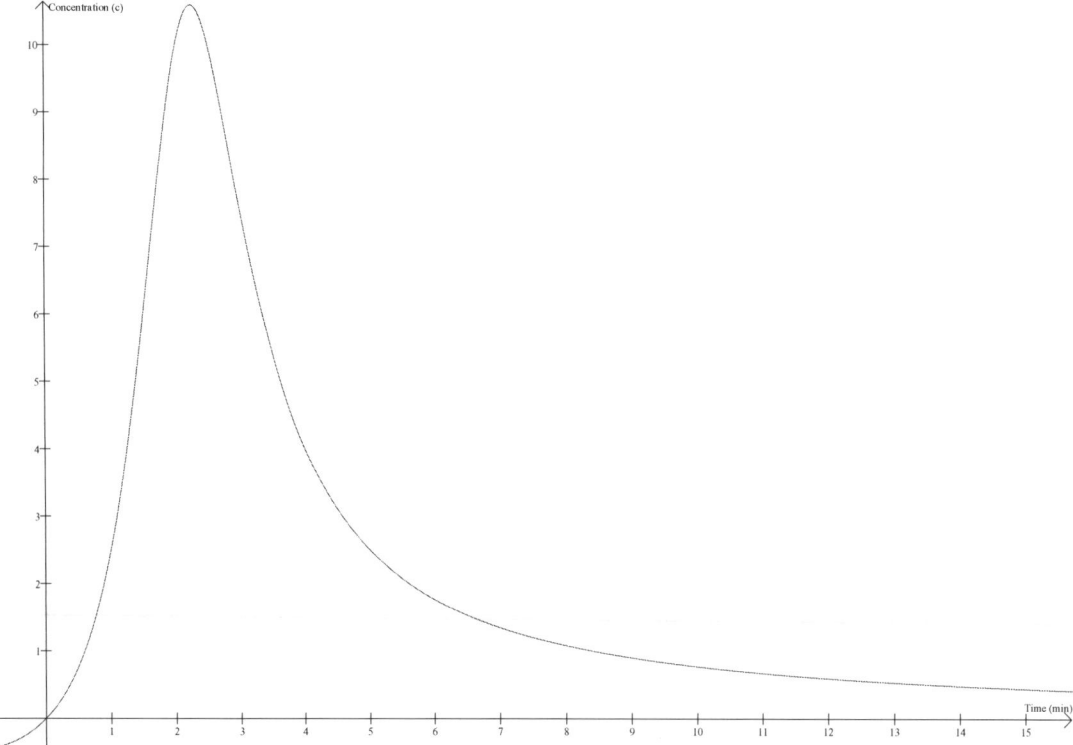

a. What is the concentration of the drug 4 hours after the injection?

b. During what period of time is the concentration increasing?

c. After how long is the concentration maximum?

d. When is the concentration greater than 5c?

e. When is the concentration smaller than 2c?

f. State the domain and range of the function.

21. The graph below shows the temperature in C° on a particular day as a function of time since midnight.

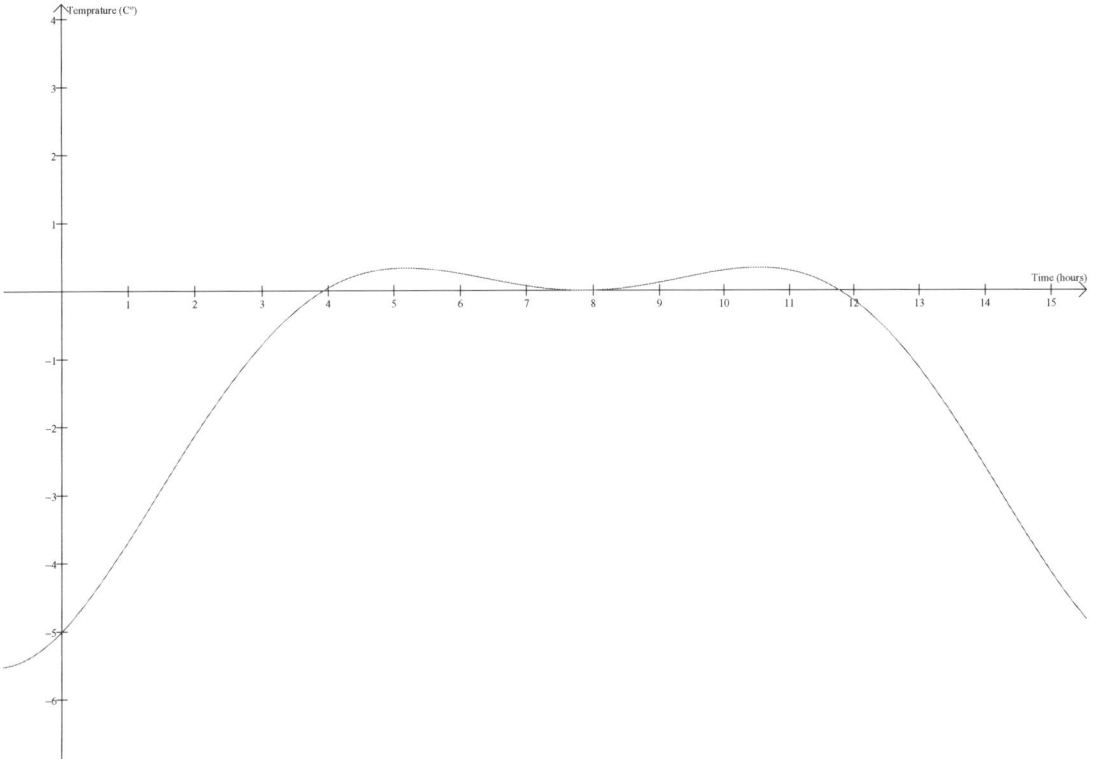

a. What was the temperature at 4:00 a.m.?

b. When was the temperature 0 degrees?

c. When was the temperature below freezing? (less than 0 degrees)

d. When was the temperature increasing?

e. State the domain and range of the function.

3.2. – LINEAR FUNCTIONS

1. Given the function: f(x) = –5, Complete the following table:

x	–5	–4	–3	–2	–1	0	1	2	3	4	5
f(x)											

- Sketch the points of the chart on a graph (use a ruler).

- State the domain of the function: _____

- State the y intercept (sketched on the graph: (____, ____)

- State the x intercept: (____, ____)

- The function is increasing on the interval: _____

- The function is decreasing on the interval: _____

- Sketch the function of the graph used for the points initially drawn

- State the range of the function: _____

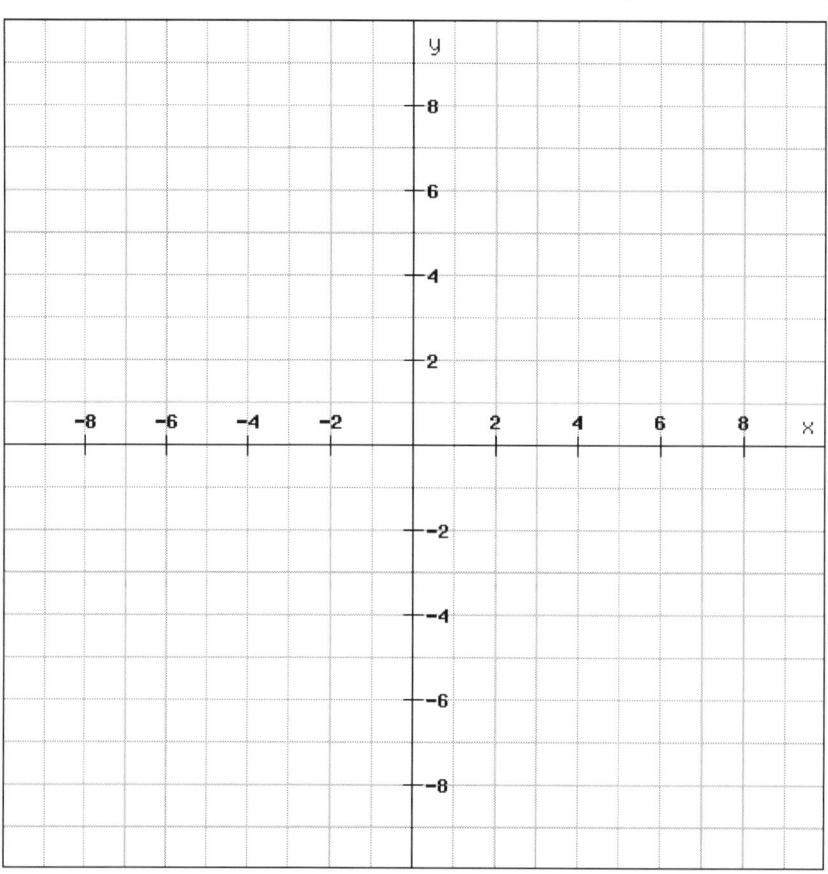

176

2. Given the function: f(x) = x + 3

- Complete the following table:

x	−5	−4	−3	−2	−1	0	1	2	3	4	5
f(x)											

- Sketch the points of the chart on a graph (use a ruler).

- State the domain of the function: _____

- State the y intercept (sketched on the graph: (____, ____)

- State the x intercept: (____, ____)

- The function is increasing on the interval: _____

- The function is decreasing on the interval: _____

- Sketch the function of the graph used for the points initially drawn

- State the range of the function: _____

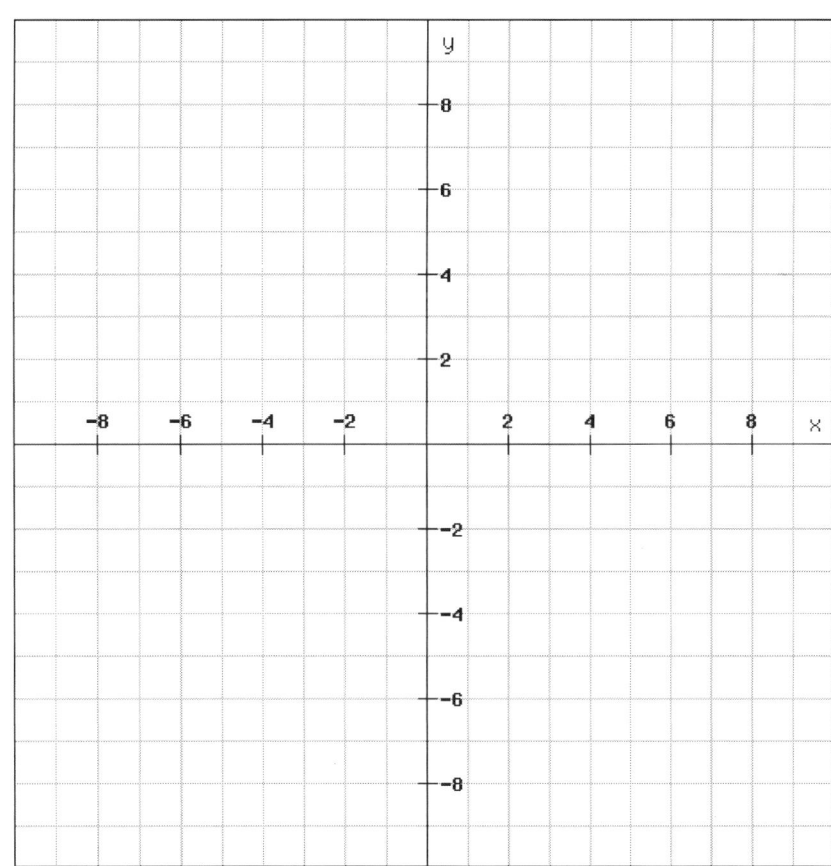

3. Given the function: f(x) = –2x – 5

- Complete the following table:

x	–5	–4	–3	–2	–1	0	1	2	3	4	5
f(x)											

- Sketch the points of the chart on a graph (use a ruler).

- State the domain of the function: _____

- State the y intercept (sketched on the graph: (____, ____)

- State the x intercept: (____, ____)

- The function is increasing on the interval: _____

- The function is decreasing on the interval: _____

- Sketch the function of the graph used for the points initially drawn

- State the range of the function: _____

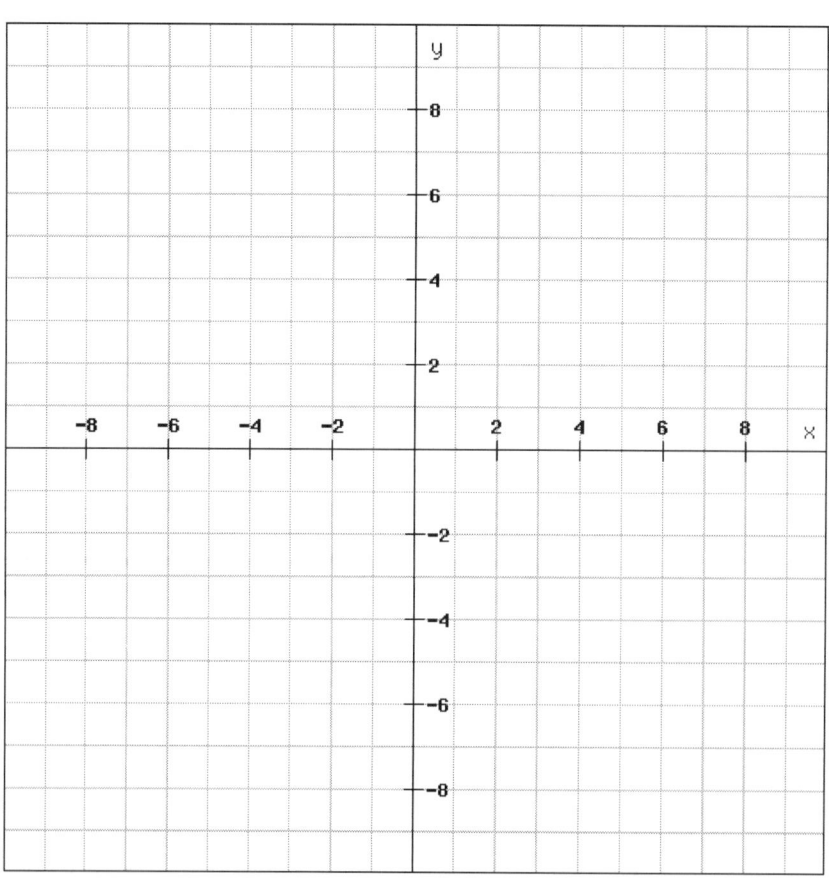

4. Given the function: f(x) = 4x – 3

- Complete the following table:

x	−5	−4	−3	−2	−1	0	1	2	3	4	5
f(x)											

- Sketch the points of the chart on a graph (use a ruler).

- State the domain of the function: _____

- State the *y* intercept (sketched on the graph: (____, ____)

- State the *x* intercept: (____, ____)

- The function is increasing on the interval: _____

- The function is decreasing on the interval: _____

- Sketch the function of the graph used for the points initially drawn

- State the range of the function: _____

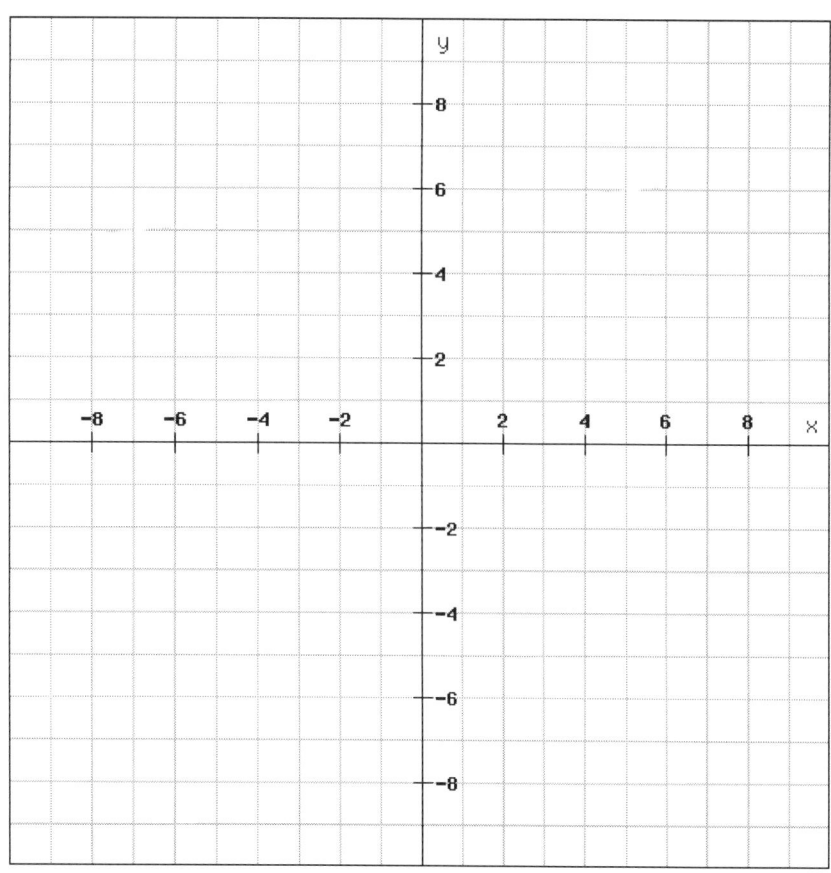

5. Given below are the equations for five different lines. Match the function with its graph.

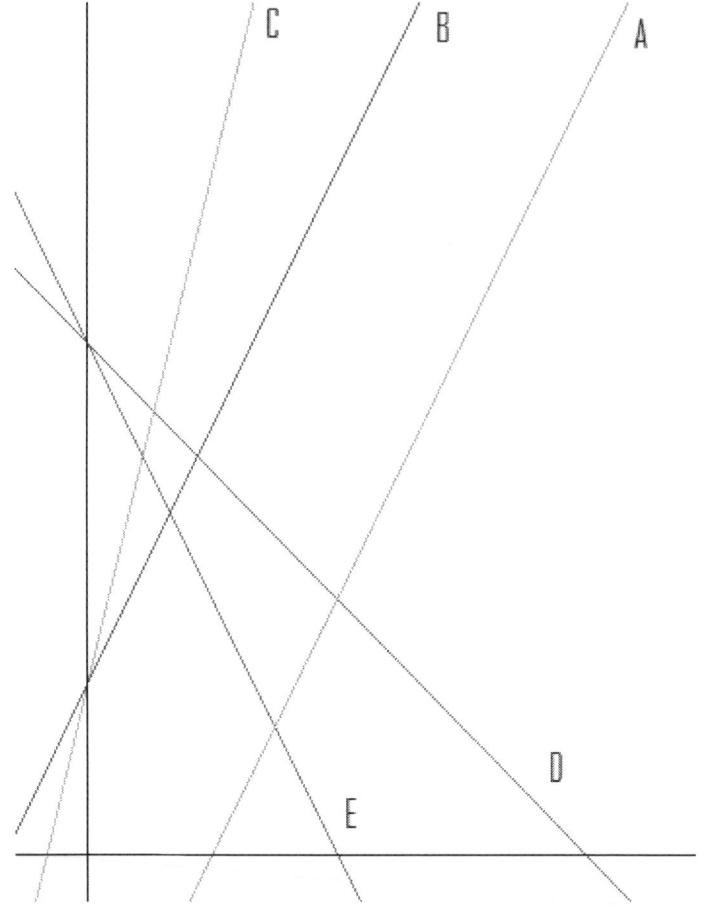

Function	On the graph
f(x) = 20 + 2x	
g(x) = 4x + 20	
s(x) = –30 + 2x	
a(x) = 60 – x	
b(x) = – 2x + 60	

6. The general functions that describes a straight line is _____

7. We know a function is a straight line because _____

8. The y–intercept (also called vertical intercept), tells us where the line crosses the _____. The corresponding point is of the form (,).

9. The x–intercept (also called horizontal intercept), tells us where the line crosses the _____. The corresponding point is of the form (,).

10. If m > 0, the line _____ left to right. If _____ the line decreases left to right.

11. In case the line is horizontal m is _____ and the line is of the form _____.

12. The larger the value of m is, the _____ the graph of the line is.

13. Given the graph, write, the slope (m), b and the equation of the line:

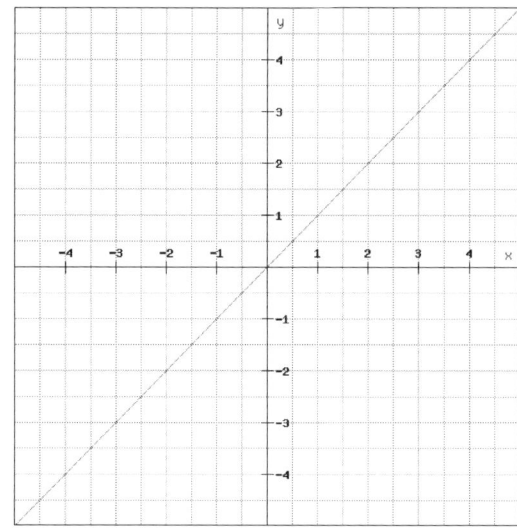 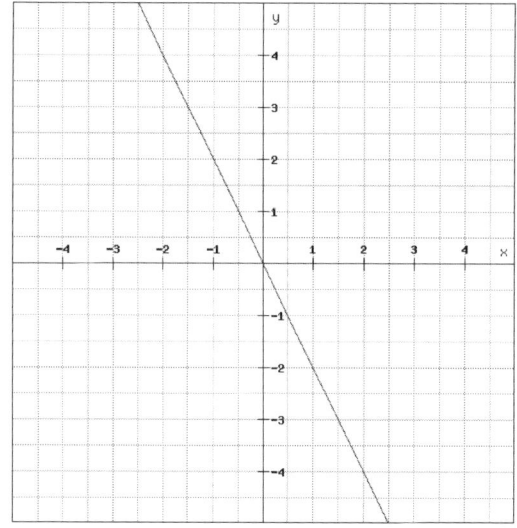

m = ____ b = ____ f(x) = _____   m = ____ b = ____ f(x) = _____

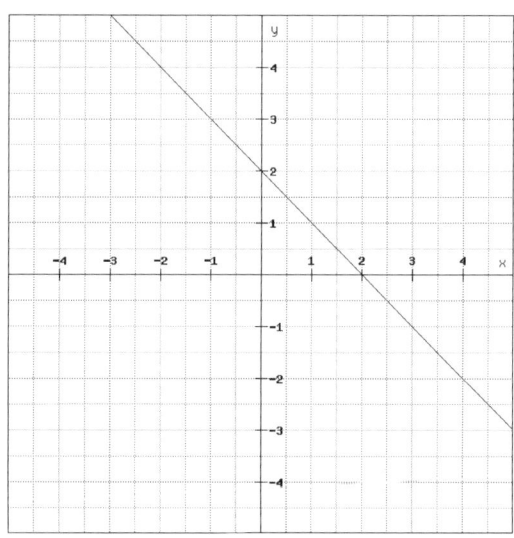 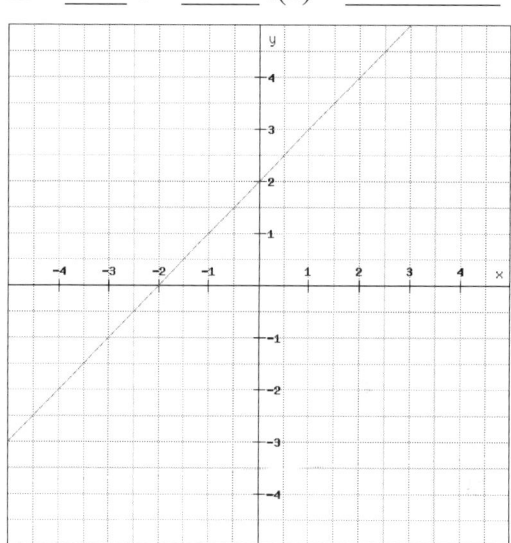

m = ____ b = ____ f(x) = _____   m = ____ b = ____ f(x) = _____

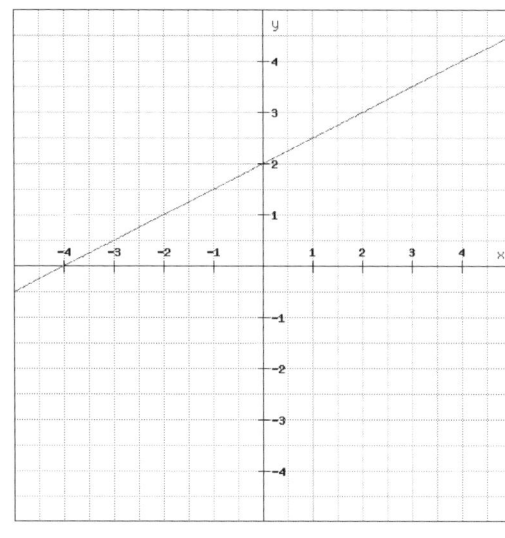 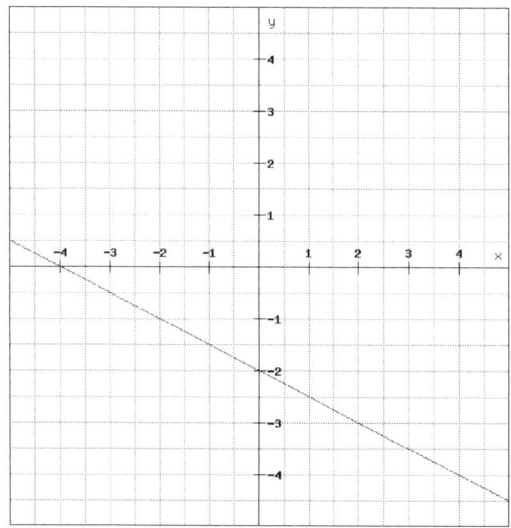

m = ____ b = ____ f(x) = _____   m = ____ b = ____ f(x) = _____

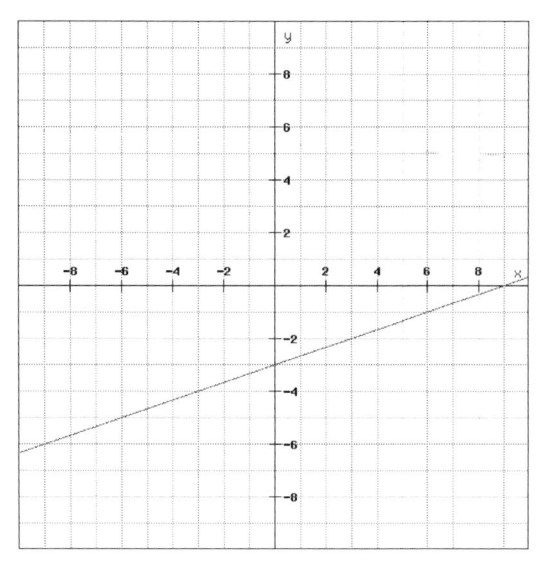

m = _____ b = _____ f(x) = _____

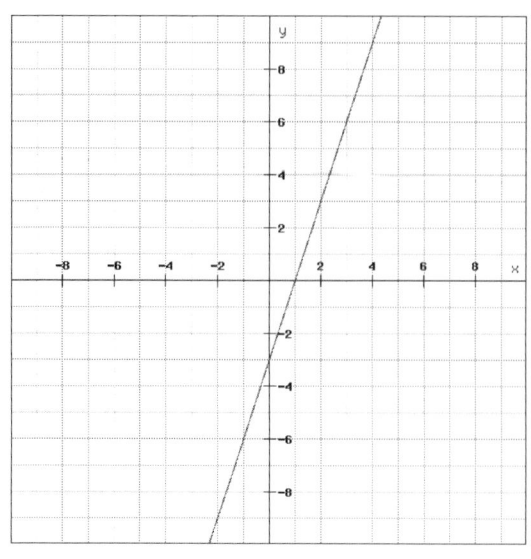

m = _____ b = _____ f(x) = _____

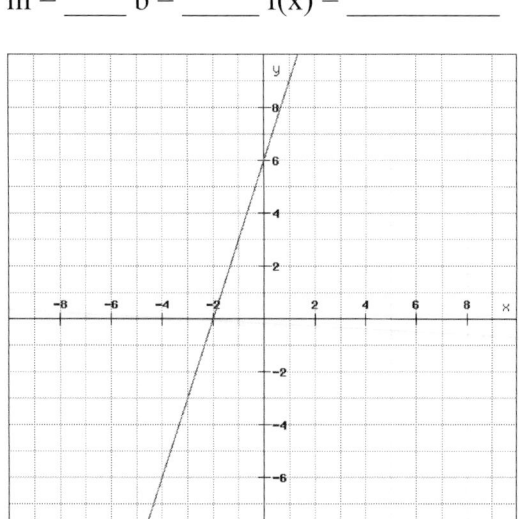

m = _____ b = _____ f(x) = _____

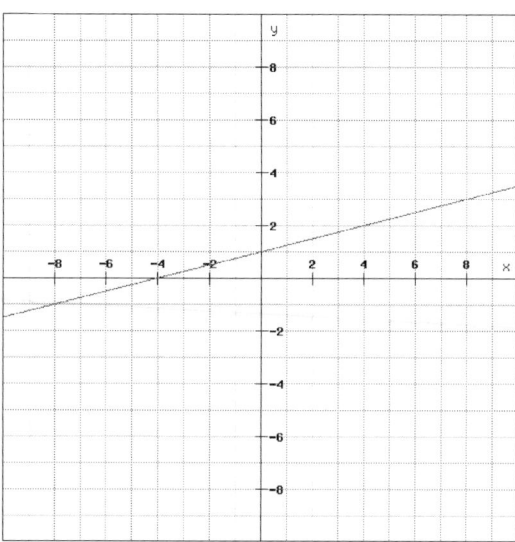

m = _____ b = _____ f(x) = _____

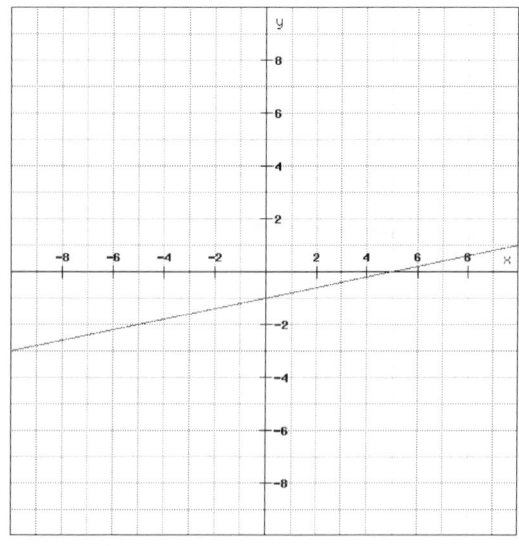

m = _____ b = _____ f(x) = _____

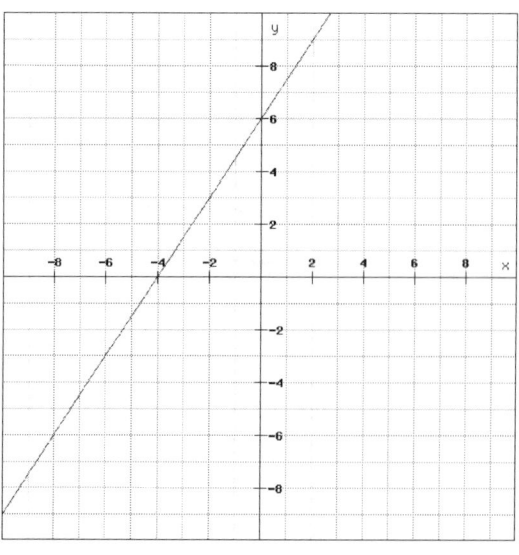

m = _____ b = _____ f(x) = _____

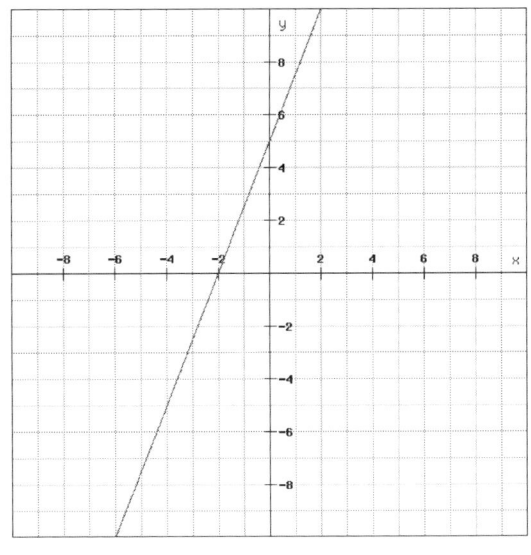 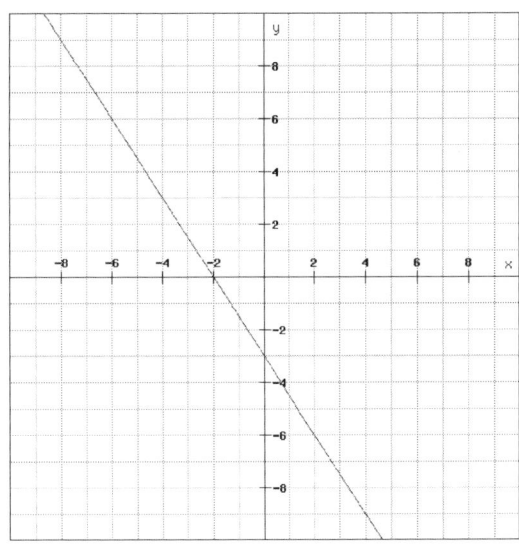

m = ____ b = _____ f(x) = _____   m = ____ b = _____ f(x) = _____

Analyze the following functions/inequlities:

1. f(x) = 1

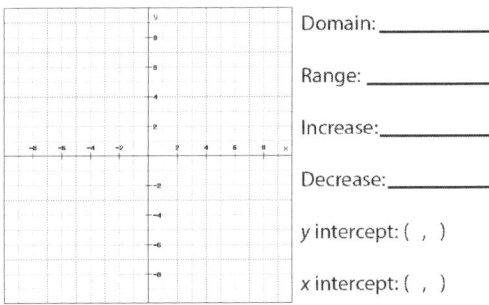
Domain:_____
Range:_____
Increase:_____
Decrease:_____
y intercept: (,)
x intercept: (,)

2. f(x) = 2

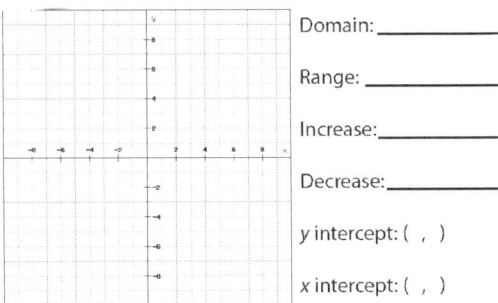
Domain:_____
Range:_____
Increase:_____
Decrease:_____
y intercept: (,)
x intercept: (,)

3. f(x) = −1

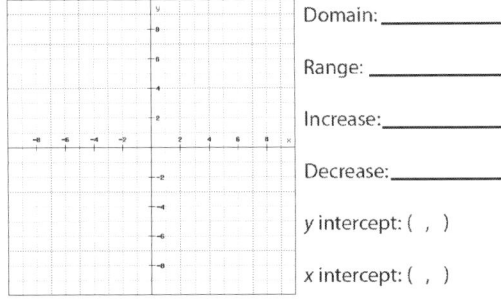
Domain:_____
Range:_____
Increase:_____
Decrease:_____
y intercept: (,)
x intercept: (,)

4. f(x) = 0

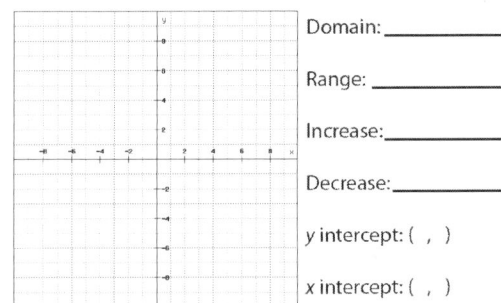
Domain:_____
Range:_____
Increase:_____
Decrease:_____
y intercept: (,)
x intercept: (,)

5. f(x) = x

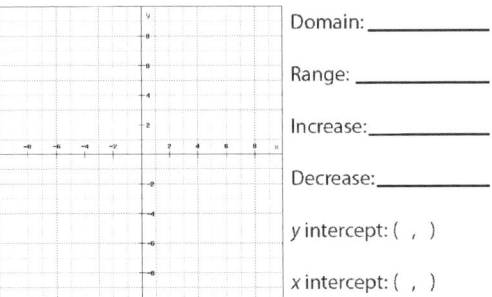
Domain:_____
Range:_____
Increase:_____
Decrease:_____
y intercept: (,)
x intercept: (,)

6. f(x) = x+1

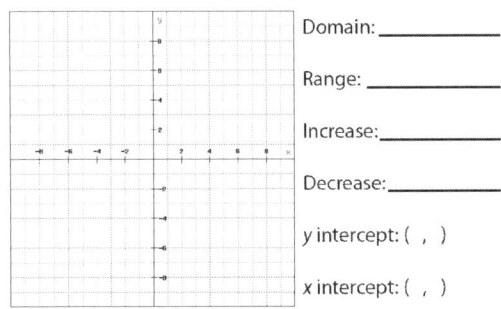
Domain:_____
Range:_____
Increase:_____
Decrease:_____
y intercept: (,)
x intercept: (,)

7. f(x) = –x

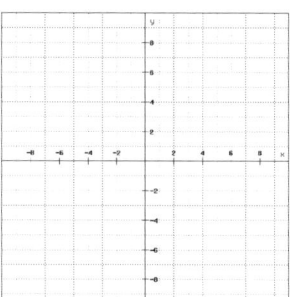

Domain: _____
Range: _____
Increase: _____
Decrease: _____
y intercept: (,)
x intercept: (,)

8. f(x) = –x–2

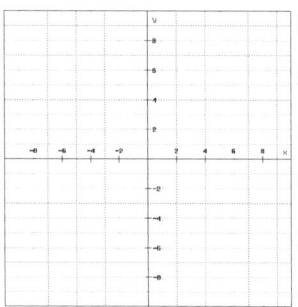

Domain: _____
Range: _____
Increase: _____
Decrease: _____
y intercept: (,)
x intercept: (,)

9. f(x) = 2x

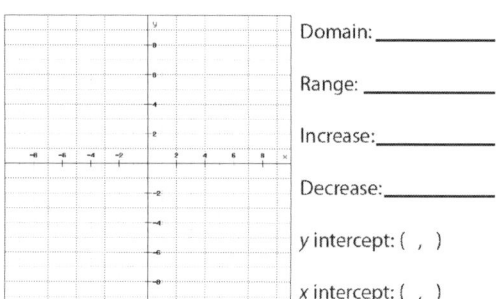

Domain: _____
Range: _____
Increase: _____
Decrease: _____
y intercept: (,)
x intercept: (,)

10. y ≤ 3x – 5

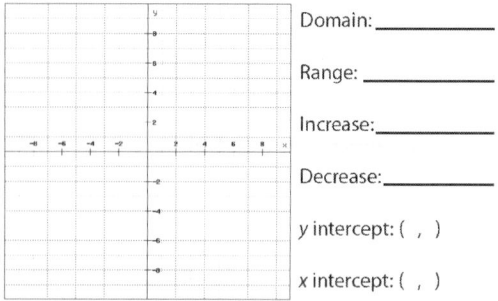

Domain: _____
Range: _____
Increase: _____
Decrease: _____
y intercept: (,)
x intercept: (,)

11. f(x) = 3 – 2x

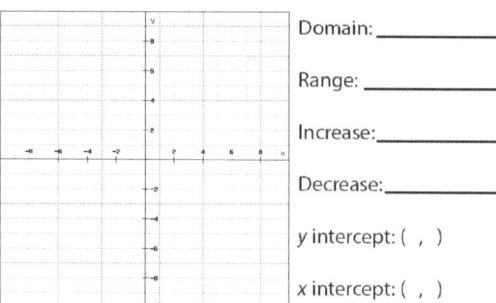

Domain: _____
Range: _____
Increase: _____
Decrease: _____
y intercept: (,)
x intercept: (,)

12. $f(x) = \dfrac{x}{3}$

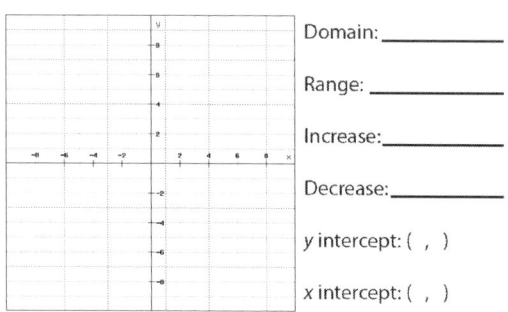

Domain: _____
Range: _____
Increase: _____
Decrease: _____
y intercept: (,)
x intercept: (,)

13. f(x) = 2x+1

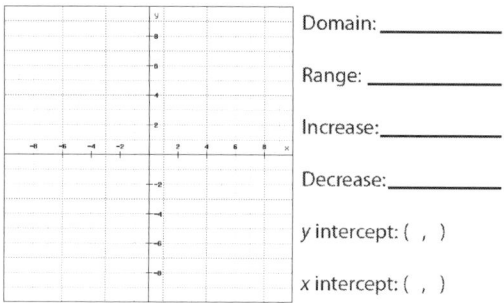

Domain: _____
Range: _____
Increase: _____
Decrease: _____
y intercept: (,)
x intercept: (,)

14. f(x) = 2x–2

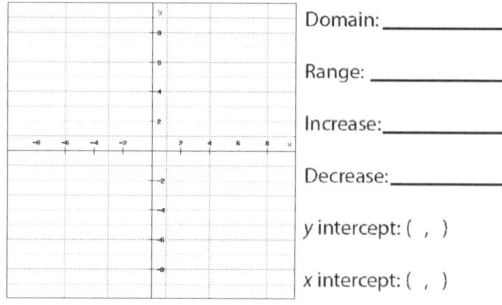

Domain: _____
Range: _____
Increase: _____
Decrease: _____
y intercept: (,)
x intercept: (,)

15. $f(x) = 3x+5$

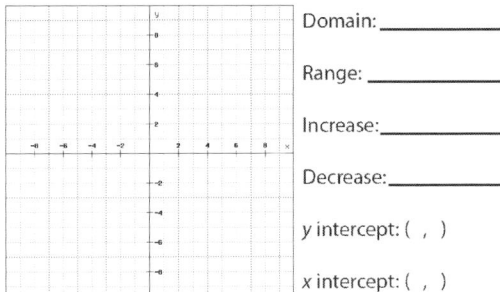

Domain: _____

Range: _____

Increase: _____

Decrease: _____

y intercept: (,)

x intercept: (,)

16. $f(x) \leq \dfrac{x}{2} - 5$

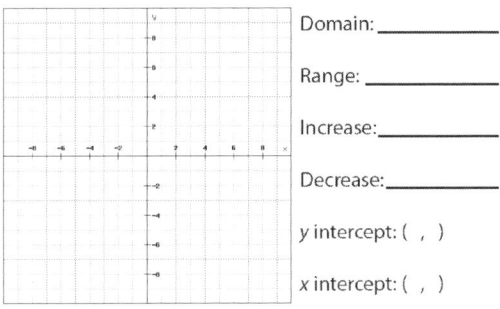

Domain: _____

Range: _____

Increase: _____

Decrease: _____

y intercept: (,)

x intercept: (,)

17. $f(x) = \dfrac{x}{4} + 6$

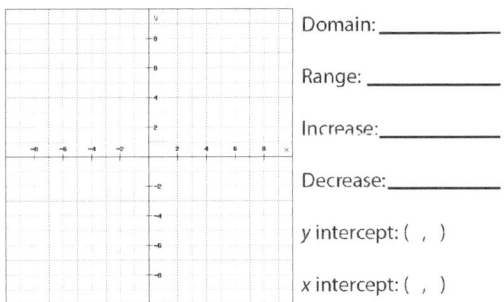

Domain: _____

Range: _____

Increase: _____

Decrease: _____

y intercept: (,)

x intercept: (,)

18. $f(x) \geq \dfrac{3x - 10}{2}$

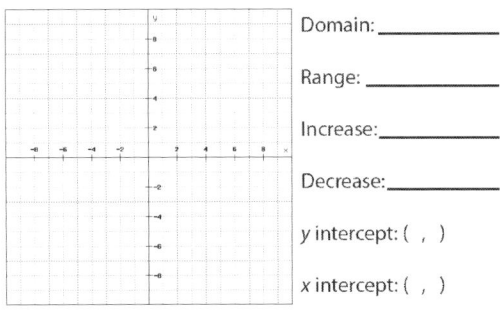

Domain: _____

Range: _____

Increase: _____

Decrease: _____

y intercept: (,)

x intercept: (,)

19. $f(x) = -\dfrac{3}{2}x - \dfrac{3}{2}$

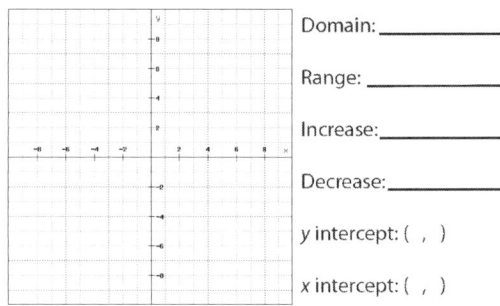

Domain: _____

Range: _____

Increase: _____

Decrease: _____

y intercept: (,)

x intercept: (,)

20. $f(x) = -\dfrac{x+3}{2}$

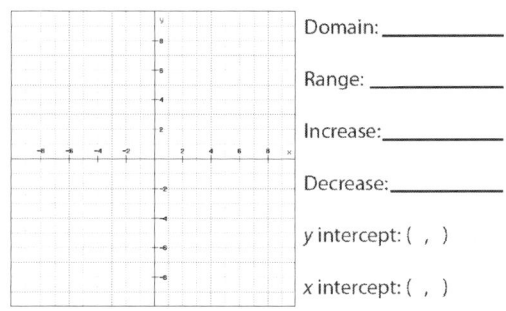

Domain: _____

Range: _____

Increase: _____

Decrease: _____

y intercept: (,)

x intercept: (,)

21. $f(x) = \dfrac{14x - 1}{4}$

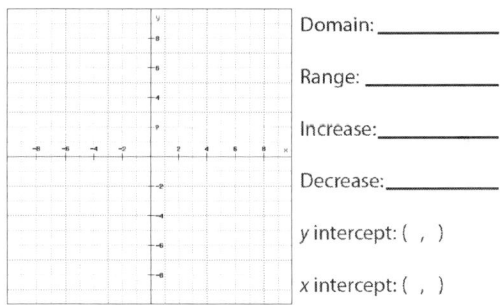

Domain: _____

Range: _____

Increase: _____

Decrease: _____

y intercept: (,)

x intercept: (,)

22. $f(x) = -\dfrac{27x - 40}{15}$

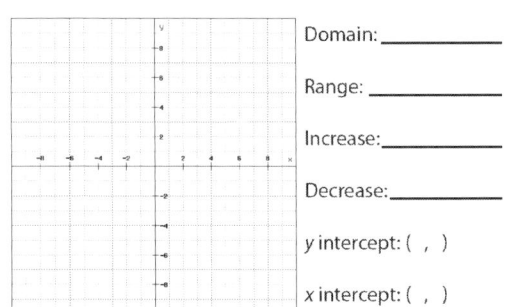

Domain: _____

Range: _____

Increase: _____

Decrease: _____

y intercept: (,)

x intercept: (,)

23. $3x + 2y = 2$

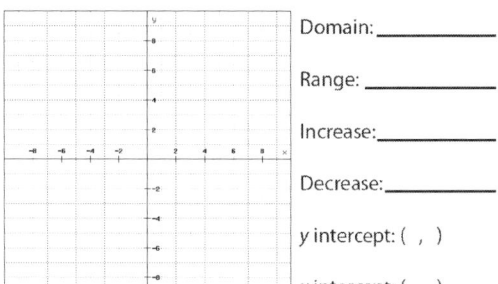

Domain:_____

Range:_____

Increase:_____

Decrease:_____

y intercept: (,)

x intercept: (,)

24. $4x - 2y - 3 = 1$

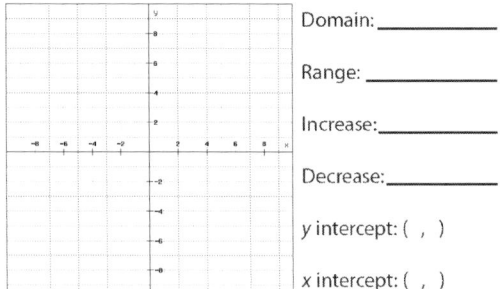

Domain:_____

Range:_____

Increase:_____

Decrease:_____

y intercept: (,)

x intercept: (,)

25. $-2y + 3x = -5$

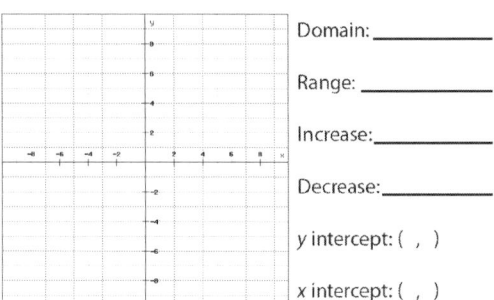

Domain:_____

Range:_____

Increase:_____

Decrease:_____

y intercept: (,)

x intercept: (,)

26. $y - x \leq 2$

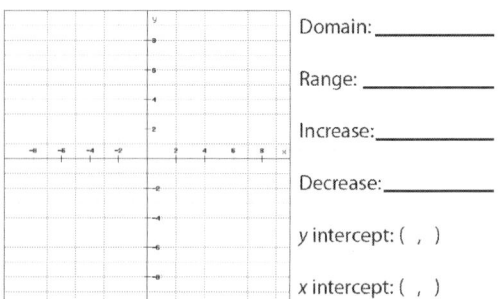

Domain:_____

Range:_____

Increase:_____

Decrease:_____

y intercept: (,)

x intercept: (,)

27. $y + 2x - 3 \geq 1$

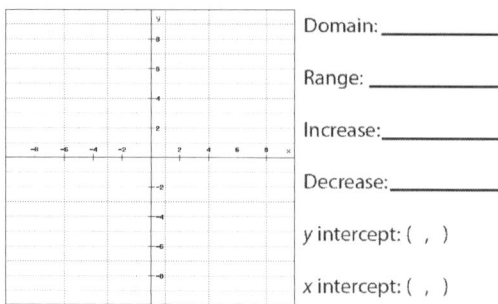

Domain:_____

Range:_____

Increase:_____

Decrease:_____

y intercept: (,)

x intercept: (,)

28. $5y + 5x = 5$

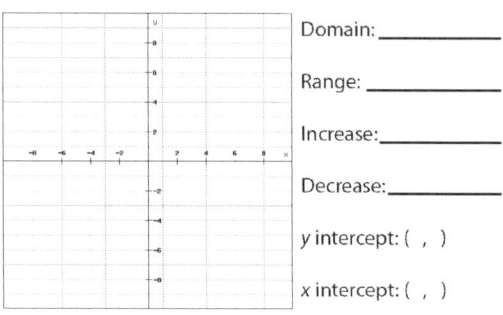

Domain:_____

Range:_____

Increase:_____

Decrease:_____

y intercept: (,)

x intercept: (,)

29. $2x - 2y - 3 = 1$

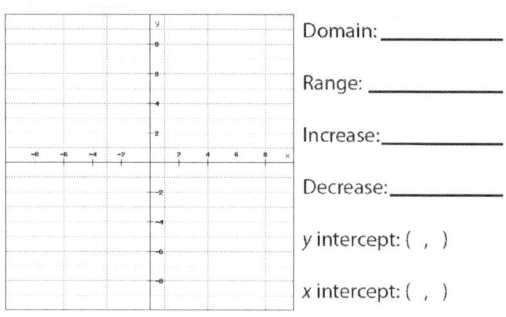

Domain:_____

Range:_____

Increase:_____

Decrease:_____

y intercept: (,)

x intercept: (,)

30. $x - 2y - 150 = 0$

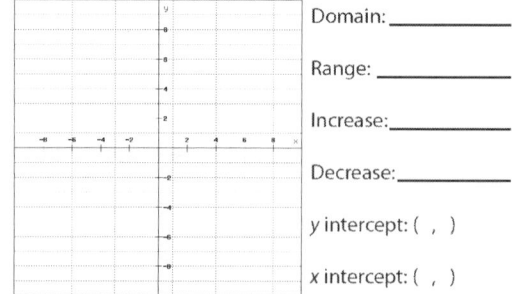

Domain:_____

Range:_____

Increase:_____

Decrease:_____

y intercept: (,)

x intercept: (,)

31. Write the equation of the line that has a slope of 2 and passes through the point (2, 4) in the forms: $y = mx + b$ and $ax + by + c = 0$, $(a, b \in Z)$

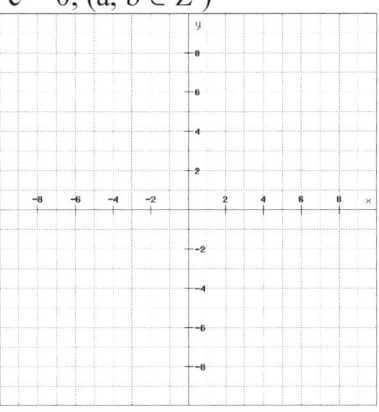

32. Write the equation of the line that has a slope of $-\dfrac{1}{2}$ and passes through the point $(-2, -3)$ in the forms: $y = mx + b$ and $ax + by + c = 0$, $(a, b \in Z)$

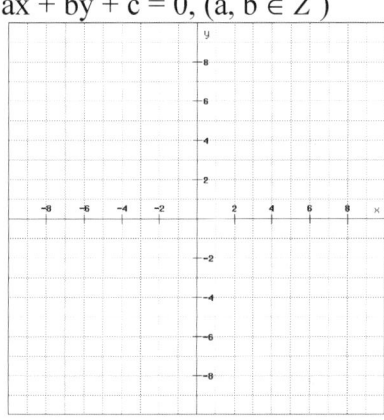

33. Write the equation of the line that has a slope of $-\dfrac{5}{2}$ and passes through the point $(-1, 2)$ in the forms: $y = mx + b$ and $ax + by + c = 0$, $(a, b \in Z)$

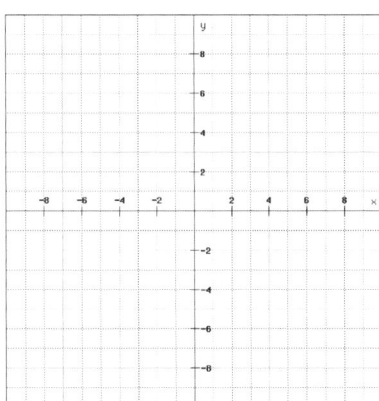

34. Find the equation of the line that passes through the points (1, 1), (2, 4), indicate its y and x intercepts and sketch it. Write its equation in the forms: y = mx + b and ax + by + c = 0, (a, b ∈ Z)

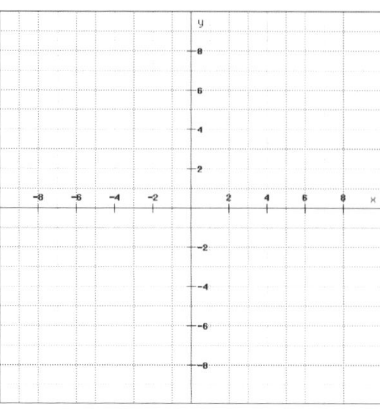

35. Find the equation of the line that passes through the points (–1, –5), (4, 3), indicate its y and x intercepts and sketch it. Write its equation in the forms: y = mx + b and ax + by + c = 0, (a, b ∈ Z)

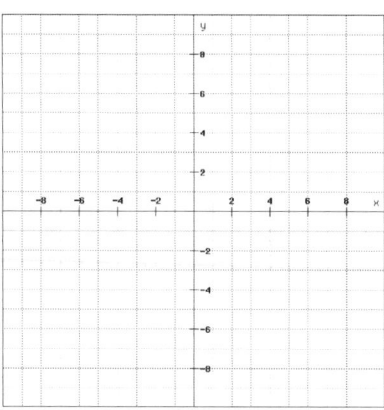

36. Find the equation of the line that passes through the points (–5, 1), (–2, 4), indicate its y and x intercepts, sketch it and write it in both formas y = mx + b and ax + by + c = 0, (a, b ∈ Z)

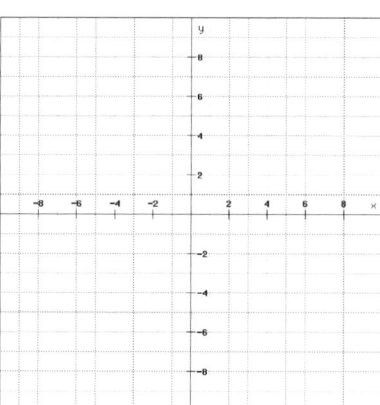

37. Write the equation of the line that is parallel to the line y = 5x – 2 and passes through the point (–2, –1). Write its equation in the forms: y = mx + b and ax + by + c = 0, (a, b ∈ Z)

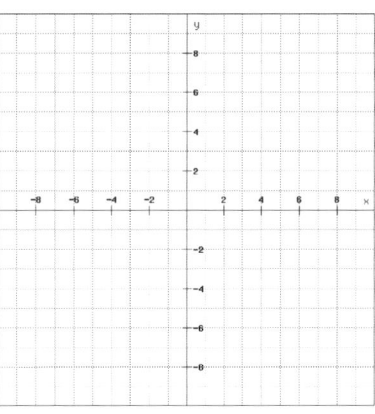

38. Write the equation of the line that is parallel to the line y = –0.5x – 1 and passes through the point (–3, 6). Write its equation in the forms: y = mx + b and ax + by + c = 0, (a, b ∈ Z)

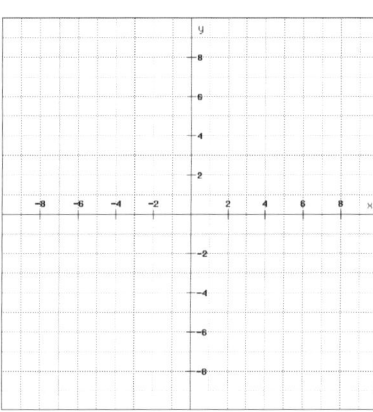

39. Sketch and write the equation of the line with a slope of $-\dfrac{1}{5}$ that passes through the point (0,2).

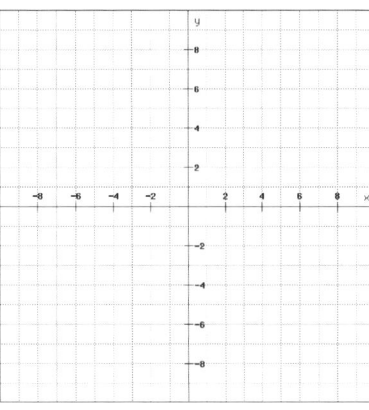

40. Sketch and write the equation of the lines with a slope: 1, 2, –3, –1, $-\frac{1}{2}$, $-\frac{1}{3}$, that pass through the point (0,0).

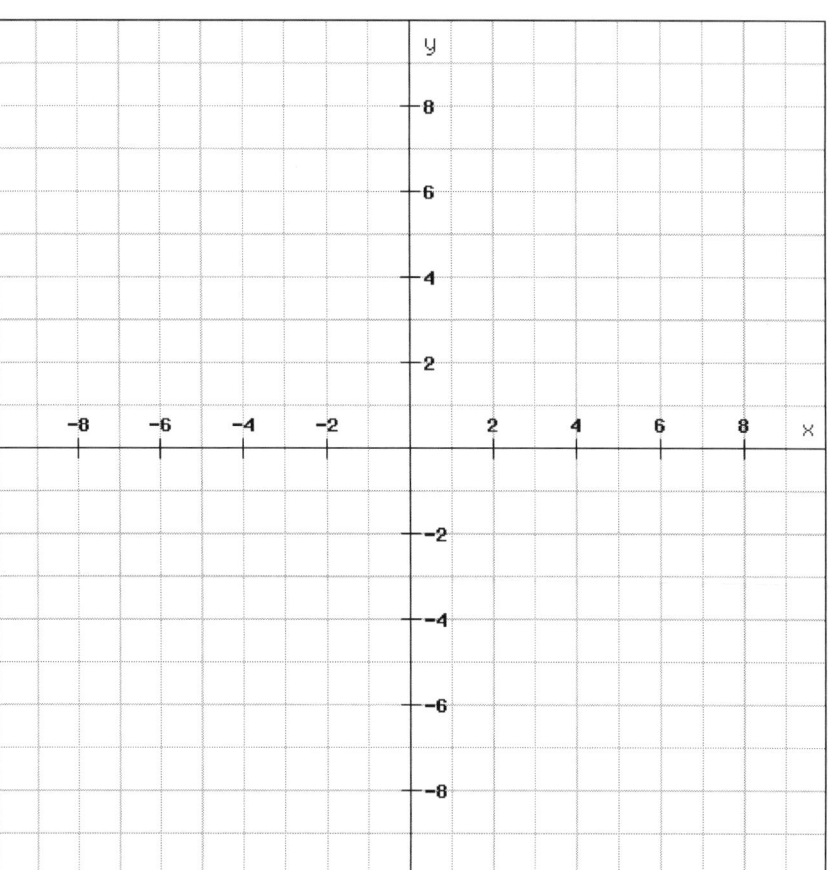

41. Sketch and write the equation of the line with a slope of –3 that passes through the point (0,–3).

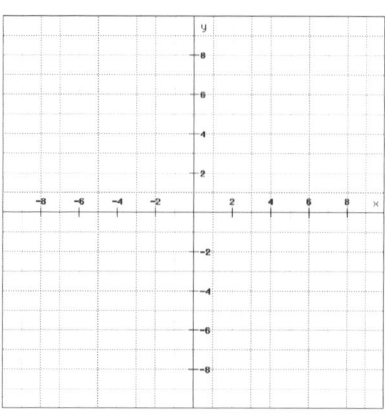

42. Sketch and write the equation of the line with a slope of 2 that passes through the point (2,0)

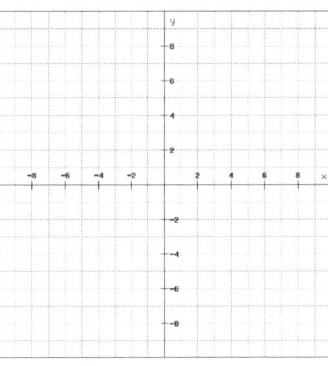

43. Sketch and write the equation of the line with a slope of $-\dfrac{1}{2}$ that passes through the point (–2,0)

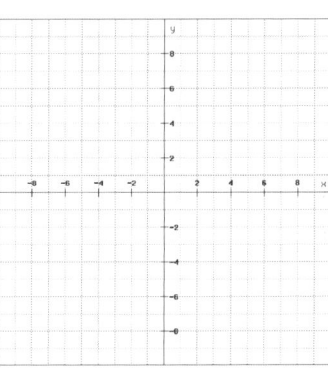

44. Sketch and write the equation of the line with a slope of 2 that passes through the point (–4,2)

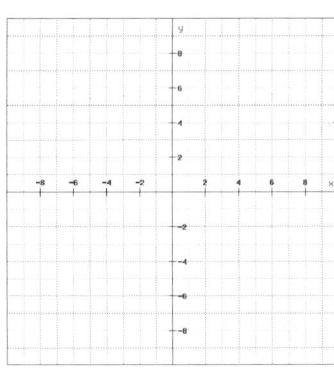

45. Find the intersection between the lines $f(x) = 2x - 3$ and $f(x) = -5x - 2$

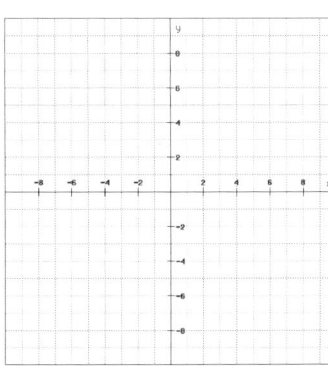

46. Find the intersection between the lines f(x) = x – 3 and f(x) = x – 4

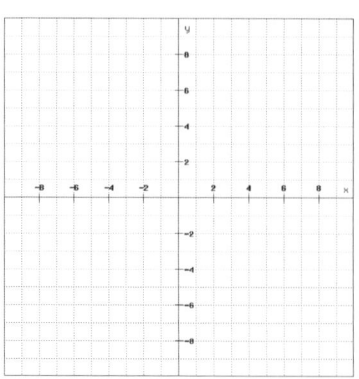

47. Find the intersection between the lines f(x) = 2x – 3 and f(x) = –2x + 7

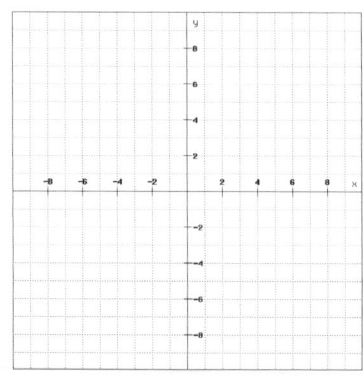

48. Find the intersection between the lines f(x) = ax – 3 and f(x) = ax + 7

49. Find the intersection between the lines f(x) = –12x – 13 and f(x) = 15x + 20.

50. Given that the lines f(x) = 2ax – 1 and f(x) = 4 – 5x + 20 do not intersect, find *a*.

192

51. Find the intersection between the lines y = 2x – 3 and 2y – 4x = – 6.

52. Given that the lines f(x) = mx – 5 and f(x) = 2x + 4 intersect at the point where x = 3, find m.

53. Given that the lines f(x) = 2x – b and f(x) = 3x + 4 intersect at the point where x = 1, find b.

54. Find the intersection between the lines 3y + 2x = 3 and 9y + 6x = 9.

55. Sketch the line $f(x) = \dfrac{-x}{2} + 3, -4 \leq x < 8$

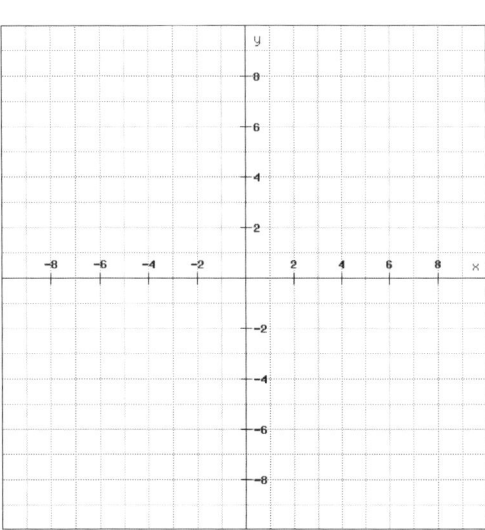

DISTANCE AND MIDPOINT BETWEEN 2 POINTS

56. Given the points (1, 2) and (5, 8). Find the distance between them. Find the midpoint. Sketch to illustrate your answer.

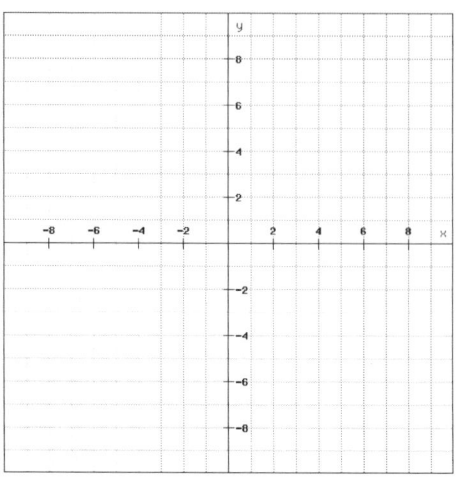

57. Given the points (–3, 2) and (5, –6). Find the distance between them. Find the midpoint. Sketch to illustrate your answer.

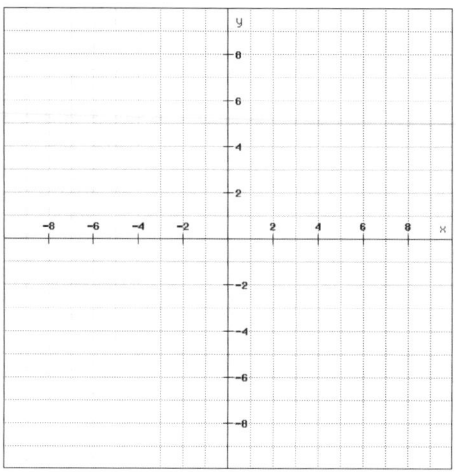

58. Given the points (–1, –6) and (–5, –1). Find the distance between them. Find the midpoint. Sketch to illustrate your answer.

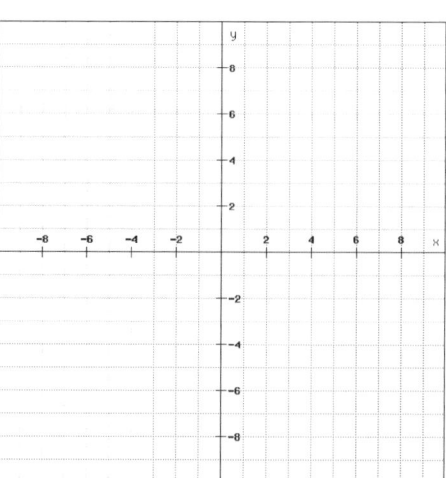

59. Given that the points (*a*, –1) and (5, 3) are 5 units away. Find *a*. Find the midpoint.

60. Given that the points (1, –4) and (5, c) are 10 units away. Find c. Find the midpoint.

61. Find the equation of all the points that are 2 units away from the origin. This equation describes a _____

62. Find the equation of all the points that are 5 units away from the point (2, –1) . This equation describes a _____

63. Given that the points (1, –4) and (5, c) are 10 units away. Find c. Find the midpoint.

64. Given the points (–8, –7) and (6, 2). Find the distance between them. Find the midpoint.

PERPENDICULAR LINES ($m \cdot m_\perp = -1$)

65. A slope perpendicular to 1 is _____, A slope perpendicular to 2 is _____

    A slope perpendicular to k is _____ A slope perpendicular to $\frac{a}{b}$ is _____

66. Find the equation of a line perpendicular to the line y = 3x – 2 that passes through the point (3, 12). Sketch to illustrate your answer.

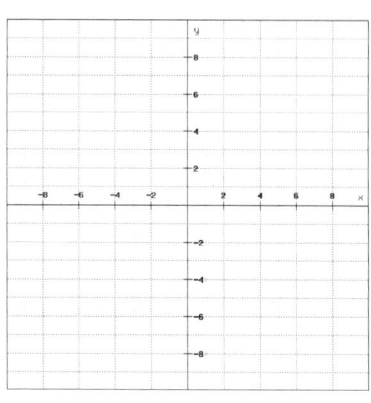

67. Find all the lines perpendicular to the line y = –3x + 4. Fin the ones that passes through the point (–3, 1). Sketch to illustrate your answer.

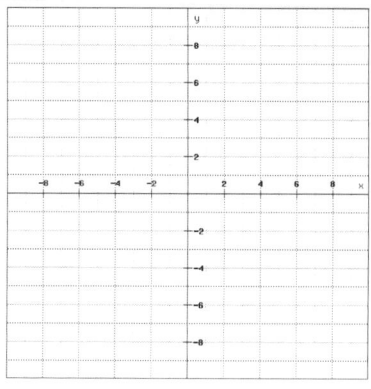

68. Find a line perpendicular to the line y = $-\frac{2}{5}$x + 1 that passes through the point (–1, –7). Sketch to illustrate your answer.

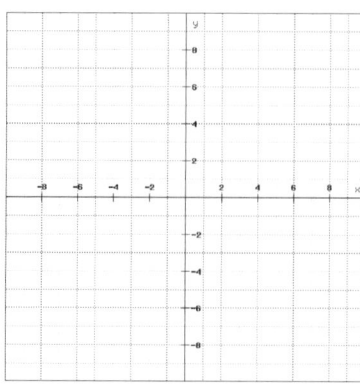

69. Given the points (–2, 5) and (4, 2).

   a. Find the equation of the line passing through them.

   b. Is the point (5, 1) on this line? Show your work.

   c. Find a perpendicular line that passes through the mid point between these points.

   d. Find all the points on the line found in c that are 0.5 units away from the point (0, 2).

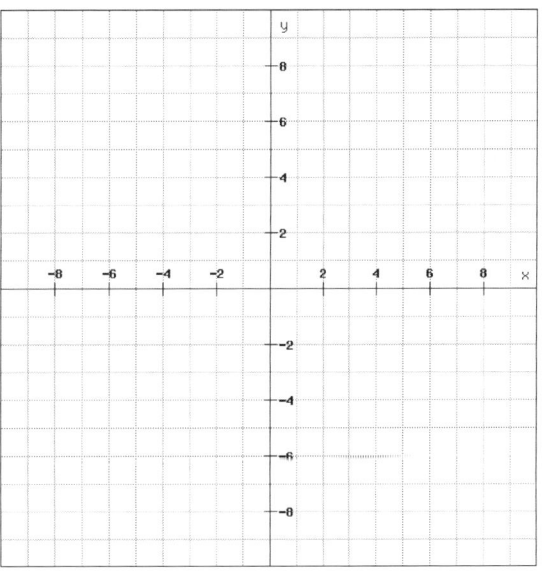

70. Find a point on the x axis that is $\sqrt{5}$ units away from the line y = 2x + 4

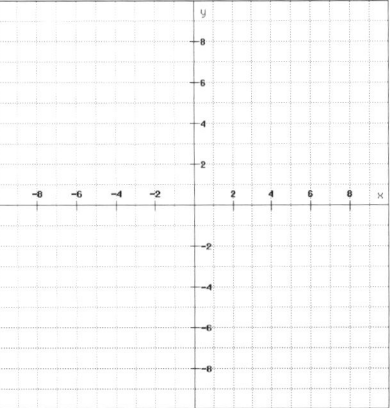

197

71. Find a point on the y axis that is 5 units away from the line y = 3x + 2

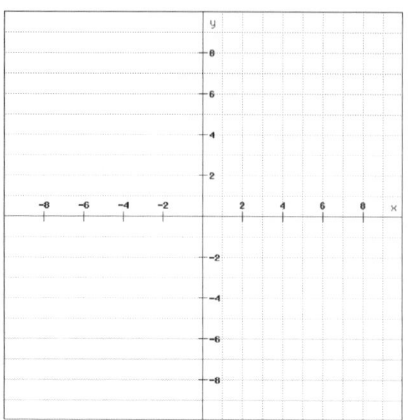

72. Given that the slope of one of the lines is 3 and that the lines are perpendicular, find the **exact** coordinates of the point of intersection of the two lines.

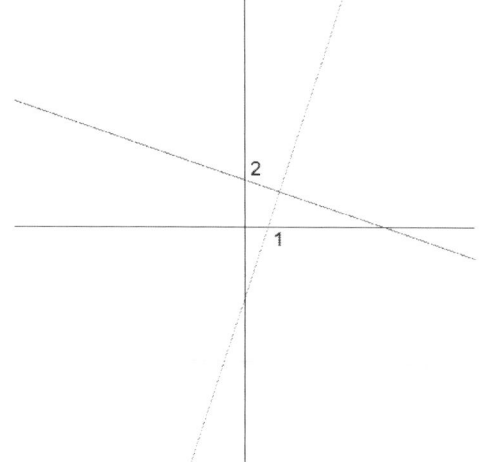

SLOPE – INTERCEPT FORM OF A LINE

73. The line $y - 3 = 2(x + 1)$ passes through the point _____ and has a slope of ___

74. The line $y + 5 = -3(x - 51)$ passes through the point _____ and has a slope of ___

75. The line $-y + 1 = (x + 3)$ passes through the point _____ and has a slope of ___

76. The line $2y + 5 = -6(x + 7)$ passes through the point _____ and has a slope of ___

77. The line $y + a = m(x + b)$ passes through the point _____ and has a slope of ___

78. The line $y - a = m(x - b)$ passes through the point _____ and has a slope of ___

79. The line $y - a = m(x + b)$ passes through the point _____ and has a slope of ___

80. Write the equation $y - 3 = 2(x + 1)$ in the explicit form

81. Write the equation $y+5=2(x+6)$ in the explicit form

82. Write down the equation of a line passing through the point (5, 2) with slope 1.

83. Write down the equation of a line passing through the point (–4, –3) with slope –2.

84. Write down the equation of a line passing through the point (6, 3) with slope $\frac{2}{3}$.

85. Write down the equation of a line passing through point (–2, –5) with slope $-\frac{2}{5}$.

86. Write down the equation of the line passing through points (–2, –5), (–7, –5),

87. Write down the equation of the line passing through points (–1, –3), (6, 5),

88. Write down the equation of the line passing through points (–1, 5), (7, –2),

APPLICATION

1. The price of a new toy (in US$) is C(t) = 20 – 0.5t, t given in days.

   a. Sketch the corresponding graph.

   b. What was the initial price of the toy? _____

   c. Find the price of the toy after 10 days

   d. What is the domain of the function, reason your answer,

   e. What is the range of the function.

   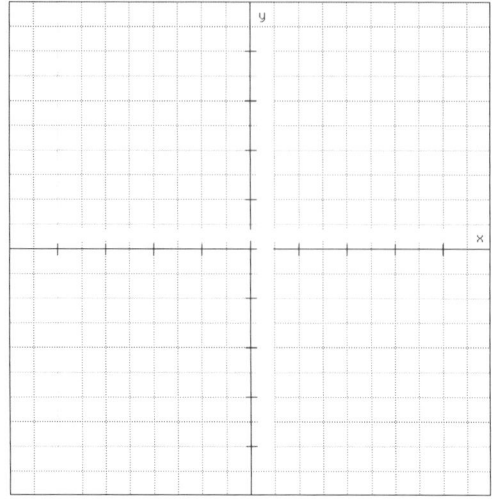

   f. What is the meaning of 0.5? Does it have units? What are they?

2. On a certain planet the temperature of the soil is 10° on the surface and 0.02° wormer with every meter of depth.

   a. Write a function to describe the temperature as a function of the depth d. State its domain and range. What are the units of the slope?

   b. Find the temperature at depth of 500m

   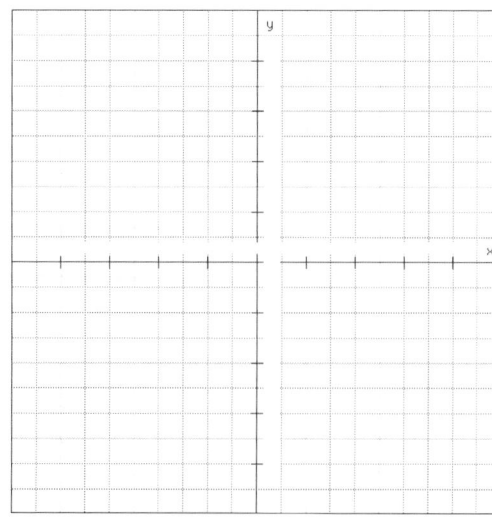

   c. Find the depth at which the temperature is 13°.

   d. Graph the function, use appropriate scale, variables and units.

3. In a factory there are 2 machines that produce a certain product. The operation cost (electricity, maintenance etc.) of Machine A is 250$ a month and the cost of production per product is 2$. The operation cost of Machine B is 200$ a month and the cost of production per product is 4$. The maximum number of products that both machines can make a month is 200.

   a. Write the functions to describe the cost C as a function of the number of products n for both machines. Indicate the domain and range of both functions. What are the units of the slope?

   b. Graph the functions, use appropriate scale, variables and units. Calculate the coordinates of important points on the graph.

   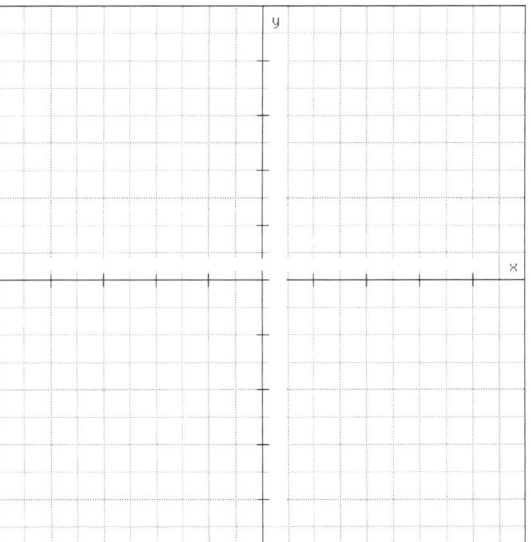

   c. Discuss in which case each machine is best.

4. A parking lot with 1200 parking spots opens at 6 am. The cars flow in a constant rate. At 10 am the parking is full.

   a. Write the function to describe the number of cars N as function of time t in hours. Indicate the domain and range of the function. What are the units of the slope?

   b. Find the number of free spots at 8:30.

   c. In case the owner needs 150 free spots at what time should he close the parking?

   d. Graph the function, use appropriate scale, variables and units.

   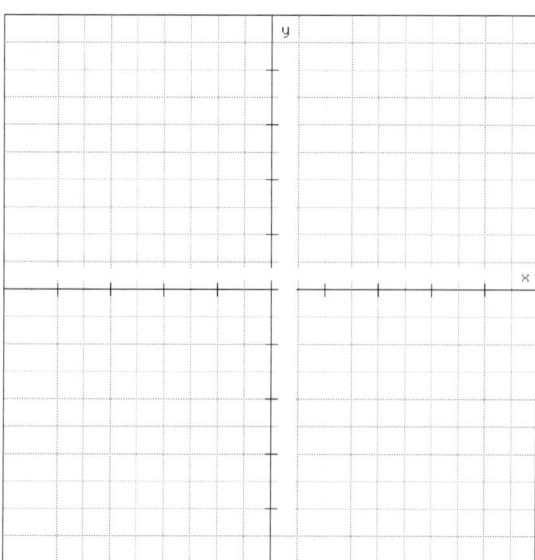

5. You need to rent a car for one day and to compare the charges of 3 different companies. Company I charges 20$ per day with additional cost of 0.20$ per mile. Company II charges 30$ per day with additional cost of 0.10$ per mile. Company III charges 60$ per day with no additional mileage charge.

   a. Write the cost function for each one of the companies.

   b. Sketch all 3 graphs on the same axes system.

   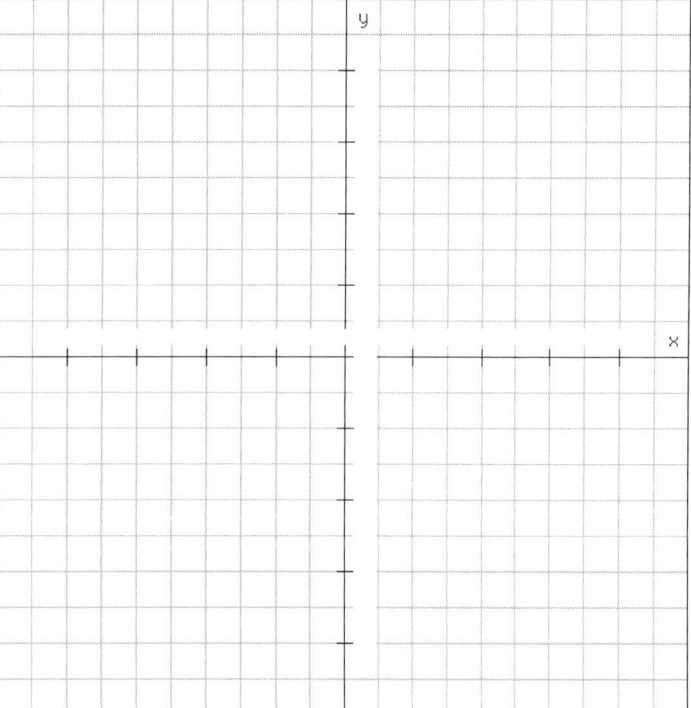

   c. Comment on the circumstances in which renting a car from each one of the companies is best.

3.3. – QUADRATIC FUNCTIONS

Introduction:

1. Given the functions: $f(x) = x^2$, $g(x) = x^2 - 2$. Complete the following table:

x	−5	−4	−3	−2	−1	0	1	2	3	4	5	6
f(x)												
g(x)												

- Sketch the points of the chart on a graph.

- State the domain of the functions: : f(x):_____, g(x):_____

- State the *y* intercepts: f(x): (___, ___), g(x): (___, ___)

- State the *x* intercept(s): f(x): (___, ___), g(x): (___, ___),(___, ___)

- Write in all possible forms:

- Find the max/min point(s): f(x): (___, ___), g(x): (___, ___)

- The functions are increasing on the interval: f(x):_____, g(x):_____

- The functions are decreasing on the interval: f(x):_____, g(x):_____

- Sketch the functions of the graph used for the points initially drawn

- State the range of the function: f(x):_____, g(x):_____

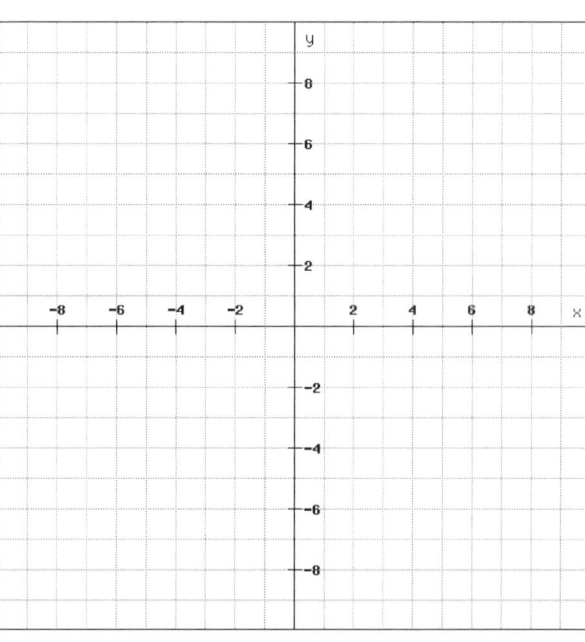

204

2. Given the functions: $f(x) = (x - 2)^2$, $g(x) = (x + 3)^2 - 2$. Complete the following chart:

x	−5	−4	−3	−2	−1	0	1	2	3	4	5	6
f(x)												
g(x)												

- Sketch the points of the chart on a graph.

- State the domain of the functions: : f(x):_____, g(x):_____

- State the *y* intercepts: f(x): (____, ____), g(x): (____, ____)

- State the *x* intercept(s): f(x): (____, ____), g(x): (____, ____),(____, ____)

- Write in all possible forms:

- Find the max/min point(s): f(x): (____, ____), g(x): (____, ____)

- The functions are increasing on the interval: f(x):_____, g(x):_____

- The functions are decreasing on the interval: f(x):_____, g(x):_____

- Sketch the functions of the graph used for the points initially drawn

- State the range of the function: f(x):_____, g(x):_____

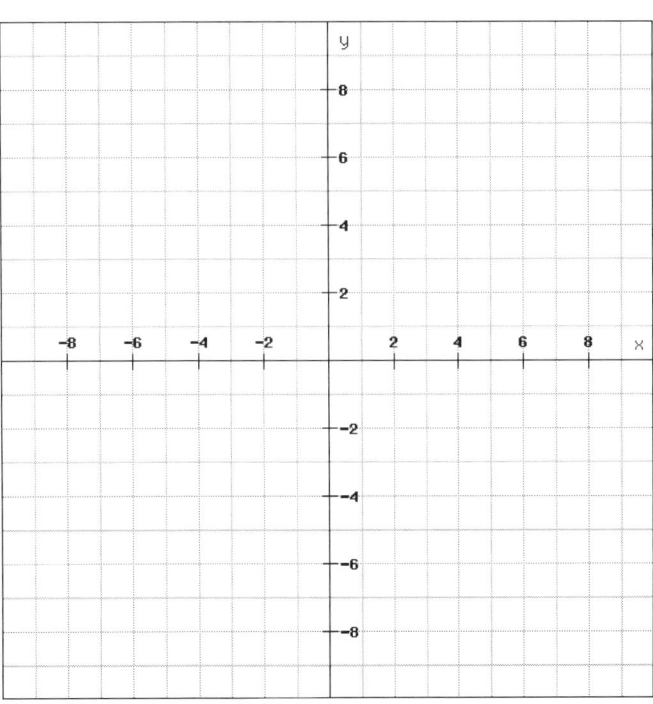

205

3. Given the functions: $f(x) = (x+2)(x-4)$, $g(x) = 2(x+2)(x-4)$ Complete the following chart:

x	−5	−4	−3	−2	−1	0	1	2	3	4	5	6
f(x)												
g(x)												

- Sketch the points of the chart on a graph.

- State the domain of the functions: : f(x):_____, g(x):_____

- State the y intercepts: f(x): (____, ____), g(x): (____, ____)

- State the x intercept(s): f(x): (____, ____), (____, ____)

   g(x): (____, ____), (____, ____)

- Write in all possible forms:

- Find the max/min point(s): f(x): (____, ____), g(x): (____, ____)

- The functions are increasing on the interval: f(x):_____, g(x):_____

- The functions are decreasing on the interval: f(x):_____, g(x):_____

- Sketch the functions of the graph used for the points initially drawn

- State the range of the function: f(x):_____, g(x):_____

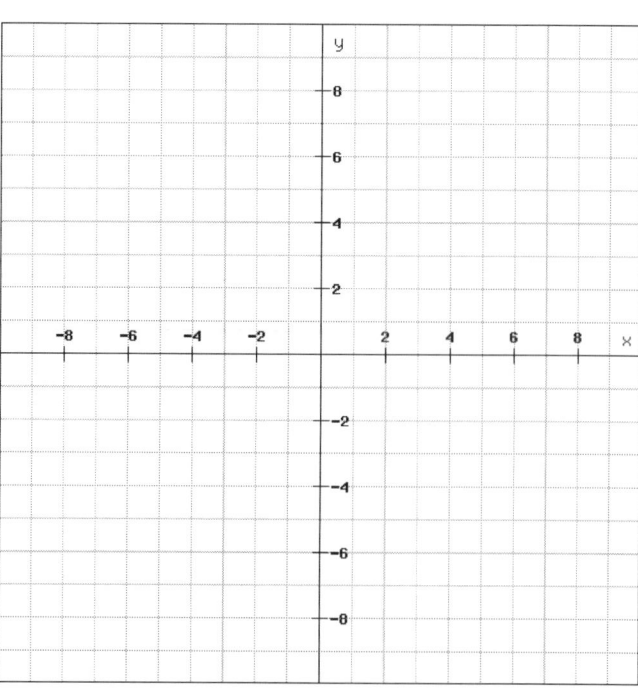

206

In general, a quadratic function f can be written in several different ways:

a. $f(x) = ax^2 + bx + c$ **standard form**, where a, b and c are constants
b. $f(x) = a(x - r)(x - s)$ **factored form**, where a, r and s are constants
c. $f(x) = a(x - h)^2 + k$ **vertex form**, where a, h and k are constants

Example:

Vertex form: $f(x) = 3(x - 2)^2 - 3$
Partial factored form: $f(x) = 3(x - 1)(x - 3)$
Standard form: $f(x) = 3x^2 + 12x + 9$

Complete the sentences:

1. The graph of a quadratic function is called a _____.

2. In factored form, the numbers r and s represent the _____ of f.

3. In vertex form, the point (h, k) is called the _____ of the parabola. The axis of symmetry of the parabola is the line _____.

4. The graph of the parabola opens upwards if _____ and downwards if _____.

5. In case $f(x) = x^2 + 1$, the function can be written in ____ form(s) only. Why?

6. In case $f(x) = x^2 - 1$, the function can be written in ____ form(s) only. Show your answer:

7. A parabola has its vertex at the point (2, 3) and goes through the point (6, 11). Find the expression of the function.

8. A parabola has its vertex at the point (− 2, 4) and passes through the point (2, − 6). Find the expression of the function.

9. Write the analytical expression that corresponds the following functions in all possible forms, assume $a = 1$ or -1 in both cases:

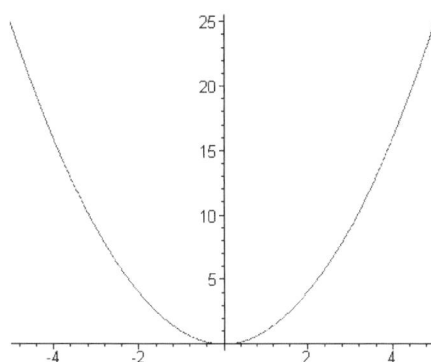 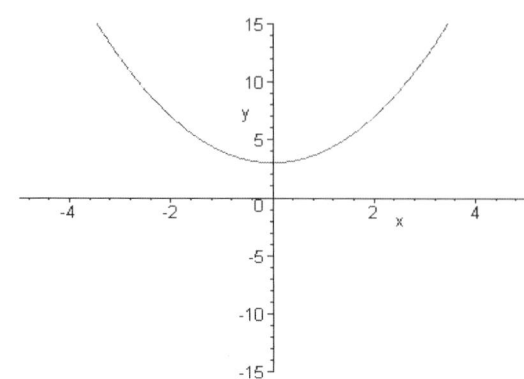

Range: _____ Range: _____
Vertex form: _____ Vertex form: _____
Factorized form: _____ Factorized form: _____
Standard form: _____ Standard form: _____

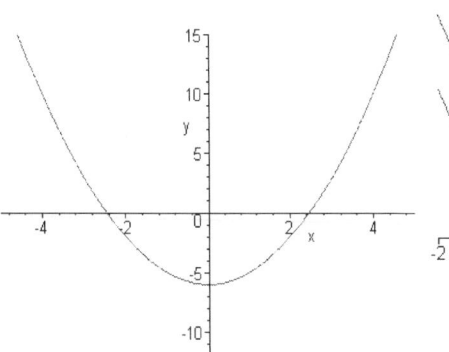 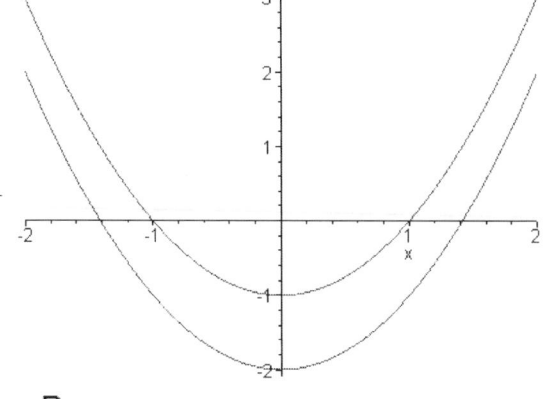

Range: _____ Range: _____
Vertex form: _____ Vertex form: _____
Factorized form: _____ Factorized form: _____
Standard form: _____ Standard form: _____

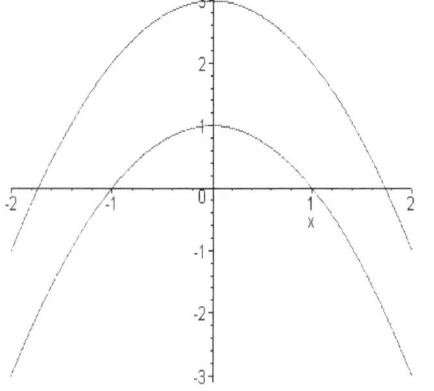

Range: _____ Range: _____
Vertex form: _____ Vertex form: _____
Factorized form: _____ Factorized form: _____
Standard form: _____ Standard form: _____

10. Complete the tables:

Function	On the graph
$f(x) = x^2$	
$f(x) = \dfrac{x^2}{2}$	
$f(x) = \dfrac{x^2}{3}$	
$f(x) = 2x^2$	

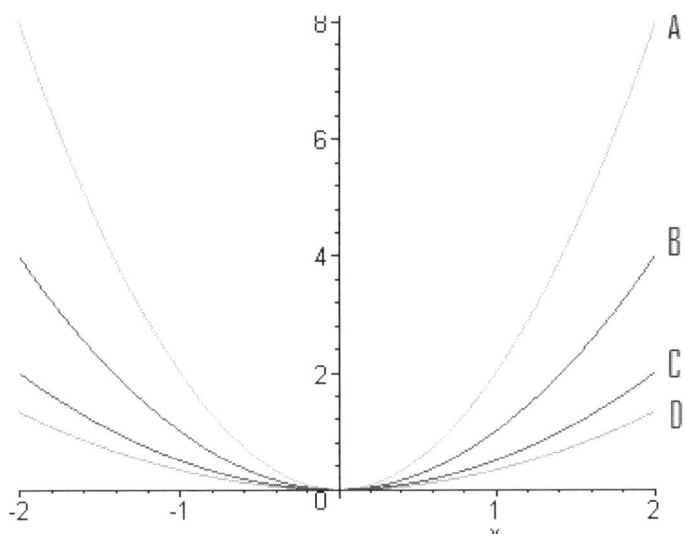

Conclusion:

11. Complete the table:

Function	On the graph
$f(x) = x^2 + 2$	
$f(x) = x^2 - 2$	
$f(x) = x^2 - 3$	
$f(x) = 2x^2 + 2$	

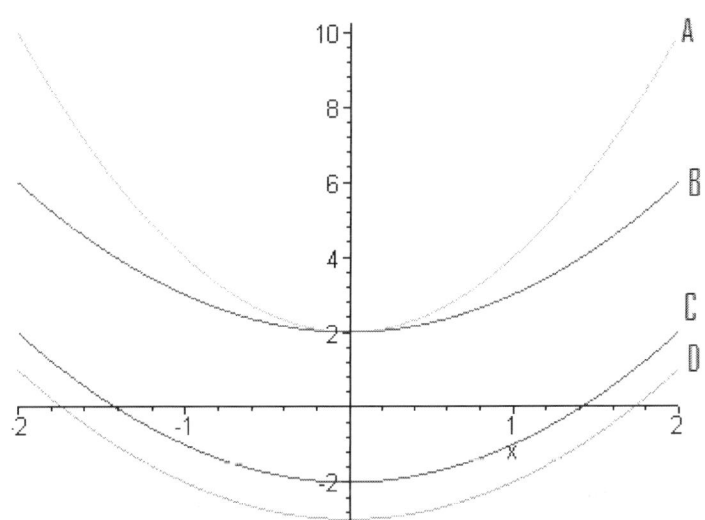

Conclusion:

12. Complete the table:

Function	On the graph
$f(x) = -x^2 + 2$	
$f(x) = x^2 - 4$	
$f(x) = -x^2 + 3$	
$f(x) = 2x^2 + 2$	

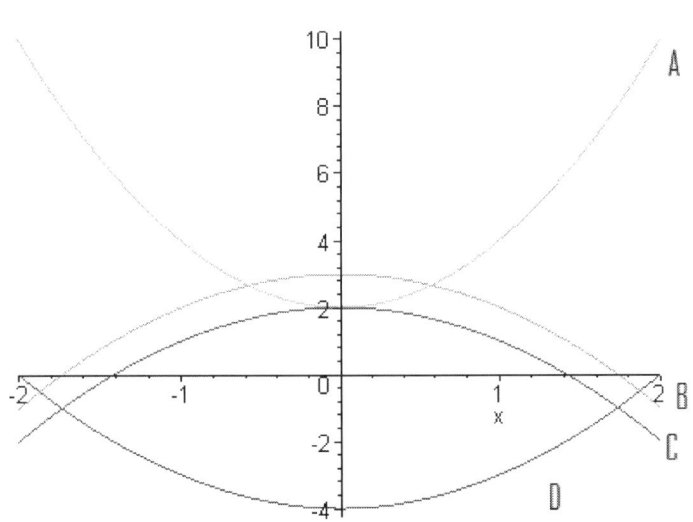

13. Write the expression of the function in all possible forms, indicate the range assume $a = 1$ or -1 in both cases:

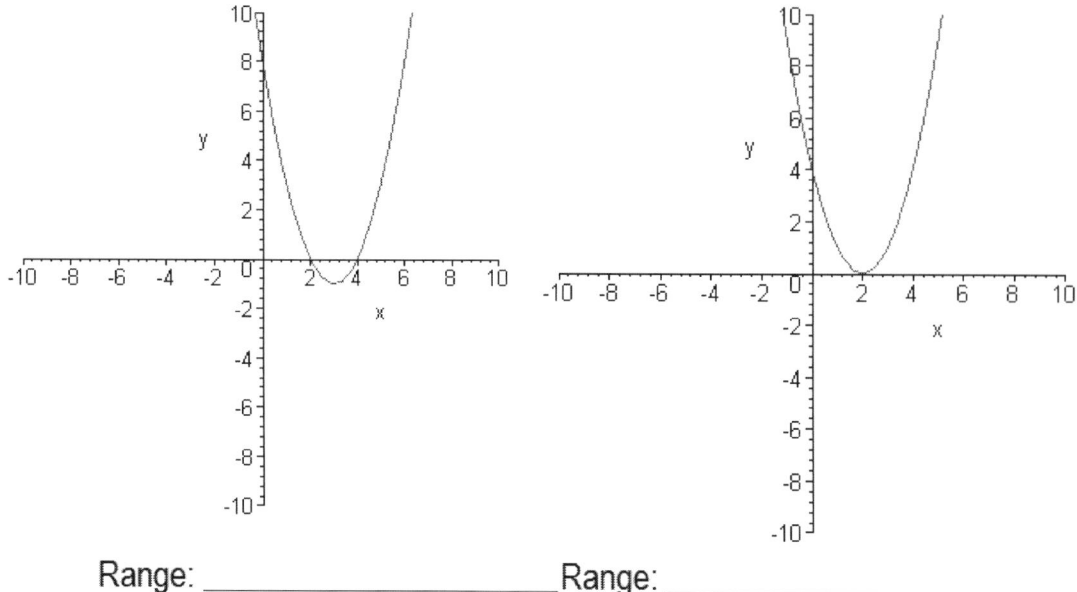

Range: _____   Range: _____
Vertex form: _____   Vertex form: _____
Factorized form: _____   Factorized form: _____
Standard form: _____   Standard form: _____

14. Write the expression of the function in all possible forms, indicate the range assume $a = 1$ or -1 in both cases:

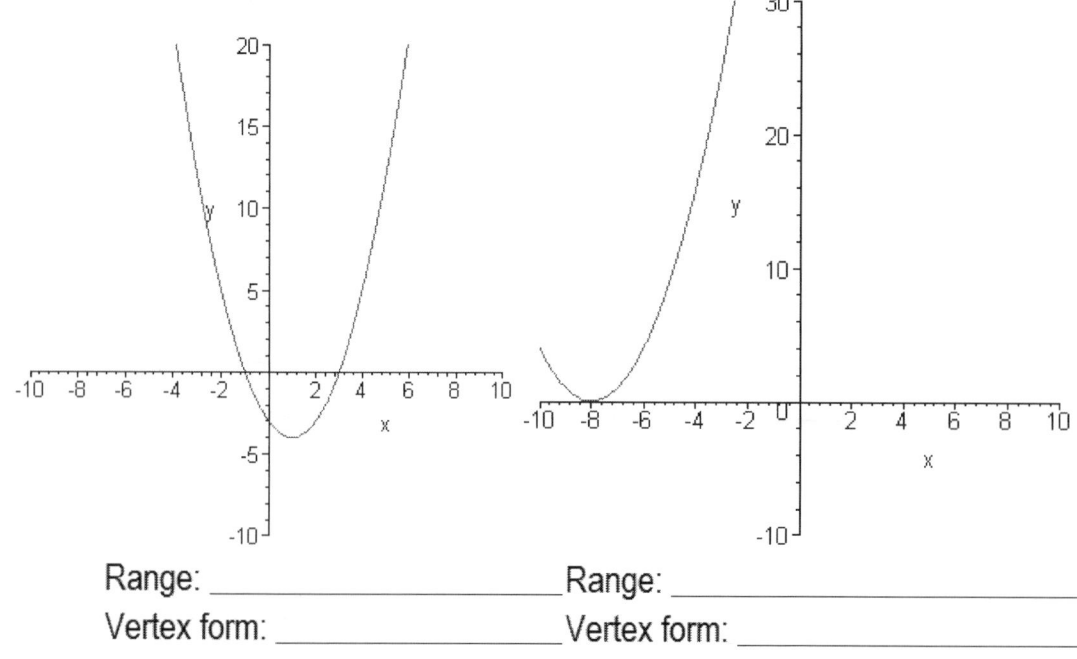

Range: _____   Range: _____
Vertex form: _____   Vertex form: _____
Factorized form: _____   Factorized form: _____
Standard form: _____   Standard form: _____

15. Write the expression of the function in all possible forms, indicate the range assume $a = 1$ or -1 in both cases:

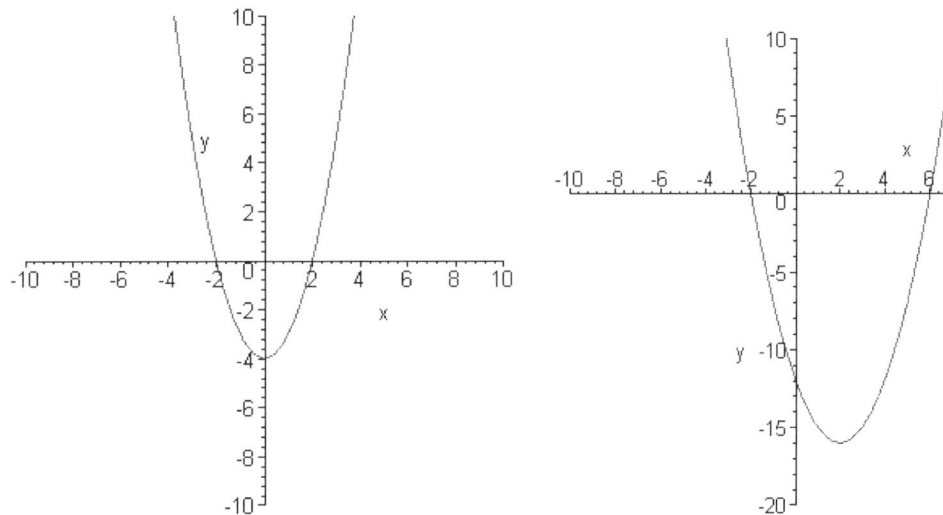

Range: _____   Range: _____
Vertex form: _____   Vertex form: _____
Factorized form: _____   Factorized form: _____
Standard form: _____   Standard form: _____

16. Write the expression of the function in all possible forms, indicate the range assume $a = 1$ or -1 in both cases:

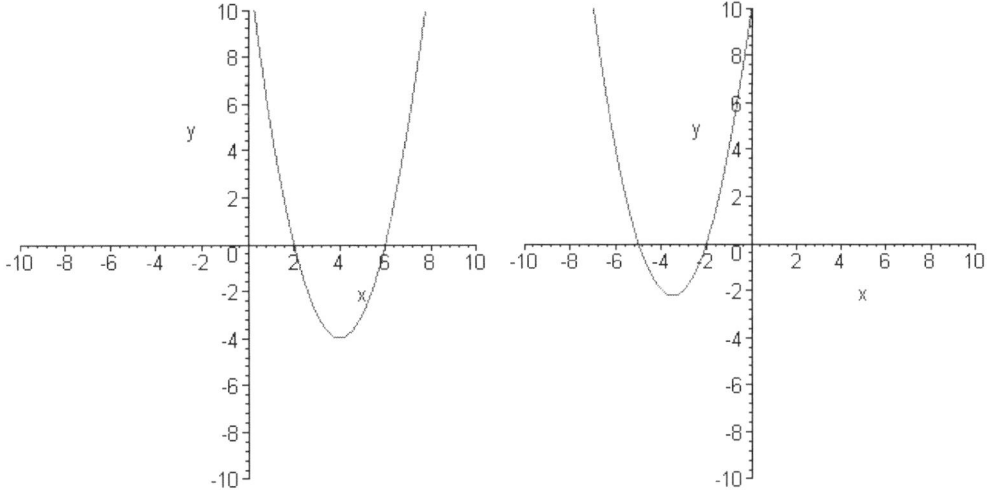

Range: _____   Range: _____
Vertex form: _____   Vertex form: _____
Factorized form: _____   Factorized form: _____
Standard form: _____   Standard form: _____

17. Write the expression of the function in all possible forms, indicate the range assume $a = 1$ or -1 in both cases:

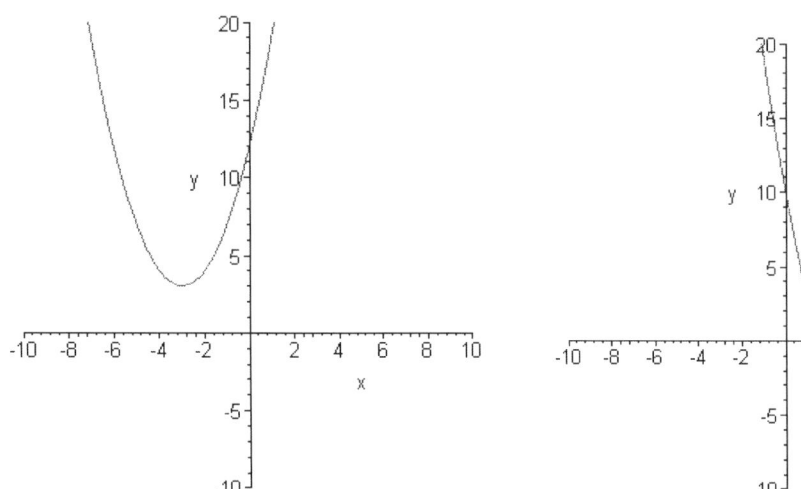

Range: _____   Range: _____
Vertex form: _____   Vertex form: _____
Factorized form: _____   Factorized form: _____
Standard form: _____   Standard form: _____

18. Write the expression of the function in all possible forms, indicate the range assume $a = 1$ or -1 in both cases:

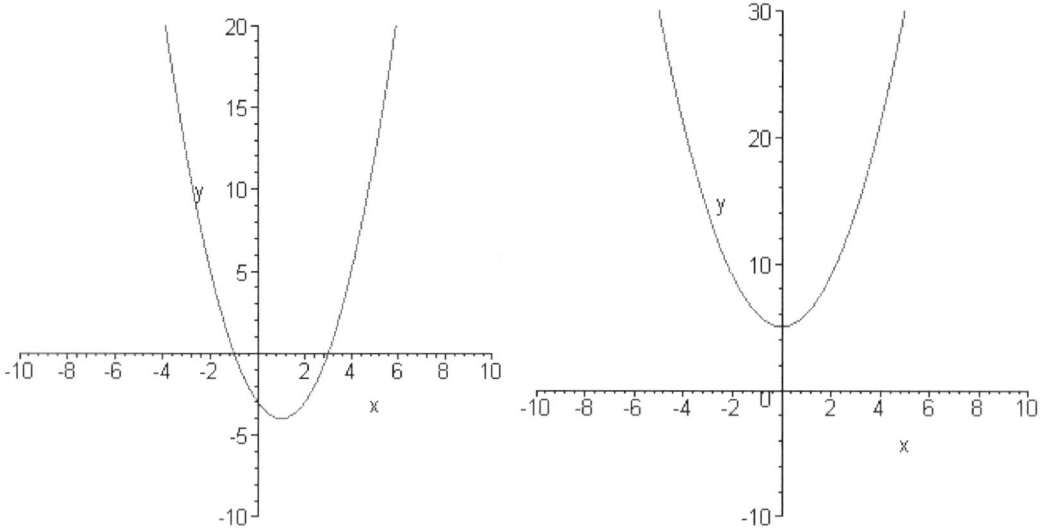

Range: _____   Range: _____
Vertex form: _____   Vertex form: _____
Factorized form: _____   Factorized form: _____
Standard form: _____   Standard form: _____

19. Write the expression of the function in all possible forms, indicate the range assume $a = 1$ or -1 in both cases:

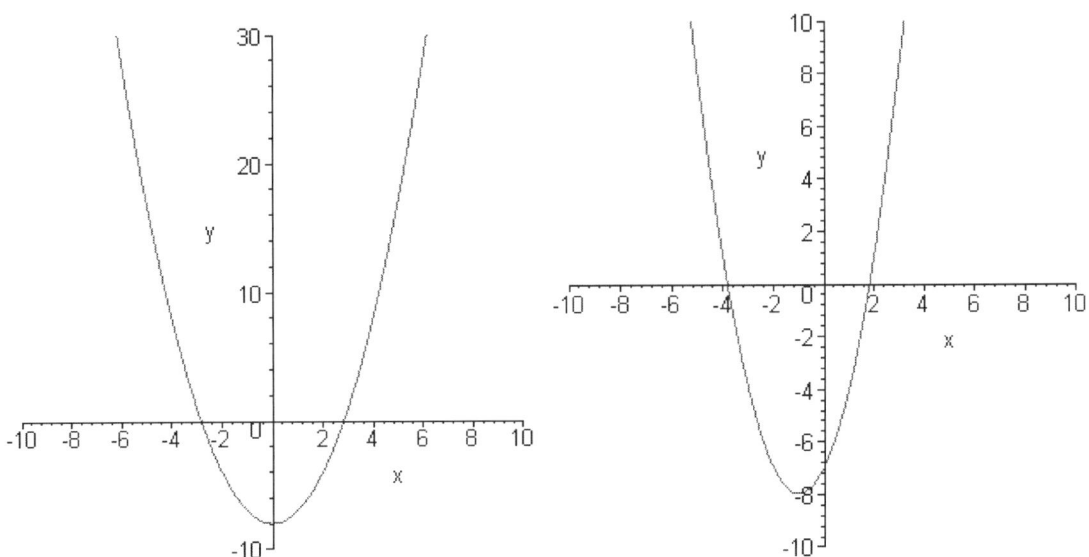

Range: _____ Range: _____
Vertex form: _____ Vertex form: _____
Factorized form: _____ Factorized form: _____
Standard form: _____ Standard form: _____

20. Write the expression of the function in all possible forms, indicate the range assume $a = 1$ or -1 in both cases:

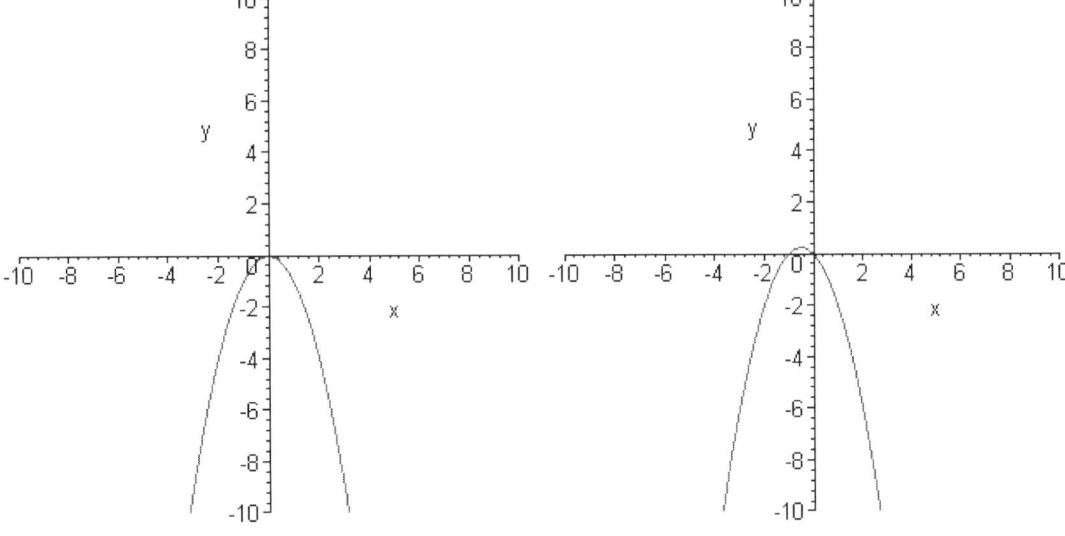

Range: _____ Range: _____
Vertex form: _____ Vertex form: _____
Factorized form: _____ Factorized form: _____
Standard form: _____ Standard form: _____

21. Write the expression of the function in all possible forms, indicate the range assume $a = 1$ or -1 in both cases:

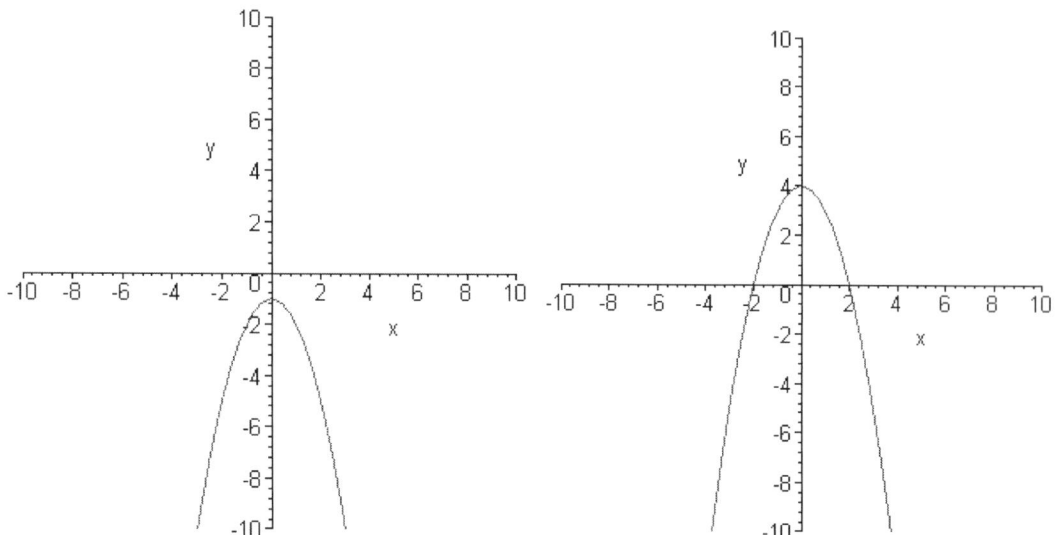

Range: _____ Range: _____
Vertex form: _____ Vertex form: _____
Factorized form: _____ Factorized form: _____
Standard form: _____ Standard form: _____

22. Write the expression of the function in all possible forms, indicate the range assume $a = 1$ or -1 in both cases:

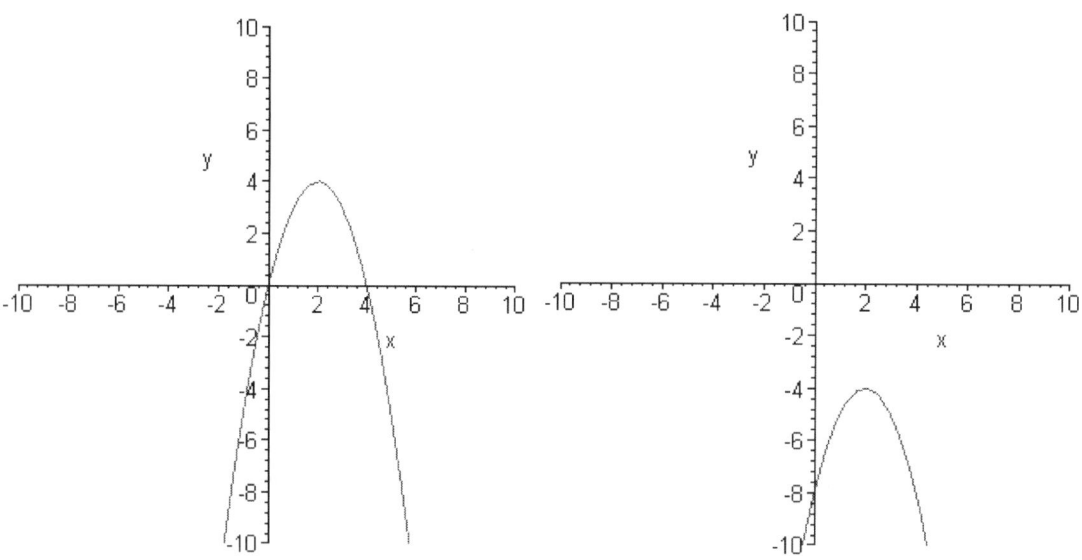

Range: _____ Range: _____
Vertex form: _____ Vertex form: _____
Factorized form: _____ Factorized form: _____
Standard form: _____ Standard form: _____

23. Write the expression of the function in all possible forms, indicate the range assume $a = 1$ or -1 in both cases:

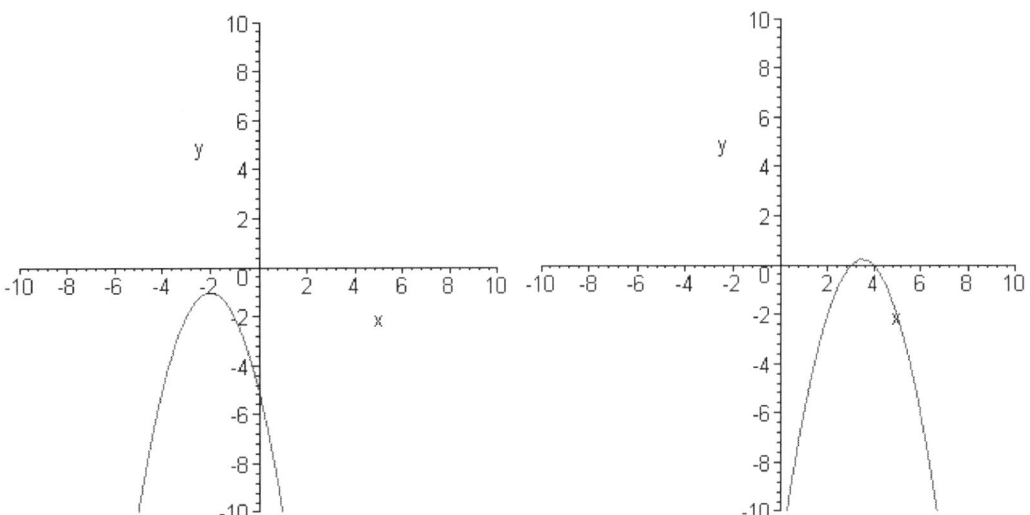

Range: _____ Range: _____
Vertex form: _____ Vertex form: _____
Factorized form: _____ Factorized form: _____
Standard form: _____ Standard form: _____

24. Write the expression of the function in all possible forms, indicate the range assume $a = 1$ or -1 in both cases:

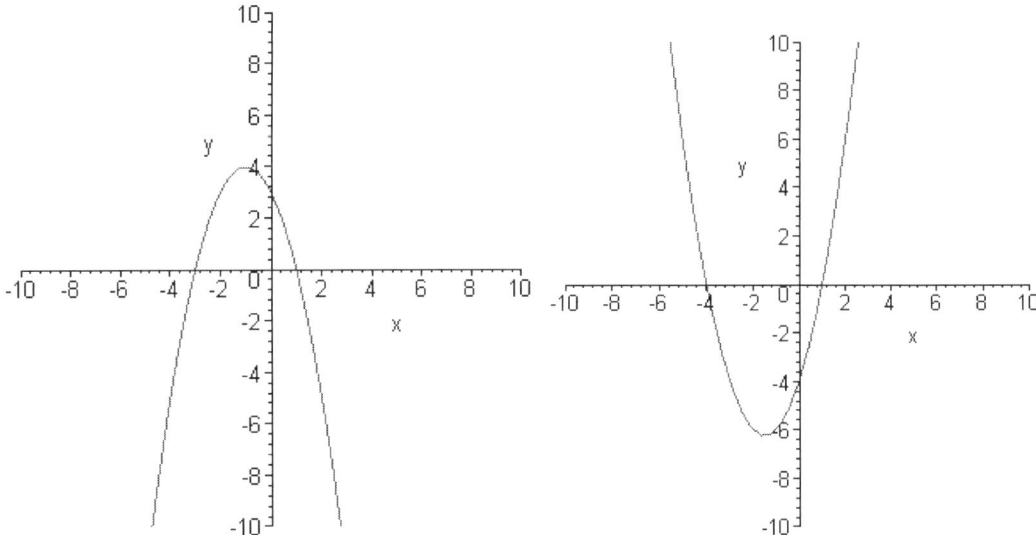

Range: _____ Range: _____
Vertex form: _____ Vertex form: _____
Factorized form: _____ Factorized form: _____
Standard form: _____ Standard form: _____

25. Write the expression of the function in all possible forms, indicate the range assume $a = 1$ or -1 in both cases:

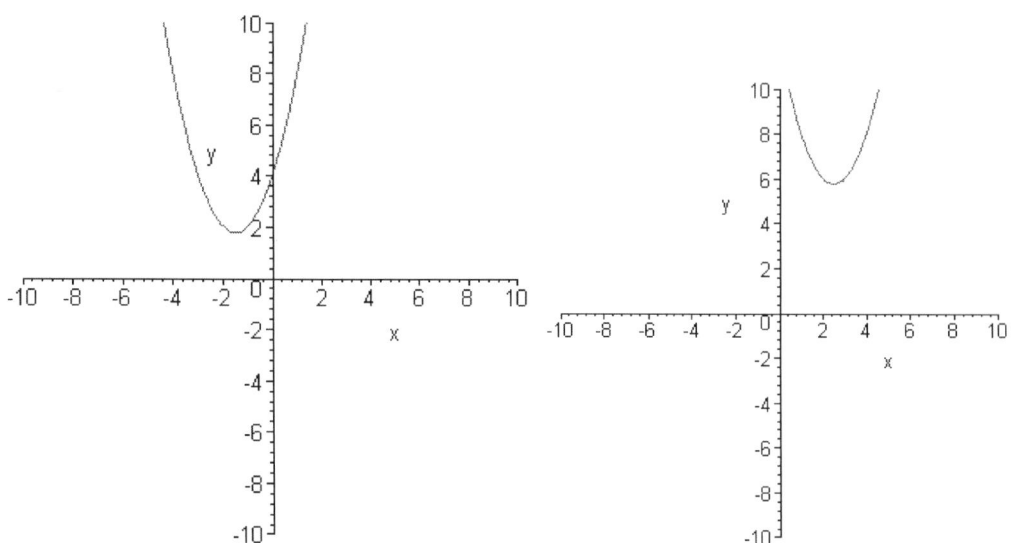

Range: _____   Range: _____
Vertex form: _____   Vertex form: _____
Factorized form: _____   Factorized form: _____
Standard form: _____   Standard form: _____

Analyze the following functions:

26. $f(x) = -3$

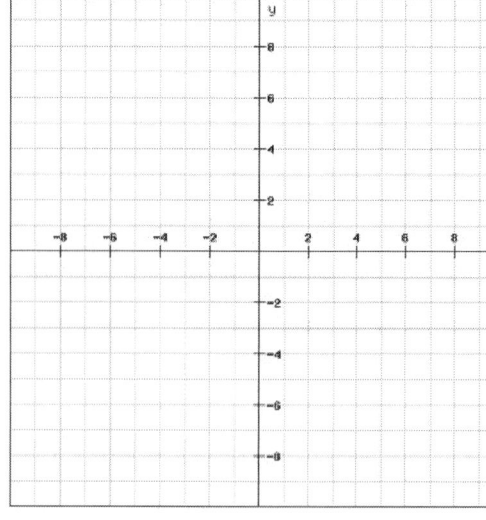

Vertex form: _____

Factorized form: _____

Domain: _____   Range: _____

y intercept:(___, ___)

x intercept(s):(___, ___), (___, ___)

Increases: _____ Decreases: _____

216

27. $f(x) = 5x$

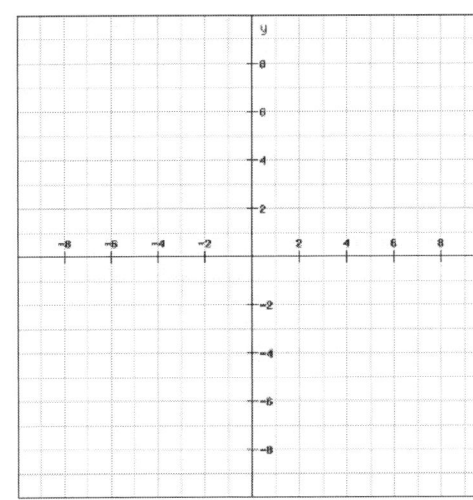

Vertex form: _____

Factorized form: _____

Domain: _____   Range: _____

y intercept:(__, __)   Vertex:(__, __) Max/Min

x intercept(s):(___, ___), (___, ___)

Increases: _____ Decreases: _____

28. $f(x) = x^2 + 8x + 19$

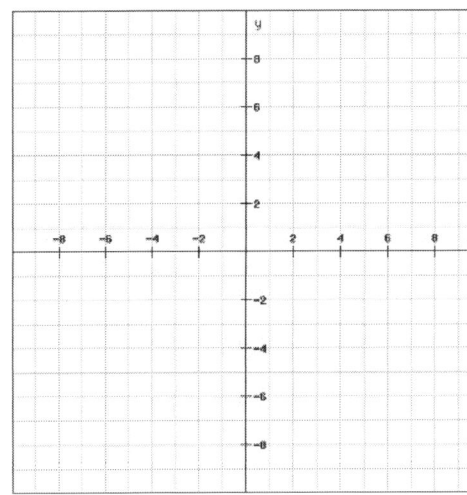

Vertex form: _____

Factorized form: _____

Domain: _____   Range: _____

y intercept:(__, __)   Vertex:(__, __) Max/Min

x intercept(s):(___, ___), (___, ___)

Increases: _____ Decreases: _____

29. $f(x) = 10x^2 - 8x - 2$

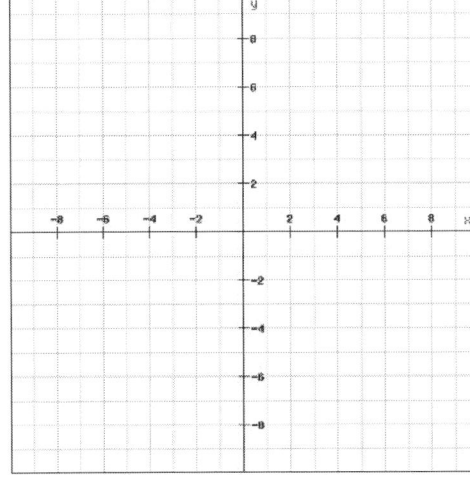

Vertex form: _____

Factorized form: _____

Domain: _____   Range: _____

y intercept:(__, __)   Vertex:(__, __) Max/Min

x intercept(s):(___, ___), (___, ___)

Increases: _____ Decreases: _____

30. $f(x) = x^2 + 4x + 1$

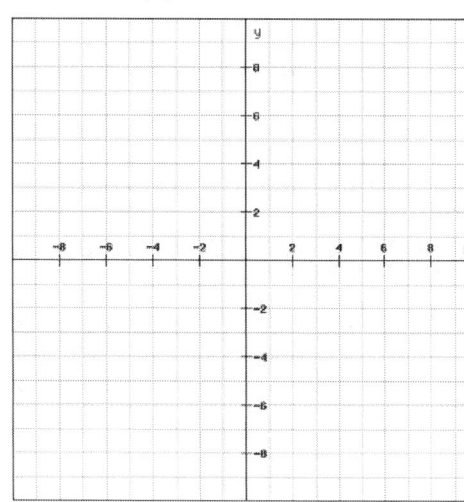

Vertex form: _____

Factorized form: _____

Domain: _____ Range: _____

y intercept: (__, __)   Vertex: (__, __) Max/Min

x intercept(s): (___, ___), (___, ___)

Increases: _____ Decreases: _____

31. $f(x) = 4x^2 - 14x + 6$

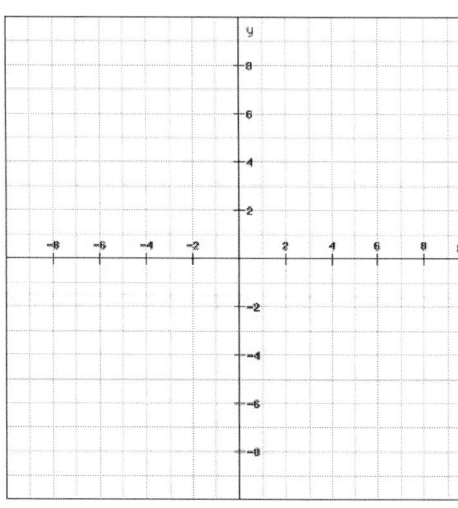

Vertex form: _____

Factorized form: _____

Domain: _____ Range: _____

y intercept: (__, __)   Vertex: (__, __) Max/Min

x intercept(s): (___, ___), (___, ___)

Increases: _____ Decreases: _____

32. $f(x) = 2x^2 - 3x - 5$

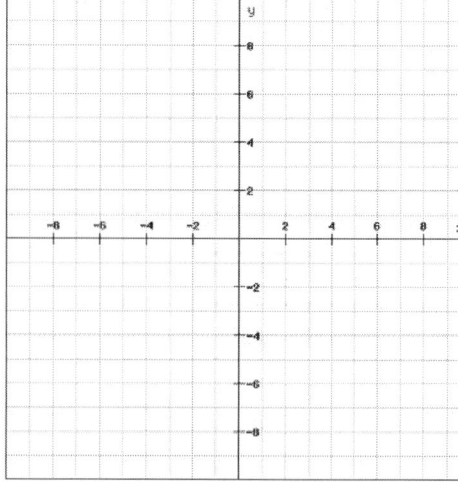

Vertex form: _____

Factorized form: _____

Domain: _____ Range: _____

y intercept: (__, __)   Vertex: (__, __) Max/Min

x intercept(s): (___, ___), (___, ___)

Increases: _____ Decreases: _____

33. $f(x) = x^2 + 3x - 10$

Vertex form: _____

Factorized form: _____

Domain: _____ Range: _____

y intercept: (__, __) Vertex: (__, __) Max/Min

x intercept(s): (___, ___), (___, ___)

Increases: _____ Decreases: _____

34. $f(x) = x^2 + 7x - 1$

Vertex form: _____

Factorized form: _____

Domain: _____ Range: _____

y intercept: (__, __) Vertex: (__, __) Max/Min

x intercept(s): (___, ___), (___, ___)

Increases: _____ Decreases: _____

35. $f(x) = x^2 + 2x + 7$

Vertex form: _____

Factorized form: _____

Domain: _____ Range: _____

y intercept: (__, __) Vertex: (__, __) Max/Min

x intercept(s): (___, ___), (___, ___)

Increases: _____ Decreases: _____

36. $f(x) = x^2 + x - 1$

Vertex form: _____

Factorized form: _____

Domain: _____   Range: _____

y intercept: (__, __)   Vertex: (__, __) Max/Min

x intercept(s): (___, ___), (___, ___)

Increases: _____ Decreases: _____

37. $f(x) = x^2 + 2x + 1$

Vertex form: _____

Factorized form: _____

Domain: _____   Range: _____

y intercept: (__, __)   Vertex: (__, __) Max/Min

x intercept(s): (___, ___), (___, ___)

Increases: _____ Decreases: _____

38. $f(x) = x^2 + 1$

Vertex form: _____

Factorized form: _____

Domain: _____   Range: _____

y intercept: (__, __)   Vertex: (__, __) Max/Min

x intercept(s): (___, ___), (___, ___)

Increases: _____ Decreases: _____

39. $f(x) = x^2 - 1$

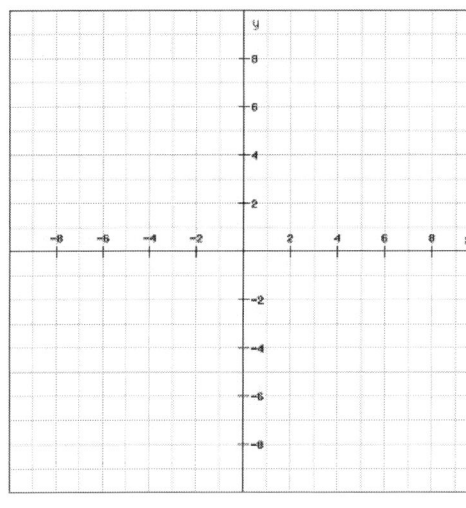

Vertex form: _____

Factorized form: _____

Domain: _____ Range: _____

y intercept:(__, __) Vertex:(__, __) Max/Min

x intercept(s):(___, ___), (___, ___)

Increases: _____ Decreases: _____

40. $f(x) = x^2 + 3x$

Vertex form: _____

Factorized form: _____

Domain: _____ Range: _____

y intercept:(__, __) Vertex:(__, __) Max/Min

x intercept(s):(___, ___), (___, ___)

Increases: _____ Decreases: _____

41. $f(x) = x^2 + 5x$

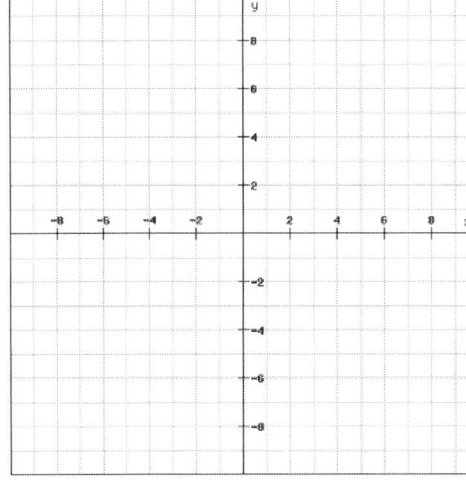

Vertex form: _____

Factorized form: _____

Domain: _____ Range: _____

y intercept:(__, __) Vertex:(__, __) Max/Min

x intercept(s):(___, ___), (___, ___)

Increases: _____ Decreases: _____

42. $f(x) = x^2 - 3x$

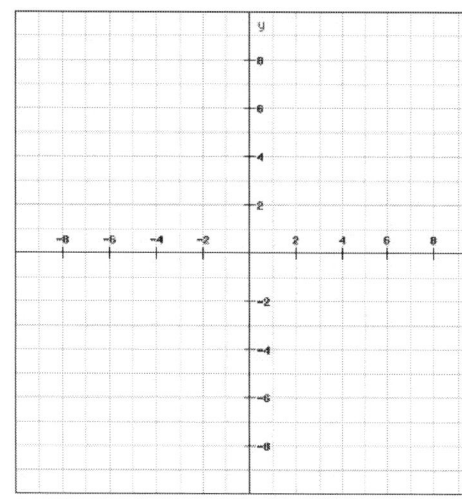

Vertex form: _____

Factorized form: _____

Domain: _____ Range: _____

y intercept: (__, __)   Vertex: (__, __) Max/Min

x intercept(s): (___, ___), (___, ___)

Increases: _____ Decreases: _____

43. $f(x) = x^2 - 7x$

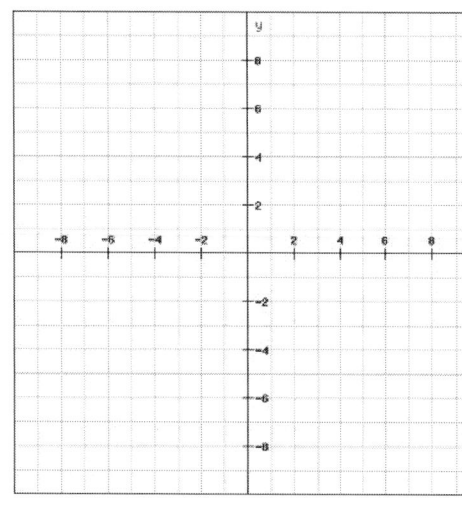

Vertex form: _____

Factorized form: _____

Domain: _____ Range: _____

y intercept: (__, __)   Vertex: (__, __) Max/Min

x intercept(s): (___, ___), (___, ___)

Increases: _____ Decreases: _____

44. $f(x) = x^2 + 4x + 6$

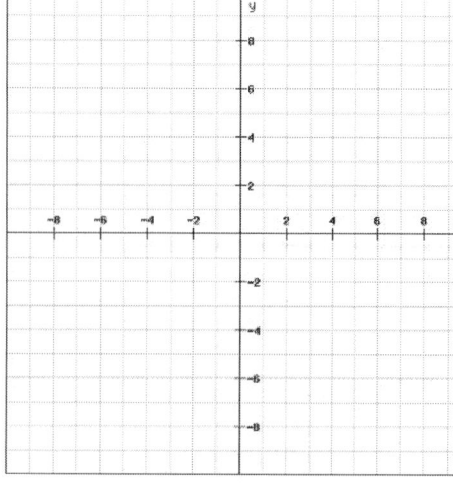

Vertex form: _____

Factorized form: _____

Domain: _____ Range: _____

y intercept: (__, __)   Vertex: (__, __) Max/Min

x intercept(s): (___, ___), (___, ___)

Increases: _____ Decreases: _____

45. f(x) = –2x² – 16x – 29

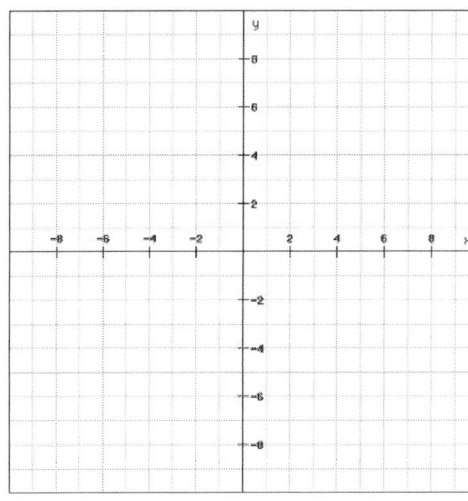

Vertex form: _____

Factorized form: _____

Domain: _____ Range: _____

y intercept:(__, __)   Vertex:(__, __)Max/Min

x intercept(s):(___, ___), (___, ___)

Increases: _____ Decreases: _____

46. f(x) = x² – 6x + 4

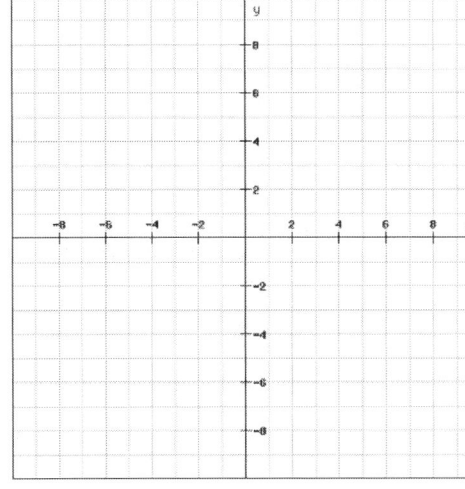

Vertex form: _____

Factorized form: _____

Domain: _____ Range: _____

y intercept:(__, __)   Vertex:(__, __)Max/Min

x intercept(s):(___, ___), (___, ___)

Increases: _____ Decreases: _____

47. f(x) = x² – 7x + 2

Vertex form: _____

Factorized form: _____

Domain: _____ Range: _____

y intercept:(__, __)   Vertex:(__, __)Max/Min

x intercept(s):(___, ___), (___, ___)

Increases: _____ Decreases: _____

48. $f(x) = x^2 + 3x + 10$

Vertex form: _____

Factorized form: _____

Domain: _____ Range: _____

y intercept:(__, __) Vertex:(__, __) Max/Min

x intercept(s):(___, ___), (___, ___)

Increases: _____ Decreases: _____

49. $f(x) = x^2 + 5$

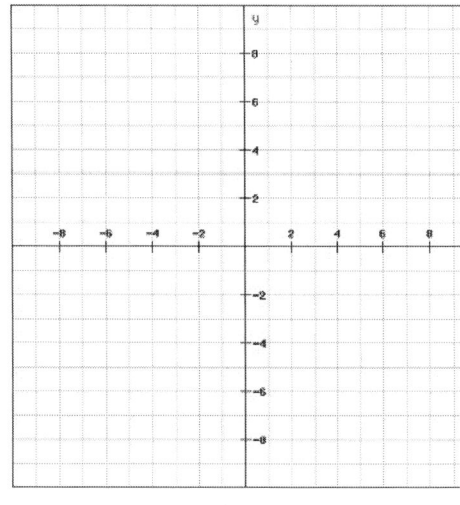

Vertex form: _____

Factorized form: _____

Domain: _____ Range: _____

y intercept:(__, __) Vertex:(__, __) Max/Min

x intercept(s):(___, ___), (___, ___)

Increases: _____ Decreases: _____

50. $f(x) = x^2 - 3$

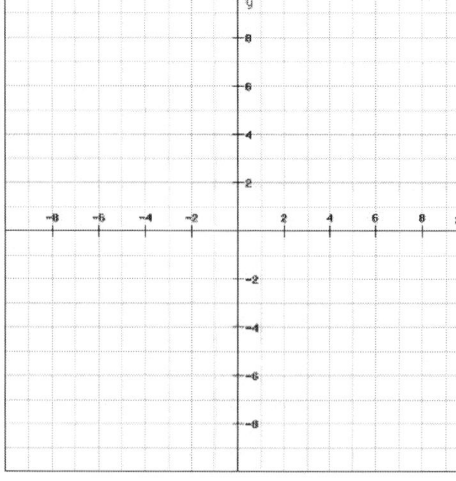

Vertex form: _____

Factorized form: _____

Domain: _____ Range: _____

y intercept:(__, __) Vertex:(__, __) Max/Min

x intercept(s):(___, ___), (___, ___)

Increases: _____ Decreases: _____

51. $f(x) = x^2 - 7x$

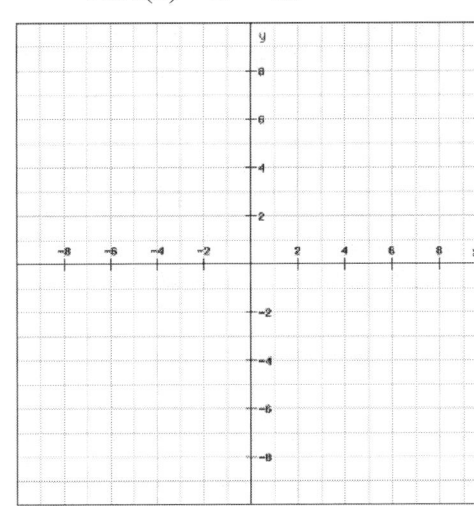

Vertex form: _____

Factorized form: _____

Domain: _____ Range: _____

y intercept:(__, __)   Vertex:(__, __)Max/Min

x intercept(s):(___, ___), (___, ___)

Increases: _____ Decreases: _____

52. $f(x) = x^2 + 3x - 5$

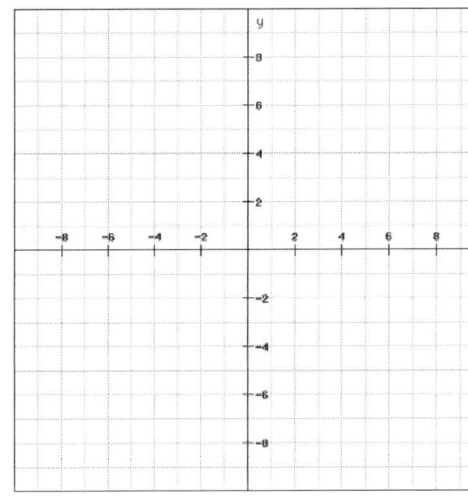

Vertex form: _____

Factorized form: _____

Domain: _____ Range: _____

y intercept:(__, __)   Vertex:(__, __)Max/Min

x intercept(s):(___, ___), (___, ___)

Increases: _____ Decreases: _____

53. $f(x) = 5x^2 - 3$

Vertex form: _____

Factorized form: _____

Domain: _____ Range: _____

y intercept:(__, __)   Vertex:(__, __)Max/Min

x intercept(s):(___, ___), (___, ___)

Increases: _____ Decreases: _____

54. $f(x) = 5x^2 - 10x$

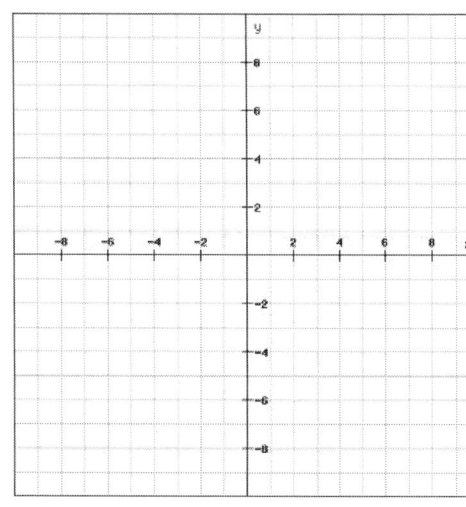

Vertex form: _____

Factorized form: _____

Domain: _____   Range: _____

y intercept:(__, __)   Vertex:(__, __) Max/Min

x intercept(s):(___, ___), (___, ___)

Increases: _____ Decreases: _____

55. $f(x) = -5x^2$

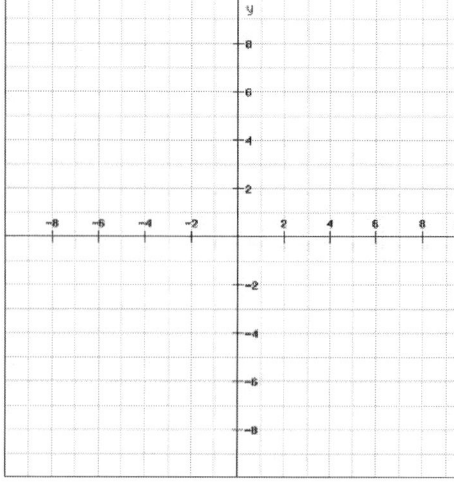

Vertex form: _____

Factorized form: _____

Domain: _____   Range: _____

y intercept:(__, __)   Vertex:(__, __) Max/Min

x intercept(s):(___, ___), (___, ___)

Increases: _____ Decreases: _____

56. $f(x) = -x^2 + 6x - 8$

Vertex form: _____

Factorized form: _____

Domain: _____   Range: _____

y intercept:(__, __)   Vertex:(__, __) Max/Min

x intercept(s):(___, ___), (___, ___)

Increases: _____ Decreases: _____

57. $f(x) = -x^2 - 6x + 2$

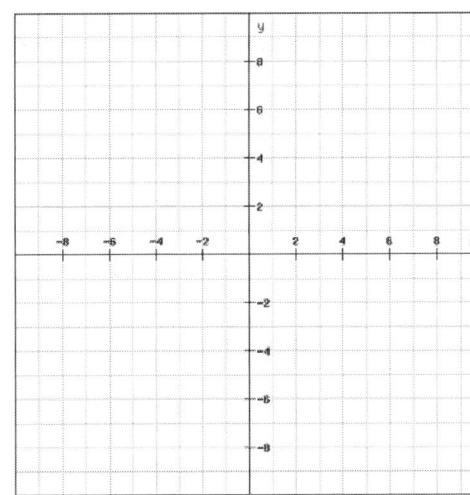

Vertex form: _____

Factorized form: _____

Domain: _____ Range: _____

y intercept:(__, __)   Vertex:(__, __)Max/Min

x intercept(s):(___, ___), (___, ___)

Increases: _____ Decreases: _____

58. $f(x) = -x^2 + x - 5$

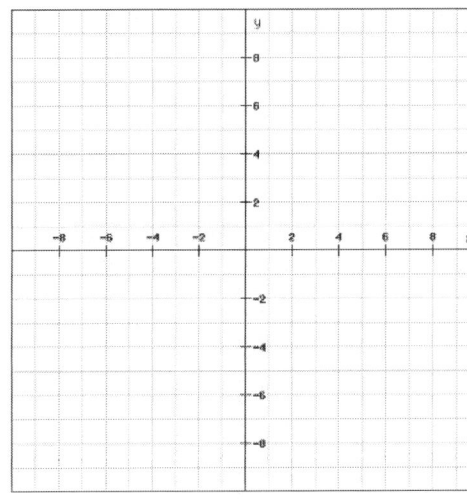

Vertex form: _____

Factorized form: _____

Domain: _____ Range: _____

y intercept:(__, __)   Vertex:(__, __)Max/Min

x intercept(s):(___, ___), (___, ___)

Increases: _____ Decreases: _____

59. $f(x) = -x^2 - 4x - 4$

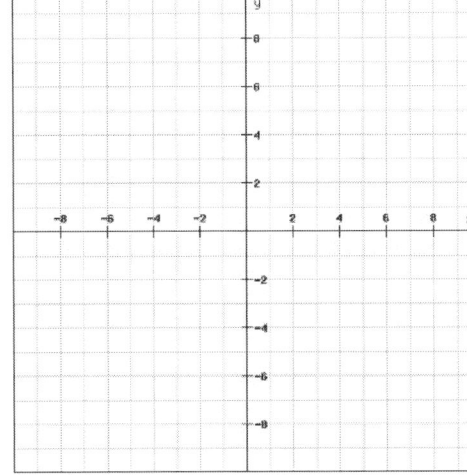

Vertex form: _____

Factorized form: _____

Domain: _____ Range: _____

y intercept:(__, __)   Vertex:(__, __)Max/Min

x intercept(s):(___, ___), (___, ___)

Increases: _____ Decreases: _____

60. $f(x) = -x^2 + 3$

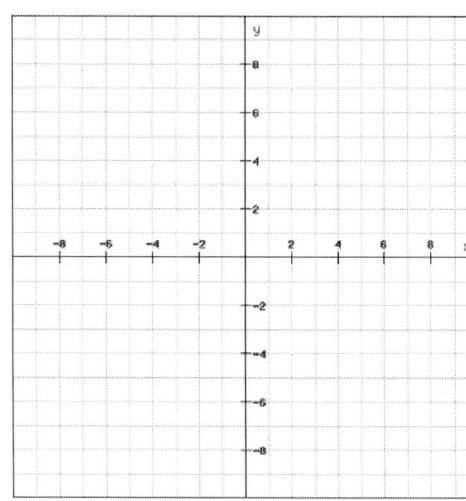

Vertex form: _____

Factorized form: _____

Domain: _____ Range: _____

y intercept:(__, __)   Vertex:(__, __) Max/Min

x intercept(s):(___, ___), (___, ___)

Increases: _____ Decreases: _____

61. $f(x) = 3x^2$

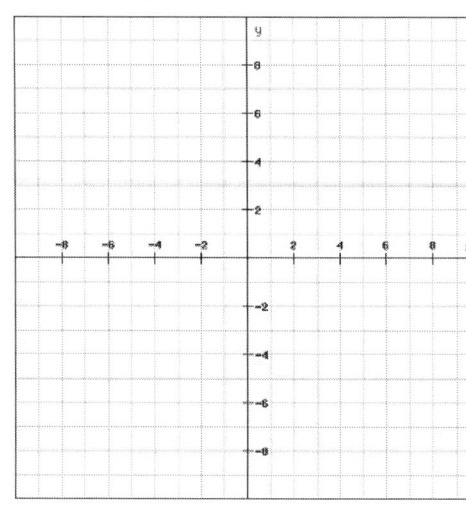

Vertex form: _____

Factorized form: _____

Domain: _____ Range: _____

y intercept:(__, __)   Vertex:(__, __) Max/Min

x intercept(s):(___, ___), (___, ___)

Increases: _____ Decreases: _____

62. $f(x) = 2((x + 3)x + 4)$

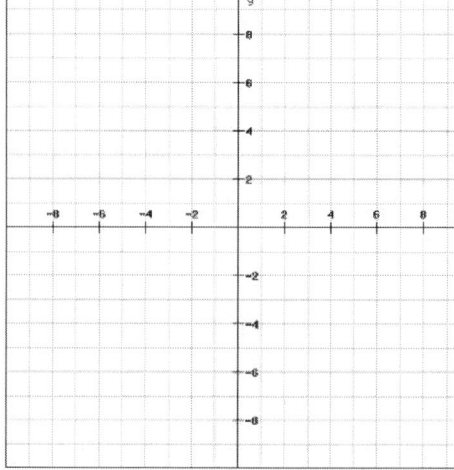

Vertex form: _____

Factorized form: _____

Domain: _____ Range: _____

y intercept:(__, __)   Vertex:(__, __) Max/Min

x intercept(s):(___, ___), (___, ___)

Increases: _____ Decreases: _____

63. $f(x) = \dfrac{2x - 4x^2}{2}$

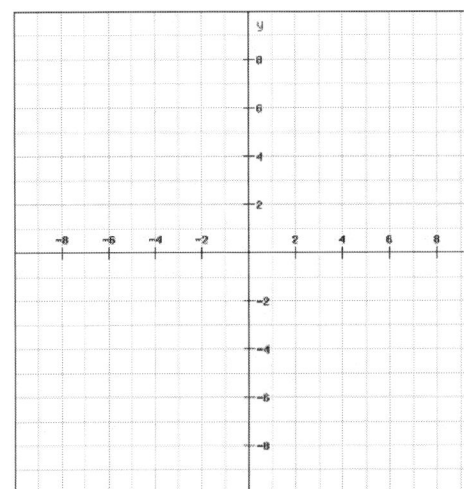

Vertex form: _____

Factorized form: _____

Domain: _____ Range: _____

y intercept:(__, __) Vertex:(__, __) Max/Min

x intercept(s):(__, __), (__, __)

Increases: _____ Decreases: _____

64. $f(x) = \dfrac{4x^2 + 8x}{4} - 2$

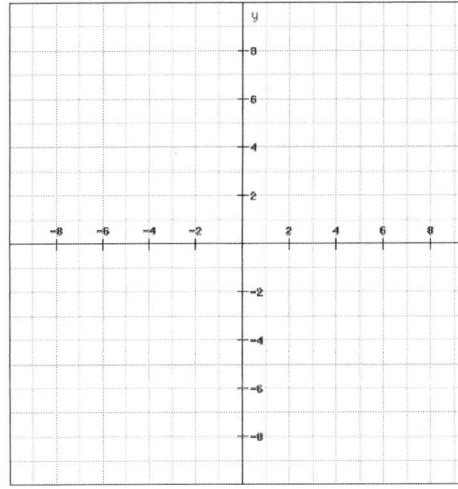

Vertex form: _____

Factorized form: _____

Domain: _____ Range: _____

y intercept:(__, __) Vertex:(__, __) Max/Min

x intercept(s):(__, __), (__, __)

Increases: _____ Decreases: _____

65. $f(x) = \dfrac{(x-3)(x+4)}{2} - 1$

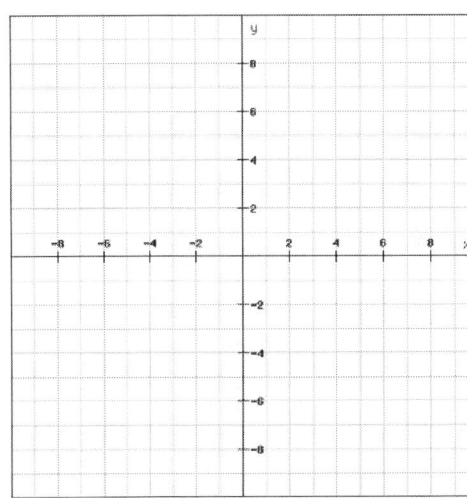

Vertex form: _____

Factorized form: _____

Domain: _____ Range: _____

y intercept:(__, __) Vertex:(__, __) Max/Min

x intercept(s):(__, __), (__, __)

Increases: _____ Decreases: _____

66. What are the coordinates of the vertex of $y = 7(x + 3)^2 + 4$? (___ , ___)

67. What are the coordinates of the vertex of $y = -2(x - 4)^2 + 2$? (___ , ___)

68. The graph of the relation $x = -5(y + 2)^2 + 6$ is a parabola. Which way does this parabola open? (up, down, left or right).

69. What value of b makes the expression $x^2 + 8x + b$ a perfect square?

70. When a quadratic function can be written as a perfect square on the graph it means that _____.

71. what are the zeros of the quadratic relation $y = 10x^2 - 20x$

72. Find the roots (zeros) of the equation $20(6 + 5x)(12 - x) = 0$.

73. The quadratic equation is used to find the _____ of the quadratic function. In case this equation has _____ it means the quadratic function is completely _____ or _____ the x axis and the value of $b^2 - 4ac$ _____. In case $b^2 - 4ac$ is _____ the quadratic function will have _____ and lastly if $b^2 - 4ac$ is _____ the quadratic function will have _____.

If $b^2 - 4ac$ __ 0 there are _____ Example: _____

If $b^2 - 4ac$ __ 0 there are _____ Example: _____

If $b^2 - 4ac$ __ 0 there are _____ Example: _____

74. What values of b make the relation $y = 6x^2 + bx + 5$ have no zeros?

75. Under what conditions will the parabola with equation $y = a(x - h)^2 + k$ have two x–intercepts?

76. How many zeros does the quadratic relation $y = -1.7(x + 13.2)^2 - 3.1$ have?

77. A parabola has its vertex in the third quadrant and opens down. A possible value for $b^2 - 4ac$ can be _____

78. Write the equation, in vertex form, of a parabola that has its vertex in the second quadrant, contains two zeros, and is narrower than $y = x^2$

79. Write the equation, in vertex form, of a parabola that has its vertex in the third quadrant, contains two zeros, and is wider than $y = x^2$

80. Give the relation $y = -4(x - 2)^2 + 7$, state its axis of symmetry:

81. Determine the value of the vertex of the relation $y = -(x - 3)(x + 1)$. Is the vertex a maximum or a minimum? Write down the axis of symmetry.

82. The parabola $y = -4(x - 2)^2 + 7$ is reflected about the x–axis. Write the equation of the image parabola.

83. The discriminant is: $\Delta =$ _____.
84. If Δ ____, then, _____
85. If Δ ____, then, _____
86. If Δ ____, then, _____
87. Write down 2 quadratic equations with 0 solutions:

88. Write down 2 quadratic equations with 1 solution:

89. Write down 2 quadratic equations with 2 solutions:

Use the discriminant to determine the <u>number of solutions</u> to the following equations

90. $x^2 - 4x + 1 = 3$

98. $x^2 - 7x - 5 = 3$

91. $2x^2 - 4x + 1 = -3$

99. $2x^2 + 4x + 2 = 0$

92. $3x^2 - 4x + 1 = -13$

100. $x^2 - 2x + 4 = 5$

93. $x^2 + 6x + 11 = 2$

101. $-3x^2 + 3x - 1 = 3$

94. $-2x^2 + 6x + 2 = -10$

102. $-2x^2 + 7x - 3 = 2$

95. $-3x^2 - 3x - 5 = 3$

103. $-x^2 + 12x + 4 = -1$

96. $3x^2 - 3x - 3 = -3$

104. $x^2 + x - 2 = -1$

97. $x^2 - 3x - 4 = -1$

105. $-8x^2 + 3x + 2 = -1$

106. Given the equation $x^2 + 3bx + 4 = 0$. Determine the number of solutions as a function of b.

107. Given the equation $ax^2 + ax + a = 0$. Determine the number of solutions as a function of a.

108. Given the equation $2x^2 + bx + 3 = 0$. Find the value of b for which the following equation has 1 solution. Find that solution.

109. Given the equation $ax^2 + bx + 1 = 0$. Find the value of b, in terms of a, for which the following equation has 1 solution. Find that solution.

QUADRATIC INEQUALITIES

Graph to solve the following inequalities:

1. $x^2 > 0$

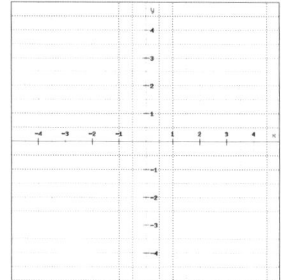

2. $x^2 \geq 0$

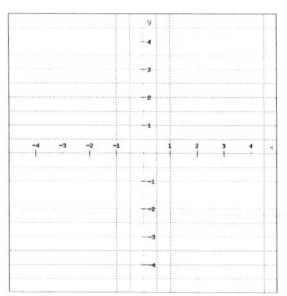

3. $x^2 < 0$

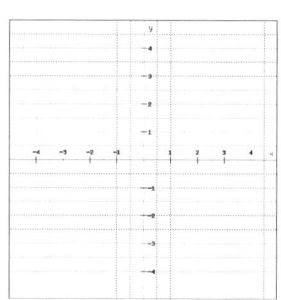

4. $x^2 \leq 0$

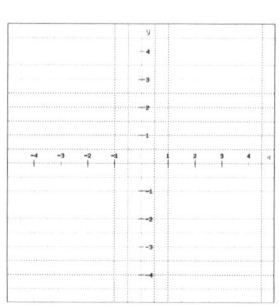

5. $x^2 - 1 > 0$

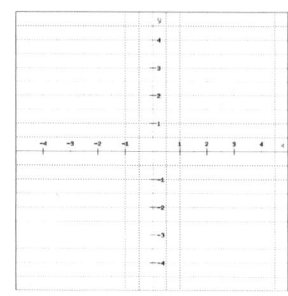

6. $x^2 - 1 \geq 0$

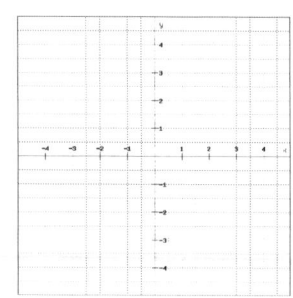

7. $x^2 - 1 < 0$

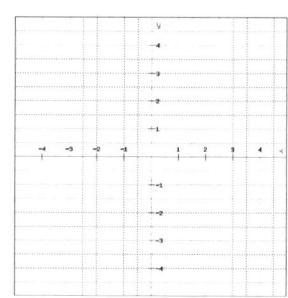

8. $x^2 - 1 \leq 0$

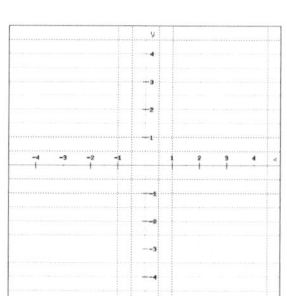

9. $x^2 + 2 > 0$

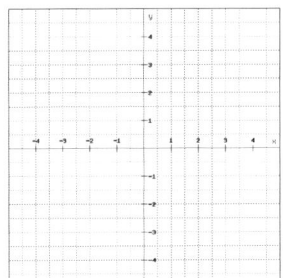

13. $6x^2 - 3x > 0$

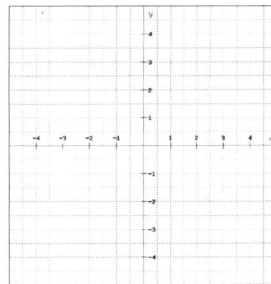

10. $x^2 + 2 \geq 0$

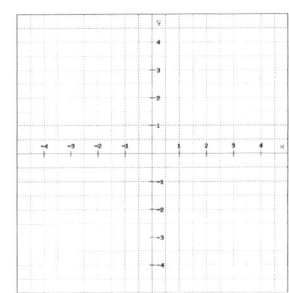

14. $x^2 + 4x \geq 0$

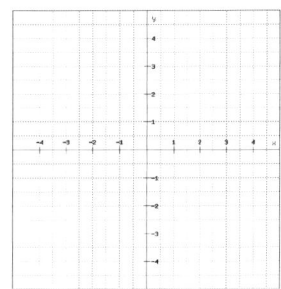

11. $x^2 + 2x + 1 \leq 0$

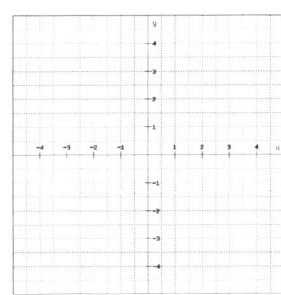

15. $x^2 - 5x < 0$

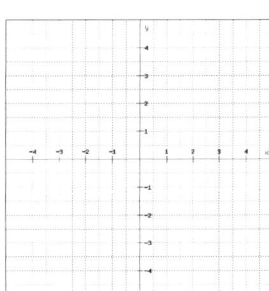

12. $x^2 + 2 \leq 0$

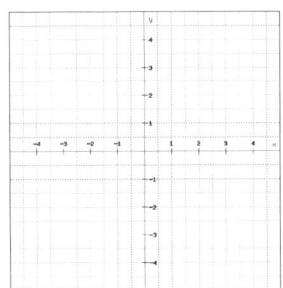

16. $2x^2 + 6x \leq 0$

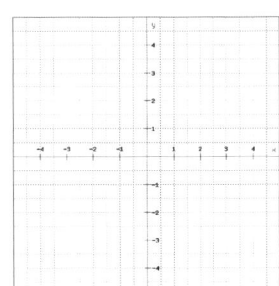

17. $x^2 - 4x + 4 > 0$

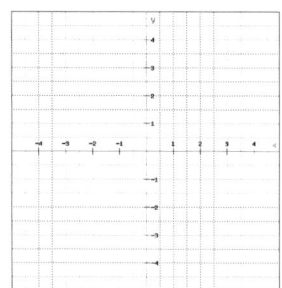

18. $-x^2 + x + 2 > 0$

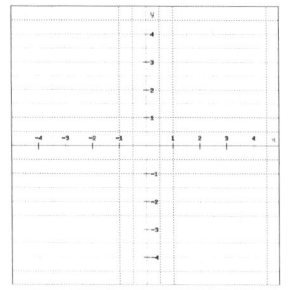

19. $-x^2 - 6x - 9 < 0$

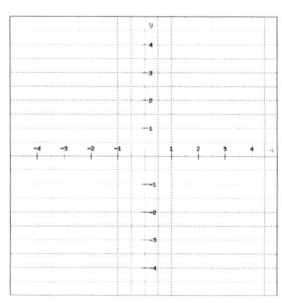

20. $-3x^2 + 7 \leq 0$

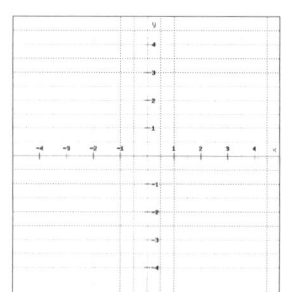

21. $x^2 - 8x + 12 > 0$

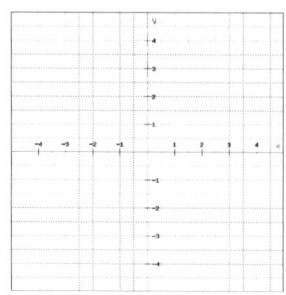

22. $-x^2 + 3x + 3 \leq 0$

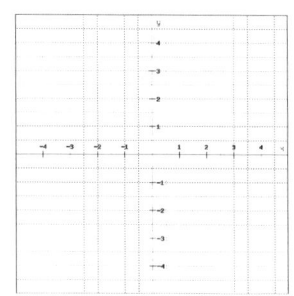

23. $-x^2 - 9x > 0$

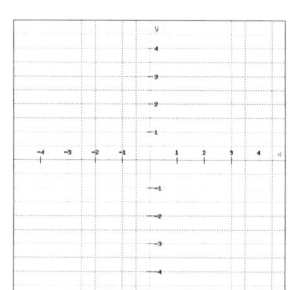

24. $-2x^2 - 3x + 10 > 0$

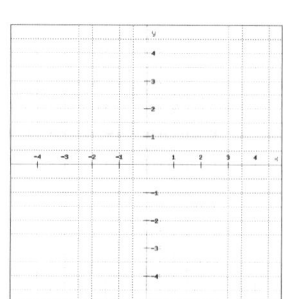

25. $x^2 + 1 > 0$

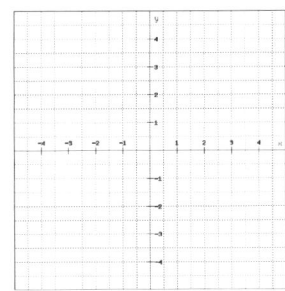

26. $-x^2 + 1 < 0$

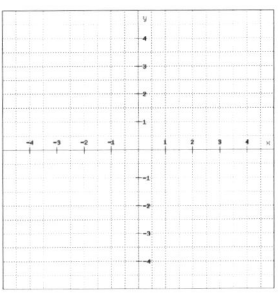

27. $-x^2 - 1 > 0$

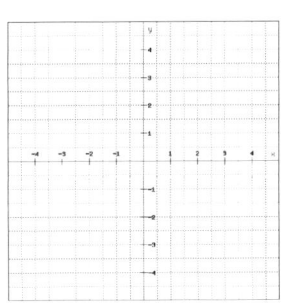

28. $-x^2 + 1 \leq 0$

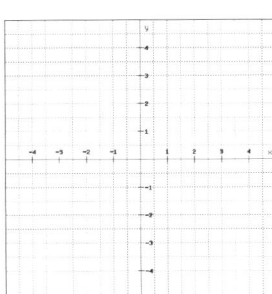

29. $-x^2 + 3 \geq 0$

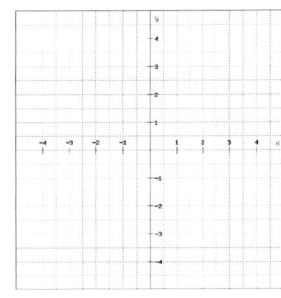

30. $-x^2 + 3 \leq 0$

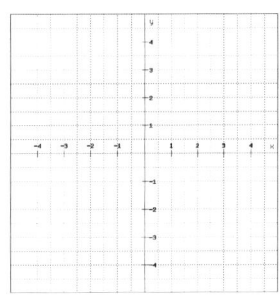

31. $x^2 - 3x > 0$

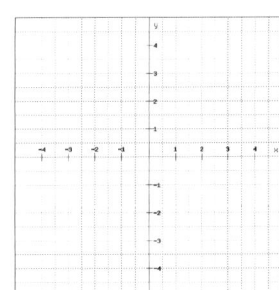

32. $x^2 - 3x < 0$

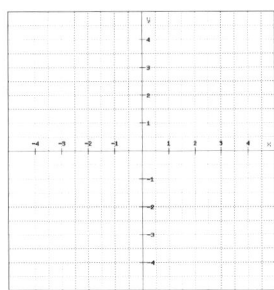

33. $2x^2 + 4 > 0$

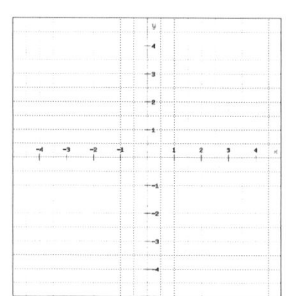

34. $2x^2 + 4 < 0$

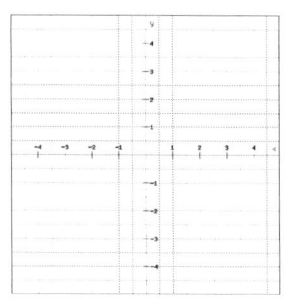

35. $-x^2 - 3x + 2 > 0$

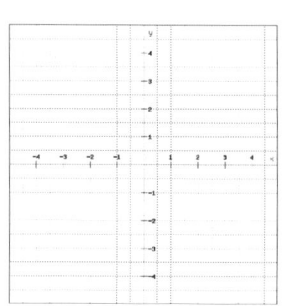

36. $x^2 - 3x + 2 < 0$

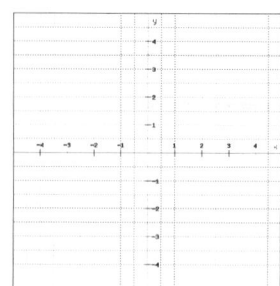

37. $x^2 + 2x - 3 > 0$

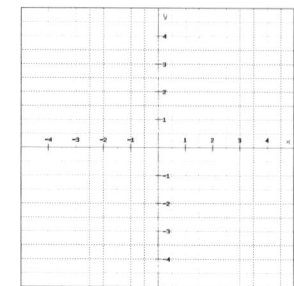

38. $-x^2 + 2x - 3 < 0$

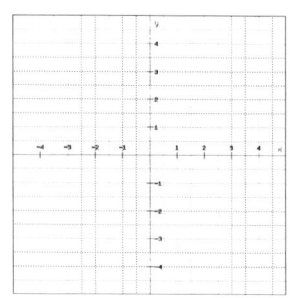

39. $-2x^2 + 8x - 10 > 0$

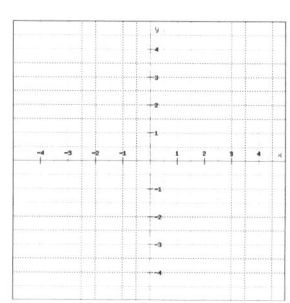

40. $-2x^2 + 8x - 10 < 0$

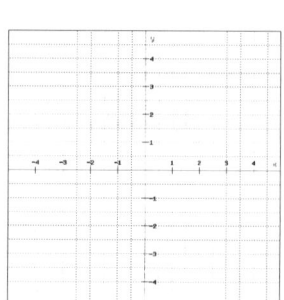

Application:

1. The height of a ball kicked upwards is given by $h(t) = 40t - 16t^2$ meters, where t is measured in seconds.

    a. Sketch the corresponding function, label the axes.

    b. Calculate $h(1)$ and give a practical interpretation to your answer.

    c. Calculate the zeros of $h(t)$ and explain the meaning in the context of the problem.

    d. Solve the equation $h(t) = 10$ and explain the meaning of the solutions in the context of the problem.

    e. Obtain the maximum height of the ball and the instant in which it reaches it.

2. The width of a rectangle is three times is length, its area is 243 m². Find its perimeter.

3. Find 2 consecutive even numbers that when their sum is squared 100 is obtained.

4. The efficiency of an engine as a function of the concentration of a certain chemical component is given by $f(x) = -0.5x^2 + x$, $0 \leq x \leq 2$.

   a. Sketch the function in its domain.

   b. Find the concentration of the chemical for which the efficiency is maximized. What is the efficiency in this case?

5. A hundred meters of fencing is available to enclose a rectangular field along side of a River, What dimensions will produce the maximum area that can be enclosed?

CHAPTER 4 – TRIGONOMETRIC FUNCTIONS

4.1. – DEGREES AND RADIANS

Since we were "young" angles were measured in degrees, we were told that the size of a circular angle is 360°. In reality the number 360° is meaningless; it is merely used because of historical reasons. If we go back to the definition of an angle in a circle it is the following:

$$X = -$$

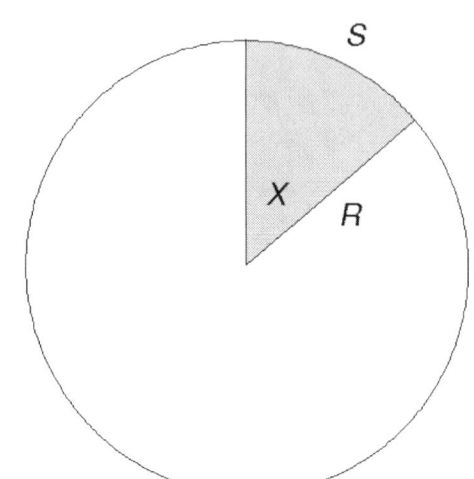

In case that S is the entire circle we obtain:

$$X = \frac{S}{R} = \frac{Length}{of-Circle} = 6.2831... = 2\pi$$

So what we see is that the angle of the entire circle is approximately 6.28 or exactly 2π. That means:

$$2\pi_{rad} = \underline{\qquad}°$$

$$1° = \frac{2\pi}{360} rad \approx 0.017_{rad}$$

$$1_{rad} = \left(\underline{\qquad}\right)° \approx 57.3°$$

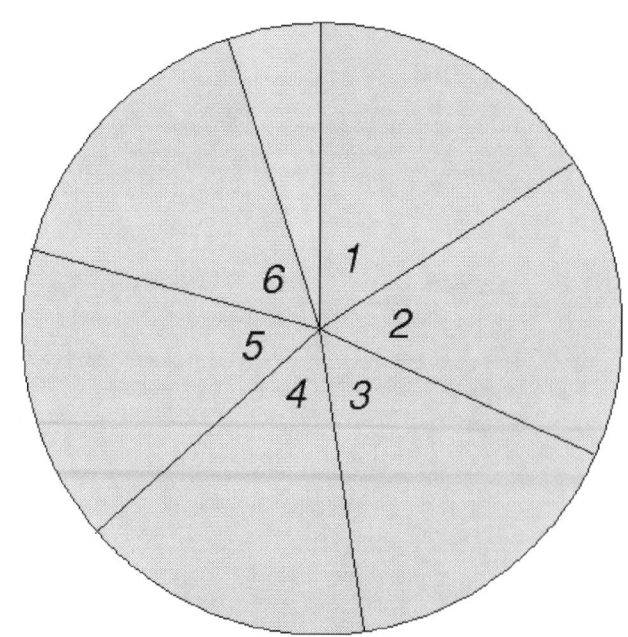

In the image we can observe that in a circle 6 radians are equivalent to a bit less than 360°, the exact number is 2π, approximately 6.28 radians.

Exercises:

1. Complete the table:

Degrees	360°	−180°	90°	45°	22.5°
Radians					

2. Complete the table:

Degrees	0°	30°	60°	−120°	150°
Radians					

3. Complete the table:

Degrees	315°	−225°	135°	330°	420°
Radians					

4. Complete the table:

Degrees	54°	18°	−36°	15°	75°
Radians					

5. Complete the table:

Degrees	10°	−9°	12°	3°	7.5°
Radians					

6. Complete the table:

Degrees	5°	1°	−10°	660°	540°
Radians					

7. Complete the table:

Degrees					
Radians	π	$\dfrac{\pi}{10}$	$-\dfrac{5\pi}{3}$	$\dfrac{12\pi}{7}$	$\dfrac{22\pi}{5}$

8. Complete the table:

Degrees					
Radians	1	2.4	3.5	−2	−3.1

9. Given the following circles, find θ or L in each one of the cases (in degrees and radians):

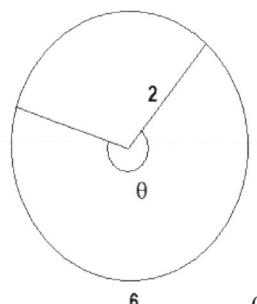

θ = _____ rad = _____ °

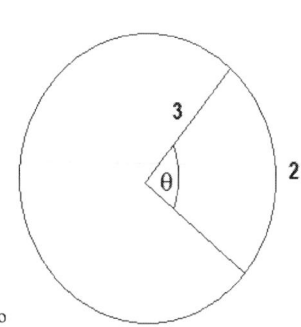

θ = _____ rad = _____ °

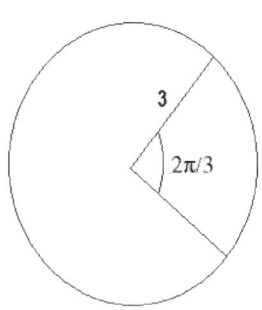

L = _____

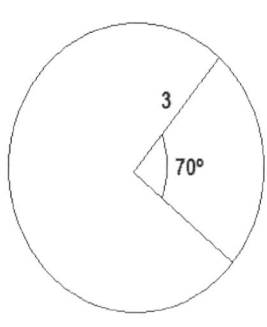

L = _____

10. The length of the perimeter of a circle with radius r is _____. The length of the arc that corresponds an angle x° is _____. In case the angle x is measured in radians it would be _____.

11. The area of a circle with radius r is _____. The area of the sector that corresponds an angle x° is _____. In case the angle x is measured in radians it would be _____.

12. Given the circle with r = 2cm :

    a. Show the arc corresponding an angle of 45°.
    b. Calculate its length.
    c. Shade Show the corresponding sector area.
    d. Calculate it.

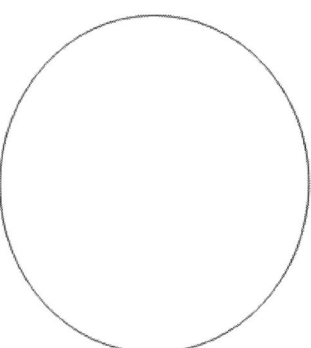

13. Given the circle with r = 3.2m:

    a. Show Shade the arc corresponding an angle of 20°.
    b. Calculate its length.
    c. Shade the corresponding sector area.
    d. Calculate it.

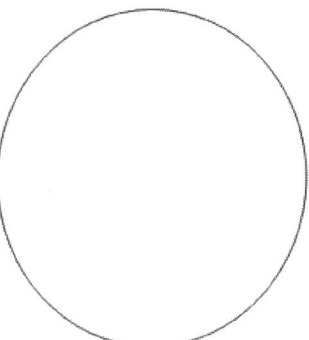

14. Given the circle with r = 3.2m:

    a. Show Shade the arc corresponding an angle of $\frac{\pi}{10} rad$.
    b. Calculate its length.
    c. Shade the corresponding sector area.
    d. Calculate it.

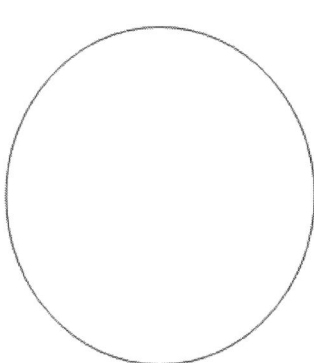

15. Given the circle with r = 3.2m:

    a. Show Shade the arc corresponding an angle of 1 radian.
    b. Calculate its length.
    c. Shade the corresponding sector area.
    d. Calculate it.

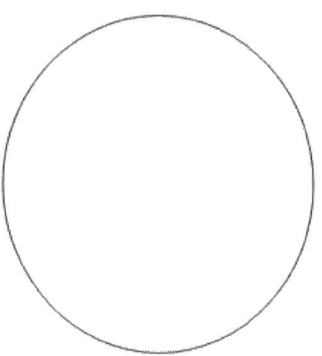

16. Given the following concentric circles with radii 3 cm and 5 cm correspondingly. Calculate the shaded area.

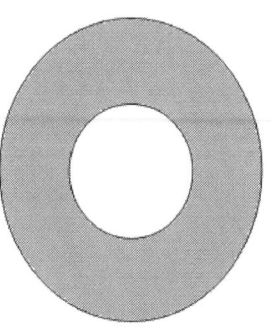

17. Given the following concentric circles with radii 10m and 14m correspondingly. Calculate the shaded area.

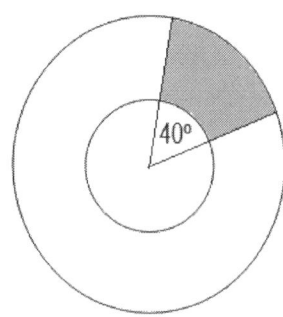

4.2. – TRIGONOMETRIC FUNCTIONS

Definition: The trigonometric functions are defined using the so called "unit circle" which is simply a circle with radius ____ :

In consequence:

$$(Sin(x))^2 + (Cos(x))^2 = \underline{}$$

This is called the Pythagorean identity

Use your calculator to find:

$$(Sin(10°))^2 + (Cos(10°))^2 = \underline{}$$

$$(Sin(1_{rad}))^2 + (Cos(1_{rad}))^2 = \underline{}$$

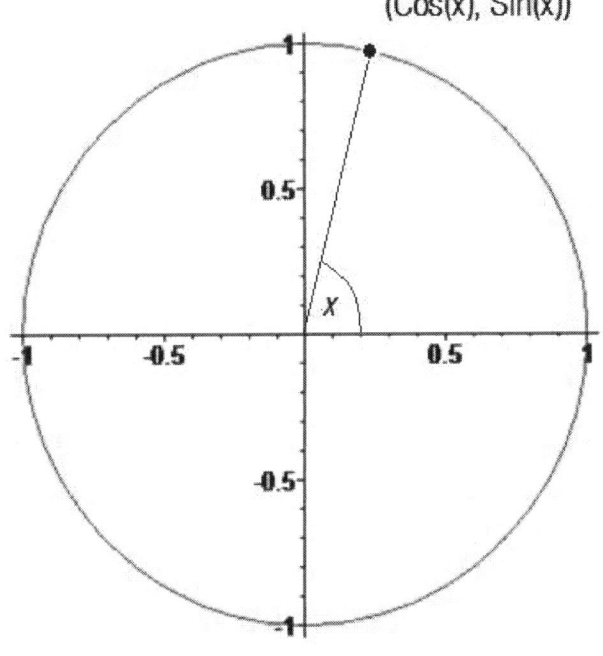

Definition of Sin(x):

1st Quadrant:

3rd Quadrant:

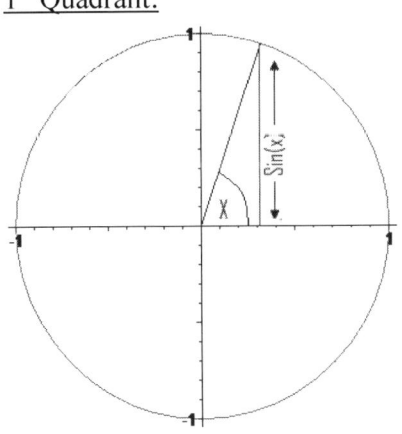
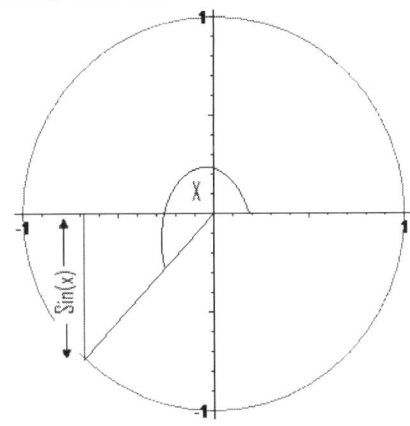

As can be seen in the _____ and _____ quadrants the Sin(x) function

points upwards, and therefore it is _____, while in the _____ and

_____ quadrants it points downwards, and therefore it is _____.

247

Definition of Cos(x):

2nd Quadrant: 4th Quadrant:

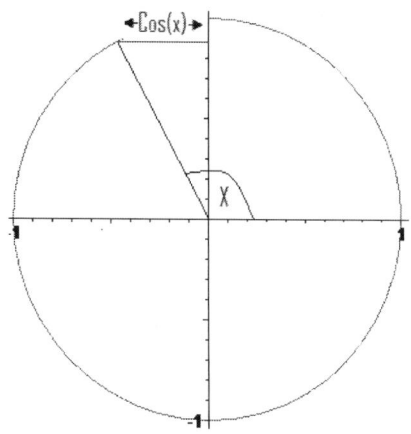

As can be seen in the _____ and _____ quadrants the Sin(x) function points upwards, and therefore it is _____, while in the _____ and _____ quadrants it points downwards, and therefore it is _____.

Exercises:

In each one of the cases sketch the unit circle and the corresponding angle and then find the corresponding value:

1. $\sin(0°) =$

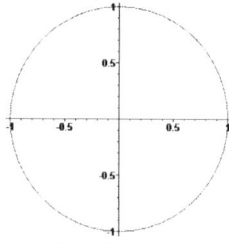

2. $\cos(0_{rad}) =$

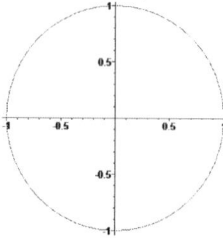

3. $\sin(0_{rad}) =$

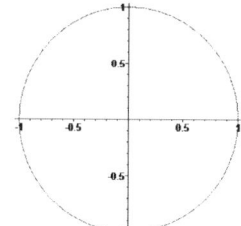

4. $\cos(0°) =$

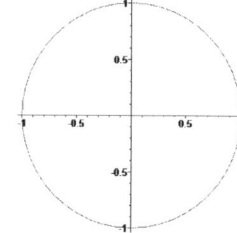

5. Sin(90º) =

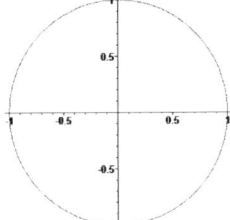

6. Cos(Π$_{rad}$) =

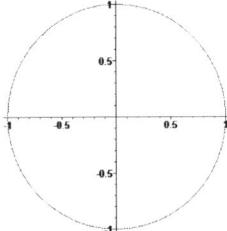

7. Sin(3Π/4 $_{rad}$) =

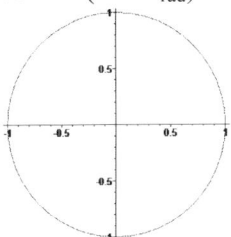

8. Cos(225º) =

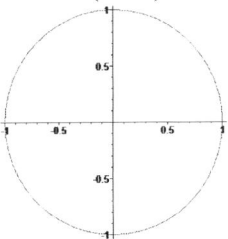

9. Sin(225º) =

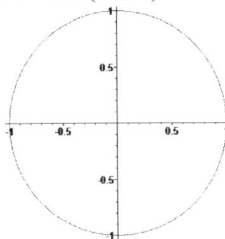

10. Cos(4Π/3 $_{rad}$) =

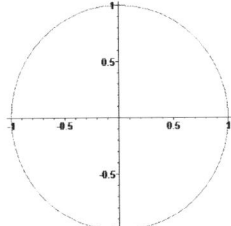

11. Sin(4Π/3 $_{rad}$) =

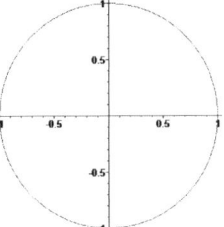

12. Cos(210º) =

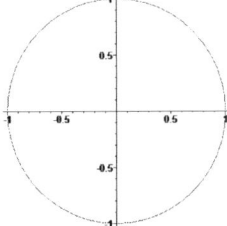

13. Sin(210º) =

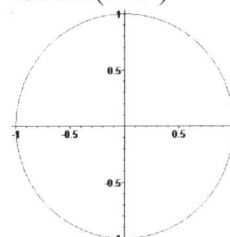

14. Sin(3Π/4 $_{rad}$) =

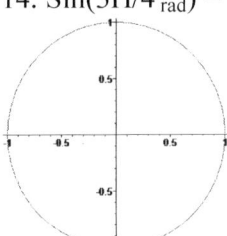

15. Cos(225º) =

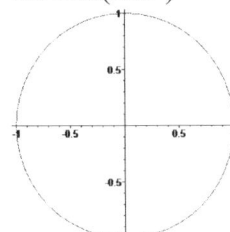

16. Sin(–225º) =

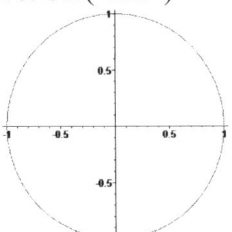

17. Cos(4Π/3 rad) =

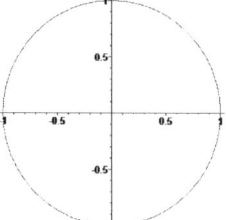

18. Sin(4Π/3 rad) =

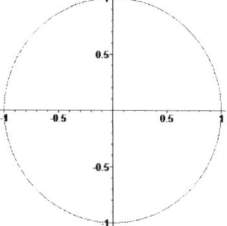

19. Cos(210º) =

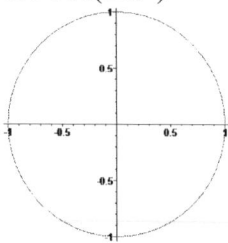

20. Sin(–210º) =

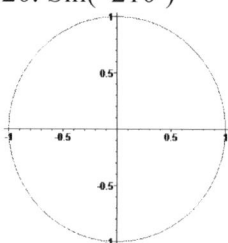

21. Sin(–Π rad) =

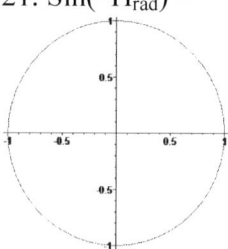

22. Cos(90º) =

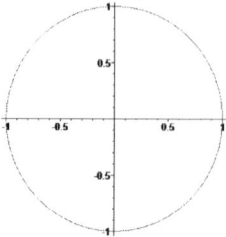

23. Sin(270º) =

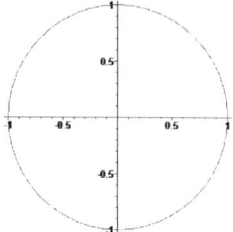

24. Cos(Π/2 rad) =

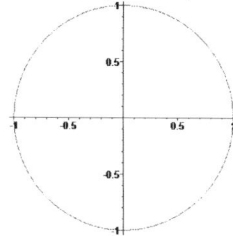

25. Sin(3Π/2 rad) =

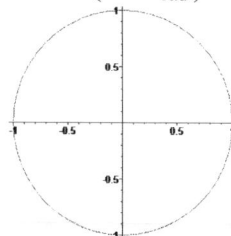

26. Cos(270º) =

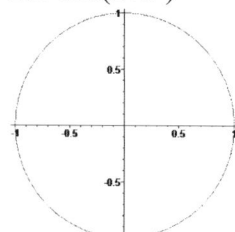

27. Sin(360º) =

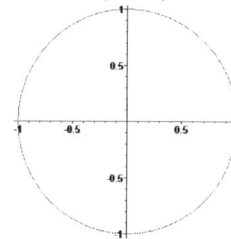

28. Cos(–Π/2 rad) =

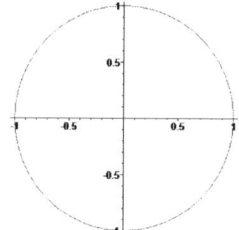

29. Sin(2Π$_{rad}$) =

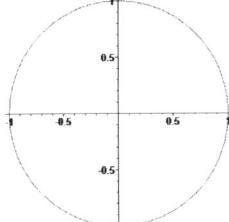

30. Cos(180°) =

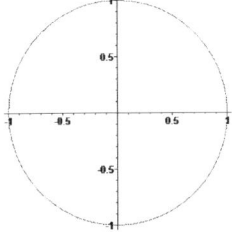

31. Sin(180°) =

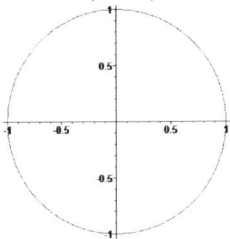

32. Cos(Π/3 $_{rad}$) =

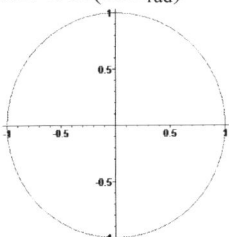

33. Sin(Π/4$_{rad}$) =

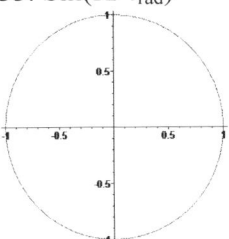

34. Cos(−45°) =

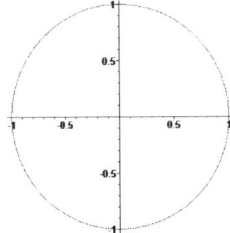

35. Sin(3Π/2 $_{rad}$) =

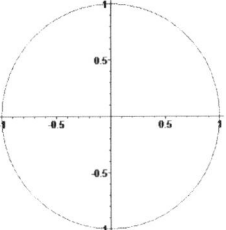

36. Cos(−2Π/3 $_{rad}$) =

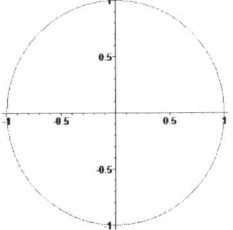

37. Sin(2Π/3 $_{rad}$) =

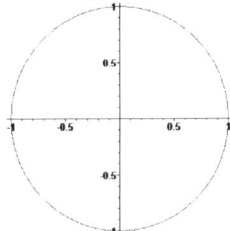

38. Cos(3Π/4 $_{rad}$) =

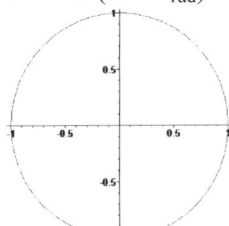

39. Cos(300°) =

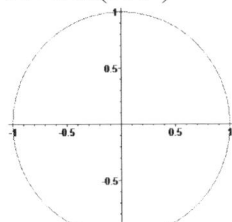

40. Sin(300°) =

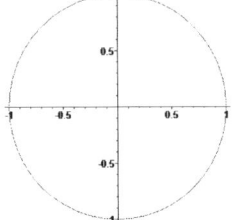

41. Cos(2Π rad) =

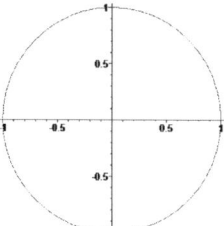

42. Sin(2Π rad) =

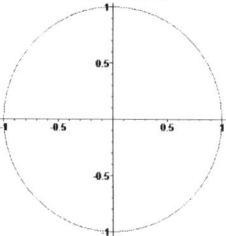

43. Sin(330º) =

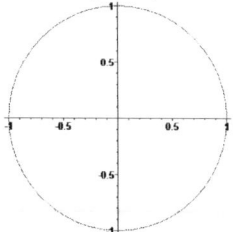

44. Cos(390º) =

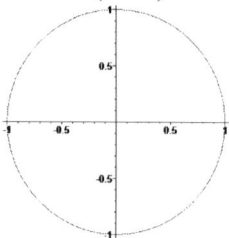

45. Cos(135º) =

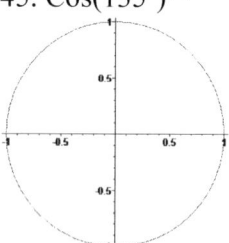

46. Sin(135º) =

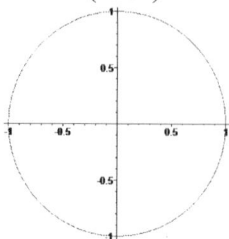

47. Sin(45º) =

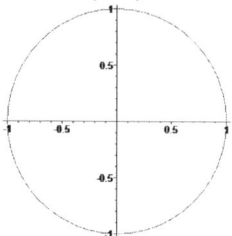

48. Cos(–3Π/2 rad) =

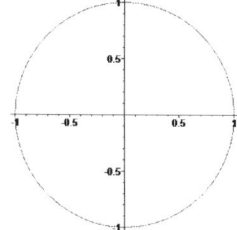

49. Cos(70º) =

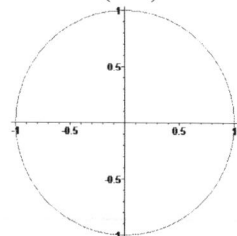

50. Cos(130º) =

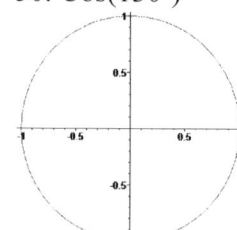

51. Cos(1º) =

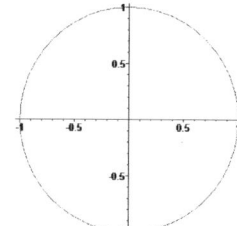

52. Cos(3 rad) =

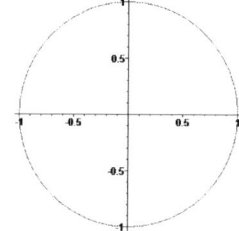

53. Sin(1_{rad}) =

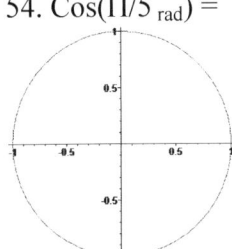

54. Cos($\Pi/5_{rad}$) =

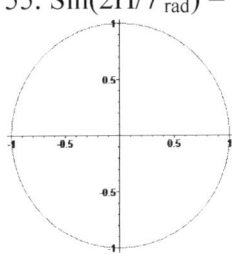

55. Sin($2\Pi/7_{rad}$) =

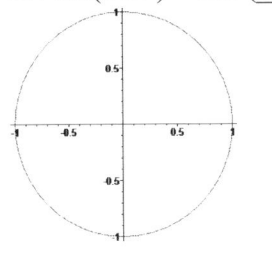

For each one of the following, fill in the blank with an angle between 0° and 360° different than the first one.

56. Sin(25°) = Sin (____)

57. Sin(145°) = Sin (____)

58. Sin(70°) = Sin (____)

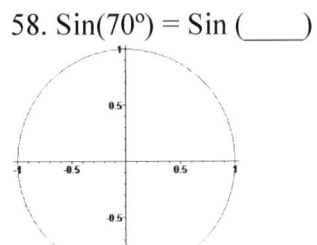

59. Sin(–20°) = Sin (____)

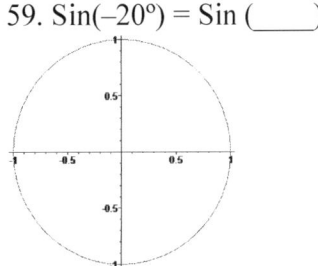

60. Sin(–30°) = Sin (____)

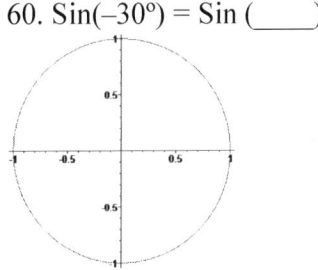

61. Sin(225°) = Sin (____)

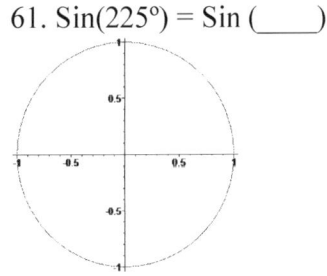

62. Sin(250°) = Sin (____)

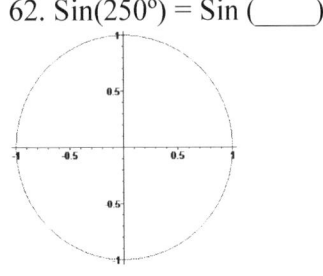

63. Cos(250°) = Cos (____)

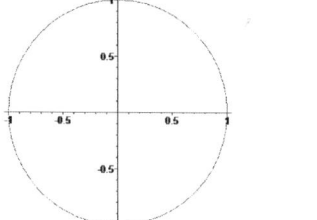

64. Cos(350°) = Cos (____)

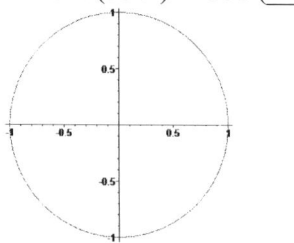

65. Cos(450°) = Cos (____)

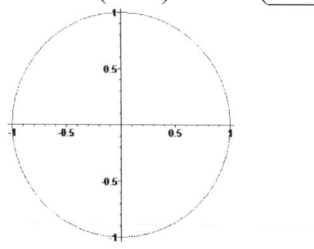

66. Cos(–250°) = Cos (____)

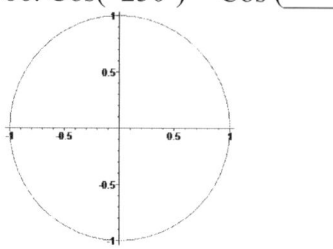

67. Cos(–50°) = Cos (____)

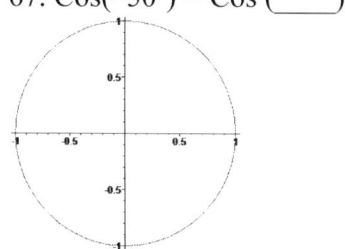

68. Cos(–73°) = Cos (____)

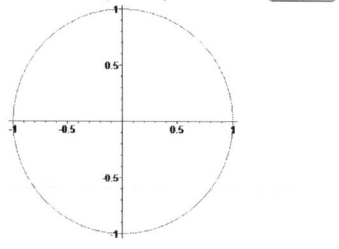

Definitions of Tan (x), Cot(x), Sec(x) Cosec(x)

$$Tan(x) = \left(\frac{\rule{1cm}{0.4pt}}{\rule{1cm}{0.4pt}}\right), Cos(x) \neq 0 \qquad Cot(x) = \left(\frac{\rule{1cm}{0.4pt}}{\rule{1cm}{0.4pt}}\right), Sin(x) \neq 0$$

$$Sec(x) = \left(\frac{1}{\rule{1cm}{0.4pt}}\right), Cos(x) \neq 0 \qquad Csc(x) = \left(\frac{1}{\rule{1cm}{0.4pt}}\right), Sin(x) \neq 0$$

In Consequence:

Tan(x) = tg(x) is positive in the _____ and _____ quadrants and negative in the _____ and _____ quadrants. Cotg(x) = Cot(x) = Cotan(x) is positive in the _____ and _____ quadrants and negative in the _____ and _____ quadrants.

69. Answer, in terms of a and b:

a. $\sin(\theta) =$ $\cos(\theta) =$

b. $\sin(\theta + 360°) =$

c. $\sin(\theta + 180°) =$

d. $\sin(180° - \theta) =$

e. $\cos(180° - \theta) =$

f. $\sin(360° - \theta) =$

g. $\cos(360° - \theta) =$

h. $\sin(90° - \theta) =$

i. $\cos(90° - \theta) =$

j. $\tan(\theta) =$

k. $\cot an(\theta) =$

l. $\sec(\theta) =$

m. $\csc(\theta) =$

n. $\tan(\theta + 180°) =$

o. $\tan(\theta + 90°) =$

p. $\cos(270° - \theta) =$

q. $\sin(270° + \theta)$

r. $\sec(\theta + 180°)$

s. $\csc(270° + \theta)$

t. $\cot(\theta) =$

u. $\cot(\theta - 180°) =$

v. $\sec(\theta + 720°) =$

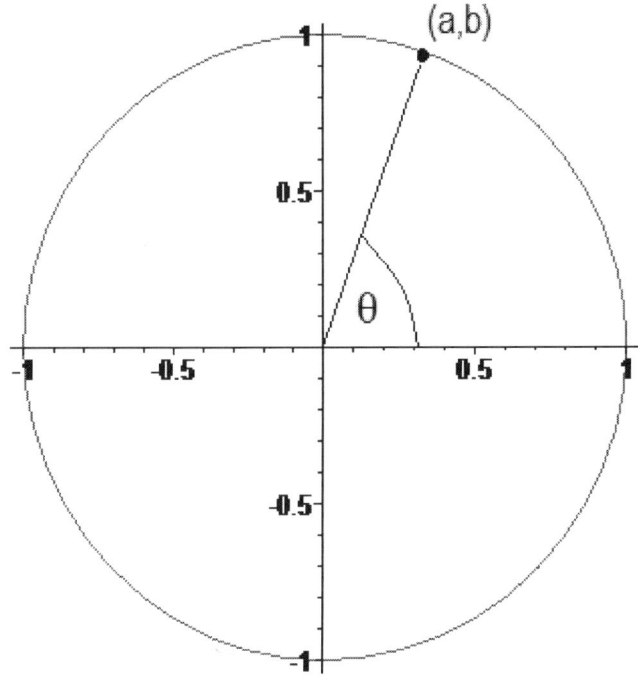

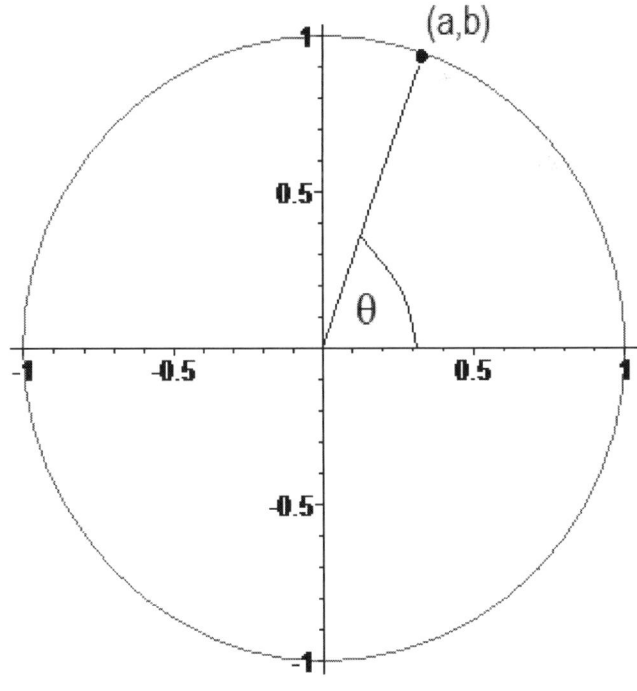

Complete the following table:

Angle in degrees	Angle in Radians	Sin(x)	Cos(x)	Tan(x)	Cot(x)	Sec(x)	Csc(x)
0	0						
30°							
45°							
60°							
90°							
120°							
135°							
150°							
180°							
360°							
390°							

Exercises:

1. Given that $\sin(x) = \dfrac{2}{7}$ and $0 < x < \dfrac{\pi}{2}$, x is in the _____ quadrant. find:

    a. $\cos(x) =$

    b. $\tan(x) =$

    c. $\cot(x) =$

    d. $\csc(x) =$

    e. $\sin(2x) =$

    f. $\cos(2x) =$

    g. $\sin(3x) =$

    h. $\cos(3x) =$

    i. $\sin(\pi - x) =$

    j. $\cos(\pi - x) =$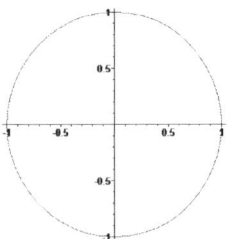

    k. $\sin(2\pi - x) =$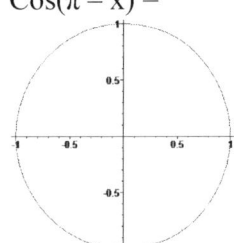

    l. $\cos(2\pi - x) =$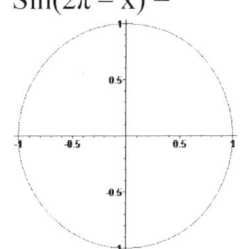

    m. $\sin(x + \dfrac{\pi}{2}) =$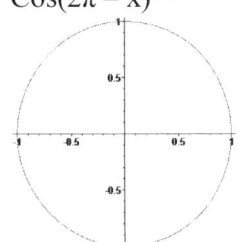

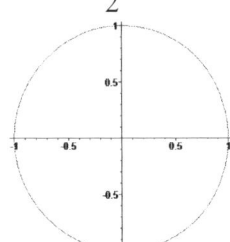

257

2. Given that $\cos(x) = -\dfrac{1}{6}$ and $\pi < x < \dfrac{3\pi}{2}$, x is in the _____ quadrant. Find:

a. $\sin(x) =$

b. $\tan(x) =$

c. $\cot(x) =$

d. $\csc(x) =$

e. $\sin(2x) =$

f. $\cos(2x) =$

g. $\sin(4x) =$

h. $\cos(4x) =$

i. $\sin(\pi - x) =$

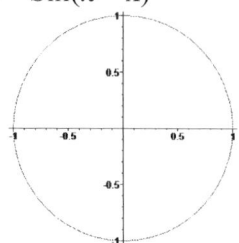

j. $\cos(\pi - x) =$

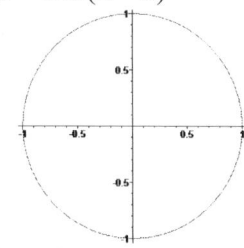

k. $\sin(2\pi - x) =$

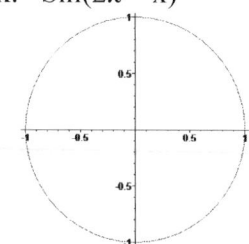

l. $\cos(2\pi - x) =$

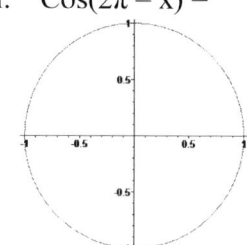

m. $\cos(x + \dfrac{\pi}{2}) =$

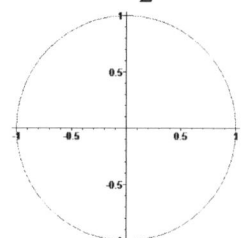

258

3. Given that Tan(x) = 3 and $\pi < x < 2\pi$, x is in the _____ quadrant. Find:

   a. Cos(x) =

   b. Tan(x) =

   c. Cot(x) =

   d. Csc(x) =

   e. Tan(2x) =

   f. Sin(3x) =

   g. Cos(3x) =

4. Given that $\sin(x) = -\dfrac{1}{3}$ and $\pi < x < \dfrac{3}{2}\pi$, x is in the _____ quadrant. Find:

a. $\cos(x) =$

b. $\tan(x) =$

c. $\cot(x) =$

d. $\csc(x) =$

e. $\sin(2x) =$

f. $\cos(2x) =$

g. $\sin(3x) =$

h. $\cos(3x) =$

i. $\sin(\pi - x) =$

j. $\cos(\pi - x) =$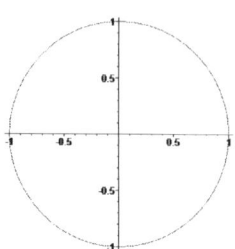

k. $\sin(2\pi - x) =$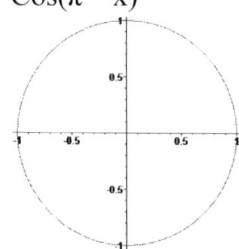

l. $\cos(2\pi - x) =$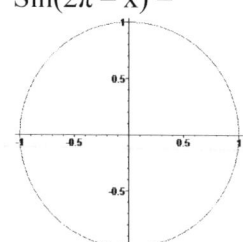

m. $\sin(x + \dfrac{\pi}{2}) =$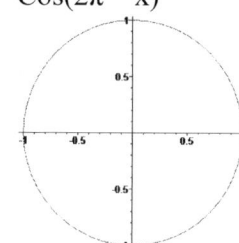

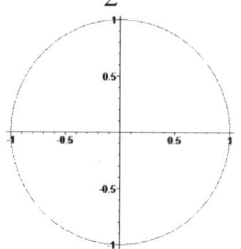

5. Given that $\cos(x) = \dfrac{1}{5}$ and $0 < x < \pi$, x is in the _____ quadrant. Find:

   a. $\sin(x) =$

   b. $\tan(x) =$

   c. $\cot(x) =$

   d. $\csc(x) =$

   e. $\sin(2x) =$

   f. $\cos(2x) =$

   g. $\sin(4x) =$

   h. $\cos(4x) =$

   i. $\sin(\pi - x) =$
   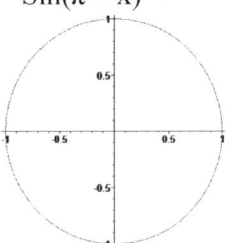

   j. $\cos(\pi - x) =$
   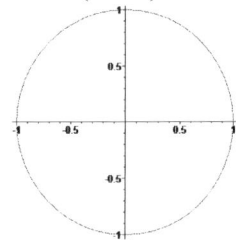

   k. $\sin(2\pi - x) =$
   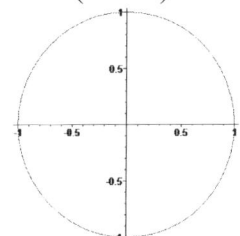

   l. $\cos(2\pi - x) =$
   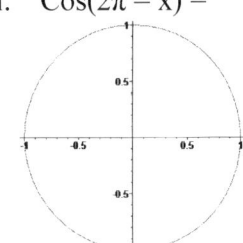

   m. $\cos(x + \dfrac{\pi}{2}) =$
   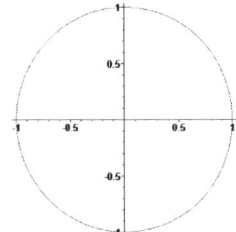

6. Given that Cotan(x) = –2 and π < x < 2π, so x is in the _____ quadrant. Find:

   a. Cos(x) =

   g. Sin(π – x) =

   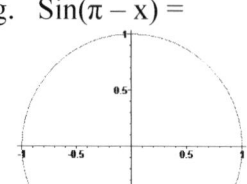

   b. Tan(x) =

   c. Csc(x) =

   h. Cos(π – x) =

   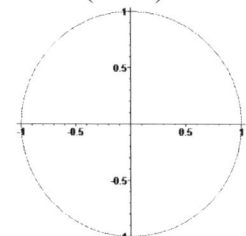

   d. Tan(2x) =

   i. Sin(2π – x) =

   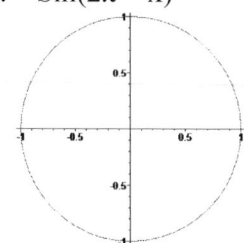

   e. Sin(3x) =

   j. Cos(2π – x) =

   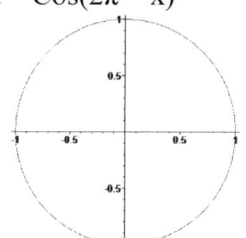

   f. Cos(3x) =

   k. $Sin(x + \dfrac{\pi}{2}) =$

   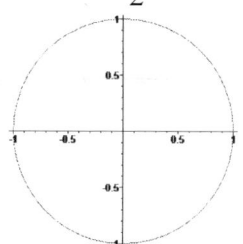

262

4.3. – TRIGONOMETRIC FUNCTIONS

1. Write next to each one of the functions if it's periodic or not. Determine the period of the periodic ones.

a.
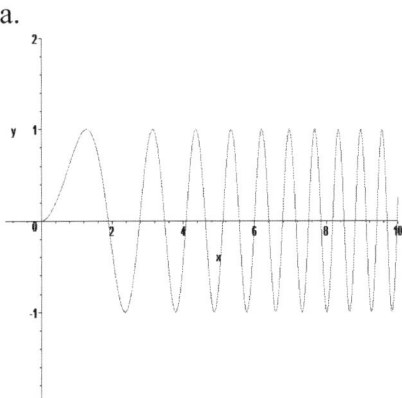

b.
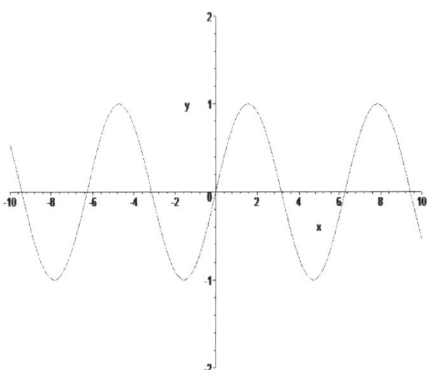

c.
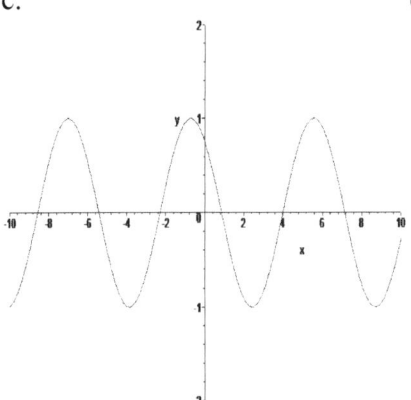

d.
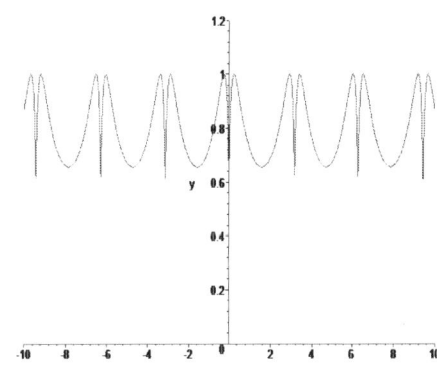

2. Given the function f(x) = Sin(x), g(x) = Cos(x), Complete the following table:

x°	0	15	30	45	60	75	90	105	120	135	150	165	180	195	210	225	240	255
Rad																		
f(x)																		
g(x)																		

- Sketch the points of the table on a graph.

- State the domain of the functions: : f(x):_____, g(x):_____

- State the y intercepts: f(x): (____, ____), g(x): (____, ____)

- State the x intercept(s): f(x): (____, ____), g(x): (____, ____)

- Write the corresponding limits and the equation of the vertical asymptote(s): ____

- Write the corresponding limits and the equation of the horizontal asymptote(s): ____

- Find the maximum point(s): f(x):_____, g(x):_____

- Find the minimum point(s): f(x):_____, g(x):_____

- State the range of the function: _____

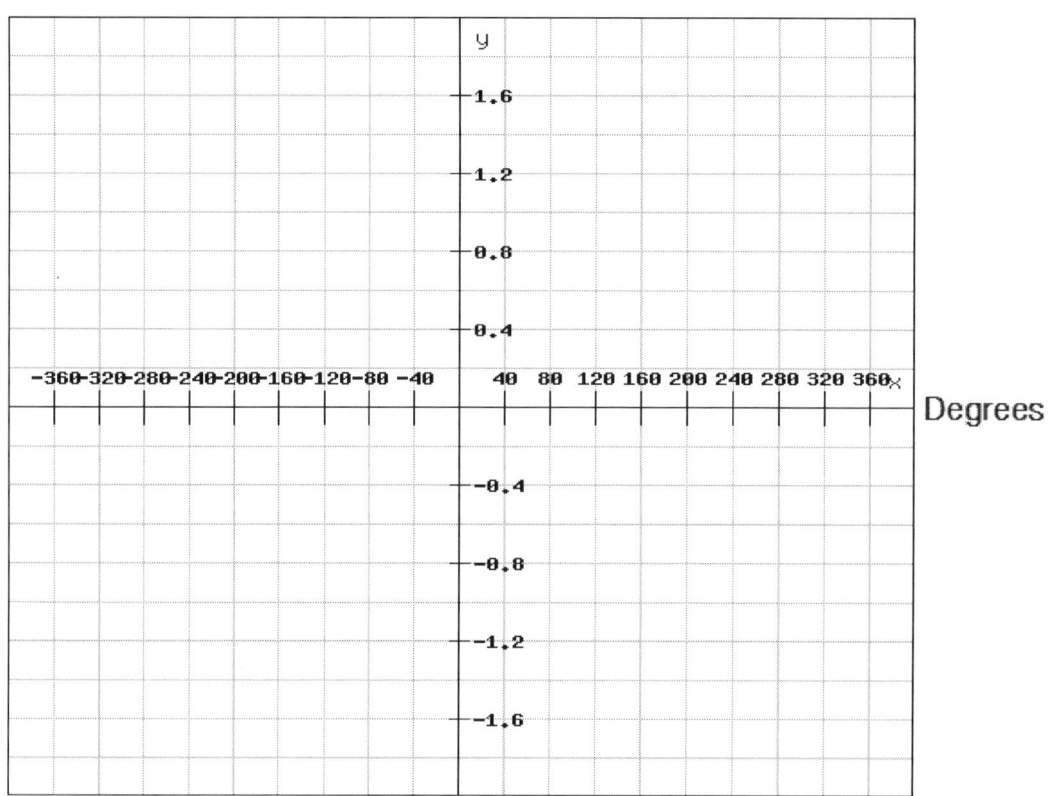

3. Given the function f(x) = Sin(x)

   a. Write in all forms the same function translated 2 positions up: _____

   b. Write in all forms the same function translated 3 positions left: _____

   c. Write in all forms the same function translated 3 positions left and 1 up.

   d. Write in all forms the same function translated 4 positions right and 1 up.

   e. Change the function so that the period would be 2.

   f. Change the function so that the period would be 3 and the amplitude 2.

   g. Change the function so that the period would be π and the amplitude 4.

   h. Change the function so that the period would be $\frac{\pi}{3}$ and the amplitude k.

   i. Change the function so that the period would be 6, the amplitude 3, then shift the function 2 positions right and 1 down.

   j. Change the function so that the period would be $\frac{\pi}{3}$, the amplitude 1.3, then shift the function 4 positions left and 2 down.

   k. Change the function so that the period would be $\frac{\pi}{5}$, the amplitude 4, then shift the function π positions left and 5 down.

4. Given the function f(x) = 3Sin(5(x – 2)) + 3

    a. Amplitude = _____

    b. Period = _____

    c. Horizontal Translation = _____ with respect to _____

    d. Vertical Translation = _____ with respect to _____ Midline: _____

    e. Range: _____

5. Given the function f(x) = –5Cos(3x – 2) – 3.4

    a. Amplitude = _____

    b. Period = _____

    c. Horizontal Translation = _____ with respect to _____

    d. Vertical Translation = _____ with respect to _____ Midline: _____

    e. Range: _____

6. Given the function f(x) = 2.4Sin(πx – $\frac{\pi}{2}$) – 3

    a. Amplitude = _____

    b. Period = _____

    c. Horizontal Translation = _____ with respect to _____

    d. Vertical Translation = _____ with respect to _____ Midline: _____

    e. Range: _____

7. Given the function f(x) = 4 – (2.4)Cos(2πx – $\frac{\pi}{3}$)

    a. Amplitude = _____

    b. Period = _____

    c. Horizontal Translation = _____ with respect to _____

    d. Vertical Translation = _____ with respect to _____ Midline: _____

    e. Range: _____

8. Given the function $f(x) = 1 + 4\sin(\frac{\pi}{3}x - 3)$

    a. Amplitude = _____

    b. Period = _____

    c. Horizontal Translation = _____ with respect to _____

    d. Vertical Translation = _____ with respect to _____ Midline: _____

    e. Range: _____

9. Given the function $f(x) = -\sin(\frac{\pi}{5}x - 1) + 1$

    a. Amplitude = _____

    b. Period = _____

    c. Horizontal Translation = _____ with respect to _____

    d. Vertical Translation = _____ with respect to _____ Midline: _____

    e. Range: _____

10. Given the function $f(x) = 4 - 3\cos(3x°)$

    a. Amplitude = _____

    b. Period = _____

    c. Horizontal Translation = _____ with respect to _____

    d. Vertical Translation = _____ with respect to _____ Midline: _____

    e. Range: _____

11. Given the function $f(x) = -\sin(\frac{x°}{10}) + 1$

    a. Amplitude = _____

    b. Period = _____

    c. Horizontal Translation = _____ with respect to _____

    d. Vertical Translation = _____ with respect to _____ Midline: _____

    e. Range: _____

12. Given the graph, complete:

   a. Amplitude = _____

   b. Period = _____

   c. Midline: _____

   d. f(x) =

   e. Range: _____

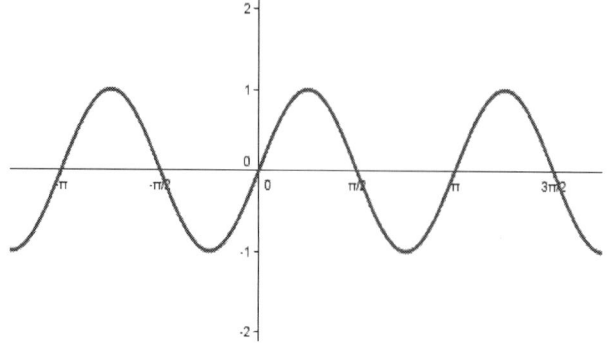

13. Given the graph, complete:

   a. Amplitude = _____

   b. Period = _____

   c. Midline: _____

   d. f(x) =

   e. Range: _____

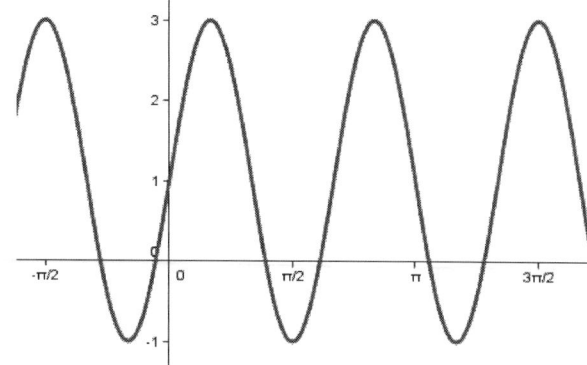

14. Given the graph, complete:

   a. Amplitude = _____

   b. Period = _____

   c. Midline: _____

   d. f(x) =

   e. Range: _____

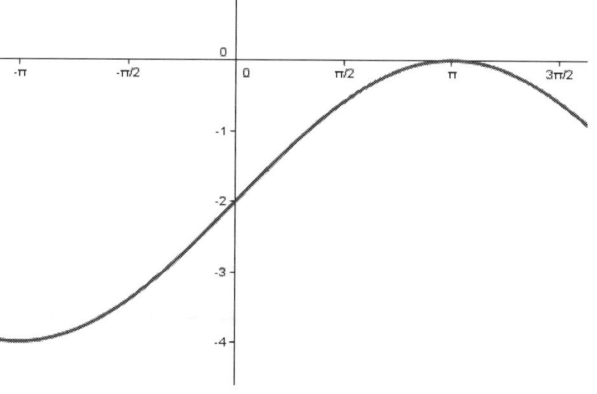

15. Given the graph, complete:

   a. Amplitude = _____

   b. Period = _____

   c. Midline: _____

   d. f(x) =

   e. Range: _____

16. Given the graph, complete:

   a. Amplitude = _____

   b. Period = _____

   c. Midline: _____

   d. f(x) =

   e. Range: _____

17. Given the graph, complete:

   a. Amplitude = _____

   b. Period = _____

   c. Midline: _____

   d. f(x) =

   e. Range: _____

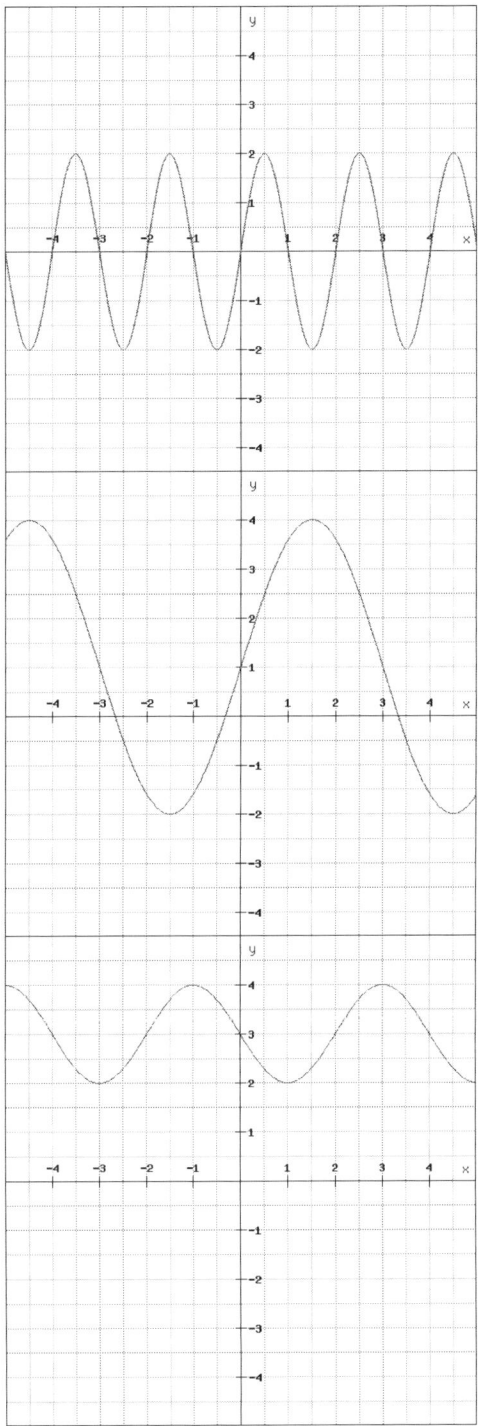

18. Given the graph, complete:

   a. Amplitude = _____

   b. Period = _____

   c. Midline: _____

   d. f(x) =

   e. Range: _____

19. Given the graph, complete:

   a. Amplitude = _____

   b. Period = _____

   c. Horizontal Translation = _____

   d. Midline: _____

   e. f(x) =

   f. Range: _____

20. Given the graph, complete:

   a. Amplitude = _____

   b. Period = _____

   c. Horizontal Translation = _____

   d. Midline: _____

   e. f(x) =

   f. Range: _____

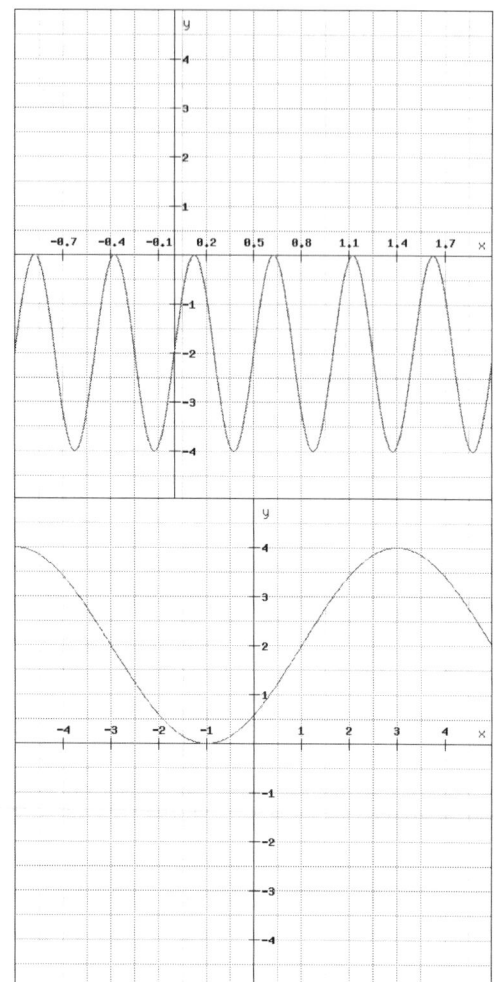

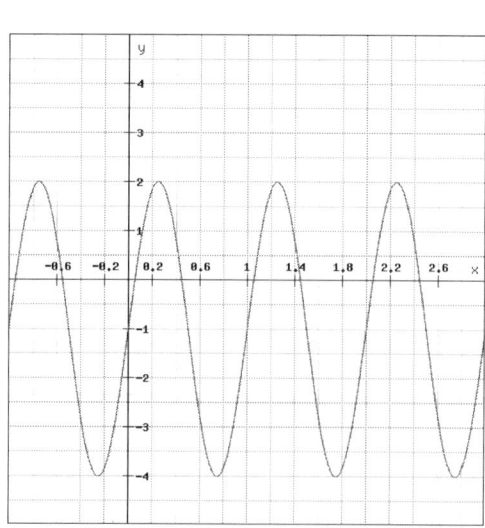

21. Given the graph, complete:

   a. Amplitude = _____

   b. Period = _____

   c. Horizontal Translation: _____

   d. Midline _____

   e. f(x) =

   f. Range: _____

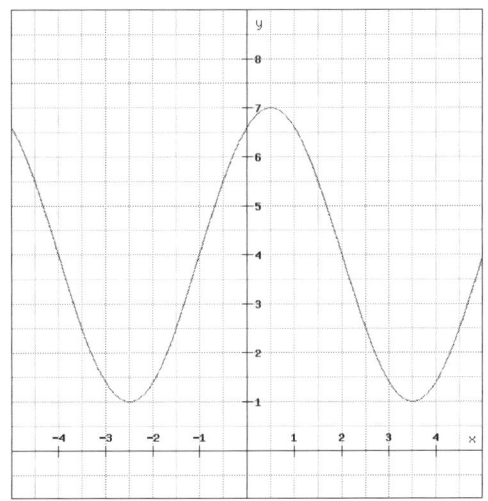

22. Given the graph, complete:

   a. Amplitude = _____

   b. Period = _____

   c. Horizontal Translation: _____

   d. Midline _____

   e. f(x) =

   f. Range: _____

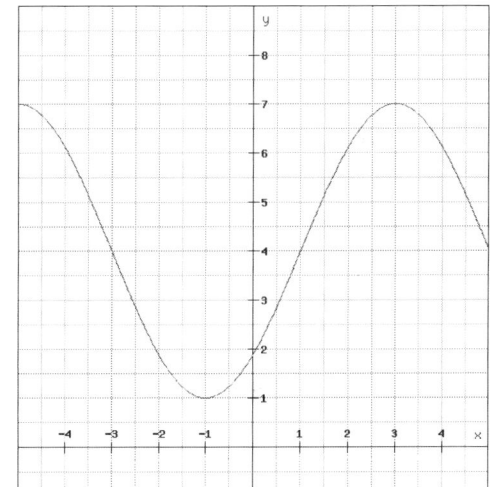

23. Given the graph, complete:

   a. Amplitude = _____

   b. Period = _____

   c. Horizontal Translation: _____

   d. Midline: _____

   e. f(x) =

   f. Range: _____

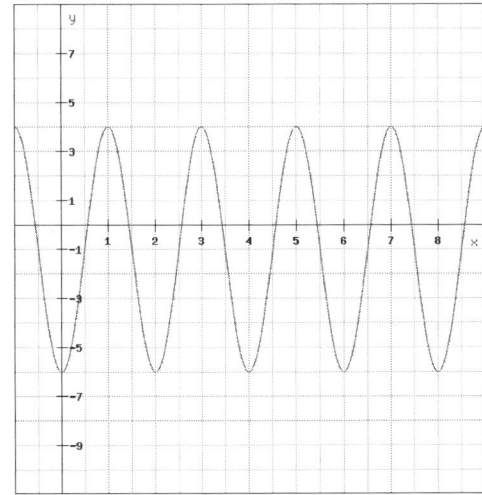

24. Given the function $f(x) = -2 + \cos(\frac{\pi}{2}x)$

   a. Amplitude = _____

   b. Period = _____

   c. Horizontal Translation: _____

   d. Vertical Translation: _____

   e. Midline: _____

   f. Range: _____

   g. Sketch the 2 periods of the function, include maximums and minimums.

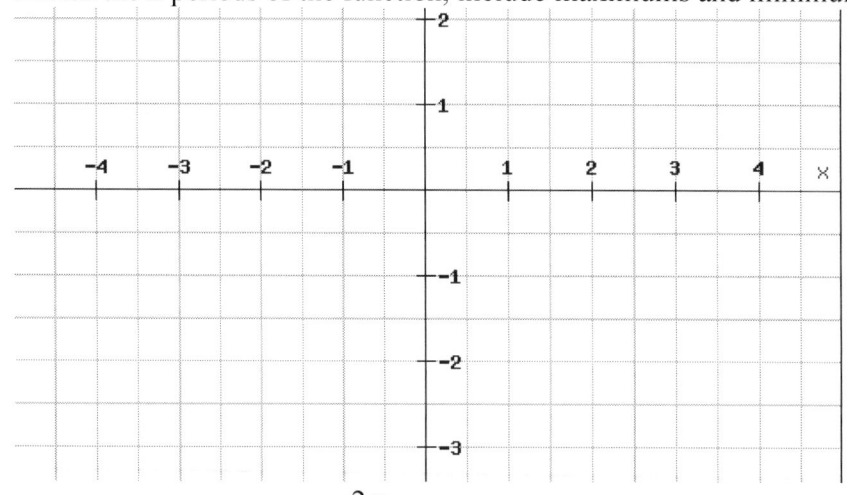

25. Given the function $f(x) = 2\sin(\frac{2\pi}{3}x) - 1$

   a. Amplitude = _____

   b. Period = _____

   c. Horizontal Translation: _____

   d. Vertical Translation: _____

   e. Midline: _____

   f. Range: _____

   g. Sketch the 2 periods of the function, include maximums and minimums.

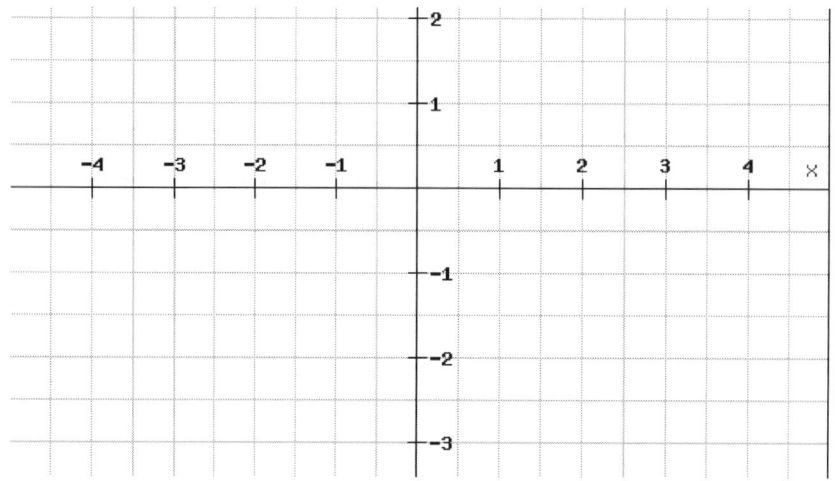

26. Given the function $f(x) = 3 - 2\cos(\pi x - \frac{\pi}{2})$

    h. Amplitude = _____

    i. Period = _____

    j. Horizontal Translation: _____

    k. Vertical Translation: _____

    l. Midline: _____

    m. Range: _____

    n. Sketch the 2 periods of the function, include maximums and minimums.

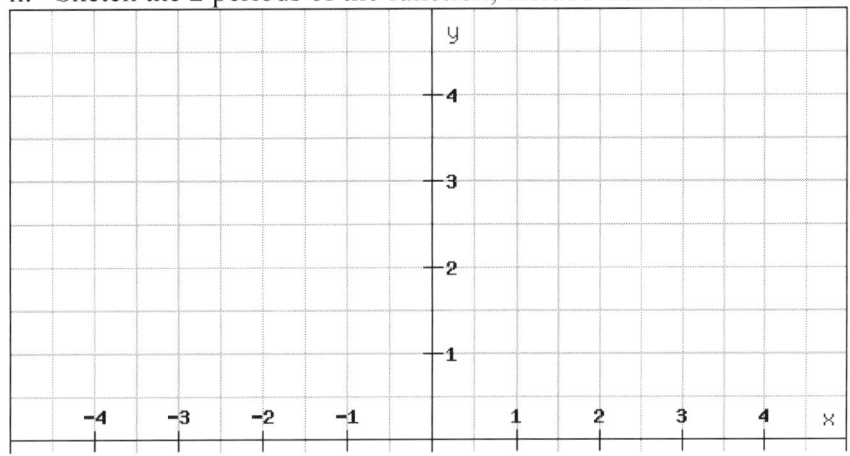

27. Given the function $f(x) = -2\sin(\pi x - \frac{\pi}{2}) + 1$

    h. Amplitude = _____

    i. Period = _____

    j. Horizontal Translation: _____

    k. Vertical Translation: _____

    l. Midline: _____

    m. Range: _____

    g. Sketch the 2 periods of the function, include maximums and minimums.

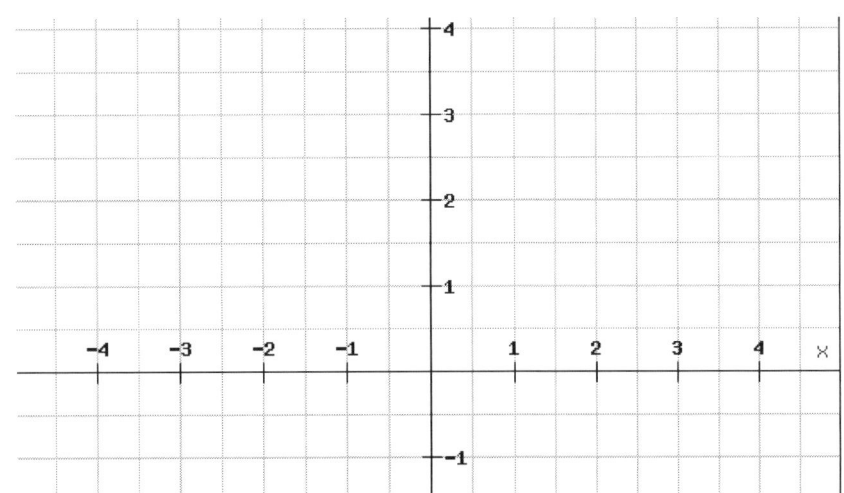

28. Given the function f(x) = Tan(x), Complete the following table:

x°	0	15	30	45	60	75	90	105	120	135	150	165	180	195	210	225	240	255
Rad																		
f(x)																		

- Sketch the points of the table on a graph.

- State the domain of the function: _____

- State the y intercept (sketched on the graph: (____, ____)

- State the x intercept(s): (_____, _____)

- Write the corresponding limits and the equation of the vertical asymptote(s):

- Write the corresponding limits and the equation of the horizontal asymptote:

- Function is increasing on the interval: _____, decreasing on the interval:_____

- Find the max/min point(s): (____, ____)

- State the range of the function: _____

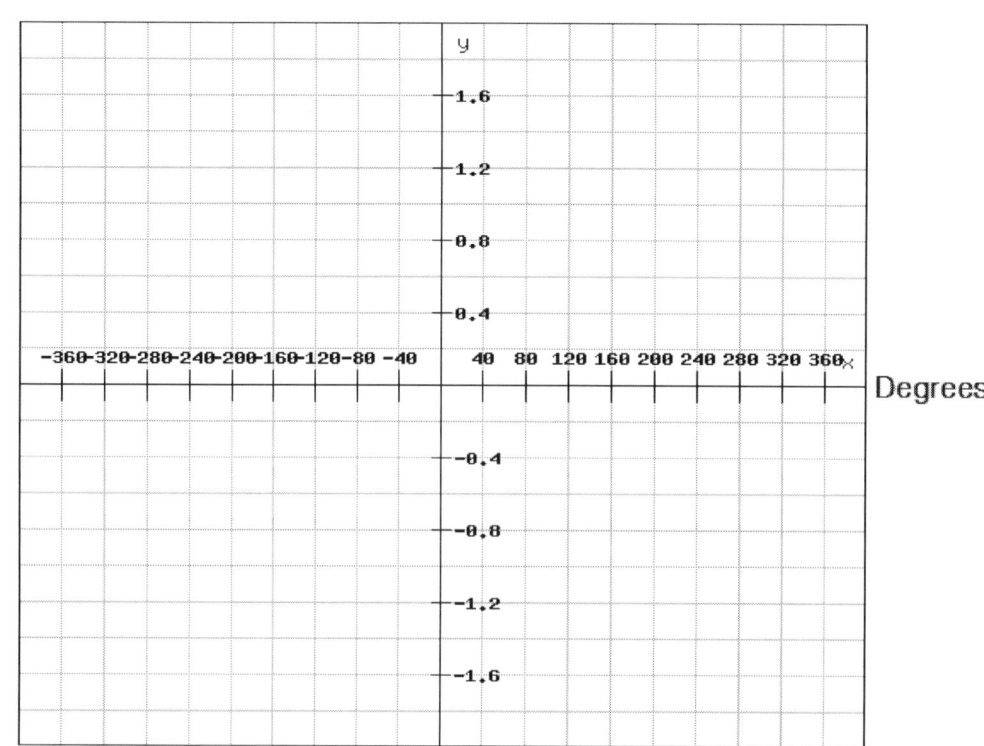

29. Given the function f(x) = Tan(x)

   a. Write in all forms the same function translated 2 positions up: _____

   b. Write in all forms the same function translated 3 positions left: _____

   c. Write in all forms the same function translated 3 positions left and 1 up.

   d. Write in all forms the same function translated 4 positions right and 1 up.

   e. Change the function so that the period would be 2.

   f. Change the function so that the period would be 3 and the amplitude 2.

   g. Change the function so that the period would be π.

   h. Change the function so that the period would be $\dfrac{\pi}{3}$.

   i. Change the function so that the period would be 6, then shift the function 2 positions right and 1 down.

   j. Change the function so that the period would be $\dfrac{\pi}{3}$, then shift the function 4 positions left and 2 down.

   k. Change the function so that the period would be $\dfrac{\pi}{5}$, then shift the function π positions left and 5 down.

30. Given the graph, complete:

   a. Amplitude = _____

   b. Period = _____

   c. Horizontal Translation: _____

   d. Midline: _____

   e. f(x) =

   f. Range: _____

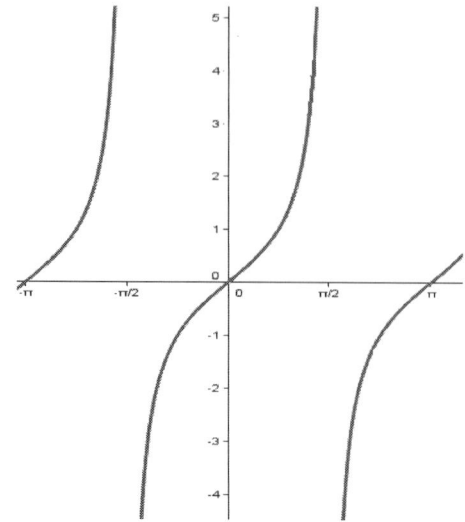

31. Given the graph, complete:

   a. Amplitude = _____

   b. Period = _____

   c. Horizontal Translation: _____

   d. Midline: _____

   e. f(x) =

   f. Range: _____

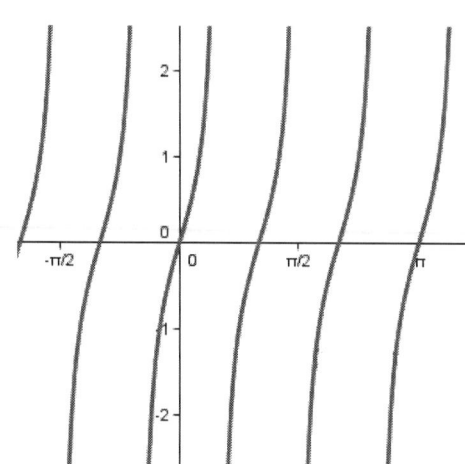

32. Given the graph, complete:

   a. Amplitude = _____

   b. Period = _____

   c. Horizontal Translation: _____

   d. Midline: _____

   e. f(x) =

   f. Range: _____

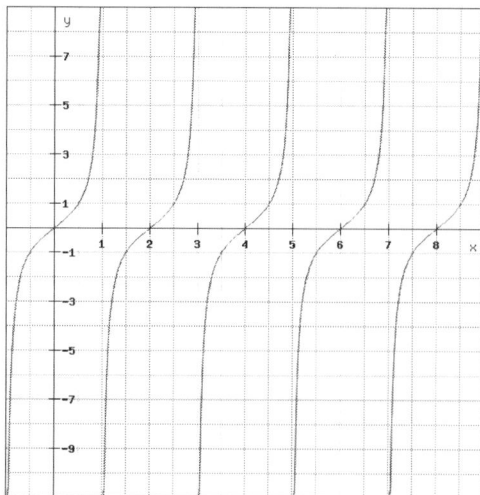

Analyze the following functions (Domain, Amplitude, Period, Range, Interceptions, maximums, minimums, sketch):

1. $f(x) = 2\sin(3x)$
2. $f(x) = \frac{1}{2}\sin(x) + 1$
3. $f(x) = 2\sin(x) + 5$
4. $f(x) = 3\sin(x) - 1$
5. $f(x) = -3\sin(x) - 3$
6. $f(x) = \sin(2x) - 2$
7. $f(x) = -\sin(3x) + 4$
8. $f(x) = -2\sin(\pi x)$
9. $f(x) = \frac{1}{2}\sin(\pi x)$
10. $f(x) = 2\sin(2\pi x)$
11. $f(x) = -\sin(k\pi x)$
12. $f(x) = \sin(\pi x + \pi)$
13. $f(x) = \sin(\frac{\pi}{2}x)$
14. $f(x) = \sin(\frac{\pi}{2}x - \frac{\pi}{2}) - 3$
15. $f(x) = 2\sin(\frac{\pi}{4}x - \frac{\pi}{2})$
16. $f(x) = -2\sin(\frac{\pi}{4}x + \frac{\pi}{2})$
17. $f(x) = \frac{1}{2}\sin(\frac{\pi}{4}x - \pi) + 1$
18. $f(x) = \sin(\pi x - 1)$
19. $f(x) = 2\cos(3x)$
20. $f(x) = \frac{1}{2}\cos(x) + 1$
21. $f(x) = 2\cos(x) + 5$
22. $f(x) = 3\cos(x) - 1$
23. $f(x) = -3\cos(x) - 3$
24. $f(x) = \cos(2x) - 2$
25. $f(x) = -\cos(3x) + 4$
26. $f(x) = -2\cos(\pi x)$
27. $f(x) = \frac{1}{2}\cos(\pi x)$
28. $f(x) = 2\cos(2\pi x)$
29. $f(x) = -\cos(k\pi x)$
30. $f(x) = \cos(\pi x + \pi)$
31. $f(x) = \cos(\frac{\pi}{2}x)$
32. $f(x) = \cos(\frac{\pi}{2}x - \frac{\pi}{2})$
33. $f(x) = 2\cos(\frac{\pi}{4}x - \frac{\pi}{2})$
34. $f(x) = -2\cos(\frac{\pi}{4}x + \frac{\pi}{2})$
35. $f(x) = \frac{1}{2}\cos(\frac{\pi}{4}x - \pi) - 2$
36. $f(x) = \cos(\pi x + 2)$
37.
38. $f(x) = 2\tan(3x)$
39. $f(x) = \frac{1}{2}\tan(x) + 1$
40. $f(x) = 2\tan(x) + 5$
41. $f(x) = 3\tan(x) - 1$
42. $f(x) = -3\tan(x) - 3$
43. $f(x) = \tan(2x) - 2$
44. $f(x) = -\tan(3x) + 4$
45. $f(x) = -2\tan(\pi x)$
46. $f(x) = \frac{1}{2}\tan(\pi x)$
47. $f(x) = 2\tan(2\pi x)$
48. $f(x) = -\tan(k\pi x)$
49. $f(x) = \tan(\pi x + \pi)$
50. $f(x) = \tan(\frac{\pi}{2}x)$
51. $f(x) = \tan(\frac{\pi}{2}x - \frac{\pi}{2})$
52. $f(x) = 2\tan(\frac{\pi}{4}x - \frac{\pi}{2}) + 2$
53. $f(x) = -2\tan(\frac{\pi}{4}x + \frac{\pi}{2})$
54. $f(x) = \frac{1}{2}\tan(\frac{\pi}{4}x - \pi)$
55. $f(x) = \tan(\pi x + 1)$

4.4. – SINE AND COSINE RULE

The sine rule: For any triangle, given the sides a, b and c and their corresponding opposite angles, A, B and C:

$$\frac{Sin(A)}{a} = \frac{Sin(B)}{b} = \frac{Sin(C)}{c}$$

How many equations are written above? ___

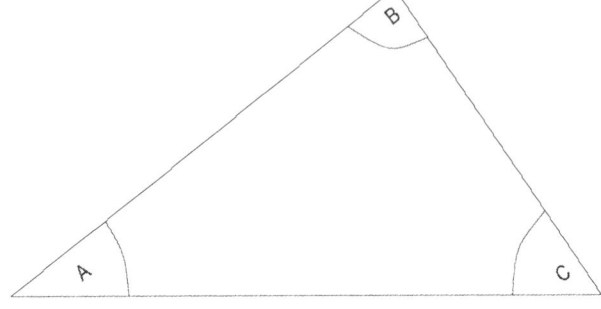

I. _____

II. _____

III. _____

The cosine rule: For any triangle, given the sides a, b and c and their corresponding opposite angles, A, B and C:

$a^2 = b^2 + c^2 - 2bc\cos(A)$

$b^2 = $ _____

$c^2 = $ _____

Given the following triangle:

a. Find AD in terms of AC and angle C.

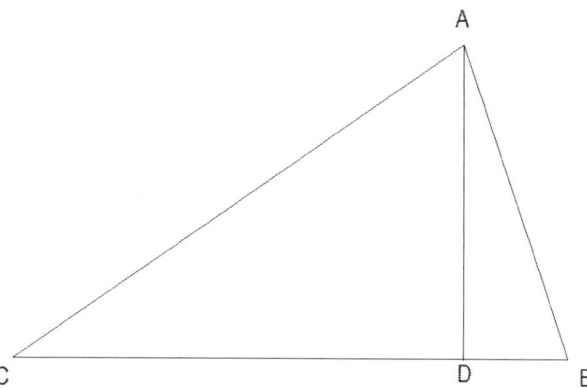

b. Find the Area of the triangle in terms of AC, CB and the angle C.
c. Conclusion:

Exercises

1. Sketch a triangle with angles: 20°, 80°, C and sides 10, b, c. Write the Sine and Cosine rule for this triangle.

2. Find all the missing sides, angles and area of the triangles below. If there is more than one set of solutions, try to find them all.

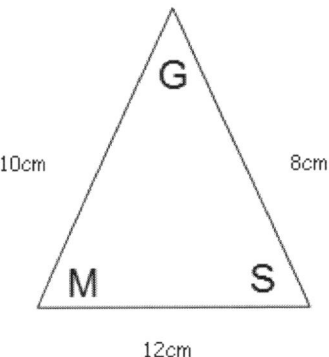

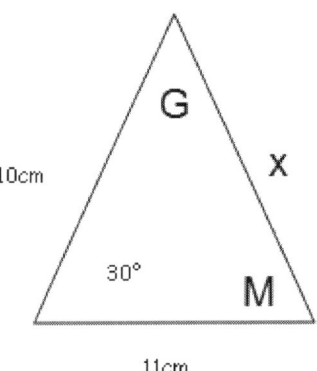

Conclusion: The cosine rule must be used in the following cases:

   I. _____

   II. _____

3. Find all the sides, angles and the area of the following triangles:
   <u>Ambiguous Case (2 possible solutions)</u>

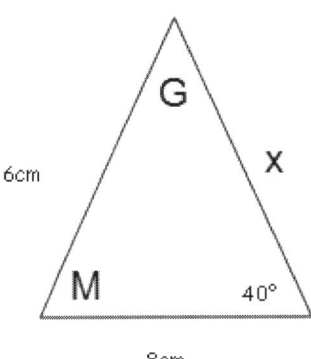

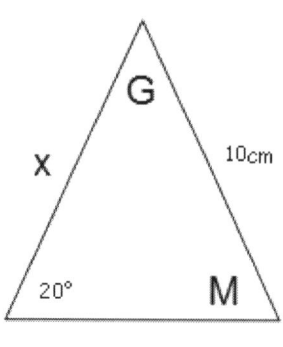

Conclusion: _____

4. Find all the sides, angles and the area of the following triangles:

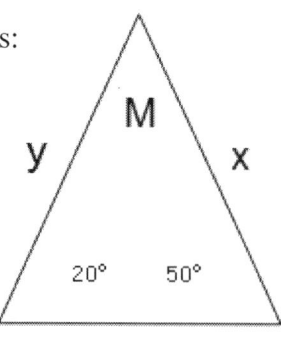

5. Find all the sides, angles and the area of the triangle:

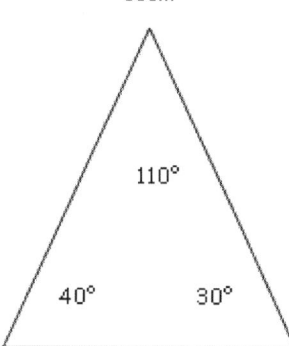

6. Find all the sides, angles and the area of the triangle:

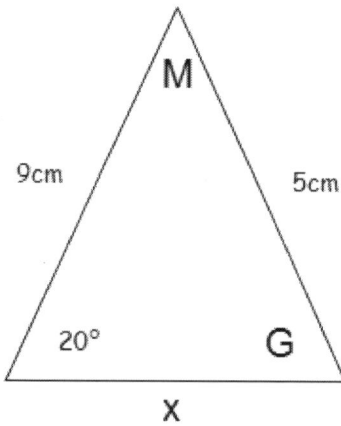

7. Find all the sides, angles and the area of the triangle:

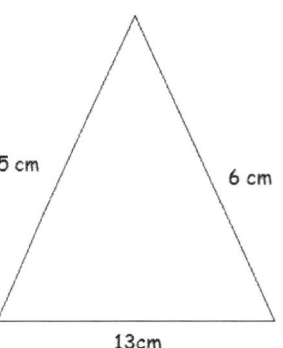

8. Find all the sides, angles and the area of the triangle:

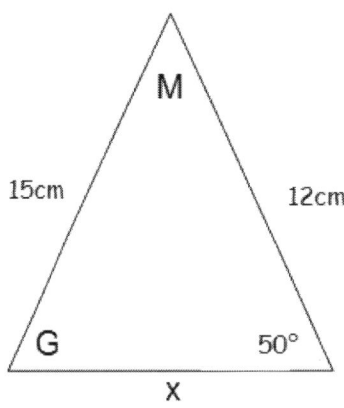

9. Find all the sides, angles and the area of the triangle:

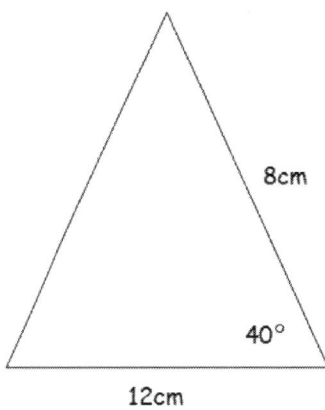

10. Find all the sides, angles and the area of the triangle:

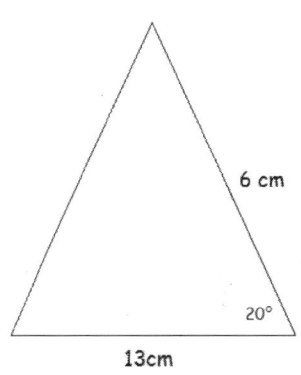

11. Can you identify how many triangles (not to scale) you could draw using the given information? In which example could you find the ambiguous case? Sketch (to scale as possible) both triangles in that case.

a.

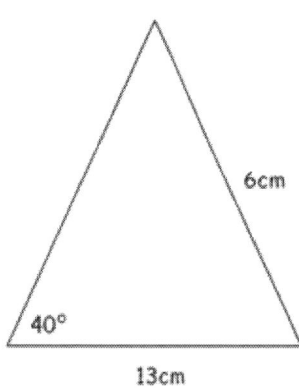

b.

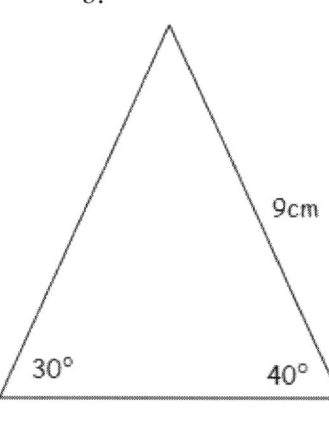

c.

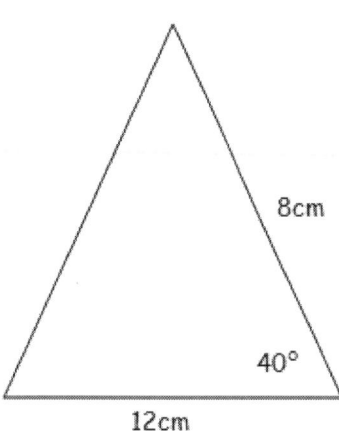

d.

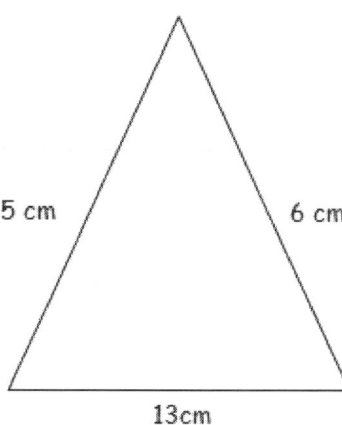

e.

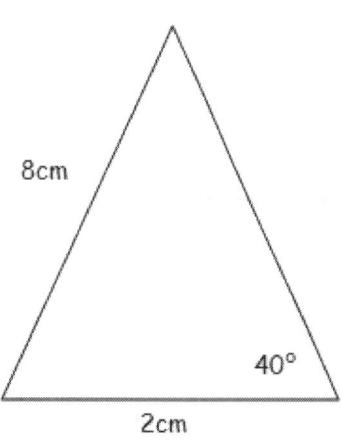

f.

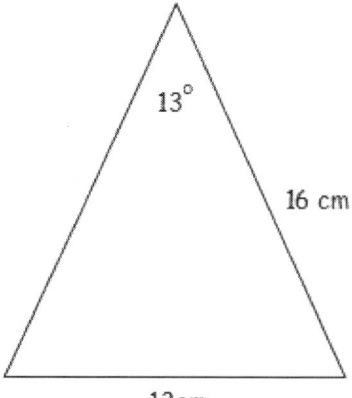

4.5. – TRIGONOMETRIC RATIOS

Following directly from the unit circle are the trigonometric ratios:

$Sin(x) = -$

$Cos(x) = -$

$Tan(x) = \dfrac{Sin(x)}{Cos(x)} = -$

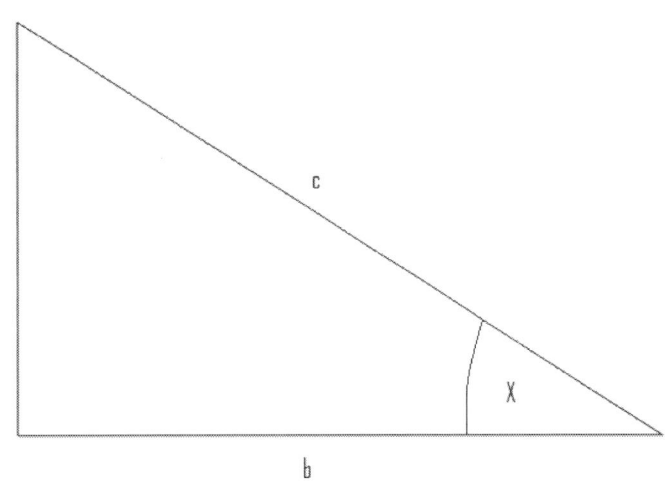

Exercises:

1. Find x and y in the following cases:

   a.

   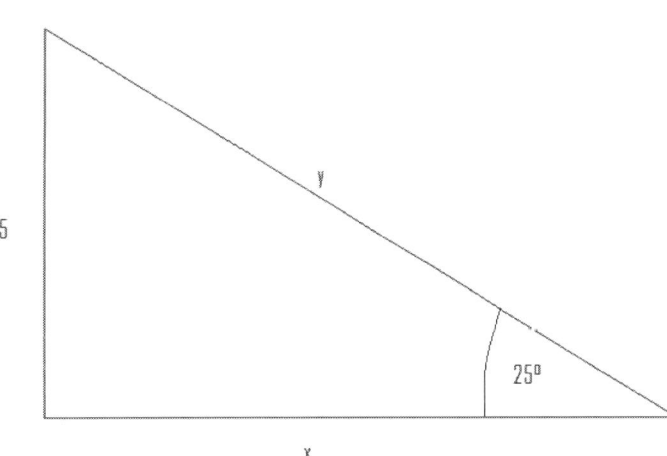

   b.

   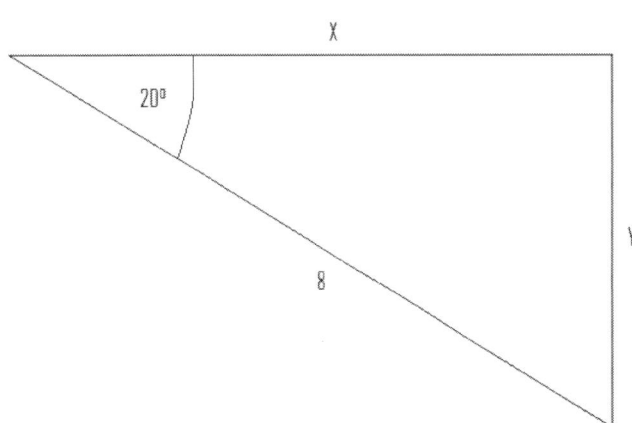

283

2. Find all the missing sides, angles, area and perimeter of the following triangle:

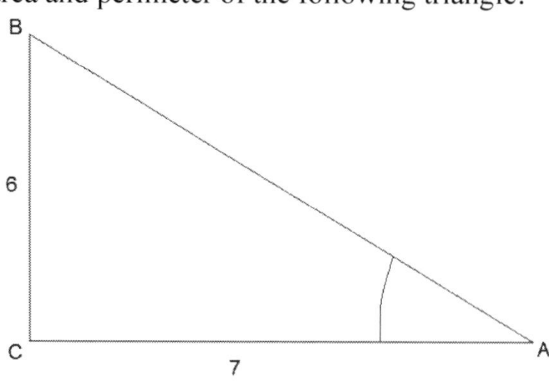

3. Find all the missing sides, angles, area and perimeter of the following triangle:

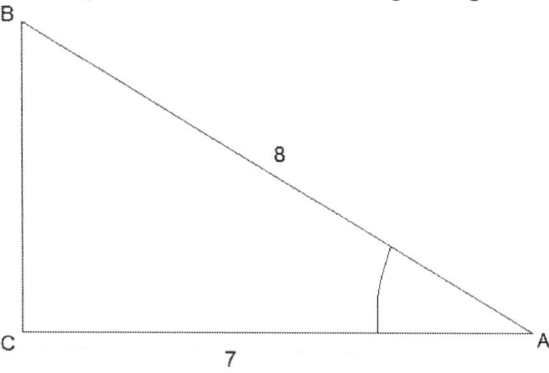

4. Find all the missing sides, angles, area and perimeter of the following triangle:

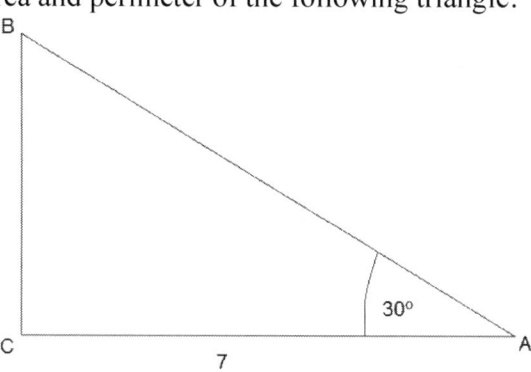

5. Find all the missing sides, angles, area and perimeter of the following triangle:

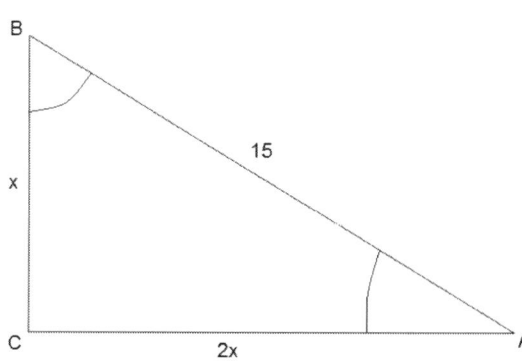

6. Find all the missing sides, angles, area and perimeter of the following triangle:

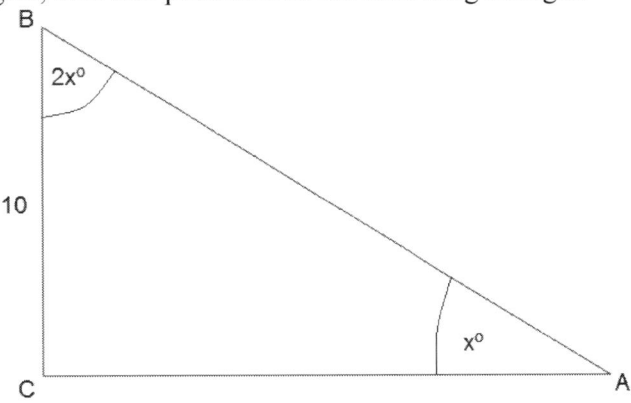

7. Find all the missing sides, angles, area and perimeter of an equilateral triangle with length side 10cm.

8. Find all the angles in an isosceles triangle whose base length is 20 cm and it is half its side length.

9. The Triangle in the diagram (not to scale) is not right angled, find X and Y.

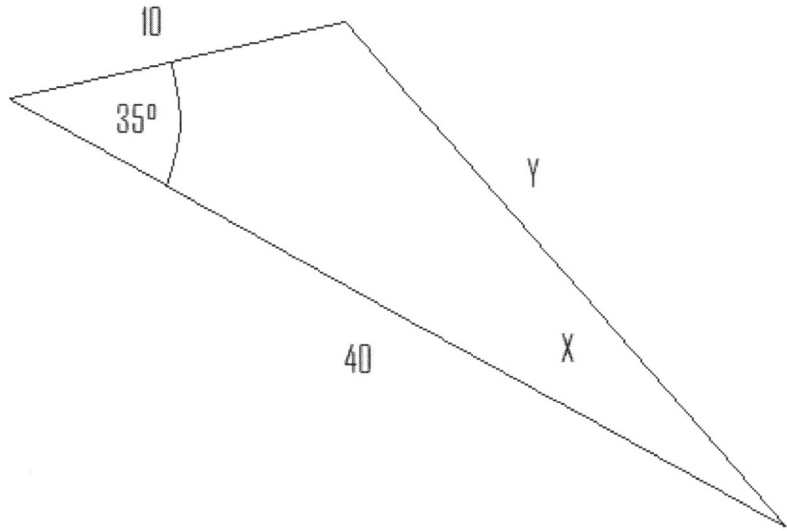

10. The shade formed by building is 100m long. The depression angle of the light as it approaches the ground is 40°.

    a. Sketch a diagram that describes the situation.
    b. Find the height of the building.

11. The height of building is 120m. The depression angle of the light as it approaches the ground is 30°.

    a. Sketch a diagram that describes the situation.
    b. Find the length of the shade on the ground.

12. In its search for food the lion is observing a certain prey located 2 m above the ground. The lion's head forms an angle of 12° as he looks at his prey.

    a. Sketch a diagram that describes the situation.
    b. Find the distance from the lion's mouth to its prey.

13. Measuring the height and distance of objects:

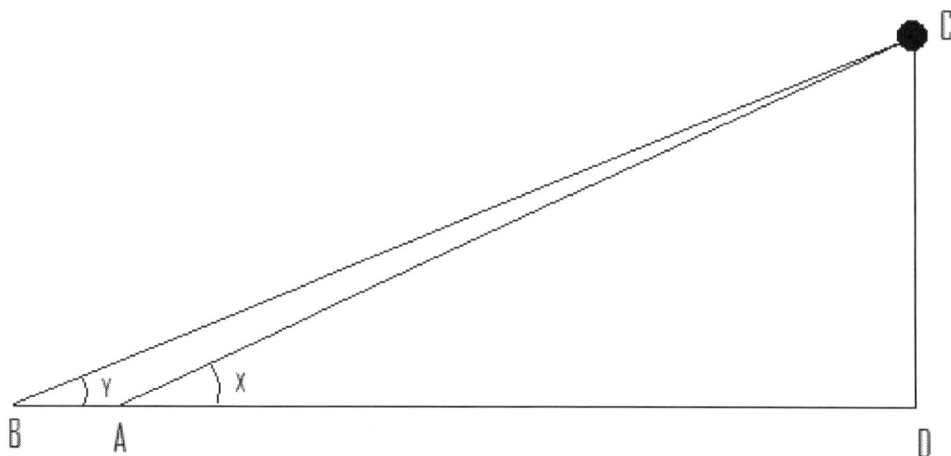

Assuming we start at point A and the object that we want to measure its distance (ground distance AD or Air distance AC) is located at point C. We need to use a device (in real life a **theodolite** is used) the measure the angle x (elevation angle), let's assume that we measured it and got 20°. Later we move a certain distance (backwards or forward) and measure the angle y. Let assume that we moved backwards 4 meters (that is AB = 4m) and the angle y is 18°. Find AD, AC, CD.

4.6. – INVERSE TRIGONOMETRIC FUNCTIONS

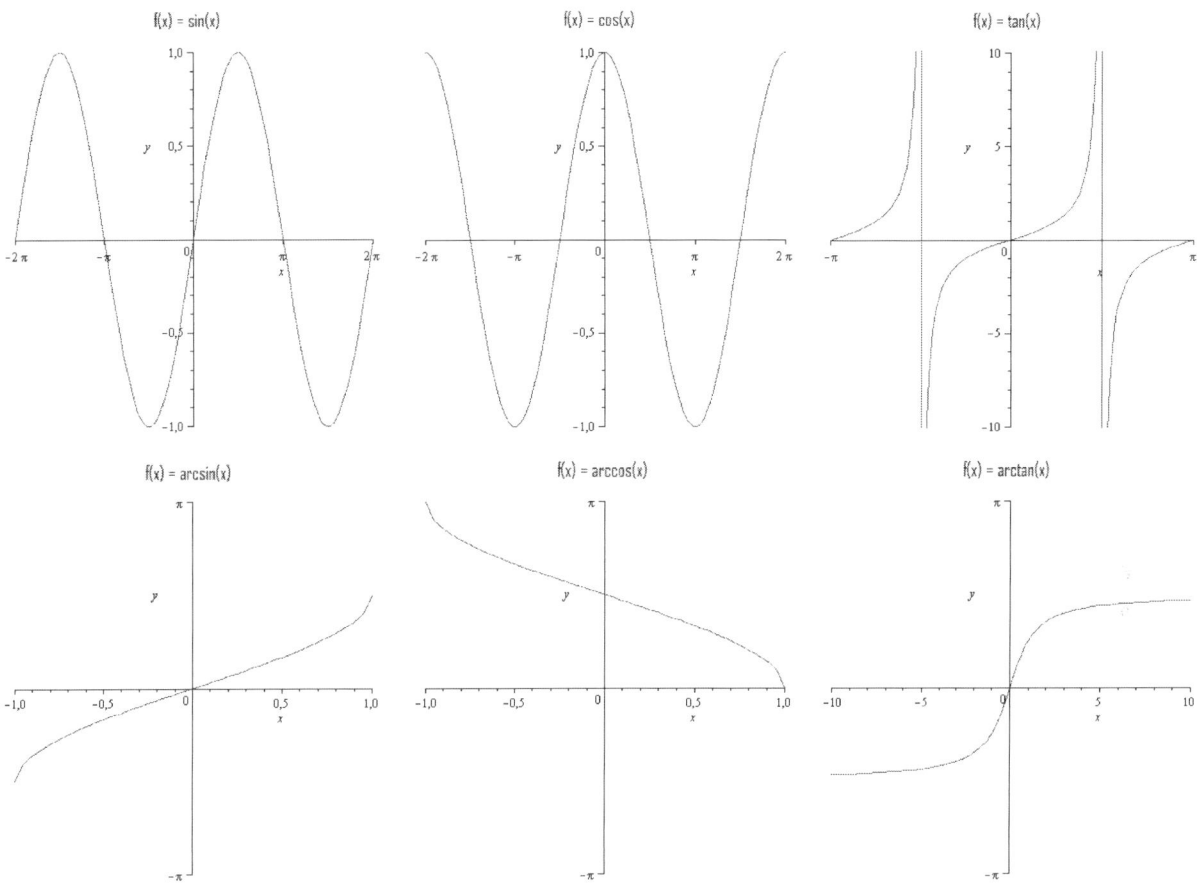

Inverse Trigonometric Function	Domain	Range	In words
$f(x) = \arcsin(x)$	$[-1, 1]$	$[-\frac{\pi}{2}, \frac{\pi}{2}]$	f(x) is the angle (whose sine is x)
$f(x) = \arccos(x)$	$[-1, 1]$	$[0, \pi]$	f(x) is the angle (whose cosine is x)
$f(x) = \arctan(x)$	$[-\infty, \infty]$	$[-\frac{\pi}{2}, \frac{\pi}{2}]$	f(x) is the angle (whose tangent is x)

Give your answer(s) in radians and degrees, use GDC only if necessary:

1. Arcsin(0) =

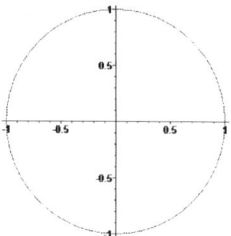

2. Arcos(0) =

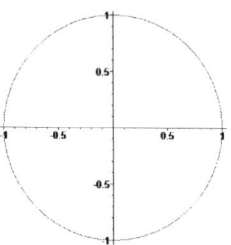

3. Arcsin(1) =

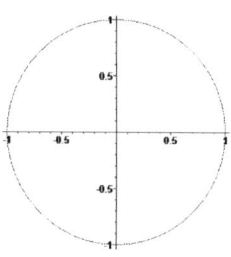

4. Arcos(2) =

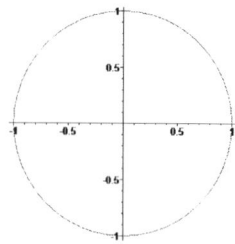

5. Arcsin(0.5) =

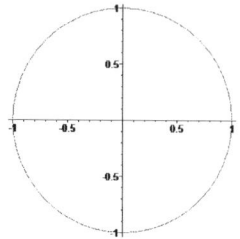

6. Arcos(−0.5) =

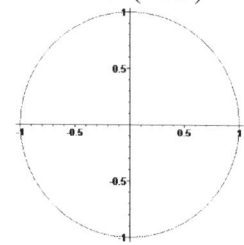

7. Arcsin($\frac{\sqrt{3}}{2}$) =

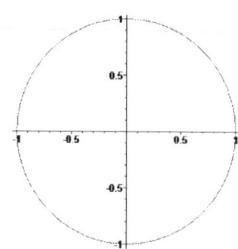

8. Arcos($-\frac{\sqrt{3}}{2}$) =

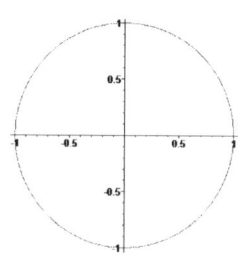

9. Arcsin($\frac{\sqrt{2}}{2}$) =

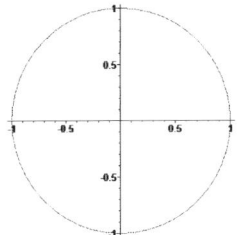

10. Arcos($-\frac{\sqrt{2}}{2}$) =

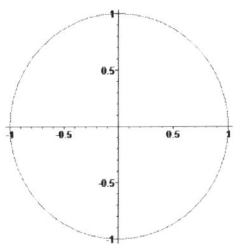

11. Arcsin($\frac{\sqrt{2}}{2}$) =

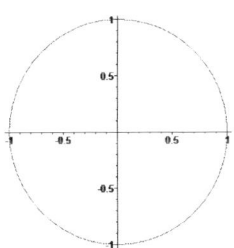

12. Arcsin(–1) =

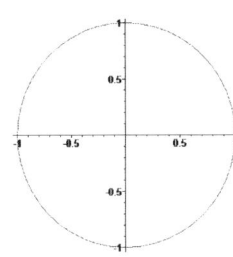

13. Arcos(–1) =

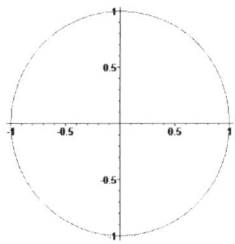

14. Arcsin(0.2) =

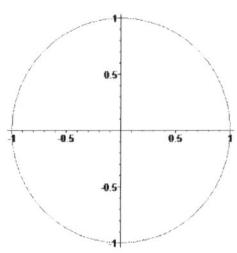

15. Arcos(–0.4) =

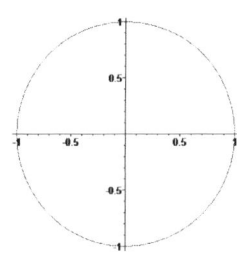

16. Arcsin(1/5) =

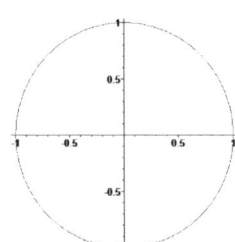

17. Arcos(–5) =

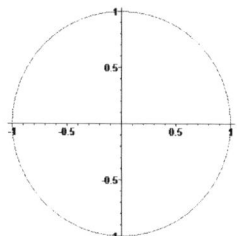

18. Arcsin(0.9) =

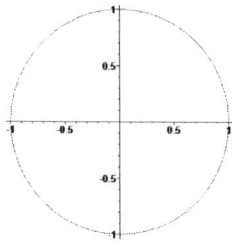

19. Arcsin(–2.4) =

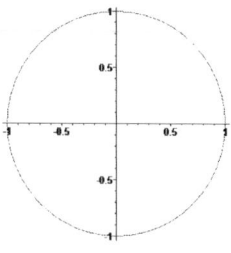

20. Arcos(0.05) =

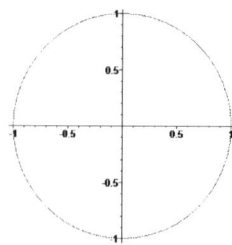

21. Arctan(–5) =

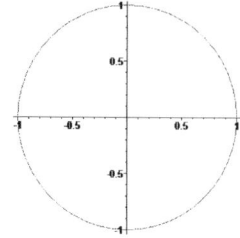

22. Arctan(1) =

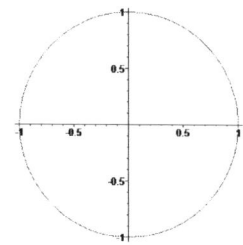

23. Arctan(–2.4) =

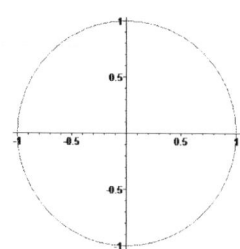

24. Arctan$(\frac{1}{\sqrt{3}})$ =

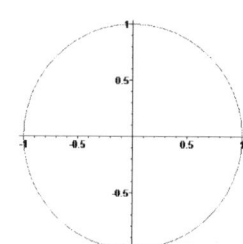

25. Arctan$(-\sqrt{3})$ =

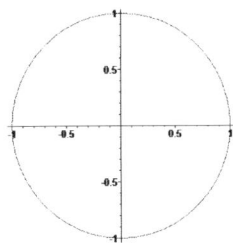

26. Arctan$(\sqrt{3})$ =

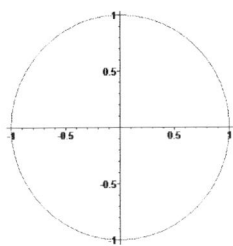

27. Arctan(-1) =

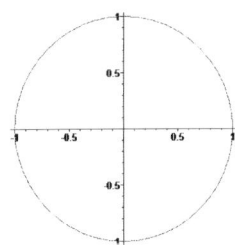

Evaluate:

28. $Arc\sin\left(\dfrac{-1}{2}\right)$

29. $Arc\cos\left(\dfrac{\sqrt{3}}{2}\right)$

30. $Arc\tan(0)$

31. $Arc\cos\left(\sin\left(\dfrac{\sqrt{3}}{2}\right)\right)$

32. $\cos\left(\arcsin\left(\dfrac{2}{5}\right)\right)$

33. $\sin\left(\arcsin\left(\dfrac{\pi}{5}\right)\right)$

34. $\csc\left(\arcsin\left(-\dfrac{2}{7}\right)\right)$

35. $\cos\left(\arctan\left(\dfrac{3}{4}\right)\right)$

36. $\csc\left(\arccos\left(\dfrac{2\sqrt{5}}{5}\right)\right)$

CHAPTER 5 – SETS

5.1. – SETS

1. A set is _____ .

2. Give 3 examples of sets:

3. Consider the set {2, 4, 6, …}

    a. This is the set of _____. The next element is ___

    b. In this set the number of elements is _____ It is an _____ set

4. Consider the set {1, 8, 27, …}

    a. This is the set of _____. The next element is ___

    b. In this set the number of elements is _____ It is an _____ set

5. Consider the set {Asia, Africa, …}

    a. This is the set of _____. The next element is ___

    b. In this set the number of elements is _____ It is an _____ set

6. A **subset** is _____. It is denoted by $A \subseteq B$

7. Given the set L = {A, B, C}

    a. State all the possible subsets of L. include the empty set.

    L1 = _____

    L2 = _____

    L3 = _____

    L4 = _____

    L5 = _____

    L6 = _____

    L7 = _____

    L8 = _____

    b. All the subsets except _____ are called **proper subsets denoted by** $A \subset B$

    c. Explain the difference between a subset and a propersubset.

    d. $A \not\subset B$ means _____ _____

    e. _____ means that A is NOT a subset of B

8. M is the set of perfect squares smaller than a 100.

    a. List the elements of M _____

    b. List the subset Q of even numbers in M _____

9. N is the set of prime numbers between 10 and 30.

    a. List the elements of M _____

    b. List the subset Q of even numbers in M _____

295

10. The **universal set** is particular for _____ and contains _____ for the problem. Usually it is denoted by the letter _____.

11. The universal set for the students in the classroom is

    U = _____

12. Given the sets U = {John, Raquel, Felix, Shan, Mila, Jessy, Pamela} and the subset of U: B = {Shan, Mila}.

    State the complement of the set B' = _____

13. The **complement of a** set _____

14. The **intersection** of 2 sets is _____. It is denoted by $A \cap B$.

15. The **union** of 2 sets is _____. It is denoted by $A \cup B$

16. For example if S = {1, 2, 3, 4, 5, 6, 7, 8, 9} and M = {2, 6, 10, 12}

    a. $S \cap M = $ _____

    b. $S \cup M = $ _____

17. Given the sets U = {John, Raquel, Felix, Shan, Mila, Jessy, Pamela} and the subset of U: B = {Shan, Mila}.

    a. $U \cap B = $ _____

    b. $U \cup B = $ _____

18. Two set are said to be "**disjoint**" in case _____

    Example:

19. Two set are equal in case _____

    Example:

VENN DIAGRAMS

Event	Set Language	Venn diagram	Probability result
Complementary event (A')	Not A		$P(A') =$
The _____ of A and B $(A \cap B)$	Set of elements that belongs to A _____ B		$P(A \cup B) =$
The _____ of A and B $(A \cup B)$	Set of elements that belongs to A _____ B _____ both		
If $(A \cap B) = \emptyset$ A and B are said to be: _____	The sets A and B are _____		$P(A \cup B) =$ $P(A \cap B) =$

20. The **commutative** property of a set means that:_____

    Example: $A \cup B =$ _____

21. The **associative** property of a set means that: :_____

    Example: $(A \cup B) \cup C =$ _____

22. The **distributive** property of a set means that: :_____

    Example: $C \cup (A \cap B) =$ _____

    $C \cap (A \cup B) =$ _____

23. Given N, the set of natural numbers, Z the set of integers, Q the set of rationals and R the set of Real numbers.

    a. Write down an element of the set $N \cap Z$: _____

    b. Write down an element of the set $Q \cap Z$: _____

    c. Write down an element of the set $Q \cap Z'$: _____

    d. Write down an element of the set $Q' \cap Z$: _____

    e. Write down an element of the set $R \cap Q$: _____

    f. Write down an element of the set $R \cap Q'$: _____

    g. Write down an element of the set $N \cap N'$: _____

24. Consider the sets: $U = \{x \in N\}$

$A = \{x \in N | 11 < x < 21\}$, B={multiples of 4}, and C ={13, 16, 18, 20}

    a. Write all the elements of the set $A \cap B$: _____

    b. Write all the elements of the set $A \cap C$: _____

    c. Write all the elements of the set $B \cap C$: _____

    d. Write all the elements of the set $B \cup C$: _____

    e. Write all the elements of the set $A \cap (B' \cup C)$: _____

    f. Write all the elements of the set $A \cap (B \cup C')$: _____

    g. Write all the elements of the set $A \cap B \cap C'$: _____

    h. True/False: $11 \in A$ True/False: $11 \in A'$

    i. True/False: $13 \in A \cap C$ True/False: $30 \notin B$

    j. True/False: $12 \in A \cap B$ True/False: $30 \notin C$

    k. True/False: $B \subset A$ True/False: $C \subset A$

25. Given the Venn diagram. Shade $A \cap B$

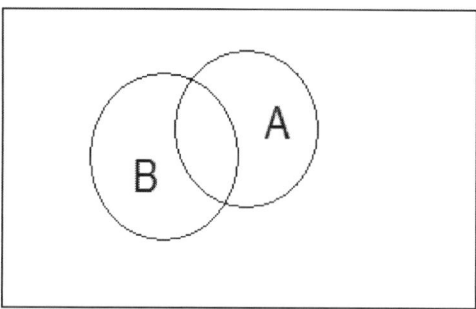

26. Given the Venn diagram. Shade $A \cap B'$

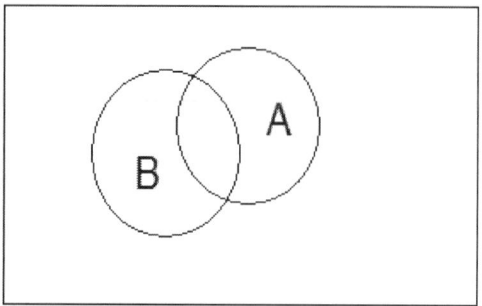

27. Given the Venn diagram. Shade B'

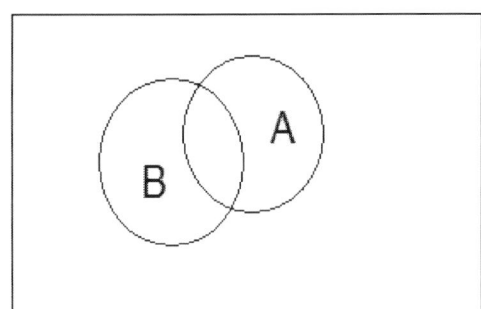

28. Given the Venn diagram. Shade A' ∩ B'

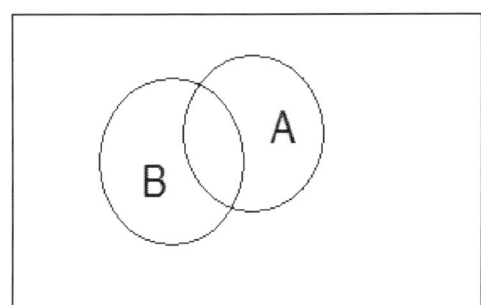

29. Given the Venn diagram. Shade A ∪ B

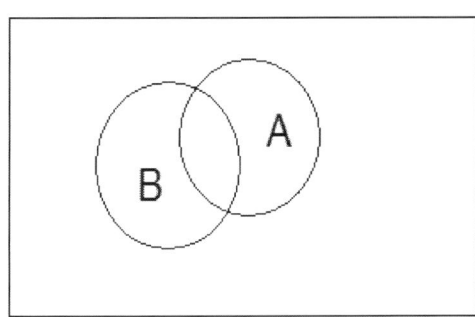

30. Given the Venn diagram. Shade A' ∪ B

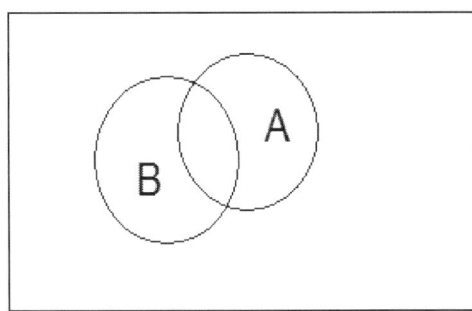

31. Given the Venn diagram. Shade A' ∪ B'

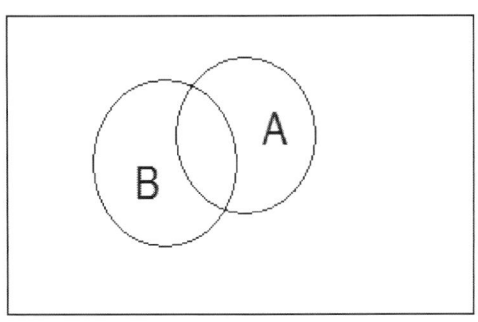

32. Given the Venn diagram. Shade A ∪ B

33. Given the Venn diagram. Shade A ∪ B'

34. Given the Venn diagram. Shade A ∩ B'

35. Given the Venn diagram. Shade A ∩ B

36. Given the Venn diagram. Shade A ∩ B ∩ C

37. Given the Venn diagram. Shade $(A \cup B) \cap C$

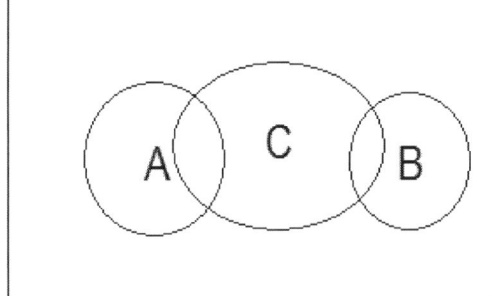

38. Given the Venn diagram. Shade $(A' \cup B) \cap C$

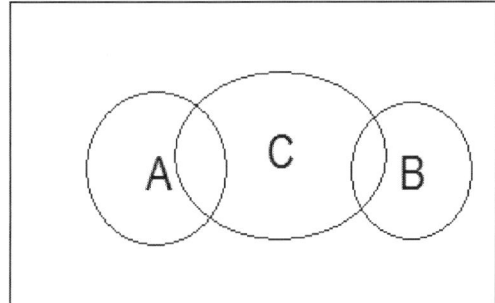

39. Given the Venn diagram. Shade $(A \cup B) \cap C'$

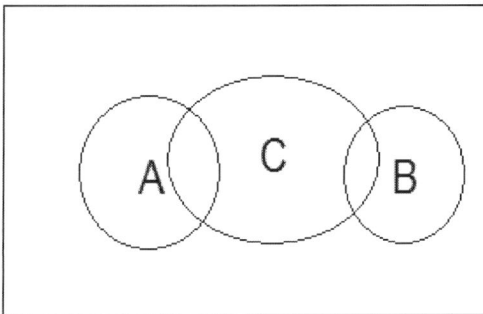

40. Given the Venn diagram. Shade $A \cap B \cap C$

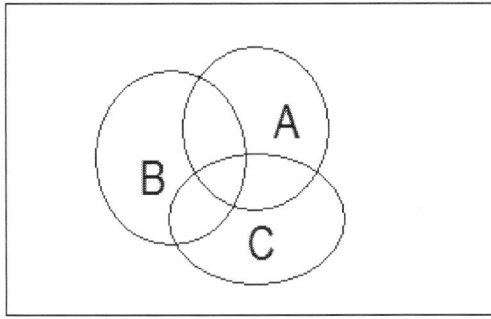

41. Given the Venn diagram. Shade $(A \cap B) \cap C'$

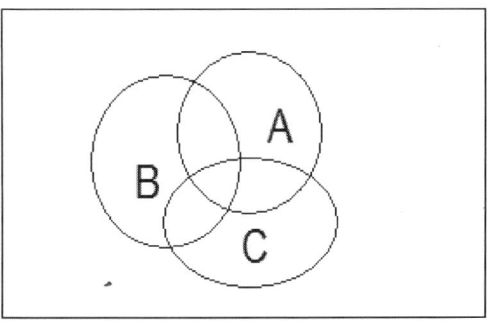

42. Given the Venn diagram. Shade $(A' \cap B) \cap C$

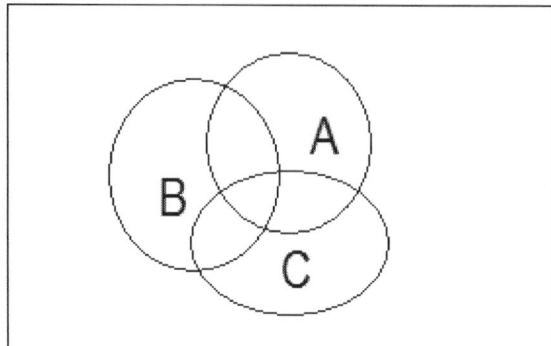

43. Given the Venn diagram. Shade $(A \cap B') \cap C$

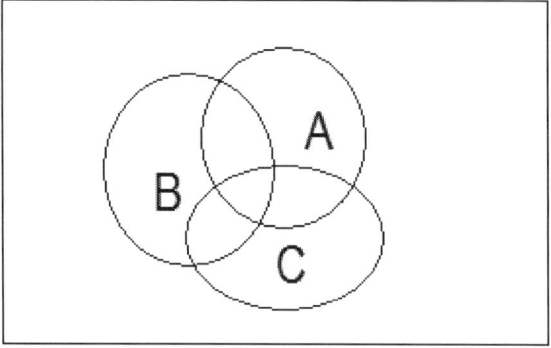

44. 50 drivers were asked about the favourite car colour. 3 choices were given: Red (X), Blue (Y) and White (Z). The results were:

        15 liked all three
        3 liked red and blue only
        9 liked red and white only
        7 liked blue and white only
        2 liked red only
        5 liked white only
        1 liked blue only

   a. Represent this information in a Venn diagram. Fill the Venn diagram with all the corresponding numbers.
   b. Write down the percentage of drivers that did not like any of the 3 colours.

45. Given the sets U = {Real numbers}, A={Negative numbers}, Z={Integers}

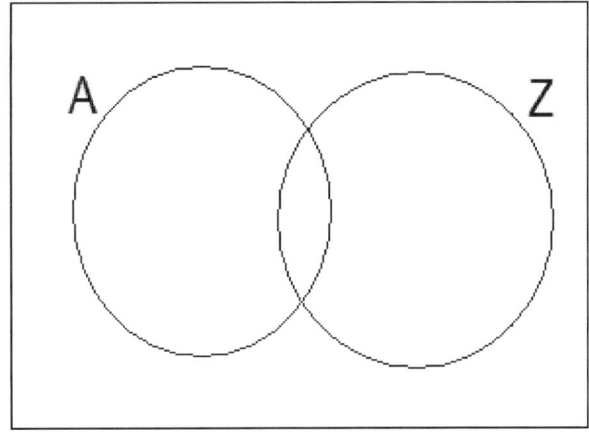

Write the following numbers in the correct region: cos(0), 0.5, $-\pi$, 5^{-2}, -7, 0

46. In a certain hospital in which there are 70 nurses, 20 work in cardiac surgery (C) and 15 others in the intensive care unit (I). 8 nurses work in both units.

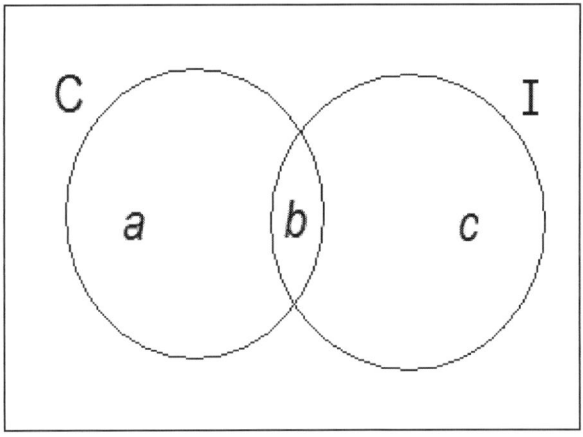

a. a = ____   b = ____   c = ____

b. Calculate the number of nurses that work outside of the cardiac surgery or intensive care units.

47. Given the following sets:

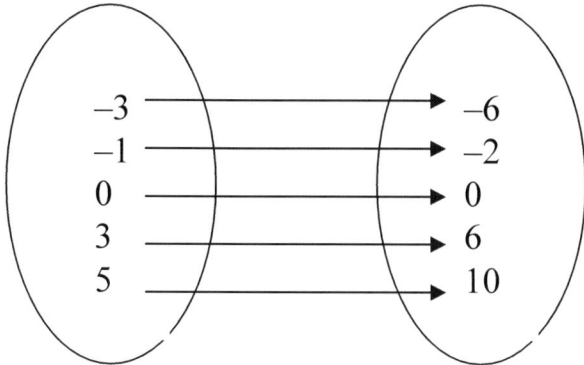

a. Write down the paires created by this mapping from one set to another:

b. Can you write a mathematical expression to express this mapping¿?

48. Given the following setts:

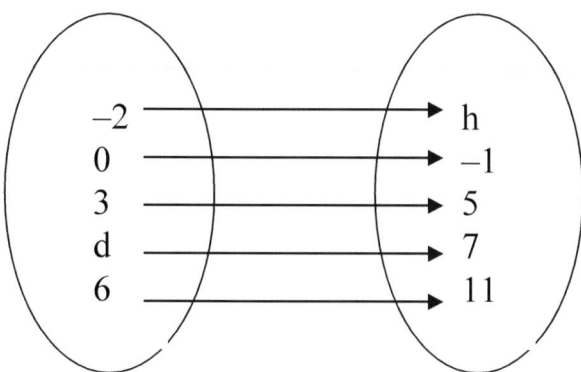

a. Can you write a mathematical expression to express this mapping?

b. Find h. Find d.

CHAPTER 6 - STATISTICS

6.1. – STATISTICS

In Statistics we try to obtain some conclusions by observing and/or analyzing data.

1. The set of objects that we are trying to study is called _____, the number of elements in the population can be _____ or _____.

2. Usually the _____ is too big and therefore we obtain a _____. This process is called _____.

3. We use the _____ to obtain conclusions about the _____.

Types of DATA

4. _____ data.

5. _____ data that can be divided to _____ or _____.

6. _____ can be counted while _____ data can be _____.

7. Give 3 examples of _____ data:

8. Give 3 examples of _____ _____ data:

9. Give 3 examples of _____ _____ data:

10. Given the following variables, classify them in the table:

    - Eye color
    - Shoe size
    - Height
    - Weight
    - Number of cars in a parking lot
    - Type of fruit
    - Number of apples sold a day in a store
    - Velocity of the wind
    - Temperature
    - Numbers of pages in a book
    - Name of writer
    - Number of students in a school

Categorical	Numerical Discrete	Numerical Continuous

11. In a certain class the eye color of students was studies. The following results were obtained:

    Brown, Black, Brown, Blue, Brown, Black, Brown, Blue, Brown, Blue, Brown, Black, Brown, Blue.

    a. How many students participated?
    b. What kind of data is this?
    c. Represent the information in a Bar Chart
    d. Represent the information in a Pie Chart (include the %)

12. In a certain math class the following grades were obtained:

    65, 72, 85, 89, 52, 71, 89, 68, 63, 76, 61, 86, 98, 79, 79, 91, 74, 89, 77, 68, 78

    a. How many students participated?
    b. What kind of data is this?
    c. Suggest a method to represent this information in a table.
    d. Use the table to create a bar graph

13. In a certain zoo the length of a certain type of animal (in meters) was studied. The following results were obtained:

    1.77, 1.60, 1.89, 1.54, 1.77, 1.65, 1.86, 1.51, 1.67, 1.94, 1.73, 1.70, 1.66, 1.58

    a. How many animals participated?
    e. What kind of data is this?
    b. Suggest a method to represent this information in a table.
    c. Use the table to create a bar graph

14. In a certain group shoe size was studied and the following results obtained:

    45, 36, 44, 38, 41, 42, 48, 39, 40, 42, 43, 41, 38, 45, 41, 38, 42, 44, 41, 41, 46

    a. How many students participated?
    f. What kind of data is this?
    b. Suggest a method to represent this information in a table.
    c. Use the table to create a bar graph

15. Choose a variable to collect information about in your classroom, state its kind, represent the information in a table and create a bar graph.

6.2. – MEAN, MEDIAN, MODE AND FREQUENCY DIAGRAMS

1. In a certain club the number of visitors per day was studied during 1 week and the following results obtained: 58, 79, 66, 78, 23, 66, 63

    a. State the number of elements in the set: _____

    b. What kind of data is this? _____

    c. Find its mean: _____   Find its mode: _____

    d. Write the information in an increasing order:

    e. Find its Median: _____   Q1 = _____   Q3 = _____

2. In a certain restaurant the amount of meat (kg) consumed per day was studied and the following results obtained: 11.5, 12.2, 14.6, 15.0, 23.2, 21.2, 10.1, 13.1

    a. State the number of elements in the set: _____

    b. What kind of data is this? _____

    c. Find its mean: _____   Find its mode: _____

    d. Write the information in an increasing order:

    e. Find its Median: _____   Q1 = _____   Q3 = _____

3. In a certain math class the number of exercises per day given for HW is the following: 5, 6, 6, 6, 4, 4, 5, 5, 4, 5, 6, 6, 7, 3, 0, 3

    a. State the number of elements in the set: _____

    b. What kind of data is this? _____

    c. Find its mean: _____   Find its mode: _____

    d. Write the information in an increasing order:

    e. Find its Median: _____   Q1 = _____   Q3 = _____

4. In the following data: 2, 2, 3, 3, 9, 9, 9 one natural number is missing. It is known that the median with the missing number is 3. Find all the possible values of the missing number.

5. In a certain math class the following grades were obtained:

   68, 79, 75, 89, 54, 81, 88, 62, 67, 75, 64, 85, 97, 77, 79, 90, 75, 89, 76, 68

   a. State the number of elements in the set: _____

   b. What kind of data is this? _____

   c. Find its mean: _____   Find its mode: _____

   d. Write the information in an increasing order:

   e. Find its Median: _____   Q1 = _____   Q3 = _____

   f. Fill the table:

Grade	Mid – Grade (Mi)	Frequency (fi)	fi x Mi	Cumulative Frequency (Fi)	Fi (%)
51 – 60					
61 – 70					
71 – 80					
81 – 90					
91 – 100					
Total					

   g. Use the table to find the mean: _____. Comment on the result compared to the previous mean obtained.

   h. Discuss the advantages and disadvantages of organizing information in a table.

   i. Is this the only possible choice for the left column of the table? Why? Discuss the advantages and disadvantages of organizing information in such a way.

j. Design a new table with a different _____

Grade	Mid – Grade (Mi)	Frequency (fi)	Fi x Mi	Cumulative Frequency (Fi)	Fi (%)

k. Use the table to find the mean: _____. Comment on the result compared to the previous mean obtained.

l. The mean of the population is denoted with the Greek letter mu: _____ and typically it is _____. The mean of the sample is denoted by _____

m. Find the modal interval in both tables:

   1st: _____ 2nd: _____

n. In general this method of organizing information is called _____

o. The 1st column is called _____ with upper interval boundary and _____ interval boundary.

p. The 2nd column is called _____

q. On the following grid paper sketch the corresponding points.

Cumulative frequency

Variable: _____

r. This graph is called cumulative frequency curve or _____

s. Find the median using the graph: _____

t. Find the first quartile (Q_1) using the graph: Q_1 = _____

u. Find the third quartile (Q_3) using the graph: Q_3 = _____

v. Find P_{30} using the graph: _____ Find P_{70} using the graph: _____

w. The <u>Inter Quartile Range</u> is in general _____ in this case it is _____

x. Find the answers to all the different parts using your GDC (Graphic Display Calculator).

6. In a certain class the following heights (in m) of students were collected:

   1.77, 1.60, 1.89, 1.54, 1.77, 1.65, 1.86, 1.51, 1.67, 1.94, 1.73, 1.70, 1.66, 1.70

   a. State the number of elements in the set: _____

   b. What kind of data is this? _____

   c. Find its mean: _____   Find its mode: _____

   d. Write the information in an increasing order:

   e. Find its Median: _____   Q1 = _____   Q3 = _____

   f. Fill the table:

Grade	Mid – Grade (Mi)	Frequency (fi)	fi x Mi	Cumulative Frequency (Fi)	Fi (%)
[1.50 – 1.60)					
[1.60 – 1.70)					
[1.70 – 1.80)					
[1.80 – 1.90)					
[1.90 – 2.00)					
Total					

   g. Use the table to find the mean: _____. Comment on the result compared to the previous mean obtained.

   h. Discuss the advantages and disadvantages of organizing information in a table.

   i. Is this the only possible choice for the left column of the table? Why? Discuss the advantages and disadvantages of organizing information in such a way.

j. On the following grid paper sketch the corresponding points.

Cumulative frequency

Variable: _____

k. This graph is called cumulative frequency curve or _____

l. Find the median using the graph: _____

m. Find the first quartile (Q_1) using the graph: Q_1 = _____

n. Find the third quartile (Q_3) using the graph: Q_3 = _____

o. Find P_{30} using the graph: _____ Find P_{70} using the graph: _____

p. The <u>Inter Quartile Range</u> is in general _____ in this case it is _____

q. Find the answers to all the different parts using your GDC.

7. In a certain class students eye color was collected:

   Brown, Black, Brown, Blue, Brown, Blue, Green, Brown, Black, Green

   a. State the number of elements in the set: _____

   b. What kind of data is this? _____

   c. Fill the table:

Eye Color	Mid – Color (Mi)	Frequency (fi)	fi x Mi	Cumulative Frequency (Fi)	Fi (%)
Brown					
Blue					
Green					
Black					
Total					

   d. Obtain the mean: _____

   e. State the mode of the set: _____

   f. Find the modal interval: _____

   g. Find the Median using the original data: _____

   h. Find the median using the table, discuss your answer.

   i. Find the answers to all the different parts using your GDC.

   j. Represent the information in a histogram:

6.3. – PROBABILITY

Probability is the science of chance or likelihood of an event happening
If a random experiment is repeated ____ times in such a way that each of the trials is identical and independent, where n(A) is the number of _____ event A occurred,

then: Relative frequency of event A = P(A) = $\dfrac{n(A)}{N}$ ($N \to \infty$)

Exercises

1. In an unbiased coin what is P(head) ?

    This probability is called _____.

2. Explain the difference between theoretical probability and experimental probability.

3. Throw a drawing pin and fill the table:

	Fell pointing upwards	Fell on its side	Total number of throws
Number of events			
Probability			

4. The definition of probability ("**Laplace law**")is:

    P(A) = $\dfrac{Number \rule{3cm}{0.4pt}}{Total \rule{3cm}{0.4pt}}$

Properties of probability

   $0 \leq P(A) \leq$ ____

   P(U) = ____

5. Given the sentence "Good day everyone". Find the following probabilities in case the choices are being made in a random way:

    a. P(choosing a vowel) =   c. P(choosing a "e") =

    b. P(choosing a "o") =   d. P(choosing a "z") =

6. In case a student is chosen randomly in your classroom. Find the probability it's a girl.

7. Find the probability of getting a prime number sum on tossing 2 dice.

8. Find the probability of getting a sum of 17 on tossing 3 dice.

9. Find the probability of being left handed in your classroom.

10. Find the probability of obtaining a sum of 5 on tossing 2 dice.

11. Find the probability of obtaining 2 tails on tossing 2 coins.

12. Find the probability that a 2 digit number divides by 3

13. Find the probability of choosing the letter b in the word probability

14. Find the probability of choosing a number that contains the digit 7 in the first hundred numbers (1 to 100).

15. Find the probability of choosing a number that contains only even digits in the first thousand numbers (1 to 1000).

16. Find the probability of obtaining a sum of 10 on tossing 2 dice.

17. Find the probability of obtaining a sum of more than 5 on tossing 2 dice.

18. Knowing that the sum of 2 dice is more than 5, find the probability it's 10

19. In a bag with 5 red marbles and 6 white marbles find the probability of drawing:

    a. A red marble.

    b. 2 consecutive red marbles (without replacement)

    c. 2 consecutive white marbles (without replacement)

    d. Red and white marbles in any order (without replacement)

    e. Sum the results of parts b to d.

    f. 2 consecutive red marbles (with replacement)

    g. 2 consecutive white marbles (with replacement)

    h. Red and white marbles in any order (with replacement)

    i. Sum the results of parts f to h.

20. In a bag with 4 red marbles 3 white and 5 blue marbles find the probability of drawing:

    a. A red marble.

    b. 2 consecutive red marbles (without replacement)

    c. 2 consecutive white marbles (without replacement)

    d. Red and blue marbles in any order (without replacement)

    e. White and blue marbles in any order (without replacement)

    f. 2 reds and 1 blue in any order (without replacement)

    g. Red, White and Blue in any order (without replacement)

CHAPTER 7

7.1. – INTERNATIONAL SYSTEM OF UNITS

1. Meter(m) is a unit of _____ Other units of _____ are: _____

2. Meter square (m^2) is a unit of _____ Other units of _____ are: _____

3. An area has units of _____ A length has units of _____

4. Kilo = __ Mili = __

Convert the units, use scientific notation in at least one of each type of exercises:

5. How many metres in 2.5 km?

6. How many metres in 0.5 km?

7. How many metres^2 in $\frac{1}{3}$ km^2?

8. How many metres in 56 km?

9. How many metres in 2500 km?

10. How many km^2 in 26 m^2?

11. How many km in 75 m?

12. How many km in 1000 m?

13. How many m in $5.2 \cdot 10^7$ km?

14. How many km^2 in $5.12 \cdot 10^8$ m^2?

15. How many mm in 3.04 m?

16. How many mm^2 in 0.5 m^2?

17. How many mm^2 in 1 m^2?

18. How many mm in 2 m?

19. How many mm in 2.5 m?

20. How many mm^2 are 1.35 m^2?

21. How many cm in $\frac{1}{3}$ m?

22. How many cm^2 in 56 m^2?

23. How many cm in 3.1 km?

24. How many mm² in 0.5 cm²?

25. How many cm in in 120 m?

26. How many mm² in 5.1 cm²?

27. How many cm in 17 km?

28. How many m in 12392 km?

29. How many mm² in 5.1 m²?

30. How many m² in 2.2 mm²?

31. How many cm in 13.12 m?

32. Complete the table:

mm	cm	m	km
14			
	65		
		3	
			5
12.5			
	3.7		
		4.78	
			1.31
			0.008

mm²	cm²	m²	Km²
14			
	65		
		3	
			5
12.5			
	3.7		
		4.78	
			1.31
			0.008

7.2. – COMMON ERRORS

1. $\sqrt{A+B} = \sqrt{A} + \sqrt{B}$ True / False, Give an example to show your answer.

2. $\sqrt{A^2 + B^2} = A + B$ True / False, Give an example to show your answer.

3. $(A+B)^2 = A^2 + B^2$ True / False, if false write the correct version.

4. $(A+B)(A-B) = A^2 + B^2$ True / False, Give an example to show your answer.

5. $(A+B)(A-B) = A^2 - B^2$ True / False, if false write the correct version..

6. $(x+2)^2 = x^2 + 4x + 2$ True / False, if false write the correct version.

7. $(A-B)^2 = A^2 - B^2$ True / False, Give an example to show your answer.

8. $(2x-3)^2 = 4x^2 - 6x + 9$ True / False, if false write the correct version.

9. $(\sqrt{a}-3)^2 = a^2 - 6a + 9$ True / False, if false write the correct version.

10. $x^2 x^3 = x^6$ True / False, if false write the correct version.

11. $(x^2)^3 = x^{(2^3)}$ True / False, if false write the correct version.

12. $\dfrac{x^{10}}{x^2} = x^5$ True / False, if false write the correct version.

13. $x^1 = 1$ True / False, if false write the correct version.

14. $x^0 = 0$ True / False, if false write the correct version.

15. $-3^2 = (-3)^2$ True / False, if false write the correct version.

16. $(4x^2) = (4x)^2$ True / False, if false write the correct version.

17. $\sqrt{7x} = 7x^{\frac{1}{2}}$ True / False, if false write the correct version.

18. $\dfrac{0}{2} = \dfrac{2}{0}$ True / False, if false write the correct version.

19. $\dfrac{14+x}{14} = x$ True / False, if false write the correct version.

20. $\dfrac{7-x}{7} = x-1$ True / False, if false write the correct version.

21. $\dfrac{a+b}{a} = 1 + \dfrac{b}{a}$ True / False, if false write the correct version.

22. $\dfrac{14+x}{14} = x + \dfrac{x}{14}$ True / False, if false write the correct version.

23. $\dfrac{1}{x+y} = \dfrac{1}{x} + \dfrac{1}{y}$ True / False, if false write the correct version.

24. An **expression** and an **equation** is the same thing.   True / False

25. $\dfrac{\left(\dfrac{a}{b}\right)}{c} = \dfrac{a}{\left(\dfrac{b}{c}\right)}$ True / False, if false write the correct version.

26. $-a^2 = (-a)^2$ True / False, if false write the correct version.

27. $a^{-2} = (-a)^2$ True / False, if false write the correct version.

28. $a^{-2} = -a^2$ True / False, if false write the correct version.

29. $a^{-2} = -\dfrac{1}{a^2}$ True / False, if false write the correct version.

30. $a^{-2} = \dfrac{1}{a^2}$ True / False, if false write the correct version.

31. $a^{-1} = -\dfrac{1}{a}$ True / False, if false write the correct version.

32. $\dfrac{1}{2} + \dfrac{1}{3} = \dfrac{1}{2+3}$ True / False, if false write the correct version.

33. $a^{-1} + a^{-1} = a^{-2}$ True / False, if false write the correct version.

34. $a^{-1} a^{-1} = a^{-2}$ True / False, if false write the correct version.

35. $a^{-2} a^{-3} = a^{-6}$ True / False, if false write the correct version.

36. $a^{-2} + a^{-3} = a^{-5}$ True / False, if false write the correct version.

7.3. – FRACTIONS REVIEW

1. Given the following circle, divide it to 2 equal pieces and shade $\frac{1}{2}$

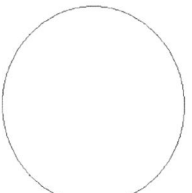

2. Given the following circle divide it to 3 equal pieces and shade $\frac{1}{3}$

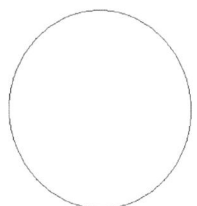

3. Given the following circle, divide it to 4 equal pieces and shade $\frac{1}{4}$

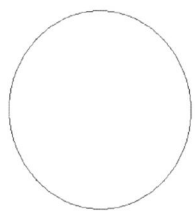

4. Given the following circle, divide it to 5 equal pieces and shade $\frac{1}{5}$

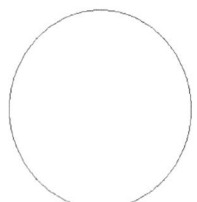

5. Given the following circle, divide it to 6 equal pieces and shade $\frac{1}{6}$

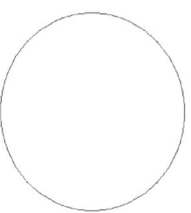

6. Given the following circle, divide it to 7 equal pieces and shade $\frac{1}{7}$

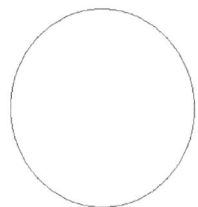

7. Given the following circle, divide it to 8 equal pieces and shade $\frac{1}{8}$

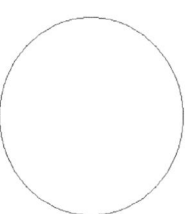

8. Given the following circle, divide it to 9 equal pieces and shade $\frac{1}{9}$

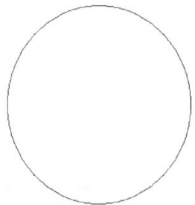

9. Given the following circle, divide it to 10 equal pieces and shade $\frac{1}{10}$

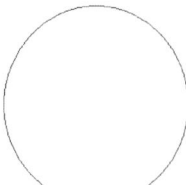

10. Given the following circle, divide it to 3 equal pieces and shade $\frac{2}{3}$

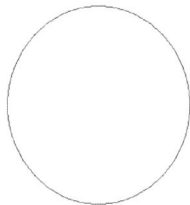

11. Given the following circle, divide it to 4 equal pieces and shade $\frac{2}{4}$

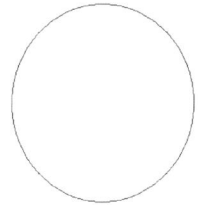

12. Given the following circle, divide it to 4 equal pieces and shade $\frac{3}{4}$

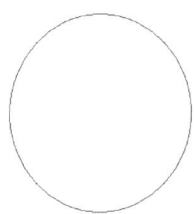

13. Given the following circle, divide it to 5 equal pieces and shade $\frac{2}{5}$

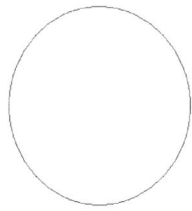

14. Given the following circle, divide it to 6 equal pieces and shade $\frac{5}{6}$

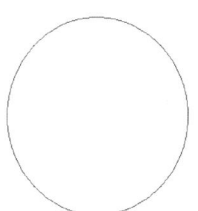

15. Given the following circle, divide it to 8 equal pieces and shade $\frac{5}{8}$

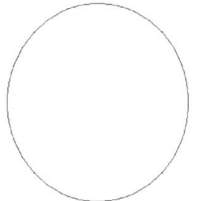

16. Given the following circle, divide it to 5 equal pieces and shade $\frac{4}{5}$

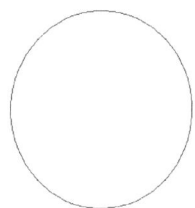

17. Given the following circle, divide it to 9 equal pieces and shade $\frac{4}{9}$

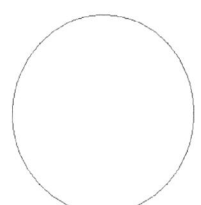

18. What fraction of the following circle is shaded:

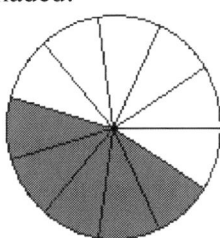

19. What fraction of the following circle is shaded:

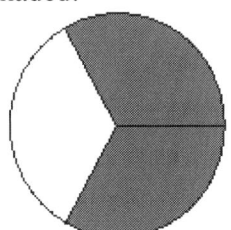

20. What fraction of the following circle is shaded:

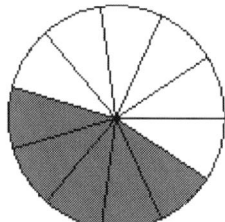

21. What fraction of the following circle is shaded:

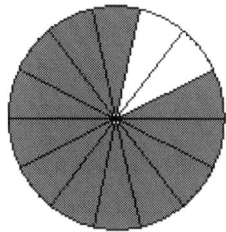

22. What fraction of the following circle is shaded:

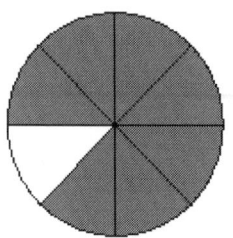

23. What fraction of the following circle is shaded:

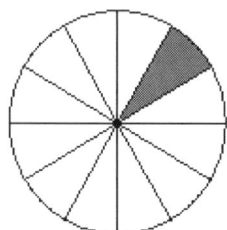

24. What fraction of the following table is shaded:

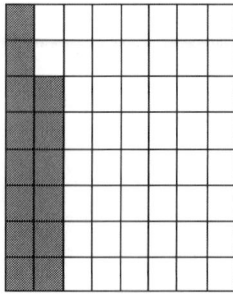

25. What fraction of the following circle is shaded:

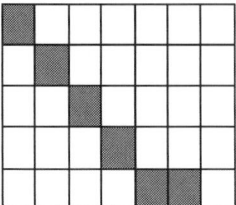

26. What fraction of the following table is shaded?

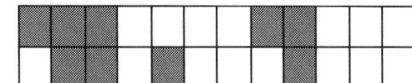

27. What fraction is shaded?

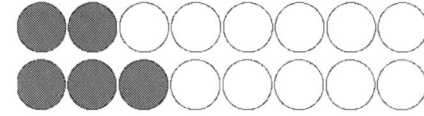

28. What fraction is shaded?

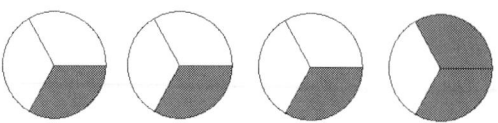

29. What fraction is shaded?

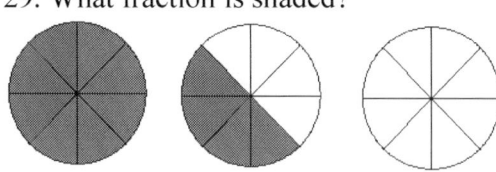

30. What fraction is shaded?

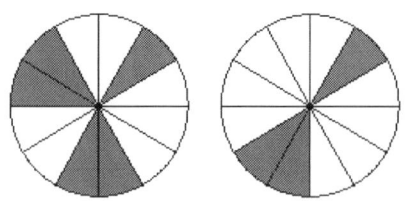

31. There were 12 cookies in the jar. John ate 5, write down the fraction of cookies john ate and the fraction that is left in the jar.

32. Lia ate 3 cookies that represented $\frac{3}{4}$ of the cookies in the jar. Write down the number of cookies in the jar before she ate. Make a sketch to show answer.

33. Rami ate $\frac{2}{5}$ of the cookies in the jar, Melissa ate $\frac{1}{4}$ of the cookies. Who ate more? Invent an imaginary jar with a number of cookies that will make the problem easy to solve.

34. How much is $\frac{1}{2}$ of 2? Shade to show your answer:

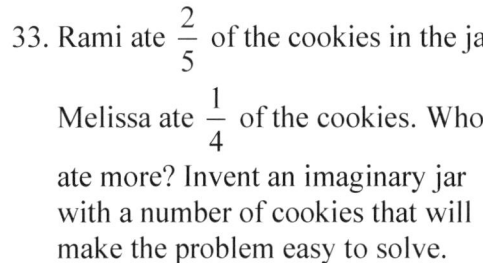

35. How much is $\frac{1}{3}$ of 2? Shade to show your answer:

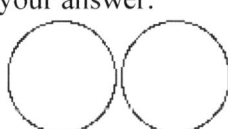

36. How much is $\frac{1}{4}$ of 2? Shade to show your answer:

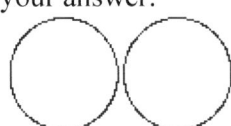

37. How much is $\frac{1}{5}$ of 2? Shade to show your answer:

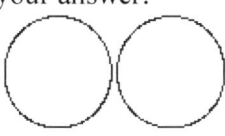

38. How much is $\frac{1}{3}$ of 5? Shade in 2 different ways to show your answer:

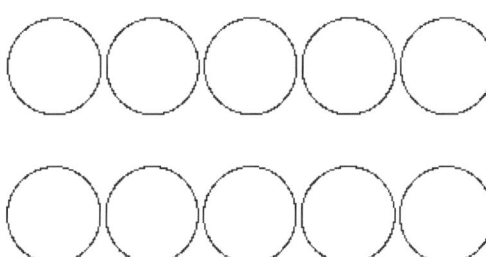

39. How much is $\frac{2}{5}$ of 4? Shade in 2 different ways to show your answer:

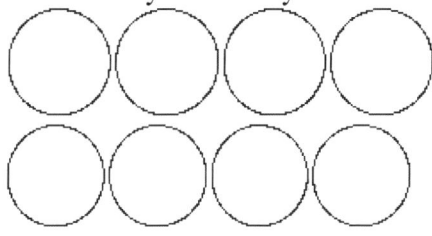

40. Sketch $\frac{3}{2}$ circles:

41. Sketch $\frac{5}{3}$ circles:

42. Sketch $\frac{7}{4}$ circles:

43. Sketch $\frac{8}{4}$ circles:

44. Sketch $\frac{7}{5}$ circles:

45. Sketch $\frac{8}{3}$ circles:

46. Nathan ate $\frac{2}{7}$ of the cookies in the jar, Melissa ate $\frac{1}{3}$ of the cookies. Who ate more? Invent an imaginary jar with a number of cookies that will make the problem easy to solve.

47. Write down the missing number(s) between 0 and 1:
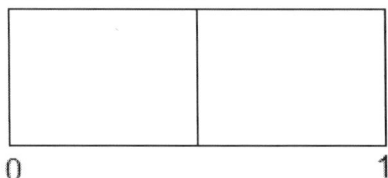

48. Write down the missing number(s) between 0 and 1:
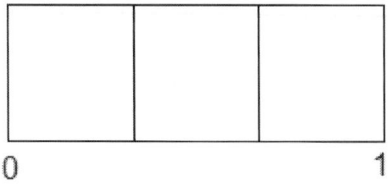

49. Write down the missing number(s) between 0 and 1:
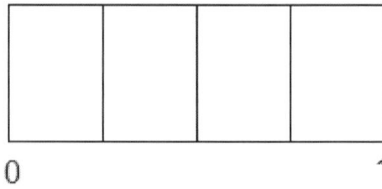

50. Write down the missing number(s) between 0 and 1:
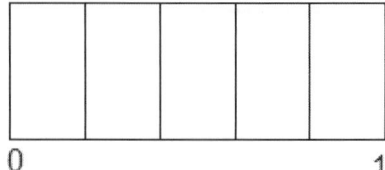

51. Write down the missing number(s) between 0 and 1:
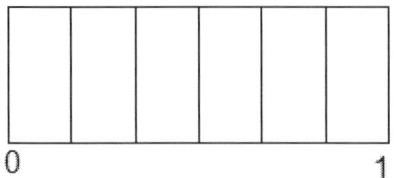

52. Write down the missing number(s) between 0 and 2:
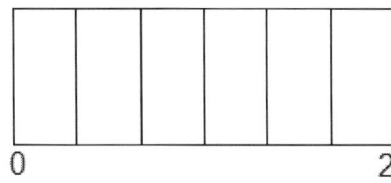

53. Write down the missing number(s) between 0 and 2:
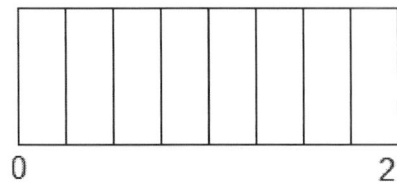

54. Write down the missing number(s) between 0 and 2:
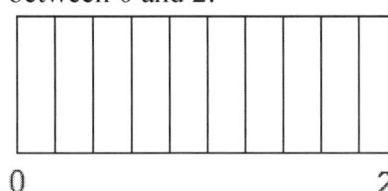

55. Write down the missing number(s) between 2 and 3:
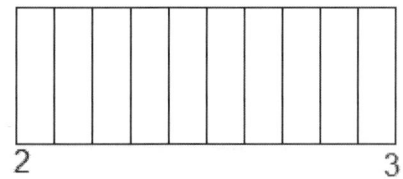

56. Write down the missing number(s) between 2 and 4:
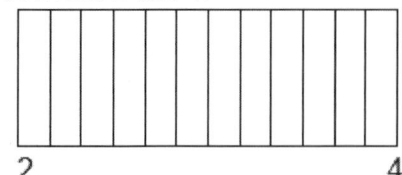

328

57. Write down the missing fractions(s):

58. Write down the missing fractions(s):

59. Write down the missing fractions(s):

60. Write down the missing fractions(s)::

    0 |————————————————————————————| [1/5]

61. Write down the missing fractions(s):

    |————[1/8]————————————[1/2]————|

62. Write down the missing fractions(s):

    |—[1]————————[3/2]—[5/3]|

63. Write down the missing fractions(s):

    |—[13/7]——[2]————————————————[20/7]|

64. Write down the missing fractions(s):

    |—[26/9]——[3]————————[10/3]|

65. Write down the missing fractions(s):

    |—[-10/9]——[-1]————————————[-4/9]——[-1/3]|

66. Write down the missing fractions(s):

    |—[-4]————————————[-2]——[-8/5]——[-6/5]|

67. Write down the missing fractions(s):

    |—[3/4]——[3/2]——[9/4]——[3]————————[6]——[27/4]——[15/2]|

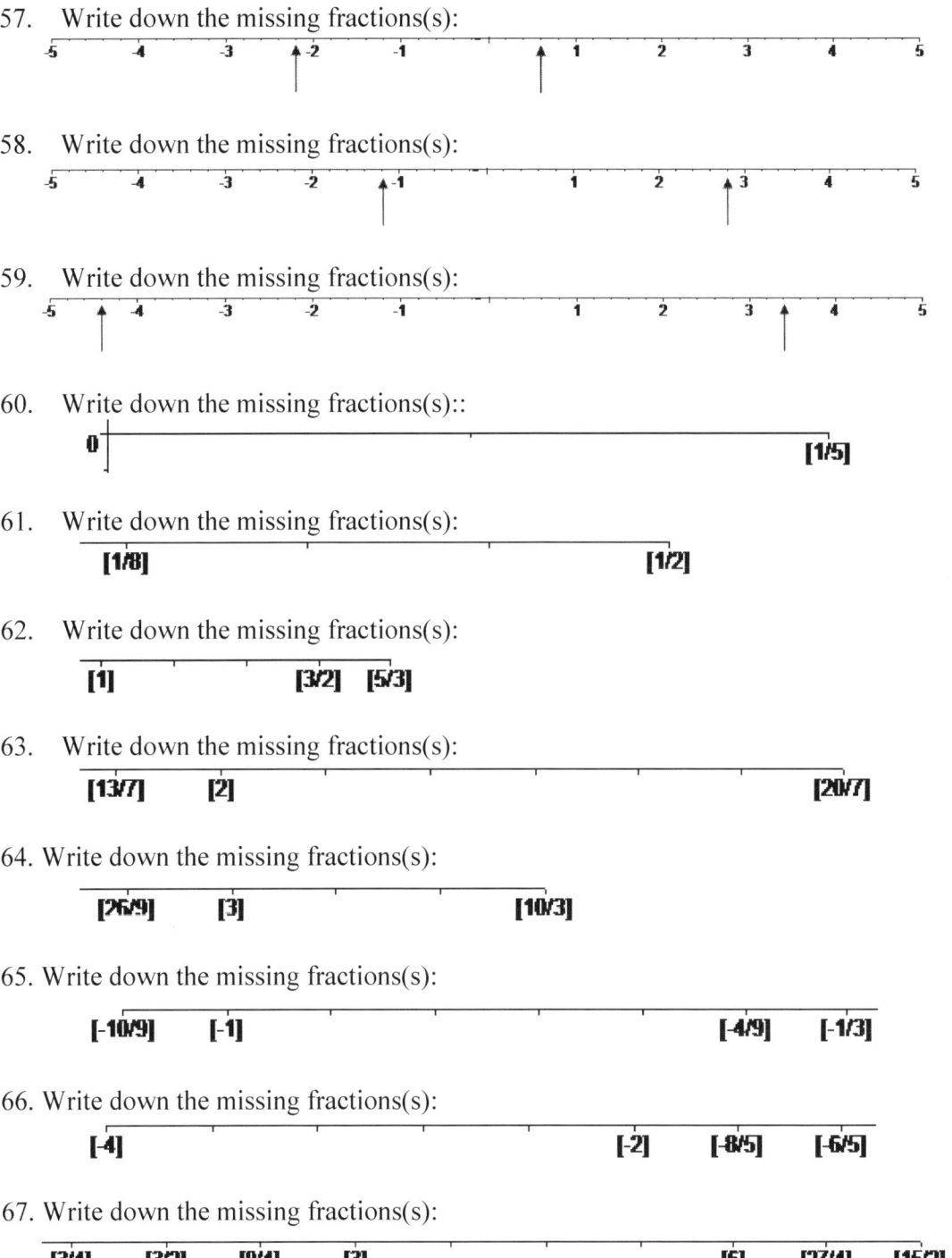

329

Made in the USA
Columbia, SC
26 August 2022